CARL HAGENBECK'S EMPIRE OF ENTERTAINMENTS

ERIC AMES

Carl Hagenbeck's Empire of Entertainments

A MCLELLAN BOOK

University of Washington Press Seattle and London

THIS BOOK IS PUBLISHED WITH THE ASSISTANCE OF A GRANT FROM THE MCLELLAN ENDOWED SERIES FUND, ESTABLISHED THROUGH THE GENEROSITY OF MARTHA MCCLEARY MCLELLAN AND MARY MCLELLAN WILLIAMS.

PUBLICATION OF *CARL HAGENBECK'S EMPIRE OF ENTERTAINMENTS* WAS ALSO AIDED BY A GRANT FROM THE MILLARD MEISS PUBLICATION FUND OF THE COLLEGE ART ASSOCIATION.

MM

Printed in the United States of America
Designed by Ashley Saleeba
12 11 10 09 08 5 4 3 2 1

UNIVERSITY OF WASHINGTON PRESS
P.O. Box 50096, Seattle, WA 98145 U.S.A.
www.washington.edu/uwpress

LIBRARY OF CONGRESS CATALOGING-IN-PUBLICATION DATA
Ames, Eric, 1969-
Carl Hagenbeck's empire of entertainments / Eric Ames.
p. cm.
Includes bibliographical references and index.
ISBN 978-0-295-98833-7 (pbk. : alk. paper)
1. Hagenbeck, Carl, 1844-1913. 2. Zoos—Germany. 3. Menageries—Germany.
4. Themed environments—Germany. I. Title.
GV1811.H2A44 2009
590'.730943—dc22 2008029702

The paper used in this publication meets the minimum requirements of American National Standard for Information Sciences—Permanence of Paper for Printed Library Materials, ANSI Z39.48-1984.

FRONTISPIECE: From Hagenbeck's 1896 patent application for a "Natural-Scientific Panorama" (color added; see fig 4.2)

CONTENTS

ACKNOWLEDGMENTS

Many people and institutions have made the writing of this book possible. I am especially grateful to the National Endowment for the Humanities for generously providing financial and research assistance. I also want to thank the Junior Faculty Development Program, the Royalty Research Fund, the Walter Chapin Simpson Center for the Humanities, and the Graduate School Fund for Excellence and Innovation—all at the University of Washington.

This project relied crucially on the work of archivists at various locations, including the Deutsche Kinemathek, the Bundesarchiv/Filmarchiv, and the Museum für Völkerkunde in Berlin; the Deutsches Filmmuseum and the Deutsches Filminstitut (especially Christoph Schöbel) in Frankfurt; the Friedrich-Wilhelm-Murnau-Stiftung in Wiesbaden; the Danish Film Institute in Copenhagen; CineGraph (Jörg Schöning) and the Staatsarchiv in Hamburg; the Buffalo Bill Historical Center in Cody; and the Denver Public Library. Many thanks, once again, to the staff at each of these institutions. I am especially grateful to the Tierpark Carl Hagenbeck in Hamburg-Stellingen, which allowed me to conduct extensive research and gave permission to reproduce various materials from its collection. There, I am particularly indebted to historian and archivist Klaus Gille, who assisted me in so many ways (supplying images, photocopies, and other materials), responded to my countless queries over the years, and discussed and thereby contributed to ideas and research in every stage of this book's progress.

For their valuable advice, feedback, or support at different moments of the project, I thank Jane Brown, Matt Erlin, Mark Feldman, Rick Gray, Tom Gunning, Sara Hall, Bradley Naranch, Andrew Nestingen, Uta Poiger, Whitney Pollack, Brigitte Prutti,

Christine Rummer, Vanessa Schwartz, Stephanie Welch, Lora Wildenthal, Sabine Wilke, and Kathleen Woodward. My greatest debt is to Anton Kaes and Mark Sandberg, my dissertation advisers at Berkeley, for supporting and encouraging this project from its beginning. While the book turned out to be very different from the dissertation, I hope they will each take pleasure in its change over time. I also want to thank my colleagues and the staff in the Germanics Department at the University of Washington for creating and maintaining a lively forum for intellectual exchange, of which I am proud to be a part.

At the University of Washington Press, I am particularly grateful to Jacqueline Ettinger, who not only believed in this project but also became my most careful and trusted reader. I could not have wished for a better editor. Thanks also to Nanette Pyne for her meticulous copyediting; to Marilyn Trueblood for guiding the manuscript through the production process; to the designer, Ashley Saleeba, who made this volume an attraction in itself; and to the Press's anonymous reviewers for their extremely helpful criticisms and suggestions.

On a personal level, I am very grateful to my parents, Gary and Barbara, whose support and encouragement have sustained me in so many ways. Finally, it is safe to say that I would not have completed this project without the love and support of Veronika Zantop. This book is for her and for Isaac, whose imminent arrival spurred me to complete the manuscript and whose presence has only widened my sense of what is possible.

COLOR PLATES

PLATE 1

"Laplanders." Watercolor based on an illustration by Heinrich Leutemann, 1875. Courtesy of Tierpark Carl Hagenbeck GmbH, Hamburg-Stellingen.

PLATE 2

"North Asia (North Siberia)." Wood engraving from *Zonen-Bilder: Nach Aquarellen von Heinrich Leutemann, mit erklärenden Schilderungen für die Jugend von Hermann Wagner* (Stuttgart: Julius Hoffmann, 1876). "Our image depicts two polar bears, which have been lured to the scene by a dead walrus. The Tungusian hunters have killed it and hauled it onto the shore. They leave, in order to get reindeers, which they would use to carry away the meat. . . . The Tungusians will have to fight for the spoils of their hunt once again. Fighting polar bears is dangerous even for hunters equipped with rifles. Despite the strength and courage of this animal, two Eskimos attack it with their spears. With the aid of their dogs, they force it to a standstill. The one hunter teases the bear, and while the latter defends himself, the other hunter stabs him in the heart" (9).

PLATE 3

"Eskimos." Illustration by Heinrich Leutemann, based on one or more of Hagenbeck's Inuit troupes. The original caption reads: (*Above*) "Summer tents; women's boat (umiak); kayak (hunting boat), with buoy made of seal skin; razorbill birds; hunting blind [on the kayak's bow]; glacier; iceberg; seal." (*Below*) "Reindeer; polar bear; women; winter houses, the one at right with umiak and kayak on top; Eskimo dogs." From *Leutemann's Bilder aus dem Völkerleben* (Fürth: Löwensohn, 1888), n. p. Amherst College Archives and Special Collections.

PLATE 4

"Carl Hagenbeck's 1885 Ceylon Expedition." Lithograph poster by Adolph Friedländer. Courtesy of the Historisches Museum Frankfurt, Frankfurt am Main.

PLATE 5

"Greetings from Carl Hagenbeck's India 1898: Exhibition on Kurfürstendamm." Berlin. Postcard of "Hagenbeck's Tea House." The sign over the awning reads: "Buy Hagenbeck's Ceylon Tea." Courtesy of Tierpark Carl Hagenbeck GmbH, Hamburg-Stellingen.

PLATE 6

"Carl Hagenbeck's Genuine Ceylon Tea—Tiger Brand." Undated poster. Courtesy of Tierpark Carl Hagenbeck GmbH, Hamburg-Stellingen.

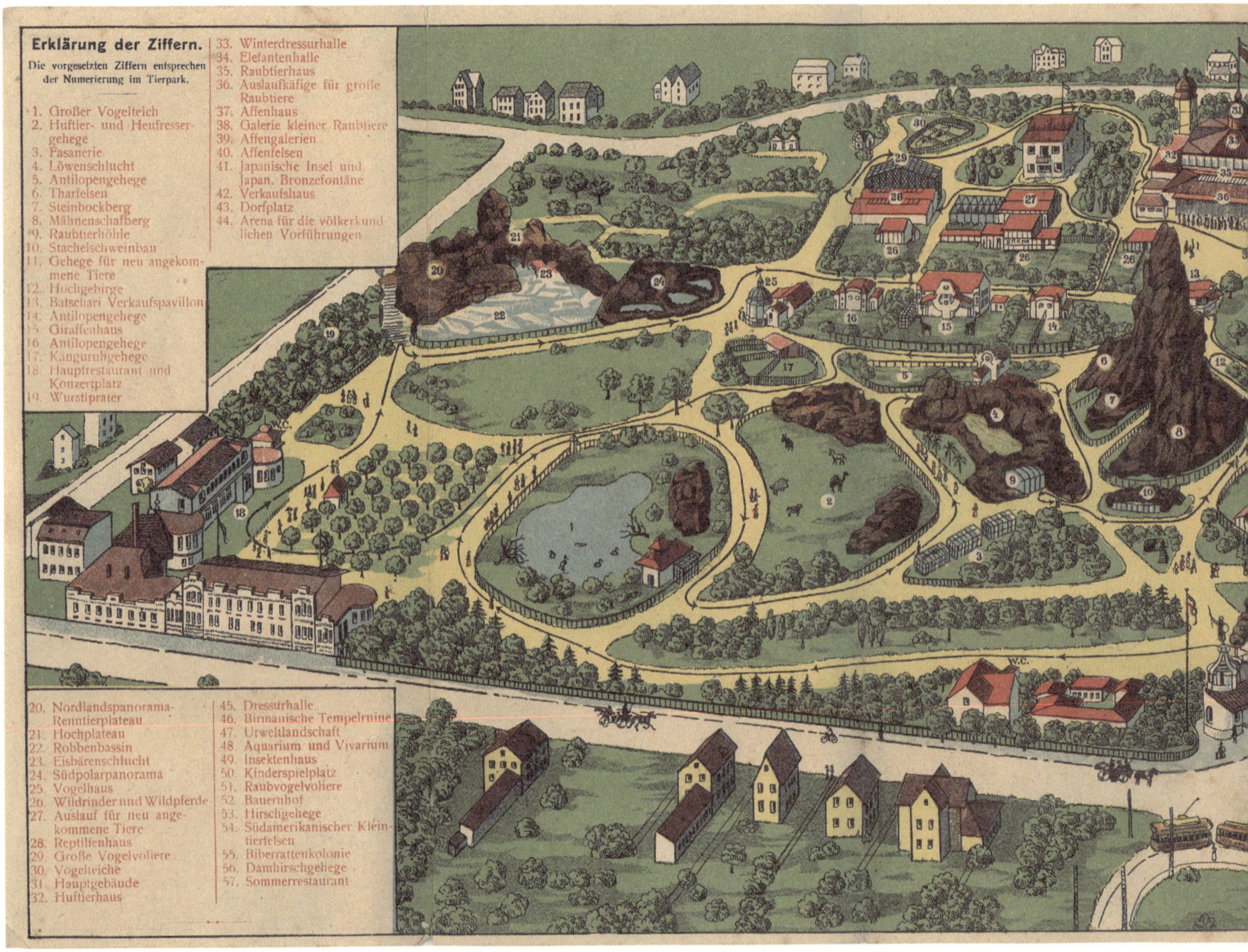

Erklärung der Ziffern.

Die vorgesetzten Ziffern entsprechen der Numerierung im Tierpark.

1. Großer Vogelteich
2. Huftier- und Heufressergehege
3. Fasanerie
4. Löwenschlucht
5. Antilopengehege
6. Tharfelsen
7. Steinbockberg
8. Mähnenschafberg
9. Raubtierhöhle
10. Stachelschweinbau
11. Gehege für neu angekommene Tiere
12. Hochgebirge
13. Batschari Verkaufspavillon
14. Antilopengehege
15. Giraffenhaus
16. Antilopengehege
17. Känguruhgehege
18. Hauptrestaurant und Konzertplatz
19. Wurstlprater
20. Nordlandspanorama-Renntierplateau
21. Hochplateau
22. Robbenbassin
23. Eisbärenschlucht
24. Südpolarpanorama
25. Vogelhaus
26. Wildrinder und Wildpferde
27. Auslauf für neu angekommene Tiere
28. Reptilienhaus
29. Große Vogelvoliere
30. Vogelteiche
31. Hauptgebäude
32. Huftierhaus
33. Winterdressurhalle
34. Elefantenhalle
35. Raubtierhaus
36. Auslaufkäfige für große Raubtiere
37. Affenhaus
38. Galerie kleiner Raubtiere
39. Affengalerien
40. Affenfelsen
41. Japanische Insel und Japan. Bronzefontäne
42. Verkaufshaus
43. Dorfplatz
44. Arena für die völkerkundlichen Vorführungen
45. Dressurhalle
46. Birmanische Tempelruine
47. Urweltlandschaft
48. Aquarium und Vivarium
49. Insektenhaus
50. Kinderspielplatz
51. Raubvogelvoliere
52. Bauernhof
53. Hirschgehege
54. Südamerikanischer Kleintierfelsen
55. Biberrattenkolonie
56. Damhirschgehege
57. Sommerrestaurant

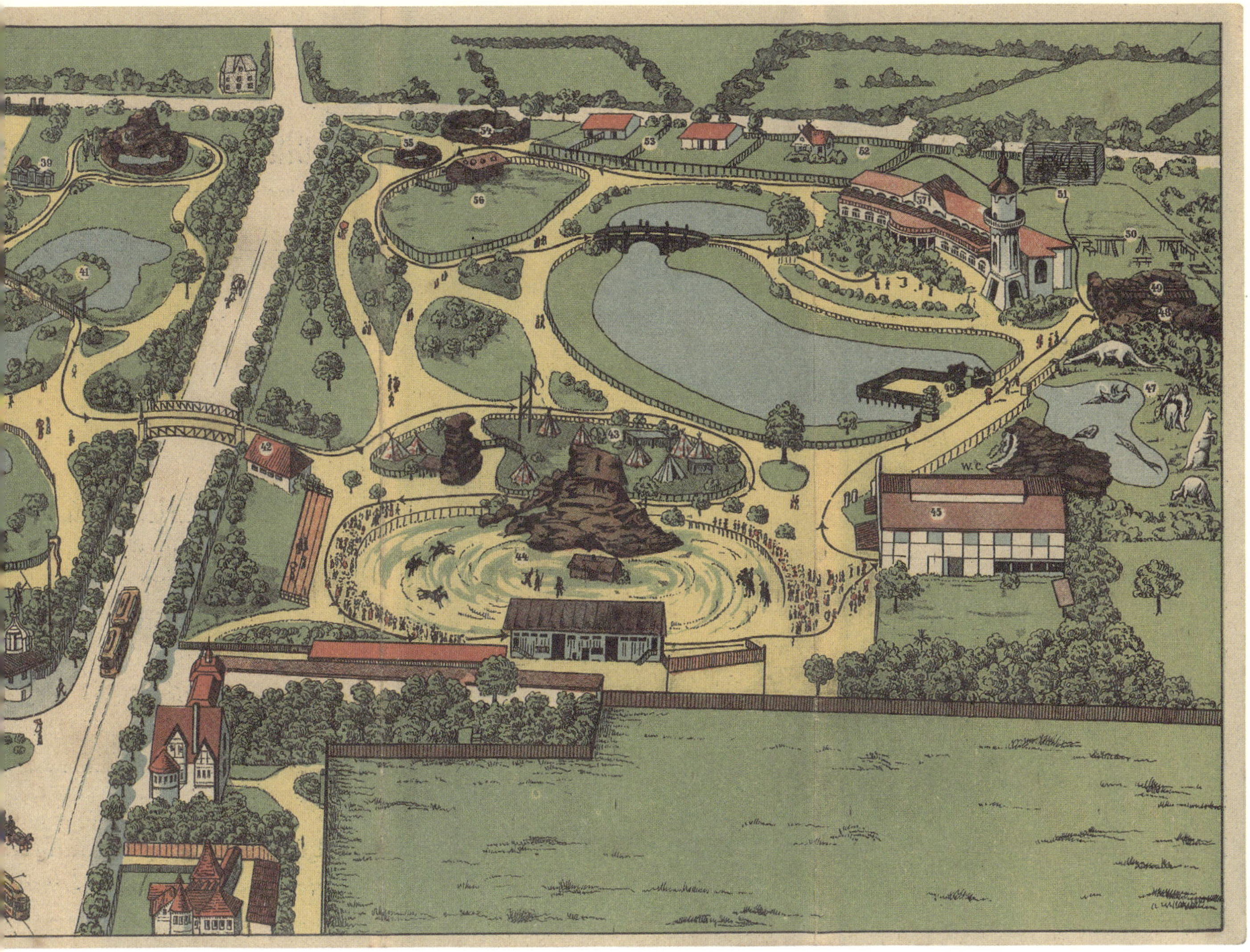

PLATE 7

Illustrated map of Hagenbeck's *Tierpark*, ca. 1913. The area for ethnographic exhibitions is at right. Courtesy of Tierpark Carl Hagenbeck GmbH, Hamburg-Stellingen.

PLATE 8

"The attack." Staged photograph of a scene from Hagenbeck's "Oglala-Sioux Indians *Völkerschau*," 1910. Courtesy of Tierpark Carl Hagenbeck GmbH, Hamburg-Stellingen.

PLATE 9

"The Arctic Sea and Its Animal World." Poster advertisement by Adolph Friedländer, for Hagenbeck's traveling panorama, ca. 1896. Courtesy of Tierpark Carl Hagenbeck GmbH, Hamburg-Stellingen.

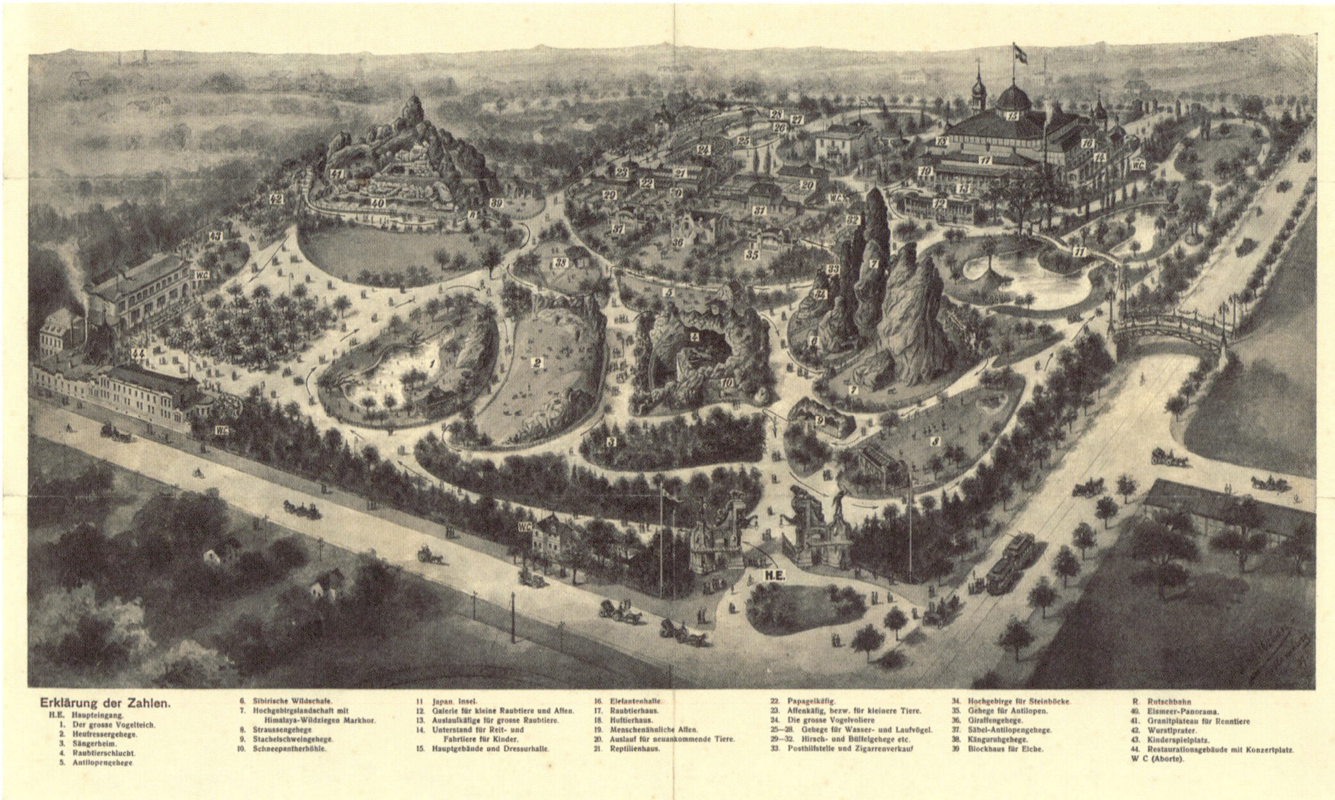

PLATE 10

"Bird's-Eye View of Carl Hagenbeck's *Tierpark*, Stellingen." The first souvenir map, illustrated by August Urban, 1907. Courtesy of Tierpark Carl Hagenbeck GmbH, Hamburg-Stellingen.

PLATE 11

"Hagenbeck's Wild Animal Show." Photo taken probably at Coney Island, ca. 1894. Courtesy of Tierpark Carl Hagenbeck GmbH, Hamburg-Stellingen.

PLATE 12

"Northern Landscape with Slide." Postcard, 1907. Courtesy of Tierpark Carl Hagenbeck GmbH, Hamburg-Stellingen.

PLATE 13

Lion attack. Lithograph poster, advertising Hagenbeck's *Tierpark* ca. 1912. Courtesy of Tierpark Carl Hagenbeck GmbH, Hamburg-Stellingen.

PLATE 14

"Polar Bear Hunt and Trapping of Seals, Sea Lions, and Walruses." Film poster by Adolph Friedländer, advertising the German release of *Polar Bear Hunt* (*Isbjørnejagt*, Nordisk, 1907; dir. Viggo Larsen). Courtesy of the Deutsches Filmmuseum, Frankfurt am Main.

CARL HAGENBECK'S EMPIRE OF ENTERTAINMENTS

INTRODUCTION

UNDER THE SIGN OF HAGENBECK

This book tells the strange and captivating story of the world-famous animal dealer and ethnographic showman, Carl Hagenbeck (1844–1913). In an age of colonial commerce and nascent globalization, the German entrepreneur brought the wild animal trade into the mainstream of Western culture by supplying huge shipments of exotic animals to zoos, circuses, and menageries throughout Europe and the United States. The agents and dealers that he employed in the animal business would also serve to recruit hundreds of native performers and collect thousands of ethnographic artifacts in a coordinated effort that eventually made Hagenbeck the most prolific ethnographic showman of the period. Over the course of his career, which ran nearly six decades, he exhibited troupes from Australia, Burma, Cameroon, Canada, Chile, Egypt, Ethiopia, Greenland, India, Labrador, Mongolia, Norway, Russia, Samoa, Somalia, Sri Lanka, the Sudan, the United States, and elsewhere. And that was not all. In 1907, Hagenbeck unveiled his revolutionary *Tierpark* in Stellingen, Germany. Its unusual design fundamentally changed the way that animals in captivity were displayed and observed by staging them in "living habitats" and eliminating barred cages and replacing them with trenches to permit unencumbered viewing. In its prime, the *Tierpark* represented more than a zoo. It was a theme park *avant la lettre*, combining animal panoramas, ethnographic performances, native villages, moving pictures, even mechanical rides—all themed around the exotic. Taken together, Hagenbeck's entertainments helped shape the preference of a mass audience not only for seeing foreign peoples and wild animals staged in natural settings, but also for plunging themselves into surround-style fantasy worlds of exotic adventure.

To some readers, this material will immediately recall the more familiar story of the international expositions, and with good reason. Hagenbeck's upward trajectory was simultaneous with the efflorescence of the world's fairs, and he exhibited at the American expositions in Chicago (1893) and St. Louis (1904). In addition, Hagenbeck's shows were similar in many ways to those that took place at world's fairs, especially in regard to ethnographic exhibitions. Commercial or proprietary shows filled the gaps between the occasional expositions and also provided fair organizers with a plentiful stock of new ideas and display practices. What makes such similarities so interesting for the purpose of this study, however, is the very absence of a major world's fair in nineteenth-century Germany. In this context, there was no single form of popular display that either supported or encompassed all other forms, as the world's fair has done in the United States.

Some distinction needs to be made theoretically separating the world's fairs—where entertainments were discursively framed within larger official themes and spatially contained within designated amusement zones—from the entertainments that appeared outside of these events, under the sign of commercial showmen. There is, however, something to be said for emphasizing their broader connections. From one angle, Hagenbeck produced his own version of a world's fair. In so doing, he also created in the *Tierpark* a type of outdoor entertainment space that would later become the legacy of the world's fair: not simply a large, temporary event, but an enduring space, namely, the theme park. Historian Neil Harris has emphasized the importance of the American expositions and of the fair experience more generally as preparing the ground for twentieth-century theme parks such as Disneyland. The present study offers a different perspective and, at the same time, aims to complement the work of Harris and others by exploring different materials, contexts, and paradigms, and by stressing their importance to our historical understanding of theme space.[1]

This book contributes to the history of visual culture by fleshing out a performance-based model of theme space, one that choreographed the use of material objects and living bodies as integral components of the display, while at the same time developing a full-bodied approach to the immersive experience of spectatorship. The late nineteenth century was an important time in the emergence of this model, and Hagenbeck was a principal harbinger of its development. To his contemporaries, the showman—indeed, just the mention of his name—conjured up a series of exoticized bodies, landscapes, and multi-sensory environments, even the audience's central position in the thick of things.

> "Hagenbeck," that is: the magic of foreign parts of the earth; the endlessness of scorching deserts, waving grass steppes, and ice-covered snow fields; the half-darkness of sweltering jungles, rugged mountains, ravines, and caves; the exotic

> hunting grounds, playgrounds, open meadows, and hiding places of rare animals; the romantic habitats of strange peoples; a totally foreign world—only one that is no longer unreachably distant, but rather accessed, made available, and literally brought near, so that it fills up our senses, and allows us to partake of its wonder.[2]

Rather than bring the world closer via technological recording, as the cinema would later do, Hagenbeck created the paradoxical terrain of an imaginary world that was physically within reach by surrounding the spectator with actual bodies, objects, and structures. This resulted in an immersive space of performance, where the possibility of interacting with the bodies on display was always a very real one, and the outcome was often unexpected.

Throughout this book, I refer to the idea of nineteenth-century theme space very specifically, and by that I mean the physical displacement of the spectacle to the spectator. By using the term "displacement," I do not mean to suggest that themed environments in the nineteenth century somehow bypassed the work of representation. On the contrary, the point of using this term is to emphasize that the work of representation consisted in the cumbersome process of collecting the different elements for a show, transporting them to Europe, and arranging them before a mass public. Hagenbeck offers an exceptionally suggestive example, because his immersive entertainments arose directly out of his primary occupation as an international animal trader. In this case, the production of theme space relied on elements that had been literally imported from other parts of the globe, only to be assembled, transfigured, re-signified, staged, and exhibited in a new context. By the same token, the act of displacement that engendered nineteenth-century theme space also implied its demise. This is especially true of the living, breathing figures that constituted Hagenbeck's themed environments. Removed from their native habitats, the different animals and peoples on display were made extremely vulnerable, their very existence put at risk.

On another level, however, a wholly appropriate emphasis on the actual movement of the spectacle to the spectator cannot adequately account for its link to later developments, most notably, the ascendance of themed environments based on principles of mechanical reproduction, such as the cinema. A strong definition would therefore need to account for the transformation of theme space, from its historical basis in the coordination of collected objects to its later occurrence in synthetic spaces of representation. This book makes a case for the interconnection of these two models, as evidenced by the transformation of Hagenbeck's entertainments over time. One of the more striking points of interconnection is the use of propinquity, the closeness and juxtaposition of otherwise distant places within the space of display. It is precisely this aspect of nineteenth-century theme space that makes it such a good example of what Michel Foucault called a "heterotopia." Unlike the utopia (or non-place), "the heterotopia is capable of juxtaposing in a single real place several spaces, several sites that are in themselves incompatible." Among Foucault's examples are the garden, the fairground, the theater, the museum, the zoo, the cinema, and the vacation village. Whatever their ontological differences, each example represents a contradictory site, where one space is transformed into another, real or imagined. Hagenbeck's immersive entertainments positively reveled in this contradiction and encouraged spectators to follow suit.[3]

Scholarly interest in the topic of themed environments—spanning theme parks, museum displays, world's fairs, period rooms, shopping centers, Wild West shows, and their cousin forms—has spread across an equally broad spectrum of academic disciplines and interdisciplinary fields. There is a wealth of literature on themed environments and related subjects in such diverse fields as tourism studies, anthropology, museum studies, social history, urban studies, geography, performance studies, visual culture, American studies, communications, entertainment studies, landscape architecture, architectural history, cultural studies, sociology, and cinema studies. Although the literature is too vast to be surveyed here, I want to make two general observations about it for the dual purpose of defining my topic and promoting fresh discussion. First, the tone of this literature tends to be more or less condescending, which has the unintended effect of stifling new ideas instead of fostering them. When other scholars have addressed issues of theme space, many seem to have done so against their better judgment. In a trenchant analysis of the criticism on Disney theme parks, for example, Greil Marcus describes the prevailing attitude as one of snobbery and the voice as one of spite. More important, the critics who seem to delight in sneering at the parks and their visitors have nothing in particular to say about the actual rides or displays there.[4]

Second, the concept of theme space has largely been conceived in terms of postmodern "simulation" and "simulacra," or, according to the paradigm of hyperreality, with a distinct set of critical postures and theoretical concerns. If the subject has a *locus classicus*, it is the work of Jean Baudrillard and his comments on the Disneyland theme park. In his analysis, Disneyland "presents itself as imaginary in order to make us believe that the rest is real, when in fact all of Los Angeles and the America surrounding it are no longer real, but of the order of the hyperreal and of simulation. It is no longer a question of a false representation of reality (ideology), but of concealing the fact that the real is no longer real." Thus, the idea of Disneyland serves to illustrate a theoretical model of the "real" in which there is no meaningful connection between sign and referent. Simulation in this system implies a form of duplication or reproduction, whose primary function is to mask the supposed absence of place, history, and origin. Loss of referentiality has thus become the defining feature in a now standard line of criticism that goes far beyond Baudrillard—only to arrive at the same basic conclusion, no matter what the actual context or material. For example, in his eulogistic portrayal of what he calls "the end of public space," architect Michael Sorkin laments the dislocation of Disneyland or its tendency to create "antigeographic space," in which there are no site-specific referents, only imaginary ones—a space constituted by layer upon layer of ungrounded simulations.[5]

The present snideness about theme space, like the postmodern celebration of it, revolves primarily around the issue of nonreferential space, so that we either bemoan the surface qualities of the themed experience or embrace its postmodern logic (in terms of "pastiche," for example). In either case, ironically, the original idea of theme space—the freighting of bodies, objects, and environments trailing their referential ties behind them as they are moved—is now nowhere recognized in the literature.[6]

To frame the Hagenbeck material in this way is to immediately confront and challenge the received idea of theme space as being essentially an American phenomenon, which starts with Disneyland and goes into other theme parks, theme restaurants, shopping malls, and so on. Intellectual elites such as Baudrillard and Umberto Eco play into this assumption and self-consciously reinforce it. Indeed, postmodern theories of hyperreality need to be historicized within a larger (and largely European) critique of American-style consumer society in the late twentieth century, as other scholars have already suggested. Rather than dismiss an entire area of visual culture by associating it with the supposed falsity of American culture (as opposed to the reality of European culture), this book contends that the idea of theme space is best approached genealogically with specific contextual rigor. The aim, however, is not one of recuperation, but rather a reexamination of the changing nature of theme space, the techniques and technologies for producing it, and the experiences associated with them.[7]

The main difference between the theme space of today and its nineteenth-century manifestation is the emphasis on signs and traces of physical presence (or what Charles Sanders Peirce would call indices) in the logic of display. The practice of ethnographic exhibition, for example, required a certain amount of public confidence in the physical token of the bodies on display, no matter what the reality of the spectacle. That is one reason why Hagenbeck and other showmen employed the discourse of authenticity and traded on the authority of science as overtly and insistently as they did, with great fanfare and publicity. Theoretically, however, theme space has no necessary indexical component; it can only simulate, so long as it presents itself as a complete environment. In the late nineteenth century, many different types of themed environments were accomplished by choreographing actual objects and bodies in the physical presence of the spectator.

Other scholars have explored museological forms of theme space, perhaps none more trenchantly than Mark B. Sandberg, whose *Living Pictures, Missing Persons:*

Mannequins, Museums, and Modernity looks at various Scandinavian wax museums and folk museums of the period. What makes this study so useful for my purposes is its particular focus on the materiality of museum-related displays as their primary means of conveying spectators through time and space. Consider the laborious process of dismantling, documenting, transporting, and re-assembling vernacular buildings for open-air museums such as Skansen in Stockholm. There, spectators were invited momentarily to occupy the reconstructed display spaces in an act of symbolic substitution, standing in, as it were, for the missing folk bodies, while being surrounded by the physical traces of their former presence. As an alternative to the postmodern idea of virtual mobility that has become almost routinely associated with the cinema, Sandberg develops a notion of "material mobility" that relies on the actual movement of objects, bodies, and structures, and is characterized by its profound allegiance to the physical world. Unlike other scholars, he emphasizes the physical limitation that such materials represent, noting the interesting theoretical impossibility of virtual travel for museum-based attractions that depend on the choreography of material objects.[8]

My approach to issues of theme space proceeds from the observation that the choreography of museum objects and mannequins is related but not equivalent to that of living, breathing animals or human beings. The difference is literally vital. If modern conceptions of the museum are characterized by their relentless effort to evoke the "living," as Sandberg claims, the idea is primarily a metaphorical one. The missing persons of the folk museum are just that—missing. Their absence is exactly that condition which makes the real and uncanny effects created via the physical presence of traces, relics, mannequins, and other forms of effigy seem so compelling (even haunting). By stark contrast, as we shall see, the performers in ethnographic troupes and the animals in zoological gardens must actually live for a significant period of time in the midst of those who observe them. A similar distinction is needed in terms of pictorial space. Hagenbeck's notion of the themed environment was clearly shaped by various kinds of images and image-making technologies, as well as by an existing iconography of the exotic. To conceptualize the entertainments in terms of pictures, however, would run the risk of flattening a multi-sensory, multi-dimensional performance space that claimed to be a self-contained environment. What Hagenbeck created was a living habitat. The idea of the habitat writ large across the nineteenth century, and the particular aliveness of Hagenbeck's shows, will help contextualize and distinguish them from adjacent forms of museum display and pictorial space. The differences are theoretically intriguing, since the viability of live objects over time, the need to allow the bodies on display to thrive, is not an issue in museum display or pictorial space, but is essential to both the *Tierpark* and the ethnographic exhibition.[9]

Hagenbeck's immersive entertainments sought to render a convincing expression of non-Western space for Western spectators to explore through their senses and momentarily inhabit with their bodies. Audiences in turn demonstrated a remarkable confidence in the showman's good reputation, in the discourse of authenticity that he employed, and in the physical token of the bodies, artifacts, and buildings on exhibit, even when they understood the spectacle's theatricality. Some commentators clearly recognized that vicarious travel via spectatorship was made possible by the actual movement of the bodies and objects on display. As one reporter put it (punning on a German saying), "Rather than travel in order to have stories to tell, we simply stay at home and let the foreigners, with their many attractions, come to us. Every troupe that has exhibited here has done everything it possibly could in order to transport, as it were, the spectator back to its homeland." As I argue, Hagenbeck's project was not about verisimilitude, illusion, or deception but about wide-scale physical dislocation of the spectacle to the observer. This movement is also the central characteristic of nineteenth-century theme space, as opposed to twentieth-century theme space and its project of virtual reality. A foundational figure, Hagenbeck refers us back to a moment when the simulated environment relied for its effect on the physical co-presence of the observer and the observed. Indeed, that was precisely what gave spectators stories to tell and what made the vicarious experience of travel so memorable and worthy of recounting.[10]

This book documents Hagenbeck's role in the history of visual culture and thereby contributes to a genealogy of theme space more generally. On the one side, the discussion can be characterized as a materialist account of Hagenbeck's immersive entertainments, with special emphasis on the interaction of performers and spectators. On the other side, the analysis of his work is an attempt to re-envision one of the ways in which theme space has been made in history. The process was neither linear nor continuous; there were accidents, conflicts, failures, repetitions, and revisions. Hagenbeck's notion of theme space took shape over time, through the many different entertainments and endeavors discussed in this study and through the various interlocking and diverging representational systems at work within them. Rather than imagine a narrative of progressive development, this book embraces the overlapping and discontinuous nature of his multifarious endeavors.

At the outset, a little biographical information will surely be helpful to most readers. Of particular interest here is the story of Hagenbeck's modest and provincial origins, which bolstered his public reputation as a trustworthy showman while adding a distinctive layer of discourse to the shows themselves. His father, Carl Hagenbeck Sr. (1810–1887), was a fishmonger by trade and a popular figure in the Hamburg district of St. Pauli. He had a standing contract with local fishermen to deliver everything that they caught in their nets, granting him first right of refusal. On 8 March 1848, a boat's crew hauled in six seals in addition to their usual catch of sturgeon. The fishmonger purchased the seals, placed them in several large wooden tubs filled with water, and exhibited them for the price of one Hamburg shilling (about one penny) per person. The first show was successful enough that he decided to take it on the road. He went inland, to Berlin, where seals were presumably even more exotic. The show took place in *Krolls Etablissement*, a huge amusement center, whose concurrent offerings included garden concerts, magic shows, and a moving panorama of the Mississippi River. Returning to Hamburg, he opened an exotic-animal business (adjacent to the seafood shop), which catered to itinerant showmen and menagerie owners. Its offerings expanded as returning sailors brought with them animals that they had acquired abroad, such as parrots, snakes, turtles, monkeys, and hyenas. He continued to exhibit animals on occasion. In 1852, for example, he set up a booth near the great Circus Renz in Hamburg and exhibited a "Giant Polar Bear from Greenland" at a price of four shillings per person.

For Carl Hagenbeck Sr., display techniques served primarily as sales techniques; all of the animals in his so-called trade menagerie (*Handlungs-Menagerie*) were available for purchase. Ticket sales became an added source of revenue, which helped offset the heavy losses and expenses that were intrinsic to the animal business. Thus, in 1856, he rented a popular Hamburg museum, or "natural wonder cabinet," and used it as a venue for attracting new customers and marketing his animals. The menagerie (which still included the giant polar bear) became one section of the larger museum, adding to its existing collections of natural history artifacts and wax tableaux depicting "world history." According to an advertisement that Carl Hagenbeck Sr. took out in a local newspaper, all of the animals were priced for sale. In each of these endeavors, he was assisted by his many children. At age eleven, his oldest son, Carl, accompanied him on a trip via omnibus to the port city of Bremen. They returned with a raccoon, two opossums, and several other "exotic" animals from North America. In 1859, Carl Sr. asked Carl Jr. to leave school and go to work full time. Given a choice between the seafood business and the wild animal trade, the fifteen-year-old boy "never hesitated for a moment."[11]

In spite of his young age, Carl Hagenbeck could not have chosen a better time to enter this particular line of business. By 1860, zoological gardens in Germany were being built at a rate of almost one per year. As a teenager, he began visiting the different European centers of the animal trade (including Amsterdam, Berlin, London, and Paris), where he became acquainted with most, if not all, of the major zoo directors, menagerie owners, and animal dealers. Previously, he and his father had relied on whatever animals returning fishermen, sailors, and travelers happened to acquire abroad and bring back to Germany. Now Hagenbeck began seeking out particular animal varieties at, for example, the annual wild animal auction in Antwerp. He also began giving specific instructions to outgoing sailors. As the company expanded, Hagenbeck gained an international reputation as an up-and-coming dealer. On 1 January

I.1 A delivery of reptiles arrives at Hagenbeck's trade menagerie in Hamburg. The famous Carl Hagenbeck unpacks a crocodile at far left. The boxes are marked "Caution! Live Animals!" Illustration by Karl Müller, 1898. Courtesy of Tierpark Carl Hagenbeck GmbH, Hamburg-Stellingen.

VORSICHT!
LEBENDE THIERE!

1866, his father relinquished his direct control over the business, putting Carl Jr. in charge, both financially and administratively, at the age of twenty-one.[12]

Over the next several years, the younger Hagenbeck developed an extensive corporate network of travelers, hunters, and outposts for the purpose of collecting and trading wild animals. The development of this network slightly preceded imperial Germany's political consolidation as a nation state, coincided with Germany's emergence as an urban-industrial society, and predated by more than a decade Germany's uneasy quest for colonial power in Africa and the South Pacific. Ironically, the proprietary nature of Hagenbeck's endeavor and its independence from the state allowed him to operate under volatile cultural and political conditions abroad. That is to say, only by maintaining an undefined yet tacitly affirmative relationship to colonialism was he able to remain in a position to conduct business during periods of violent, state-sponsored repression and native rebellion, not only in the German colonies but also in territories controlled by American, British, Danish, Dutch, and other colonial powers. The global scope of Hagenbeck's company was for him both a means of economic survival and a particular source of pride. "No trade company is forced to conduct practical geography to such a comprehensive extent as an animal emporium," he wrote. "The territory in which it must search for its objects encompasses *the entire world.* In the tropical forests of Africa, in the jungles of India and Sri Lanka, in the vast steppes of Siberia and Mongolia, scouts must be sent out in advance, followed by globetrotters and hunters with their teams of native laborers." The Hagenbeck Company was a colonial enterprise whose range of operation extended necessarily beyond the German colonies, spanning trade routes and communication lines that circled the globe.[13]

Hagenbeck's contemporaries were particularly impressed by the idea that he marshaled large numbers of people and coordinated modern systems of circulation for such unusual ends. "At the moment," wrote one reporter who visited the company's headquarters in 1902,

> Hagenbeck has Whites and Mongolians and Indians and Negroes, all in all probably 5–6,000 people, en route through the most diverse parts of the world. And the man who mobilizes this regiment, the man who oversees the logistics and directs his troops as a commander, from a central point in Hamburg, the man who simply sends a dispatch by telephone from his desk or from the main telegraph office to the innermost reaches of Asia or Africa: "Trap thirty wild sheep and ten tigers," or "catch fifteen giraffes and send ten zebras on the next steamship to Hamburg," and does so with the same indifference as someone who telephones a deliveryman: "Send me ten bottles of wine,"—this man, who elevated himself from a fishmonger's son to a millionaire, is the embodiment of simplicity.

I.2 Hagenbeck in his office, ca. 1907. Courtesy of Tierpark Carl Hagenbeck GmbH, Hamburg-Stellingen.

Though Hagenbeck probably had no more than fifty animal trappers working for him at any one time, and the number of native laborers and performers more likely ran in the hundreds (not thousands), the reporter's use of hyperbole is indicative. The complexity of Hagenbeck's project was often highlighted and juxtaposed with the "simplicity" of his personality. (The Abraham-Lincoln "look" was one that he carefully groomed as an outward sign or expression of his inner humility, virtue, and integrity.) At the same time, the reporter's focus on logistics also reflected a widespread fascination for what took place behind the scenes of Hagenbeck's organization. Some observers compared his legendary facility to that of a military commander. Others equated him with "practical world conquerors" and captains of global industries, such as Alfred Krupp, Werner Siemens, and John D. Rockefeller. Indeed, Hagenbeck was a mover and a shaker working in a different realm. Many believed that he enjoyed a monopoly over the international wild animal trade, and the tremendous scale of his operation seemed to corroborate this idea. To mention his name was to summon more than the accomplishments of an individual person. "Hagenbeck" became a byword for a particular set of cultural practices—namely, the collecting and exhibiting of wild animals and foreign peoples—which, though extraordinary in a sense, were also quite prevalent in the late nineteenth century.[14]

At stake in this enterprise was physical access to distant objects, bodies, and spaces. The railway, steamship, and telegraph infrastructure that Hagenbeck required for the wild animal trade also informed his entire repertoire of display practices. Indeed, his work provides evidence that modern modes of circulation and display needed one another, in order to render foreign space readily available and accessible—the shared dream of imperial mastery, capitalist expansion, and mass spectatorship. Hagenbeck's themed environments created safe spaces of alterity, where spectators could enjoy the sensory experience of physical proximity to cultural difference, while removing many of the internal stresses of this experience by staging and reshaping it as fantasy.

In making my case, as the reader will observe, I have set aside the argument, found elsewhere in the literature, that themed environments such as zoos, museums, and ethnographic villages represent diagrams of social control or models of cultural domination. On this point I agree with a handful of scholars, including James Clifford, Elizabeth Hanson, and Carla Yanni, who investigate the relationship of power and display but at the same time emphasize the historical diversity, complexity, and contingency of themed environments. To give only one example, Hanson has argued that "few zoos maintained unity over time that would allow the writing of a master narrative of order and power." The claim that themed environments have a single all-encompassing function, be it to justify colonial conquest or to illustrate scientific knowledge, oversimplifies the nature of these entertainments as cultural and historical phenomena. More important, such arguments have been made at the expense of understanding the very cultural processes by which theme space has been made, regulated, marketed, consumed, experienced, and interpreted. This is not to suggest that historians of visual culture should turn away from issues of power. On the contrary, we can look for evidence of the exertion, negotiation, and resistance of power among various agents, even under radically asymmetrical political conditions, without front-loading the argument or reducing the evidence so as to illustrate a ready-made theory. Thus, questions of power, race, assimilation, and displacement are among the first to be addressed in my study, because they are crucial to our historical understanding of Hagenbeck's enterprise.[15]

This book begins with a discussion of the "Business of Collecting" (chapter 1) because all of Hagenbeck's entertainments were originally based on and linked to the international wild animal trade. By his own account, the "devouring capital" of the animal business led him to explore other possible revenue sources, beginning with the production of ethnographic exhibitions. How exactly did the animal trade relate to the assembly of ethnographic troupes? What were the principles governing the selection and recruitment of native performers? Why would anyone join such a troupe? Under what kinds of terms and conditions did the negotiations take place? Particular emphasis is given to issues of cultural displacement, which largely determined the recruitment of colonial subjects but also came to bear on the various performances in Europe.

In the mid-1870s, Hagenbeck developed his approach to showmanship in the context of live ethnographic performance. It resulted in a key form of habitat display, namely, the "Living Habitat" (chapter 2). Initially, at least, Hagenbeck took for his visual model a popular form of geographical illustration called the "zone picture." The Arctic sea, the African desert, and the Siberian steppe were some of the zones that he claimed to represent by arranging native peoples along with their tools and domesticated animals in a single, coherent space of display. There was a racial logic to the boundaries between zones, and this logic was generally reinforced by Hagenbeck's exhibitions. At the same time, and in sharp contrast to other forms of visual culture, there was always the potential in live performance for some kind of reciprocity to break out between participants and spectators. In fact, colonial propagandists became so troubled by this possibility that they lobbied successfully for a federal ban against the recruitment and display of German colonial subjects. What arises from this historical controversy is not only the connective dynamic of mass culture, but also the capacity of theme space to accommodate rival forms of racism.

One of the most interesting developments that this book traces is the narrativization of theme space or what I call "Hagenbeck's Turn to Fiction" (chapter 3). Over time, a dramatic shift in emphasis takes place in the practice of ethnographic exhibition: from a seemingly positivistic mode of representation to a blatantly performative one, in which participants enact fictional roles that are literally assigned to them. A major impetus for this development was the arrival of Wild West shows in Germany around 1890. What Hagenbeck saw in the Wild West was the powerful effect of myth and melodrama, as opposed to the rational veneer of science and education. Much of the material on the Wild West in Germany has not previously been made available in English, so this chapter holds particular interest for American historians of visual culture. Chapter 3 also explores the changing relationship of ethnographic fantasy to the commercialization of theme space, concentrating on the use of branding, that is, the added value that a brand name gave to shows and products. Hagenbeck's themed environments were corporate spaces, where entertainment and merchandise were creatively linked and grouped around a certain theme, where mass spectators were directly addressed as consumers, and vice versa. The full-blown effect of each development—narrativization and commercialization—defined the shows that were held between 1907 and 1914 at Hagenbeck's *Tierpark* in Stellingen. There, fictionalized performances coexisted with "living villages," mountainous landscapes, and other monumental sets spread out across the park. In other words, the park became an extraordinary type of diegetic universe—a fictional story world, where narratives of exotic adventure unfolded before the spectator's eyes, where visitors thought of themselves as exploring an elaborate fantasyland teeming with foreign peoples and wild animals.

When it first opened in 1907, Hagenbeck's *Tierpark* was unlike any zoological garden in the world. Chapter 4 thus explores the alterity of the *Tierpark*, with particular focus on its aesthetic aspect. The ethnographic exhibition was a significant precursor to the *Tierpark*, but it was the nineteenth-century panorama that served as the actual model of inspiration and transformation. Curiously, it was the idea of the panorama that led Hagenbeck to re-envision the living habitat as a space for displaying wild animals. In the mid-1890s, he tested and even patented a process for exhibiting large groups of wild animals in natural settings. The idea of the panorama also inspired the design for an exciting alternative to the nineteenth-century zoological garden. Indeed, the entire park was originally conceived as a vast open-air panorama, with spectators immersed in a variety of simulated landscapes, each based on the extensive use of *faux terrain* and deep trenches instead of cages. Of special interest here is the role of trained artists, especially sculptors, in designing and implementing the various exotic settings or "motifs," as they were called. The sculptural aspect of the park, its spatial embodiment of exotic landscapes, its haptic and tactile qualities, also introduced new possibilities for immersive effects.

The legacy of nineteenth-century theme space for early film culture is the subject of chapter 5. Beginning in 1907, Hagenbeck supplied various kinds of big game for a controversial series of fictional safari films. What most interests me about these films is their insistent staging of hunters and animals within the same frame space, a practice strongly reminiscent of Hagenbeck's project. By 1913, the *Tierpark* had begun renting space to film production companies, and a number of fictional features would be made on the park's grounds, including two that were directed by the young Fritz Lang. After the war, the Berlin-based Decla Film Company agreed to purchase Hagenbeck's park and transform it into a modern studio complex. A forgotten site of early German cinema, the Decla Film City in Hamburg-Stellingen has never been excavated. If the *Tierpark* was really so popular and commercially successful, then why was it slated to become a film studio? What was it that drew film companies to Stellingen of all places? What kinds of productions did the *Tierpark* support, and what impact did they in turn have on its existing displays and collections? This chapter identifies a number of unexpected connections between the park's theme space and filmic diegesis, including some of the ways in which they both created a convincing impression of foreign space and situated the viewer in relation to it.

The main contribution of this book lies in its conceptual framing of theme space so as to account for long-range continuities as well as for discontinuities in the tradition. The Hagenbeck material turns out to be extremely useful for addressing questions of change over time, which is partly what gives this study its broad relevance for cultural history. It is the double nature of Hagenbeck's themed environment—as grounded in the material world of collecting, on the one hand, and in the imagination of diegetic space, on the other—which makes it such a rich context for current discussions of theme space in general. The Conclusion reflects on the implications of "Hagenbeck" for our historical understanding of theme space and its motivating fantasy of being immersed in the exotic.

CHAPTER 1

THE BUSINESS OF COLLECTING

In the autumn of 1874, Hagenbeck imported to Germany a group of six "Laplanders" (Sami), in addition to the herd of thirty-one reindeer that he was already having shipped from above the Arctic Circle in Norway. The idea of adding people to the group has been attributed to Hagenbeck's friend, Heinrich Leutemann (1824–1905). A freelance journalist, newspaper illustrator, and animal painter, Leutemann had a particular set of skills that would serve him well as the showman's first publicist and self-styled adviser. In each capacity, he shaped the aesthetic of Hagenbeck's ethnographic exhibition. He also had a hand in shaping its legacy. As Hagenbeck's first biographer, that is, Leutemann set the terms on which the *Völkerschau* (or "foreign peoples show") would later be remembered and reconstructed. His *Lebensbeschreibung des Thierhändlers Carl Hagenbeck* (Life story of the animal dealer Carl Hagenbeck, 1887) was more than just an interesting read for audiences at the time. Later, it became the primary written source for in-house biographies as well as for Hagenbeck's own memoir. Leutemann's work is also revealing for a study of nineteenth-century theme space, particularly in relation to ethnographic exhibitions, because it offers unique insight into the historical practice of recruiting native performers. The role of native agency in this process is precisely what distinguished the *Völkerschau* from other types of themed environments.

Of particular interest here is Leutemann's account of the initial troupe, the Sami. Actually, he wrote two very different accounts. The first, an 1875 article titled "Nordic Guests," was published in *Die Gartenlaube*, a middle-brow family magazine with national distribution. The second was the official version published more than a decade later as a chapter in Hagenbeck's life story. Each version has a vested interest in its subject. The article promotes the troupe; the biography puffs the showman. The original version is not necessarily the more accurate of the two, but it is the more extensive, including a number of fascinating details that are later omitted and have long since been forgotten. Some of these details (which have yet to be examined in the scholarship) bear repeating, especially insofar as they complicate our received ideas about the origins and underlying assumptions of Hagenbeck's ethnographic enterprise. The article, for instance, states that it was Hagenbeck (not Leutemann) who proposed collecting foreign people as well as exotic animals for the purpose of exhibiting them together. Leutemann takes credit for suggesting that Hagenbeck purchase "all of the objects that these people used—tents and equipment, skates, snowshoes, dogs—in short, everything that is characteristic of the life of this nomadic people brought from Lapland." Such variations demand further scrutiny, partly because it is difficult to obtain any evidence whatsoever about the historical practice of collecting. Out of necessity, I rely almost exclusively on German and Western sources, which raises a methodological issue, for troupe members doubtless had different viewpoints and experiences of the recruitment process. With this in mind, let me begin by combining Leutemann's two accounts and using the variations as a way of at least suggesting the complexity of agency, perspective, and exchange that characterized the assembly of ethnographic troupes.[1]

The official account of the very first troupe, as told by Leutemann in 1887, begins with the troupe's arrival in Germany:

> With utmost excitement, I traveled to Hamburg in September, as soon as I received notice [from Hagenbeck] that the ship was about to arrive there, and—since we were both equally impatient—raced up the Elbe in a friend's boat, in order to intercept the steamship en route. As the incoming ship passed by, we climbed aboard through a hatch and all of a sudden found ourselves in between decks, right where the Lapp woman, with her infant and a four-year-old girl, had made herself comfortable. The sight was decisive in convincing us that the enterprise would succeed—even more so when, walking up onto the deck, we found three yellow-brown, dwarfish Lapp men together with their reindeer. The accompanying agent, a Norwegian trader and photographer who had recruited the Lapps and traveled with them to Germany, gave his initial report (he also spoke German). The unloading began and, while the herding of reindeer took a great deal of energy and created the wildest scenes, everything was ultimately brought to Hagenbeck's. The first show began just a few days later. Its success exceeded even our greatest expectations, for the stream of spectators began early in the morning and, although a large space had been set aside for them, the crowds were so immense that the service entrance had to be opened in order to let people out.

Hagenbeck's ethnographic enterprise had hardly begun, and yet the key figures had already been assembled: the entrepreneur and his adviser, each excited by the prospect of turning a profit; the foreign agent or traveler, an independent businessman who along the way serves many different functions as trader, recruiter, photographer, and translator; a group of indigenous people (men and women, children and adults) accompanying a number of animals from the same region; and last but not least, an eager, surging crowd of spectators, too many to be accommodated all at once. Drawing extensively on this account, Hagenbeck would later claim that the troupe was so popular because "our guests were, indeed, unchanged natural people (*Naturmenschen*), still unfamiliar with Europe's affected politesse." Unlike other groups of Sami, whose survival depended on trade, tourism, and other forms of contact with Europeans, the "mountain Lapps" exhibited here made their own tools and clothes, and remained "almost completely dependent on the reindeer."[2]

Compare this arrival scene and its cast of characters with those of Leutemann's 1875 article, "Nordic Guests." Assuming that the motivation here was to promote the current show by generating interest and shaping expectations, consider his approach and the elements of the troupe that he highlights for prospective audiences at future stops along the tour. To begin with, Leutemann acknowledges that Sami "have been exhibited for years in Germany and Austria," but he does so only to dismiss these shows as so many examples of "affected savagery." Predictably, he sets the scene for Hagenbeck's troupe. What follows, however, is unexpected. As a point of interest, Leutemann gives the Norwegian names of most (but not all) of the performers: The woman is Ella Maria Rasti; no first name is given for her husband, who is called simply Herr Rasti, nor for their two children; the other two men in the troupe are Lars Nielson and his son Jacob. "As the first names . . . already suggest," Leutemann adds, relaying to his audience some information that he received from the recruiter, "the Lapps are Christians; it is known that they were baptized and instructed by traveling priests and school teachers, respectively."[3]

The complexity of perspective that was shared by organizers and participants becomes even more evident in the scene of their first encounter. By this account, rather than stumble upon a naïve Lapp woman engrossed by her children, Leutemann and Hagenbeck confront a traveling performer who apparently knew what she was doing.

> She looked at us with a questioning but uninhibited gaze, and the expression in her eyes had something so familiar and intelligent about it that now it doesn't surprise me at all that, after I gave her a one-Mark piece, we later became good friends. . . . Frau Rasti behaved very tactfully upon receiving the aforementioned coin. When she saw that I had drawn pictures of some of their equipment, she immediately opened a crate and, unprompted, pulled out a copper can in the

form of a teapot and a tool for cleaning the inside of reindeer skins, and set them out for me to draw. Her husband, when she handed him the received money, gave me neither a word nor a glance. He spun the coin around in his fingers until the wife took it back from him. In return for his increase in wealth, by contrast, Jacob gave me a clear, already learned "Danke!" Lars, the most advanced, even gave me a friendly handshake, as well.

No such gestures appear in later accounts of the troupe. Only the 1875 article shows participants and organizers engaging in social transactions mediated by vision, money, language, and touch. The exchange is uneven, to be sure. The entire account is based on a set of paternalistic assumptions about Sami as quaint, simple, "natural" people. At the same time, it includes fascinating moments of cross-cultural identification and dialogue that complicate such easy assumptions. Leutemann reports,

> The elder Nielson is an open person, and he is already studying German. One of the first evenings here, he risked a carriage ride with us through the streets of Hamburg, but refused to take another, for the whole thing seemed to him more like a ride to hell. But Lars has a sense of humor, too. In Berlin, he had fun throwing a lasso around an inappropriate spectator who was standing on the stage, but the insolent (*unverfroren* [literally, unfrozen]) Berliner caught it in his hand.[4]

The original account is especially remarkable for what it suggests about the awareness not only of performers but also of historical spectators. Some Germans—at least those who read Leutemann's article—were informed that the Sami were "people," and not mere objects of ethnography. They had names, backgrounds, personalities, Christian beliefs, a sense of humor, a bit of schooling, and even some knowledge of German. That was the hook, it seems, a way to make the troupe interesting to readers as potential customers. The assumption of naïveté, whether on the part of spectators or performers, is one that we as historians of visual culture make all too readily; both sides probably had more information than we tend to assume. Similarly, the assumption of cultural homogeneity must also be questioned. Rather than imagine and project onto native performers a framework of authenticity or "purity," we can look to the Rastis and the Nielsons as testifying to the effects of trade, travel, missionary work, and other forms of cultural assimilation that also circumscribed the history of ethnographic exhibition.

Though none of these transactions appear in Hagenbeck's life story or in other accounts of his ethnographic enterprise, they invite us to explore a more complicated scenario of cultural encounter, displacement, and exchange, beginning with the recruitment of native performers. After the first tour had ended with great success,

Hagenbeck treated his wife and Leutemann to dinner at an upscale restaurant in Hamburg's zoological garden. There, he outlined his plan to assemble a second troupe. "The money is still just lying there in the street," said Hagenbeck with enthusiasm, "You only need to know how to pick it up."[5]

✦ ✦ ✦

This chapter looks at the business of collecting as the basis for Hagenbeck's project, with particular focus on the assembly of ethnographic troupes. In so doing, it also lays a foundation for this book's larger claim that nineteenth-century theme space took shape as a hyperbolic collecting project. The task here is to analyze the means of cultural production in the context of ethnographic exhibition. Part of a worldwide network devoted to the accelerating exchange of consumer goods, Hagenbeck's ethnographic enterprise began as an epiphenomenon of the wild animal trade and eventually became semi-autonomous as an immensely popular form of commercial entertainment. He assembled groups of natives and animals for the sole purpose of displaying them for profit within a burgeoning industry of leisure and mass consumption. According to his biographer, Hagenbeck provided "an undeniably great service: He gave to the millions of people who are unable to search out their fellow human beings living in remote parts of the earth, formed differently in their habitats, the sight of them here among us." Indeed, Hagenbeck's "service" can be understood as providing local access to living, breathing foreign peoples, trailing the signs of the native setting behind them, by means of their physical dislocation and display. The *Völkerschau* both stimulated and responded to "the desire of contemporary masses to bring things 'closer' spatially and humanly," which Walter Benjamin would later attribute to cinema.[6]

Whereas Benjamin places emphasis on mechanical reproducibility and its effects, what interests me is the distinctive aliveness of human and animal display, and the decisive physicality of collecting for such a purpose. In contrast to the more familiar modes of museum collecting, on the one side, and technological recording, on the other, the production of an ethnographic troupe involved recruiting itinerant performers, in addition to acquiring large numbers of ethnographic artifacts and domesticated animals and transporting them all to Europe for the purpose of mounting a single, integrated group display. The resulting exhibition would be assembled several months later, thousands of miles away, and it would need to remain viable over an extended period of time, as it traveled from city to city. When a show ended its tour, the animals and the artifacts would typically be sold to interested buyers, often becoming part of other collections, whereas the people would be transported back to their homelands. That was the idea, anyway.

With his far-flung network of travelers and trappers, Hagenbeck was uniquely positioned to assemble itinerant troupes abroad. The point is not simply that Hagenbeck treated indigenous performers as commodities (which he did); it is his coordination and exploitation of this movement that most interests me. Special attention is devoted to the mechanics of collecting foreign peoples—the selection principles, administrative obstacles, physical conditions, and assimilation issues that defined the whole process of recruitment. In fact, I conceived of this chapter as an extended reply to the particular questions that I received from all sorts of people when I shared with them this material in particular. Where did the troupes originate? How were people recruited, and on whose terms? To what extent did individuals actively shape the recruitment process? Who were the performers, generally speaking, and why did they participate? None of these questions can be answered definitively, but they can be addressed and explored through a wealth of archival fragments. The results of this inquiry, however partial or speculative they must be, have considerable implications for our historical understanding of ethnographic performance.[7]

Recruitment began as a mode of collecting that was particular to live ethnographic performance and connected in many ways to the global trade in wild animals. If the idea of collecting seems obvious on some level, it is nonetheless crucial, especially when linked, as it is here, to issues of cultural displacement. The Hagenbeck material suggests that most performers were already (at least) once displaced within the colonial context. His troupes included native guides, hunters, traders, interpreters, house servants, migrant workers, and Christian neophytes. The troupes also attracted seasoned professionals, who made a living as itinerant ethnographic performers. From this perspective, the salient issue is not the myth of first encounter or untouched naturalness, but the factors of native agency and self-determination that shaped and often complicated the business of collecting for live ethnographic shows. So, besides developing the idea of recruitment as a mode of collecting, this chapter also explores the idea that native performers joined ethnographic troupes as a way of negotiating the lived experience of cultural displacement. Although Hagenbeck sought to control the business of collecting, he was certainly not the only one who had a stake in it.

Vertical Integration

Hagenbeck's ethnographic enterprise relied on an existing infrastructure, a rapidly expanding network of transportation and communication lines, which he was already using in the context of his animal business. As an international dealer, he had greater access to this network than was commonly available or affordable to urban audiences or even to professional scientists and entertainers. Between 1866 and 1886, he reportedly traveled an average of 50,000 kilometers a year by rail and steamship. He did so

1.1 "Animal transport with Elan antelope from the interior of Africa," ca. 1900. Photograph from Carl Hagenbeck, *Von Tieren und Menschen* (1909). Courtesy of Tierpark Carl Hagenbeck GmbH, Hamburg-Stellingen.

mostly in order to generate business—visiting almost every major zoo, circus, and menagerie, attending the annual fall zoo animal auction in Antwerp, meeting shipments at various ports—not in order to do the actual legwork of animal trapping or recruiting. For that he developed a corporate network of agents and outposts in Africa, Asia, Europe, and the United States. He and those who traveled for him used various systems of travel and communication, including foreign as well as German shipping lines and railways. The modern systems of circulation that enabled the dealer to trade animals more widely and efficiently would now support the entertainer in assembling and mobilizing foreign peoples. The task was to coordinate the available networks, while exploiting them in a new context. As Leutemann wrote in 1887, "the expansion of Hagenbeck's business activities, the animal trade as well as the ethnographic exhibition, was only possible in our era; earlier it would have been unthinkable. Only in the now highly developed system of railways and shipping lines, in connection with the telegraph and everything else that makes commerce flow today—only in this system was Hagenbeck in a position to plan and carry out these activities."[8]

The process of expanding his company to include ethnographic entertainments can perhaps best be described in terms of vertical integration (a concept often used by film historians to describe the emergent film industry). By this I mean the unification of production, distribution, and exhibition under a single managerial entity. The long-term effect of this process was to unify many different points along the same supply route, in this case, "from jungle to zoo."[9] Hagenbeck expanded his activities in both directions at once. Upstream, so to speak, he began assembling troupes of foreign peoples and collecting ethnographic artifacts in addition to wild animals. Here, as in the animal trade, he sought to minimize the cost and maximize his control of each stage of the process, creating his own pool of travelers and recruiters, many of whom also worked for him in other capacities. Downstream, he expanded from the animal trade into the entertainment industry; in addition to supplying buyers with wild animals he became an exhibitor of ethnographic shows. Beginning with the *Völkerschau*, Hagenbeck developed a dazzling array of entertainments, even as he continued the internal expansion of his animal business, which remained at the company's core. The analogy makes even more sense if we acknowledge that Hagenbeck's business was never totally integrated. It certainly embodied most of the basic functions of animal trapping, ethnographic exhibition, and zoological display (the same cannot be said for Hagenbeck's competitors), but the company also needed flexibility, especially in regard to certain tasks that could not be easily internalized. For example, menial tasks such as portage and cooking, which were absolutely necessary for large-scale hunting expeditions, but had no overspill in the performance arena, would still be doled out to natives who worked on a temporary basis. To be precise, then, the expansion of Hagenbeck's enterprise should really be described as a loose sort of vertical integration.[10]

Hagenbeck recalls the origins of his ethnographic enterprise, interestingly, as a sort of economic recovery plan, which was developed in the context of the wild animal trade. "The first impulse was the fact that the animal trade slowly began to sink in the mid-1870s, and I was thus forced to think about expanding my corporation in some other way." Until then, he had concentrated on a single line of business. The unprecedented number of circuses and zoological gardens that were established across Europe in the 1860s had provided him with more than ample reason to plan for future growth in the markets he knew best. In Germany, this long period of growth in the animal trade intensified during the so-called *Gründerjahre* (or founders' years), a period of economic euphoria in the early 1870s, immediately following political unification, when hundreds of new firms were established and patriotic burghers invested as never before in joint-stock companies (including a number of zoological gardens). Like all states of euphoria, it was not to last. The stock market crash of 1873 stifled the air of prosperity and confidence that businessmen in Germany had exuded for but a few short years.[11]

The details of Hagenbeck's account have been disputed, but the upshot is clear. Three points stand out, in particular. First, Hagenbeck's *Völkerschau* was first created in the context of what was then known as the Great Depression. The showman might not have accurately interpreted the economic situation, as other scholars have emphasized, but in his perception of crisis he was not alone. Second, Hagenbeck rationalized his ethnographic enterprise as an effort to recover some of his sunk costs in the animal trade (overseas freight and transport were by far the highest expenses he incurred), to maximize the infrastructure he already had in place, and to squeeze more out of standing orders and the labor that was required to fill them. The *Völkerschau* was not more financially reliable than the animal trade was, but the initial investment had already been made and the infrastructure of collecting was already in place. The possibility that ethnographic shows could offset lost profits in the animal trade was an outcome of vertical integration. Third, the animal trade's decline was partly a result of the very revolution in shipping technology and organization that made the transport of live animals faster and safer than ever before. As the international market for exotic animals expanded, prices steadily fell. Lower prices in turn eroded the dealer's profit margin, which is precisely why Hagenbeck began looking for new sources of revenue, beginning with ethnographic troupes.[12]

The plan was simple. Although the conditions of overseas transport had improved with the technology of shipping, the traffic in wild animals continued to rely on the presence and vigilance of human handlers. The use of native labor both to capture wild animals and to accompany them on long overseas journeys remained standard practice in the international animal trade. Hagenbeck's idea was to take the very people he employed at other points of the supply chain and exhibit *them* in Europe. Integration thus relied on the extension and transfer of native labor from the field of collecting to the arena of exhibition. What began as a strategy for economic recovery in the animal trade soon developed into a formula to be repeated and elaborated, resulting in a further extension of the company into the entertainment industry.

The Great Depression of the late nineteenth century initiated a new phase of encounter between capitalism and the "rest," an era of unprecedented expansion and acceleration of commodity flows across the globe. As other scholars have shown, radical developments in technology, logistics, and consumption at this time created new branches of big business whose fortunes were closely tied to those of particular parts of the world. Hagenbeck's ethnographic enterprise offers a prime example of this (however archaic or extraordinary it might seem to us today). The fact that this new branch of the business was based in the wild animal trade—a situation of cultural encounter and a form of colonial commerce in its own right—makes the example of Hagenbeck all the more interesting. So before we examine the mechanics of collecting, it may help to gain a sense of the context in which native peoples were initially recruited to be performers. Some familiarity with this context is also necessary in order to understand Hagenbeck's particular type of theme space, for many of his shows included dramatic reenactments of spectacularized scenes from the wild animal trade.[13]

1.2 En route to Europe, one of Hagenbeck's travelers (probably Hermann Boger) feeds the animals on deck, ca. 1890. Courtesy of Tierpark Carl Hagenbeck GmbH, Hamburg-Stellingen.

The Context of the Wild Animal Trade

The international traffic in wild animals, perhaps the only area of colonial trade that was dominated by Germans, created an important context for the emergence of Hagenbeck's ethnographic enterprise. While the destinations of his expeditions and the locations of his animal holding stations provided the cultural themes for particular shows, these routes and places first established the local conditions of recruitment. Changes in the international animal trade due to market forces or political events had sweeping implications for all his overseas ventures, including the availability of native performers. The business of human display was related to several different markets within the animal trade, two of which deserve emphasis here: namely, the markets for zoo and circus animals. Together, they constituted what Hagenbeck called his "business constellation," an extended area of intense trading and collecting activity—a constellation whose shape would often change over time.[14]

Throughout the 1860s and 1870s, the center of this constellation was the Sudan, a region of Africa controlled by Egypt and the British colonial government. As zoological gardens were being built around the world at the rate of almost one per year, Hagenbeck invested heavily in the Sudan, with expected returns in the international market for zoo animals. In 1864, he hired one of the most famous trappers of his day, the Austrian Lorenzo Casanova, who had already operated in the region for more than two decades before he began working exclusively for Hagenbeck. By 1865, Casanova had established Hagenbeck's first animal catching station (*Tierfangstation*) in Kassala. Casanova's work in the Sudan helped formalize the international business of animal trapping and transport, while boosting its public reputation as a respectable profes-

1.3 "John Hagenbeck's Elephant Depot in Ceylon," ca. 1900. Photograph from Carl Hagenbeck, *Von Tieren und Menschen* (1909). Courtesy of Tierpark Carl Hagenbeck GmbH, Hamburg-Stellingen.

sion. Hiring this legendary trapper also had the effect of raising Hagenbeck's profile as a major international dealer by the age of twenty-one, which in turn lured many other hunters, collectors, and businessmen to him, all seeking to make their fortunes by joining his outfit. So when Casanova died, in 1870, Hagenbeck continued his domination of the animal trade by contracting independent collectors, such as the German businessman Bernhard Kohn and the self-styled globetrotter Josef Menges, and coordinating their overseas operations largely via mail and telegraph. Hagenbeck further expanded his operation by currying favor with international businessmen and colonial administrators. The greatest American trapper of the period, Frank Buck, commented that "every German consul in the smallest port of Asia or Africa had been a Hagenbeck agent on the side." British consuls were perhaps even more important to his activities in the Sudan and (later) in Sri Lanka. At its fullest extent, his network encompassed as many as fifty collectors with animal catching stations in Asia, Africa, Europe, and the United States. These agents and stations would also provide the infrastructure for Hagenbeck's ethnographic enterprise.[15]

The holding station in Kassala was the primary setting in which Hagenbeck's agents traded with Arab and African dealers and eventually began recruiting some of them to join ethnographic troupes. In his 1876 report on the German animal trade in northeast Africa, Menges describes the station as a specialized form of trading post and the dealer's activity as a safe and predictable form of overseas business. "For the most part, the dealer stays in Kassala, leads a quite comfortable, unfettered life there, and lets his brown business friends deliver the animals right to his doorstep. During his stay in Kassala, a dealer can get hold of the following animals: giraffes, elephants, buffalo, hyenas, lions, leopards, various antelope, ostriches, eagles, vultures, secretary-birds, wild chickens, etc."[16] That same year, Kohn received a letter that set in motion the first Nubian troupe. In it, Hagenbeck gave him "the task of recruiting for me as part of the next transport a number of really interesting natives, and bringing them back to Germany, along with their animals, tents, tools, and hunting equipment." The troupe consisted almost entirely of young men. "There was also a woman, named Hadidje, the first Nubian woman to reach Europe," according to Hagenbeck. "These beautiful people belonged to various tribes." What united them as a troupe, apart from their non-Western origins, was their shared occupation in the animal trade. Advertising paraphernalia for the show identified the men as "Hamran hunters," a name that conjured up images of the legendary sword hunters of the Sudan. In fact, Kohn recruited not sword hunters, but some of the very people with whom he regularly traded. The performance dramatized scenes from the animal trade in Kassala as a representation of life in the Sudan; it was a living advertisement for Hagenbeck's company. The Nubian Caravan was so popular among audiences—shows took place not only in German cities, but also in Paris and London—that Hagenbeck went on to organize three more such caravans, between 1877 and 1879, with the assistance of various agents in Kassala.[17]

The ethnographic exhibition was also shaped by the international traffic in circus animals. This was especially true of the 1880s, when several major showmen vied for audiences in the United States. Hagenbeck made his first big push into the American market in 1881, when he hired William A. Conklin, director of New York's Central Park Menagerie, to be his official American representative. As a broker, Conklin helped import big game from the Sudan directly to the United States. In so doing, he enabled Hagenbeck to compete against the German brothers Charles and Henry Reiche, who had operated an office in New York City and sold animals there since 1847. When Hagenbeck arrived on the scene, competition in the American circus revolved around the hyperbolic display of elephants. By 1882, for example, P. T. Barnum and his rival Adam Forepaugh each had more than twenty elephants. As a result, wrote Hagenbeck, "It was raining big delivery orders, and that was a great stroke of luck for me in more ways than one." Indeed, the competition for circus animals had the inadvertent effect of bringing more native performers to Europe, and creating a new cultural theme. The elephant trade led to Hagenbeck's first "Ceylon" show in 1883. He even drew attention to this nexus in his memoir: "A new exhibition of peoples developed along the circuitous route of this year's elephant imports, and one can see therein how the chain was made, link by link."[18]

1.4 Hagenbeck with Somali performers, ca. 1895. Courtesy of Tierpark Carl Hagenbeck GmbH, Hamburg-Stellingen.

If the chain of associations was obvious for Hagenbeck and his contemporaries, today it needs to be made explicit. In 1880, the Mahdi uprising against the British (as the war of liberation was called) brought colonial commerce in the Sudan to an abrupt halt. Sudanese fighters ransacked Hagenbeck's station in Kassala, killing Bernhard Kohn. "In one fell swoop," wrote Hagenbeck, without commenting on the loss of his agent, "the African animal trade was totally ruined." As far as the dealer was concerned, he needed a new source of supply. "To that end, I sent my colleague, the famous globetrotter Joseph Menges, who had previously represented me in the Sudan, now to Ceylon. He went there initially as a pioneer, to scout out what was to be had there in the way of elephants. Menges took a comprehensive survey, traveling to the remotest corners of the island, and establishing business connections along the way. In his tracks followed two other travelers, who were sent there to organize the actual purchase and transport of elephants."

Between 1883 and 1885, Hagenbeck exported from Sri Lanka some of the largest animal shipments ever assembled. The first year alone he transported sixty-seven elephants to the United States. "It was a matter of course that the human exhibitions, which carried on uninterrupted, would enter the new region, as well." From the new holding station or "elephant depot," as it was called, Hagenbeck's agents, including his nephew Johannes Castens, his half-brother John Hagenbeck, and a new traveler named Eduard Gehring, organized an immensely popular series of at least five different Ceylon shows, which they brought to Europe each summer from 1883 to 1889. The circuitous route of the elephant trade led from Germany to the Sudan, to the United States, to Sri Lanka, to Germany, and ultimately back to Africa. When the African animal trade re-opened elsewhere, in Somalia, Hagenbeck dispatched Menges to the area, where he established a new holding station and later assembled another ethnographic troupe for Hagenbeck.[19]

The colonial networks of transport, communication, and exchange allowed Hagenbeck to establish his ethnographic enterprise within the context of the wild animal trade. Since he had been selling animals to zoos, circuses, and other buyers for several decades, the infrastructure for collecting was already in place. His station in Kassala, a site of colonial encounter and exchange, set the scene for the assembly of ethnographic troupes. Native trappers, dealers, and handlers—the very people whom Hagenbeck's agents engaged on a routine basis—would now be selectively recruited and brought back to Europe for the purpose of display. Several different animal markets would come to bear on the assembly of ethnographic troupes. In this case, the frenzied market for circus elephants in the United States led Hagenbeck, circuitously, to organize a series of Sri Lankan troupes and display them in Europe. Each example here can also be seen as part of a larger process that is the vertical integration of Hagenbeck's company. Initially, ethnographic exhibition had a secondary place within the company and a compensatory function in relationship to the animal business. As the show became an immensely popular form of commercial entertainment in its own right, it gained a certain degree of independence from the animal trade, without completely detaching from it. The inner workings of this process manifested themselves in specialization—especially at the stage of collecting, when Hagenbeck hired a "traveler" for the sole purpose of recruiting people, leaving the animals to be supplied from another part of the company. Specialization helps shed light on the links as well as on the differences between recruitment and other modes of collecting for theme space.

The Task of the Traveler

Of all the collectors associated with Hagenbeck's *Völkerschau*, one stands out in particular—one who admittedly (and to his mind, regrettably) had nothing to do with the wild animal trade. His name was Johan Adrian Jacobsen (1853–1947), and for a history of theme space he represents the development of a full-blown collecting project

1.5 "Hagenbeck's Traveler," Johan Adrian Jacobsen (at right), pictured here with the Norwegian general consul at Hagenbeck's *Tierpark* in Stellingen, ca. 1910. Copyright: Museum für Völkerkunde, Hamburg.

in the context of ethnographic display. Through Jacobsen, we see how the recruitment of performers extended to new environments with no direct connection to the animal business. While some of Hagenbeck's troupes continued to be organized around the animal trade, other troupes, such as those assembled by Jacobsen, developed a rather different relationship to the places and cultures that they claimed to represent. In branching out from the animal trade, Hagenbeck's shows explored the vicissitudes of the ethnographic imagination more broadly, while tracking the latest changes in audience expectations and preferences. Within this process of development, the practice of recruitment became a specialization in its own right.

Unlike Kohn or Menges, Jacobsen was hired by Hagenbeck for the sole purpose of recruiting native peoples and collecting ethnographic paraphernalia. On some occasions, he doubled as a show's impresario, accompanying the troupe from city to city, but he was a traveler by profession. Most of the troupes he assembled would also feature exotic animals, but they had been collected elsewhere and delivered by other agents. This arrangement became a source of some disappointment. "I have only two regrets in my life," wrote Jacobsen in his diary, "and they are: first, that I didn't collect animals for Hagenbeck from the beginning, as then I'd be a made man like Menges," and "second, that in my youth I didn't become an animal trainer, for that way too I would've been able to make a good living. Collecting peoples alone—there are so few occasions to do so, and so few peoples who allow themselves to be collected." For all his aspirations, Jacobsen remains a noteworthy figure precisely because of his failures and limitations, his reluctant specialization in "collecting peoples alone." What makes him even more important, from a historical perspective, is that he documented his experiences in thousands of letters and journal entries as well as in numerous publications. Parts of his story are worth recounting and analyzing more closely, because they give us a look at the process of recruitment in action, from the traveler's viewpoint. They also offer fascinating insight into issues of native participation and resistance.[20]

Born on a small island above the Arctic Circle, Jacobsen came to Hamburg in 1874, an uneducated Norwegian immigrant searching for employment and hungry for experience. Having worked as both a sailor and a fisherman in Norway, he joined the crew of a commercial ship bound for Chile, where he held odd jobs at local fishing outfits and shipyards, before returning to Hamburg in 1877. By then, Hagenbeck had completed preparations for his second Nubian troupe, and he was already organizing another. For variety's sake, Hagenbeck planned to shift the focus from Africa back to the Arctic and import a group of Inuit from Greenland. In this case, he needed to hire a traveler. The twenty-three-year-old Jacobsen presented himself with brio as ready and eager to go. When asked if he was really up to the task of assembling an ethnographic troupe, Jacobsen replied, "Yes, why not?"[21]

That very evening he left for Copenhagen, which was then the colonial gateway to Greenland. His first task was to secure official permission to bring a group of Inuit to Europe. At the office of the Danish interior minister, he conveyed "Hagenbeck's desire to present an ethnographic exposition so that one would obtain in Germany a concept of the life and work of this unique people." Permission denied, he appealed to one of Hagenbeck's acquaintances, the director of the Royal Danish Trading Company, Hinrich Johannes Rink, who was also a renowned expert on Greenland and the Inuit. Instead of offering assistance, Rink cast even more doubt over the project, emphasizing the health risk to the recruits and the potential effect that an experience of Europe might have upon their return to Greenland. As it happened (and it often did), Hagen-

1.6 The Greenland "Eskimo" troupe at the *Jardin d'Acclimatation* in Paris. Photo by Pierre Petit, 1878. Copyright: Museum für Völkerkunde, Hamburg.

beck's network of personal contacts provided the necessary backing. The director of the Zoological Garden in Copenhagen, it turned out, was also the interior minister's father-in-law, and the two of them worked out an agreement that allowed the expedition to take place under the supervision of the Danish government and its colonial inspectors in Greenland. Hagenbeck guaranteed that, after the show had ended, the entire troupe would be returned to Greenland on a Danish-owned ship, and he made "a considerable deposit" in Copenhagen.[22]

From Copenhagen, Jacobsen traveled via commercial whaling ship to the west coast of Greenland. The voyage lasted several weeks, as the crew hunted whales en route and sailed against adverse weather. In early July the ship reached Baffin's Bay and the trading post at Umanak. Jacobsen's introduction to the job of collecting was at once abrupt and difficult. "I immediately started making my ethnographic collection among the Eskimo who lived there, but to engage a family seemed impossible." Throughout his trip he encountered native reluctance to recruitment, but not to exchange; artifacts were aplenty, participants were not. Nor was the Danish colonial governor of assistance. "On 12 July I met the governor, the 'inspector,' and asked him for his help with my problem, but he seemed to be very uncertain about taking people to Germany. On 17 July I went to Disko Bay in the sailboat *Thorwaldsen*, but it seemed impossible to get any people there." Five days later, after a series of fruitless visits to villages, missions, and trading posts, he arrived in the town of Jacobshaven. There, he appealed to several local Germans and Scandinavians, including a doctor, a trader, and a Moravian missionary. He won over the missionary, who had already sold Jacobsen several ethnographic artifacts, by arguing that the intended show "would mainly demonstrate that the Eskimos living under Danish rule were by no means the savages, for which people took them to be." With assistance from local authorities, he eventually managed to recruit three men (Okabak, Kojange, and Kokkik), one woman, and her two children. Through an interpreter (the trader, whose father was a German and mother was an Inuit), Jacobsen promised them money and a chance to see the wider world. An employment contract was drawn up by the governor. Upon learning of its terms, the Inuit protested. Wages had not been allotted for the days (possibly weeks) of travel to and from Greenland. The Inuit negotiated better terms, and the contract was modified accordingly. Once an agreement had been reached, the new recruits allowed themselves to be examined and vaccinated by a local doctor, who found them all to be in good health and able to travel. At this point, Jacobsen endeavored to complete the task of outfitting the Inuit for their performances in Europe. By his own account, he "bought many ethnographic objects like large and small skin boats, tents, dogs, sleds, fishing and hunting gear, jewelry, clothing, and tools." Most of these items were purchased in order to be used first as props and later auctioned to the highest bidder; some of them, namely, the kayaks and skin boats (umiaks), were only half-built at the time, to be finished as part of the exhibition and sold to interested spectators.[23]

The troupe arrived in Hamburg on 29 September 1877, the first official stop on a year-long tour. There, six polar bears and twelve seals from Hagenbeck's trade menagerie were added to the show before it went out on the road. Throughout the tour, Jacobsen served as its impresario. His friend, Adolf Schoepf (whose father of the same name was director of the Dresden zoo), accompanied Jacobsen and worked as the show's manager. On 26 October they arrived in Paris, where the troupe performed for almost two months at the *Jardin d'Acclimatation*, followed by appearances at the zoological gardens in Brussels, Cologne, Berlin, Dresden, Hamburg, Hannover, and Copenhagen. Attendance in Paris was particularly strong, but the troupe drew large crowds throughout the tour; at Hagenbeck's menagerie in Hamburg, for instance, more than 44,000 people attended the shows on Easter weekend. In mid-July of 1878, the entire troupe returned safely to Greenland, as promised. Okabak's family reportedly brought home more than four thousand Danish crowns (along with two wagons filled with gifts), and Kojange another eight hundred in earnings. This was a tremendous amount in the colonial context, and a sum that Jacobsen would later bandy about as a lure for recruiting other native performers.[24]

Over the next few years, Jacobsen continued to assemble ethnographic troupes for Hagenbeck, each from the Arctic north. In 1878, he returned to his homeland of Norway, where he recruited a group of nine Sami. The following year he purchased a ship for Hagenbeck, *Der Eisbär* (The Polar Bear), which he had specially equipped for animal hunting as well as for transporting ethnographic troupes. In 1880, he led a crew of seal and whale hunters back to Greenland. As the first European ship to arrive in Jacobshaven that year, the crew received a warm welcome from a fleet of kayakers, who performed rolls and demonstrated their harpooning skills: "All in hopes of being noticed and recruited, for Okabak, Kojange, and Kokkik, the Eskimos who were in Europe 3 years ago, were now well-to-do people, and have long inspired the wish among their acquaintances to share in the same good fortune." The mood in Jacobshaven was festive, and Jacobsen sought to take advantage of it. "The numerous Eskimos coming on board were all well served. The entire ship was often filled with them. Then the organ-grinder piped up, and no Eskimo could resist these sounds. A spontaneous ball was arranged; the deck became a dance floor." These scenes and others were later described in an illustrated brochure, which was based on Jacobsen's diary, and gave a detailed account of the recruitment process for interested German spectators (see fig. 1.7). The actual purpose of bringing the organ-grinder—and the marionettes mounted on top of it—according to the brochure, was "to entertain the Eskimo population and encourage them to join the troupe." Jacobsen claims to have recruited several members of the original troupe, who allegedly wanted to return for another tour. They were joined by a number of newcomers drawn by the promise of wealth. Both sides had agreed to terms when the Danish government intervened, once again, only this time Jacobsen failed to reach a compromise with the colonial inspector. A further request for permission to hire a native guide and interpreter for a recruiting trip to northern Greenland was also denied.[25]

With some desperation, then, Jacobsen began casting about for alternatives. He sailed to the island of Labrador, where he encountered some resistance from the Moravian mission in Hebron. "Here I gathered some ethnographic artifacts from the native Eskimo. I found some especially rich graves. To engage a family to go to Europe was impossible because the German missionaries there, who were otherwise friendly toward me, urged the Eskimo not to go." He succeeded, however, in hiring a Christianized Inuit by the name of Abraham Ulrikab (age thirty-five) to work as his guide and interpreter. Jacobsen promised him a new suit if he succeeded in persuading someone to join the troupe and make the trip to Europe. Abraham's nephew, Tobias (age twenty-one), piloted the boat that they took to the settlement of Nakvak, the northern outpost of the Hudson's Bay Company and home to several traditional Inuit families who refused to be converted by roving missionaries. There, with assistance from an English trader named Mr. Ford, he recruited a "heathen" family of three: a shaman named Terrianiak (age forty), his wife, Paingo (whose age was estimated to be fifty), and their teenage daughter, Noggasak. Joining them—against the will but with the knowledge of the missionaries—were the interpreter, Abraham, his wife, Ulrike (age twenty-four),

1.7 "Eskimo ball on board *Der Eisbär* in Jacobshaven." Illustration by M. Hoffmann, 1880. Courtesy of Butler Library, Columbia University, City of New York.

their two daughters, Sara (age four) and Maria (less than a year old), as well as his nephew, Tobias. The acquaintance with Ford also became crucial in another way. Abraham agreed to participate on the condition that his mother, who would remain in Hebron, be given "enough food and supplies for the next year," in addition to the wages that he and his family would earn for their performance in Europe. This was "of course, a condition that was very happily granted" by the Hudson's Bay Company. Presumably, Ford and Jacobsen struck a deal of their own, on the side.[26]

The troupe of eight Inuit arrived in Hamburg at the end of September 1880. A certain Frau Jacob was hired "for the mothering of this troupe," to cook and do laundry for the performers, as she had done for previous troupes. After a month of performances in Hamburg, they visited Berlin and Prague, where Jacobsen rejoined the troupe, followed by stops in Frankfurt am Main, Darmstadt, Krefeld, and Paris. Later destinations were to have included London, Petersburg, Vienna, and Herrnhut (a Moravian village near the German-Polish border and the symbolic home of the modern church). They never reached those destinations.[27]

In January 1881, the show came to an abrupt and tragic end. All eight of the performers contracted smallpox and died in rapid succession. First, doctors in Darmstadt misdiagnosed Noggasak for an ulcer and Paingo for rheumatism. Then, in Krefeld, Sara presented with the same symptoms, including chills and vomiting. Frau Jacob stayed behind and took care of the girl until she died. Finally, Jacobsen had the remaining members immunized against smallpox, upon their arrival in Paris, but by then it was too late. Writing from his bed in Saint-Louis-Hospital, where he was also recovering, Jacobsen seems to have agonized over the consequences of his actions, as suggested by a diary entry dated 16 January 1881. "Did I really have to lead these poor brave people from their homeland only to find their grave in foreign soil? How did everything come to pass so differently from my intention?"[28]

The task of the traveler was to care for the troupe's well-being in every sense—at least, that is how it was defined in contracts of employment and that is how it was represented to missionaries and government officials. To what extent did he actually fulfill this task? That was the crucial question. In terms of medical care, for example, Hagenbeck's traveler generally attended to minor conditions such as fevers, diarrhea, and bite wounds. For more serious injuries and illnesses, either doctors were called in or performers were taken to local hospitals. Doctors were also employed abroad to screen and immunize new recruits, as noted in the case of the 1877 Greenland troupe. In Labrador, by contrast, there were as yet no doctors at the mission station, and the Hudson's Bay Company had no vaccination supplies, so it was decided that the Inuit would be immunized in Germany. By the time they arrived in Hamburg, Jacobsen was so ill that he had to be immediately hospitalized. Hagenbeck hired Schoepf as the troupe's impresario until Jacobsen was able to join him. In the exchange, they neglected, once again, to have the Inuit immunized. When the show came to Berlin, several members of the Moravian church visited the troupe, and one of them filed a positive report in the December 1880 issue of the church's newsletter. "I think it is my duty," wrote Brother Dewitz, "to correct possible wrong opinions and to acknowledge in gratitude at this moment, that the physical and mental well-being of the Eskimos is cared for in liberality and with great effort."[29] A personal appearance by Hagenbeck, who came to Berlin expressly to meet with church leaders, evidently influenced the report, which cited his presence as a sure sign of his interest in the group's welfare. By the end of the month, two of the performers would already be dead.[30]

This is the context in which Jacobsen parted company with Hagenbeck and took a new job as traveler for the Royal Museum of Ethnography in Berlin. The museum's founder and director, Adolf Bastian, had already commissioned the Inuit performers to create objects for the museum during their visit. Now he expressed interest in acquiring the show's collection of artifacts. Within a week of their death, "Bastian not only purchased the collection, he set in motion plans to hire the collector." For his part, Jacobsen would later recall the Labrador show as a turning point in his career; the death of the Inuit marked for him the symbolic end of his life as a businessman, and the beginning of a new one. It would not last for long. Although he made some of the largest acquisitions in the museum's history, he failed to land a permanent job there for lack of academic training.[31]

Jacobsen's museum work is interesting for my purposes, because it opens up the possibility for comparison and contrast between different "objects" of collecting. The very skills and experiences that he had gained as Hagenbeck's traveler—organizing expeditions, negotiating colonial bureaucracy, soliciting assistance from German and Scandinavian businessmen abroad, exploiting available infrastructure, selecting ethnographic artifacts, trading with native dealers, even robbing native graves—would also serve him well as "Traveler for the Royal Museum." Bastian made this explicit when he wrote in 1883, "The museum was fortunate in securing the services of a collector so well qualified as Herr Jacobsen, who had the advantage of special preparation in his long association with Herr Carl Hagenbeck, Hamburg, for whom he has made many collections for purposes connected with business." In each capacity, moreover, the collector's task similarly entailed identifying and accumulating selected pieces of the physical world to be extracted, carted away, and transported to Europe. These pieces might accrue a different kind of value—namely, display value—as a result of their displacement.[32]

The contrast between Jacobsen's work for Hagenbeck and Bastian can best be understood in terms of their respective objects and the mode of collection that each in turn required. For example, when the museum sent him to Alaska, in 1881, Jacobsen moved at "lightning speed," purchasing (even stealing) whatever artifacts he could at one station, looking in some villages for as little as one hour, and hastily moving on to the next. He allowed no time to systematically label and organize his collection, no time to fret over its various holes and duplicates, before he packed up the objects and sent them to Europe. To assemble an ethnographic troupe required a different approach. Jacobsen had to think in terms of creating a single, coherent, self-contained group for the sole purpose of public display. In addition to recruiting people, he had to outfit them with appropriate-looking costumes and props. In negotiating with performers, moreover, the traveler encountered forms of agency and resistance that had no equivalents in the process of collecting material artifacts. To give only one example, when Jacobsen found interest among local peoples, he had to negotiate not only with individuals, but also with larger groups or families. The questions came from all sides. *How can you guarantee our safe return? What is it that we'd have to do in Europe? Can I bring my spouse with me? Won't you take my other, very talented son, too? Who will provide for my parents while I'm away? How long is the passage?* A traveler had to answer such questions either directly or through an interpreter, and the recruitment process usually involved staying in one place for days (not hours) at a time.[33]

That was not all. Once the various members of the troupe had been assembled, the traveler had to keep them all together, while negotiating their various needs and demands throughout the entire journey. For this reason alone, Jacobsen preferred the relative ease of collecting artifacts. "You see in principle," he confided in a letter to his fiancée, "I like the position at the museum better than with Hagenbeck, one gets a lot of honor during the trip and is linked to far less worry, because once the collections are packed into a box I have little to worry about—but with the people the worries just start the day one has hired them."[34] In February of 1882, for example, Jacobsen was released from his duties as museum collector in order to assemble for Hagenbeck a troupe of "Long-heads" from British Columbia. With the assistance of his friend George Hunt (another dealer for the Hudson's Bay Company, and the same person who would later assist the anthropologist Franz Boas and the photographer Edward S. Curtis), Jacobsen recruited three men and two women from Koskimo village on Vancouver Island. After a four-day potlatch, a series of visits to other villages, where troupe members stopped to take ceremonial leave of their relatives, and several interventions by others who urged them not to go, the group arrived at Fort Rupert two weeks later. There, they encountered what might be described as a kind of native infrastructure, a local network of resistance that channeled the people back to their village. By Jacobsen's account, the Fort Rupert natives repeatedly emphasized how close they were to home, "to make them realize how easy it would be to leave me" and reminded them "of the difficulties of their trip this far, stressing how much worse it would be to go to Europe for a whole year, when they would be rocked on the sea and be seasick without a break." Shortly before their scheduled departure, five natives from Koskimo arrived and implored the group, once again, to return with them. The next night, wrote Jacobsen, the entire troupe deserted him "without even saying good-bye."[35]

By following some of Jacobsen's routes and activities, we gain a more nuanced understanding of the traveler's task at precisely the moment when the assembly of ethnographic troupes became an area of specialization. It also helps situate the practice of recruitment "on the ground." We see the assistance as well as the resistance that he received from native guides, Creole interpreters, European traders, and colonial administrators. The example of Jacobsen demonstrates the carryover between recruitment and museum collecting, while emphasizing the important differences between these cultural practices, especially the issues of persuasion, viability, and attrition. His was a position of power, to be sure, but it required him to negotiate with native performers, who had their own reasons and conditions for participating.

Selection, Negotiation, and Professionalization

The informing context of power appears most vividly in the process of selecting ethnographic performers, but so does the role of native assimilation and resistance. Various forms of evidence—diaries, letters, photographs, publicity materials, and employment contracts—offer insight into the governing principles of selection, and the extent to which such principles were actually followed. By selection I mean the process of determining, first, which kinds or groups of people were deemed suitable for ethnographic display, and second, whether or not a particular individual was desirable for a given troupe. Such decisions were keyed in part to audience expectations, what showmen believed would be widely appealing and marketable to a commercial audience. Audience preferences changed over time, to be sure, as did the expectations of native participants. The professionalization of performers became more and more a factor of recruitment and display. What follows, then, is not a stepwise account of the selection process but an attempt to synthesize what little is known about it, and to complicate this material by emphasizing the role of native self-determination.

The German expert on *Völkerschauen*, Hilke Thode-Arora, has suggested that Hagenbeck's recruiters worked with a set of imaginary and mostly visual criteria. Three of these criteria predominated: "a certain degree of otherness (*Fremdheit*), physically distinctive features, and 'picturesque ways' or customs, which lend themselves to presentation." The vagueness of these criteria is due in part to the level of generalization, which aims to encompass a wide diversity of troupes. The category of physical distinctiveness, for example, extends from spectacular displays of physical abilities (including contortion, dancing, and animal handling) to unusual somatic features (such as skin color or body shape). Whether travelers such as Jacobsen consciously applied these or any other criteria is doubtful. As it unfolded, the selection process could be as intuitive as it was calculated. It helps, then, to identify an exemplary moment of inspiration and see where it leads.[36]

Consider the Koskimo natives of 1882, the troupe that got away. Jacobsen was in Bastian's employ, buying artifacts on Vancouver Island, when he wrote the following letter to Hagenbeck on 3 November 1881. "I have things which people who have lived among the Indians for 20 years have not seen—particularly for dancing, e.g., masks and rattles. When these guys start dancing with them—then it looks fine, the house is lit in the middle with a big fire—then all kinds of figures dance around it—ravens, eagles, owls, fish, devils, all kinds of human faces—in short, there is probably not a single carnival where you can see more dramatic figures than in the Indian dances." As for the women, Jacobsen was struck by the labrets that they wore, especially those made of bone or stone—materials that for him connoted ancientness. In proposing to assemble a Koskimo troupe, which is what he did in this letter, he was careful to write in terms that would resonate with Hagenbeck as a showman.[37] A kinetic scene taken from everyday life, complete with lights, music, and dramatic figures, using costumes and props for great effect—this is the kind of scene that could grab the attention of spectators in Europe. Hagenbeck was hooked. "I have already read today's letter from you 3 times and will read it several times more until I have enough of it because from this morning I have been thinking of nothing else but of the Indians you think you can bring." After personally appealing to Bastian for Jacobsen's release, Hagenbeck sent new instructions.

> HAMBURG, 5 JANUARY 1882
>
> Dear Jacobsen,
> I was in Berlin 8 days ago and spoke with Bastian about getting permission from the [Berlin] Society [for Anthropology], so that you could bring me Indians from that area, and he agreed to speak with the gentlemen. . . . I just received a letter from Herr Bastian, wherein he informs me that I have been granted permission, and that as of now you are in my employ. . . . So, you must now see to getting long-headed Indians along with whatever these people need. What you do and how you negotiate is entirely up to you, as you alone know what is necessary. I also leave you a free hand as to how these people are paid. From this time forward, everything that you purchase there is on my account, though I naturally have to give the museum first pick. You will receive your old salary from me, plus 10 percent of all earnings and photograph sales. If you bring these Indians, if the women have flat heads and tattoos and wear bones in their noses and lips, then I'm convinced that we'll make a huge profit. . . . Wishing you much luck, I send kind regards.
> Yours,
> Carl Hagenbeck

Each of the criteria that Thode-Arora has suggested—cultural otherness, physical difference, and dramatic customs—can also be gleaned from Hagenbeck's letter. When it came to selection, Hagenbeck deferred to his traveler on the scene. Jacobsen received no further details or instructions. If Bastian provided any sort of ethnological guidelines or suggestions that might have aided Jacobsen in the recruitment process, Hagenbeck never conveyed them to his traveler. Instead, he gave Jacobsen a financial stake in the show, a tangible incentive to make business-minded decisions.[38]

Beyond the criteria that Thode-Arora has suggested, a principle of variety governed some decisions on the cultural level, especially in the effort to distinguish between consecutive troupes. The first two shows that Hagenbeck had assembled, the Laplanders and the Nubians, suggest an interest in creating dramatic juxtapositions between peoples from different geographical regions or zones, in this case, the Arctic and the tropical. Leutemann was explicit about this point when he described the latter show: "The glaring contrast of now being presented with the dark, slender sons of the hot zone, who move with such passion and grace, after previously seeing the children of the north here, contributed much to enhance the effect." If a troupe was exceptionally popular and profitable, however, variety gave way to repetition: hence, the extended series of shows featuring Nubians in the late 1870s and Sinhalese in the early 1880s. Hagenbeck's far-flung network allowed him to cast a very wide net, offering a longer succession and a greater diversity of ethnographic troupes than any other showman of the period.[39]

The scientific discourse informing the selection of particular individuals presupposed the existence of anthropological types. The theoretical concept of type, which museum curator and anthropologist Elizabeth Edwards has called "the abstract essence of human variation," was extremely flexible, widely interpreted, and shot through with internal contradictions. Nevertheless, it was generally agreed that through the use of visual technology—above all, photography—the characteristics of type (however defined) could be made visible and thereby observed. In nineteenth-century Germany, this idea is perhaps best illustrated by Carl Dammann (1819–1874), a Hamburg photographer who assembled and published various albums of racial types, including the large-format *Anthropologisch-Ethnologisches Album in Photographien* (1873). What distinguishes this project, according to Edwards, is its concern with demonstrating "the nature of human and cultural variety" (as opposed to visualizing Darwinian evolution, which Edwards identifies with the British context). It is important to emphasize, however, that the idea of the anthropological type was a minor factor in the recruitment of ethnographic performers, especially in comparison to representational practices, such as public exhibition and advertising. As far as recruiters were concerned, native performers should appear to be typical inhabitants of a certain region or members of a particular ethnic group, but what counted as "typical," "characteristic," or "representative" in this context was obviously not governed by a system of scientific classification. As John Hagenbeck recalled, concerning the Sri Lankan troupe he assembled in 1885: "Aside from dancers I also engaged for our European tour a large number of elephant drivers, magicians, contortionists, snake-charmers, and other characteristic figures of Indian folk life, as well as women with their children." By this logic, the anthropological type and the circus artiste were virtually indistinguishable. In the process of assembling an ethnographic troupe, where a bottom-line logic of time and money held sway, recruiters employed more widely accepted constructs such as cultural clichés and racial stereotypes, which would presumably be legible and identifiable among mass spectators, and could also be reconciled with scientific categories—without being hampered by such material in the collecting phase.[40]

The notion of assembling characteristic figures further implied a principle of social diversity within the troupe. It was especially pronounced in terms of age and gender, as suggested by archival photographs such as figure 1.6, which depicts the Inuit troupe

1.8 "Director Willy Möller recruiting at a Bisharin settlement," from the program brochure, *Die Bischaris* (1899). Courtesy of Tierpark Carl Hagenbeck GmbH, Hamburg-Stellingen.

that Jacobsen assembled in Greenland. Though organized on a considerably smaller scale than that of later shows, the Greenland troupe demonstrates the principle of representative diversity: seated on the sled are Okabak (whose Danish name was Kaspar, age thirty-six), his wife Maggak (in Danish, Margarethe, twenty-four), and their two daughters, Ane (three) and Katarina (two); standing behind them are Kokkik (whose Danish name was Hans, twenty-eight) and Kojange (twenty-one). From the viewpoint of its iconography, the photograph is obviously based on a much older ethnographic trope: that of the mother nursing her child. By the same token, the photograph, like the troupe it portrays, is meant to demonstrate what Jacobsen called "the family life of foreign peoples." In the early shows, as we shall see, the everyday life of families became a key context for representing Hagenbeck's notion of the ethnographic, while at the same time allowing for the possibility of spectator identification spanning men and women, children and adults. In terms of recruitment, the family embodied the basic ideal of anthropological variety that collectors held in mind.[41]

Over time, the selection process was shaped and reshaped by audience expectations, as Hagenbeck and other impresarios interpreted them. The Bisharin Caravan of 1899 offers a fascinating example. Assembled and directed by Willy Möller, an independent businessman who made an entire career of organizing ethnographic shows, the troupe consisted of fifty-two men, seventeen women, and four children. The Bisharin (also spelled Bishari) were, and still are, a Sunni Muslim tribe that belongs to the nomadic Beja ethnic group. Living in the area of the Sudan between the Nile and the Red Sea, at the time they were well known within the international animal trade as camel-herders. In the program brochure, Möller describes for his audience the tremendous difficulties that had to be overcome to assemble the group. In framing it as the outcome of his heroic efforts as a collector, however, Möller inadvertently highlights the very constructed nature of his troupe. Around 1890, impresarios competed for spectators through the hyperbolic inflation of the show's scale, with some troupes consisting of several hundred performers. In terms of scale, Möller's troupe was modest, but it admittedly overshadowed the size of an actual nomadic community. "The main difficulty in getting together a troupe of the strength that I wanted lay in the fact that the Bisharin are only used to living in small and totally dispersed troupes; it took months of hard work to bring this endeavor to a close." In the process, Möller recruited some people whose relationship to the Bisharin was tenuous, but whose presence in the troupe was deemed essential. In particular, "the artisans (*Handwerker*) who accompany the troupe are not all Bisharin but people from Upper Egypt, as well. As the Bisharin have no industry of their own, I was forced to take these Egyptians, but I nonetheless selected only those who stand in direct contact with the Bisharin so as to meet their needs." A stock figure of ethnographic display, the native artisan had by this time become so prevalent that no troupe, regardless of its theme or origin, seemed complete without one. Here it should be made explicit that consumers expected not merely to see craftsmen at work, they expected to be able to purchase their goods as either artifacts or souvenirs.[42]

Ultimately, however, for all the criteria that collectors might have employed, from anthropological ideals to audience expectations, recruitment hinged on the question of agency: Who was willing and able to go? The search for participants was so costly and laborious that travelers invariably made concessions so as not to return empty-handed. We see this not only in unrealized troupes, such as the Koskimo of 1882, but also in troupes that were actually exhibited. In the summer of 1885, for example, Jacobsen returned to British Columbia in yet another effort to hire a group of "Long-heads." His younger brother, Fillip, was sent ahead, ostensibly to speed the process, but he failed to recruit any people in advance. The brothers met in Victoria, where they managed to assemble a group of eleven Kwakiutl, including two long-headed women. George Hunt agreed to accompany them to Germany as the troupe's interpreter. While Hunt and the Jacobsen brothers made a collecting trip to Vancouver Island, the members of the Kwakiutl troupe changed their mind and fled, as the Koskimo had earlier. At this point, Fillip recalled encountering nine Bella Coola (Nuxalk), who were en route to the hop fields of Washington. "There was nothing else to do," Jacobsen reasoned,

“but to make an attempt in this direction.” They caught up with the Bella Coola in the port city of Victoria.[43]

1.9 The “Bella Coola” troupe in Breslau, 17 February 1886. Copyright: Museum für Völkerkunde, Hamburg.

There, after long negotiations, the migrant workers agreed to the terms of a contract, which was drawn up by lawyers on 25 July 1885. The Indian Superintendent in Victoria, Israel Wood Powell, certified that the agreement had been made and that its terms had been interpreted and explained to the performers in his presence. Among the various “Articles of Agreement,” each Bella Coola agreed to “exhibit himself before the Public in the performance of Indian Games and recreations in the use of Bows and arrows in singing and dancing and speaking and otherwise in showing the habits manners and customs of the Indians.” The scheduled work day lasted from eight in the morning to six in the evening, with a half-hour break for lunch, seven days a week. Each performer would earn twenty dollars a month. For his part, Jacobsen agreed to “pay all reasonable and necessary expenses,” including food, lodging, clothing, transportation, medical care, “and funeral expenses in case of death.” The troupe was to return to British Columbia by 1 August 1886. Finally, Jacobsen was required to post a security deposit of one thousand dollars in the event of default.

When informed of this stipulation, Hagenbeck protested, emphasizing his good reputation, and asked why such a deposit had not been required in the past. The development behind this policy was the increasing professionalization of native performers, and government efforts to regulate it.[44]

Professionalization was not entirely new in this context. Trained performers such as acrobats, snake charmers, and elephant drivers had often been recruited for Hagenbeck's troupes. Professionals were not categorically excluded, despite all claims to the contrary. In some contexts they were preferable, not least of all "because it was easier to work with them," as Anne Dreesbach has recently observed; "they were already accustomed to performing in front of an audience." Moreover, the general interest and willingness of native participants seems to have changed over time. With the spread of Hagenbeck's reputation and network of agents, people from around the world tried to make their fortunes in Europe by joining one of his shows. Some people fled from Hagenbeck's traveler, others came to him. In other words, the process of recruitment also involved a certain degree of self-selection.[45]

1.10 The Somali entertainer Hersi Egeh Gorseh worked with Hagenbeck for more than thirty years. Courtesy of Tierpark Carl Hagenbeck GmbH, Hamburg-Stellingen.

The idea of native professionalization and entrepreneurialism is perhaps best illustrated by a Somali participant named Hersi Egeh Gorseh. Between 1895 and 1927, he joined at least five different African exhibitions and served in almost as many roles. He was an animal handler, a performer, a recruiter, an impresario, and more. By 1909, the show was old hat for him, when he and his family returned to Hamburg with a troupe of eighty performers, assembled by Gorseh himself, for the grand Ethiopia exhibition, which he was also hired to direct. "He at least is no stranger to Europe," wrote one journalist, "even if he now appears in his capacity as native director of a *Völkerschau* caravan for the very first time." In this role, he also participated in advertising and public relations, giving interviews to local reporters and meeting with prestigious visitors and other "friends of the company" before the show's premiere. In full regalia, Gorseh "sat down at the coffee table and conversed with the group as best he could in a colorful mix of

CONTRACT.

ARTICLES OF AGREEMENT, made and entered into this 16. day of Feby. 1910, by and between Adrian Jacobsen, a citizen of Hamburg, and domiciled in Hamburg, as representative for Carl Hagenbeck, Hamburg (hereinafter called the Impressario), and an Indian James Red Horse of Pine Ridge Agency, South Dakota, (hereinafter called the Performer).

Witnesseth: That the Impressario has and by these presents does engage the Performer, for the Tierpark in Hamburg or eleswhere in Germany. to take part in a performance known as Carl Hagenbeck's Show, for a period of 37 weeks, services hereunder to begin on or about April, 15th 1910 the approximate date of arrival in Germany.

The Performer hereby agrees to act in the capacity of general utility in Hogenbecks Show, and to do whatever in reason and justice may be required of........ while in the service of the Impressario, and which may be necessary and incident to such employment, not inconsistent with the laws of morality and the ordinary rules of propriety.

The Performer further agrees to keep sober and obey the regulations governing the establishment of the Impresario. If the Performer fails to observe faithfully said regulations, or if.... is inattentive to business or become incapacitated by reason of injury, sickness or other cause from properly performing in the Hagenbecks Show the Impresario shall have power to abrogate this contract, subject to said Impresario providing the Performer with a return ticket to the Indlan Agency from which he came, with sufficient money for subsistence and other necessary expenses incident to the return trip.

In the event that the contract is abrogated because of the refusal or failure of the Performer to observe the regulations above mentioned or to perform his duties in a proper manner. said Performer shall forfeit all salary due.... at the time of said abrogation, Provided however, that the Commissioner of Indian Affairs consents there to and not otherwise.

The Performer hereby covenants not to rehearse, act, or perform in any capacity for any person or persons gratuitously or for profit in any other theatre or place of amusement, nor directly or indirectly aid or assist in any other production or show before the termination of this agreement. In case of any violation of the above covenant the Impresario shall have the right, by injunction ~~or other~~ legal process, to obtain damages and restrain the performer from so working, or assisting in any other performance in any way whatever.

The Performer agrees to provide one set of Indian clothes, head-dress, moccasins, and such other equipment as may be necessary and suitable to the character which may be allotted to him or her.

The service of said performer shall consist of not more than twenty-six (26) performances per week or ten (10) working hours per day.

No salary in addition to that herein specified shall be paid for rehearsals.

The Impreario agrees that for the faithful performance of this contract by said Performer he will paid to the latter, the salary of $24.00 dollars per Month from the day of departure of the Performer from New York until his return thereto.

The Impresario further agrees to pay all expenses of the Performer, including steamship and railroad fare both from and returning to the Indian Reservation; to furnish him ample accomodations as to sleep and lodging; and also to furnish him with good substantial food, consisting of fresh meat, fish, vegetables, bread and butter, etc., etc.,

The impresario agress also to take proper care of the Performer in case of illness and to provide him with all needful medical attendance and medicine.

The Impresario further agrees to take necessary precautions to guard the Performer from improper influences while absent from his home, and that he will not be furnished intoxicating liquors of any kind or permitted to obtain them while away from his reservation.

In case of fire, war panic, other calamity or force major over which said Impresario has no control, he shall have the right to terminate this contract, upon which termination the salary payable hereunder shall cease, but all other provisions of this contract shall remain in full force and effect until complied with by the Impresario.

It is hereby agreed that the Impresario shall have the option of extending the time of this contract for a period not exceeding ten (10) weeks.

Arabic, English, and German." The result was good publicity for Gorseh as well as for Hagenbeck. "Gorseh not only manages the liveliest, most interesting, nothing short of dramatically moving performances, war games, riding shows and parades in the great arena like a skillful director, he is also an extraordinarily clever businessman."[46] Indeed, Gorseh and his family created a business of their own by importing sewing machines from Germany to Somalia. According to Thode-Arora, "his family went on to establish a monopoly in high-speed textile industry and became rich in the process." A professional entertainer, an able manager, a resourceful entrepreneur, Gorseh successfully adopted a model of production developed elsewhere. The resemblance is worth noting: Gorseh as Hagenbeck's double. Although the two men were most likely not perceived on equal terms, their exchange attests to the important role of collaboration where perhaps we least expect it. Gorseh's "close personal relationship" with Hagenbeck was admittedly unusual, but his entrepreneurial motivations were by no means exceptional.[47]

The professionalization of native performers can be seen as culminating in the Sioux troupe of 1910, which was also the most popular group that Hagenbeck ever assembled (for a discussion of the performance, see chapter 3). The fact that he recruited a troupe of Plains Indians—indeed, a Wild West show—further demonstrates that visual clichés and audience expectations informed the selection of cultural themes as well as performers. This time Hagenbeck sent Jacobsen directly to Pine Ridge Reservation in South Dakota. His instructions for the collector, written in English, were remarkably vague and formulaic: "I want you to engage for me: 30 Indian warriors, including one interpreter who knows the Sioux language, and furthermore 10 squaws and children, being 40 persons in all. With these Indians we must of course get all the necessary clothes, shirts, feathers, moccasins, head-dresses, etc." After several decades of Wild West shows and Karl May novels, more specific criteria were unnecessary; they went without saying. When it came to recruiting cowboys, he urged Jacobsen to simply avoid "drunkards and quarrelers."[48]

1.11 Page one of the employment contract for James Red Horse. Each performer's contract was signed by the troupe's interpreter Charles Géroux, approved by the U. S. Indian Superintendent at Pine Ridge, Major John R. Brennan, and later certified by the Bureau of Indian Affairs in Washington, D.C. The agency also provided boilerplate language for the contract. Courtesy of Tierpark Carl Hagenbeck GmbH, Hamburg-Stellingen.

The selection process here was characterized by federal regulation and local competition. First, the Bureau of Indian Affairs supplied Jacobsen with a standardized employment contract as well as with letters of introduction to government agents at the Rosebud, Pine Ridge, and Standing Rock reservations. As instructed by Hagenbeck, Jacobsen went directly to Pine Ridge on account of its relatively good reputation among showmen and recruiters. Indeed, he was one of six agents who had converged on Pine Ridge Reservation at the same time, each working for a different company. Yet another agent had just departed, after recruiting more than forty people for a trip to Brussels, and Buffalo Bill's agent was scheduled to arrive shortly. This level of competition was intense but not unprecedented. By this time, several generations of Sioux had performed in Wild West shows throughout the United States, with some troupes coming to Germany as early as 1883. The professionalization of "show Indians," as they were called in the business, had mixed implications for Jacobsen, as performers were very informed about the experience of overseas travel and of life on the itinerant entertainment circuit.[49]

To assist him in negotiating with so many performers Jacobsen was accompanied by George W. Everette (a.k.a. "Texas Tex"), an experienced circus cowboy and an old acquaintance of the Hagenbeck family, who later served as the Sioux troupe's leader in Hamburg. In addition, Jacobsen hired a translator by the name of Charles Géroux, who (along with his family) would also accompany the troupe to Germany. Further assistance came directly to Jacobsen. "A typical Indian was here today," he wrote in his diary, "Thomas American Horse. The same person became chief this year after his father died. He thinks he could assemble a large number of people from his tribe alone. We sent him out to recruit around the reservation." In this case, Jacobsen clearly had certain physical as well as cultural criteria in mind. For example, he insisted on hiring only people with long hair. "Many, however, had their hair cut, whether voluntarily, because they liked the 'new fashion' or involuntarily, such as all those who attended school (where long hair was prohibited) or had recently been in jail." As long hair was also preferred by the Oglalas for traditional dances, Jacobsen observed that people with short hair were apparently permitted to don "wigs made from their own hair." Imagine the scene in Germany: if native performers of any kind were seen dancing in wigs, Hagenbeck would almost certainly be accused of fraud. On this point there was no room for compromise. By contrast, although Jacobsen had initially declared that he would not hire any English-speakers, he later had to abandon this policy, because it excluded too many candidates, making it very difficult for him to assemble a troupe of the scale that Hagenbeck wanted. Ultimately, Jacobsen assembled a group of forty-two Indians and ten cowboys.[50]

In contrast to the Bella Coola contract, which covered the entire troupe, this time Jacobsen signed forty-two contracts with forty-two Native American actors. As far as wages, male performers each earned twenty-four dollars per month, female performers a mere twenty dollars per month, the latter being the same amount that the Bella Coola earned in 1885, for the same number of hours. In contrast to that agreement, moreover, members of the Sioux troupe were required not to demonstrate Indian ways and customs, but rather "to take part in a performance known as Carl Hagenbeck's Show" (as well as in an unspecified number of unpaid "rehearsals"). In addition to articles on transportation, salary, work periods, living expenses, and medical coverage, the 1910 contract adds a no-compete clause, prohibiting involvement of any kind in other shows in Europe. Of particular interest is the article on props: "The Performer agrees to provide one set of Indian clothes, head-dress, moccasins, and such other equipment as may be necessary and suitable to the character which may be allotted

1.12 Members of Hagenbeck's Sioux show aboard the S.S. *President Grant*, 1910. Lying on the deck is the collector, Johan Adrian Jacobsen (*far left*), as are several members of the ship's crew. Copyright: Museum für Völkerkunde, Hamburg.

to him or her." The language is telling. By the early 1910s, the process of collecting foreign peoples had indeed become a form of casting, with recruiters looking not for "anthropological types," but for actors able to fill scripted roles that would literally be assigned to them.[51]

Professionalization had far-reaching implications for ethnographic performance, of which I will have more to say later. Here it is enough to point out that the governing principles of selection changed over time, as recruiters, spectators, and performers jointly participated in the making of ethnographic troupes. If some principles were fundamental—namely, the visual potency, cultural alterity, and social diversity of a given troupe—most of them had to be improvised on the spot. In practice, Hagenbeck's traveler made numerous concessions out of necessity, depending on the local context of recruitment. The professionalization of native performers, and their expanded role in the recruitment process, was perhaps the single most significant development in this context. Assisting recruiters, joining troupes, negotiating terms of employment, demanding that conditions be met, protesting broken promises, disseminating knowledge about previous tours and agents, even organizing and directing troupes of their own, native performers exerted considerable influence at the level of recruiting, in ways that we have yet to fully acknowledge. On another level, the importance of native agency and self-determination raises the question of whether cultural displacement was perhaps a necessary condition for the very possibility of exhibiting "natural peoples."

Cultural Displacement

In her well-known essay, "Objects of Ethnography," Barbara Kirshenblatt-Gimblett argues that "the artfulness of the ethnographic object is an art of excision, of detachment, an art of the excerpt." This idea goes for collecting as well as for exhibition. A more accurate term than "the ethnographic object," she suggests, would be "the ethnographic fragment," because it brings out the metonymic logic that so often structures ethnographic display as an arrangement of selected parts made to stand in for a notional whole. By ethnography, Kirshenblatt-Gimblett understands "a poetics of detachment," a term that "refers not only to the physical act of producing fragments but also to the detached attitude that makes that fragmentation and its appreciation possible." Not only artifacts but also human beings can be subjected to this process, a point that she supports with the example of Hagenbeck's *Völkerschau*. The notion of excision offers a very useful way of theorizing the means by which the show constructs its object by rendering it portable and therefore available to display. It has deeply informed my concept of nineteenth-century theme space, providing further reason to emphasize, as I do, the physical dislocation of the spectacle to the spectator. Characteristic of Hagenbeck's show, according to Kirshenblatt-Gimblett, is its strategy of blurring the distinction between humans and animals in representing the ethnographic. In this observation, however, the analytical model shifts very subtly from the ethnographic fragment to the biological continuum (which the show did not purport to represent, for reasons discussed in chapter 2). More important, the notion of "excision" doesn't quite capture the idea and the practice of recruitment, which was particular to the assembly of ethnographic performance troupes. A metaphorical emphasis on detachment and its cognates, however fitting it might be for other versions of the ethnographic, fails to capture the specificity of recruitment as a mode of collecting and the various transactions it engendered.[52]

A closer look at some of these negotiations has led me to emphasize a slightly different idea: that of displacement. In contrast to excision or detachment, this term helps expose native agency as a distinguishing feature of recruitment and, by extension, live ethnographic performance. It also makes explicit the cultural abjection of performers within the native setting, before they were recruited, and in some cases even helps explain why they decided to join a troupe in the first place. In the United States, for example, the two major contexts for recruitment were Indian reservations (such as Pine Ridge) and the travels of migrant workers. When Jacobsen and his brother went in search of the Bella Coola, they made tracks not for the village by that name but rather for the city of Victoria, then the regional center of native trade and migrant labor. Like so many Northwest Coast peoples, the Nuxalk men were on the move that summer, en route to the hop fields of Washington State, searching for work. We know that they spoke English as well as Chinook (a trade language in British Columbia), in addition to their native tongue. And we know this because Maria Cronau, wife of the well-known German traveler and painter Rudolf Cronau, invited them to dinner at her house in Leipzig and wrote about her experience of the troupe in the local newspaper. At a minimum, as Thode-Arora has pointed out, "there had to be some previous contact via traders, missionaries, or colonial administrators, just as there had to be a common language of commerce, which allowed for a basis of understanding." And yet the notion of contact hardly begins to describe the necessary conditions for the possibility of assembling ethnographic troupes. Displacement offers a wider and more powerful conceptual lens, for two main reasons. First, it creates a context for understanding the surprising richness and diversity of social interaction among performers and audiences (such as dinner at the Cronau house), where much more took place than the flexing of colonial muscle or the proverbial exchange of gazes. Second, it opens up the fascinating possibility that native performers sought to negotiate the very experience of colonial abjection and cultural assimilation by joining an ethnographic troupe.[53]

Claims to the contrary notwithstanding, the prospect of joining an itinerant performance troupe became attractive, in a certain sense, to some of the same native peoples who were living under extreme conditions of social and cultural marginalization. Recruiters were vaguely aware of this phenomenon and clearly tried to exploit it. There were endless degrees of complicity, and the results were sometimes disastrous. In the spring of 1878, for example, Hagenbeck received word that "a group of Indians [from South Asia] . . . were staying in London, who had come there in the service of the English, but could now be easily engaged to perform. With the clear understanding that they had to be authentic natives, and that they must appear in native costume, and only after receiving confirmation from a scholar who verified their authenticity, he now undertook an Indian show—with elephants, naturally, as this was self-evident, and he already had them anyway." On this occasion, rather than dispatch one of his own trappers or travelers, as he had earlier, Hagenbeck would assume control of an existing troupe that was allegedly ready to go. As the group consisted of former domestic servants who had made their own way to Europe, Hagenbeck wanted some guarantee of their "naturalness" before he closed the deal, hence the scholar's work

1.13 The "Hindu group" in Hamburg, 1878. Courtesy of Tierpark Carl Hagenbeck GmbH, Hamburg-Stellingen.

of verification. So, when the performers disembarked in Hamburg, the showman stood and watched in disbelief. "They were all wearing European clothes."[54]

The people he encountered that day were *ayahs* and *lascars*, abandoned servants and sailors, who were part of a growing population in London's East End. In her interesting case study of an 1886 Indian troupe in London, anthropologist Saloni Mathur has demonstrated that assembling a troupe in this context doubled as a technique of social control, a way of dealing with "subaltern colonial figures among London's urban poor," by creating temporary jobs for them and shipping them back to India when the show ended. Hagenbeck confronted a similar group of "destitutes," only in this case they had been further displaced and shipped to Hamburg. These performers were caught up not only in an urban policy of social control, but also in a blatant instance of commercial fraud. Instead of sending them back to London (assuming that was even an option), Hagenbeck devised a plan of action and went ahead with the show.[55]

Often, when a new troupe arrived at the docks, Hagenbeck made a public spectacle of it, parading the newcomers in full regalia from the harbor through the city, for the citizens of Hamburg to see and start discussing. More than just a form of free publicity for the show (as it is usually understood), the parade was an important type of performance in its own right, one that co-opted public space by moving through it, and transformed unwitting pedestrians into curious spectators. In this instance, however, he quietly hustled the performers through the backdoor of his menagerie. Though they had just arrived from London, they were immediately put to work on (literally) refashioning their outward appearance. According to Leutemann,

> a sewing workshop was set up, under the direction of an Indian woman who earlier—much earlier—must have been very beautiful, and thus knew how to give orders. They made Indian costumes from morning to night. When the performers . . . were put into these costumes, their appearance was satisfactory, if a bit drab and homogeneous. A hut was made out of mats and bamboo, and some Indian tools were scared up, too. But the unfamiliar task of making an elephant saddle, which was supposed to serve as a chair for several of the women, required great effort and worry.

The very artifacts (or props) that the performers would use in the show had already been once collected; they were purchased from a local dealer in ethnographic goods. To this collection was added a group of six worker elephants, which had already been trained by Hagenbeck's brother, Wilhelm. None of these former domestic servants knew how to drive an elephant, let alone make a saddle. So Wilhelm assumed the role of impresario, too, in order to help integrate the elephants into the show. The native participants, for their part, had to be taught how to perform the roles of "kornacks" and "artisans" that they were expected to play. The troupe's first engagement, at the Hamburg Zoological Gardens, failed to draw crowds as large as earlier shows had. "After such completely authentic and exciting troupes," wrote Leutemann, "this Indian group that appeared in Hamburg could not help but have a lesser effect."[56]

The "Hindu group," as it was often called, "deserves special mention" in Leutemann's otherwise upbeat account of the *Völkerschau* and the process of assembling an ethnographic troupe, as "an example of how not to go about it." The travel suits and kid gloves that the passengers wore upon their arrival only seemed to confirm the idea that they were "no longer natural people, but corrupted by European influence." As a cautionary tale, it serves in Leutemann's biography to emphasize the importance of controlling every aspect of the collecting process. In subtle ways, it also implies that Hagenbeck's troupes were typically superior to this one; that even an honest businessman such as Hagenbeck could be duped (a victim of the English agent who assembled the fraudulent troupe); and that the German businessman would learn from the experience, rather than make the same mistake twice. Shortly thereafter, he was allegedly offered the opportunity to take over a troupe of Native Americans that had been assembled in the United States. This time he refused, wanting nothing to do with a preassembled troupe. As Leutemann averred, "he would never again undertake anything similar to this so-called Hindu group. I could at least take comfort in having warned him in the first place. But the strongest warning against future mishaps was, of course, the loss of 36,000 Marks."[57]

Control over the means of production might have been the entrepreneurial upshot, but what seems most interesting about this anecdote is the unexpected visibility of cultural assimilation. The conditions of displacement were not exceptional (despite Leutemann's claims to the contrary); they were constitutive. Every ethnographic troupe, no matter what its composition or context of origin, was tailor-made for European audiences. The only question was how to re-dress the performers and camouflage the signs of their assimilation. In this case, it meant literally redesigning travel suits as ethnic costumes and hiding the seams as much as possible. The failure of this particular effort only highlights the signs of travel and assimilation that had to be negotiated by every ethnographic troupe, no matter how it fared with commercial spectators. At the same time, however—and this is the larger paradox—the very process of recruitment only exacerbated the very conditions that the show would try to conceal. In other words, as Kirshenblatt-Gimblett has argued, there is a way in which the process of collecting "implicates exhibition in the disappearance of what it shows."[58]

Another context of cultural displacement deserves more attention: the context of foreign missions or outposts for evangelizing abroad. Religious missions shaped the practice of collecting native performers in various ways. Indeed, the members of Hagenbeck's first troupe, the Sami of 1874, had been baptized and educated by traveling missionaries, as noted at the beginning of this chapter. In an article promoting the 1878 Inuit troupe, Leutemann stressed a series of related points:

> namely, that these wild-looking people, with their formless fur clothing, are all Christians, baptized, confirmed, married and buried formally by Danish priests; that they have been educated by native teachers (who were trained at a Greenland seminary) in reading, writing, arithmetic, some geography, history, and natural history; that they even use paper money in their transactions with the government (which has a monopoly on trade); and that, for example, the aforementioned [performer] Herr Okabak has decent handwriting—and one could hardly ask for more than that.

On a different note, it appears that some performers cultivated an ironic relationship to Western religion, offering frankly to either take it or leave it, depending on what the impresario needed—that is, to land a contract. The leader of the 1885 Bella Coola

1.14 "Heathen Eskimo family from Labrador." Photograph by Jacob Martin Jacobsen, hand-written caption by Johan Adrian Jacobsen. Shown here are the shaman Terrianiak (*right*), his wife Paingo, who was also a shaman, and their daughter Noggasak (*center*). Carte de visite, 1880. Copyright: Museum für Völkerkunde, Hamburg.

troupe, Tom Henry reportedly said to Jacobsen: "It's too difficult to be a Christian when the missionary goes away. I convert back again to Indian religion and go with you. I will dance and tell white people about us."[59]

The issues that are particular to this context come into sharper focus if we return to the ill-fated members of the Inuit troupe from Labrador and their relationship with the Church of the United Brethren, or Moravians, a Protestant missionary sect established in the late fifteenth century. Of the estimated two thousand Inuit who lived in Labrador at the time, Jacobsen noted in his travel diary, approximately "1,500 people (namely Eskimos) belong to the parishes of their mission stations." There were six stations in Labrador when he arrived in 1880, the oldest ones having been established in the previous century. The missionaries in Hebron, a station founded in 1830, had considerable influence not only over the troupe that Jacobsen assembled, but also over the form in which it was later displayed. Indeed, it is precisely the Moravians' missionary zeal, or what one scholar has called their "compulsion for documentation," that makes this troupe so relevant and useful for the purposes of my study.[60]

The troupe consisted of two distinct groups—a "Christian" family of five and a "heathen" family of three—according to a widely understood dichotomy first constructed by the Moravians in Labrador. The baptized couple, Abraham and Ulrike, actively participated in the mission and its various day-to-day activities. According to Brother Kretschmer, the missionary in Labrador who wrote many of the reports and inquiries about the troupe's well-being, Abraham "plays the violin, the clarinet, the guitar, [and] understands a little English. His wife, Ulrike . . . served 4 years as a maid and 2¾ years as a nanny in our house, [she is] a good pupil with Brother Erdmann, [and] knows a little German." Kretschmer explained the church's position on the recruitment of Abraham and Ulrike as follows: "I told them that we absolutely cannot allow our baptized people to be exhibited and observed outside in Europe for money, like wild animals. They could not however understand our reservations." In his diary, Jacobsen commented on this position without reflecting on the implications of his own activities. "To undertake such a journey to Europe is seen [by the missionaries] to be synonymous with leading them [the Inuit] to their doom. It is sad," he wrote, "that a people are so suppressed, and still more so that Europeans demonstrate such power." A more caustic and public critique was voiced by Frankfurt's daily newspaper, *Nachrichten*, on 3 December 1880: "the Danish government in Greenland as well as the Moravians in Labrador have their own important reasons for keeping their subjects locked away, if possible from the whole outside world. They especially and firmly oppose a visit to Europe, fearing that these [people] could on the occasion get to know some unpleasant things about the real value of the hunting products they bartered away as well as about the real price of the materials they received in exchange."[61]

1.15 Photograph of Abraham Ulrikab (*center*) and his family standing before a hut at one of the exhibition venues, 1880. Copyright: Museum für Völkerkunde, Hamburg.

The missionaries stationed at Hebron refused to sign a contract with Jacobsen and voiced their opposition to the recruitment of Abraham and his family. "While it is happening with our knowledge," Kretschmer reported to his superiors, "it is entirely happening against our will." Of the "heathen family" he wrote simply, "they wanted to move to Ramah [another mission station] and convert." Nowhere does he protest against their display in Europe. Of prime concern for the missionaries, indeed the basis for their protests against displaying "our baptized people" (and not the pagan members of the troupe), was the public image of the Moravians it would project, and their inability to control that image or the behavior of Abraham and his family in Europe.[62]

The very reasons that Abraham gives for joining the troupe are shaped by his personal relationship to the missionaries, by his experience of the mission station, and by the ideological framework that the church espoused. He wrote of settling his debt (of £10) to the mission's store, of wishing to see Europe, and of visiting other parishes there, including his former "teachers" or missionaries. Kretschmer noted these wishes and added another: namely, "the desire for European splendors is too strong." Whether or not this held true for Abraham, it was an argument that missionaries often cited when criticizing the ethnographic exhibition as a challenge to their authority. On a more basic level, the opportunity to repay his debts must have been attractive to Abraham, especially as he and his family were living in conditions of great poverty. The troupe was promised "daily earnings of 3 Marks per man, 2 per woman, 1 for the child." Brother Kretschmer acknowledged, "that naturally adds up to a lot."[63]

On this occasion, the circumstances of recruitment also suggested a certain governing principle of exhibition. As Hartmut Lutz has recently noted, "the Moravians had asked Jacobsen to keep the two groups apart, so that their neophytes would not be contaminated by Terrianiak's heathenism, which might cause them to backslide in their religious beliefs." Throughout the tour, two separate huts would be built at each venue, to be occupied by the different families, as requested. In this way, too, the families were juxtaposed to each other and, by extension, to the "civilized" members of the audience. Even Brother Kretschmer expressed (in advance of the actual show) an awareness of the consequences of this dichotomy for spectatorship and a vested interest in the outcome: "We shall learn next year whether these people [Terrianiak and his family] or ours were considered alike, whether a difference was observed between the baptized and the heathen." Indeed, it was precisely this contrast that Christian groups found lacking in ethnographic exhibitions generally, which became a major reason for their criticism of the practice.[64]

At the zoological garden in Frankfurt, the two huts were placed on opposite sides of the music pavilion. Spectators compared and contrasted the two families, but the conclusions they reached were sometimes, well, unorthodox. For example, one world-weary observer lamented the cultural effects of Christianization, and in a romantic gesture celebrated the "freedom" of heathens, instead. In his words,

> the whole "national costume" very quickly disappears, at least in the family converted to Christianity. The women at the mission are already even ashamed of it, and particularly like to follow European fashion and wear wool skirts. Only with much trouble could the members of Abraham's family be persuaded to return to their forefathers' custom during their stay in Europe. But this did not happen unconditionally either, because we can see European vests and shirts peeking out from under the seal skins the men wear.

Such visible signs of assimilation made the Christian family less interesting to this observer, especially when compared to "the so-called wild Eskimos, the ones who could preserve their freedom to a certain extent and keep themselves independent from the missionaries." In Berlin, the well-known pathologist Rudolf Virchow was allowed to physically examine the performers. His published report asserts the existence of significant differences between the two families not only in their religious practices and social behaviors, but also, significantly, in terms of their physical appearances.[65]

While some aspects of cultural displacement were acknowledged and even featured in publicity materials as points of historical or cultural interest, other aspects were either withheld or concealed for an effect. The 1911 Northland Exhibition, held in Berlin, offers a striking example of both strategies operating simultaneously. Unlike previous shows that Hagenbeck sponsored, this one consisted of four different habitat groups: namely, Samoyeds, Labrador Inuit, Sami, and Swedish folk dancers. The latter were admittedly professional performers from Skansen, the famous open-air museum in Stockholm. The presence of "Swedes" in the troupe is exceptional within the Hagenbeck materials, but nonetheless instructive. As "civilized people" they represented utterly familiar figures; the guidebook even acknowledges that "nothing Swedish is foreign to us anymore." And yet here they are, as part of a larger *Völkerschau*. "When the exhibition's organizers decided to include a number of Swedish men and women anyway, they did so in order to complete and enliven the overall picture." The Skansen performers are thus explicitly linked to Sweden's rural past, framed in picturesque terms and offered up for ethnographic study, mainly for the sake of dramatic contrast, in juxtaposition to the Inuit, Samoyeds, and Sami at the other end of the spectrum. The contrast, however, seems to break down almost immediately. While the guidebook contains many telling passages, one must suffice: "With the acceptance of Christianity, the Lapps have not abandoned their own ways and customs, and they generally resist the temptations that the contact with civilization brings with it, although it cannot be denied that there are everywhere pressures to make them sedentary. The coastal Lapps have long owned block and stone houses. For example, Marie Papila Winie in our troupe is the owner of a permanent block house, which she operates as a guest house, providing a lodging place for tourists." Rather than envision a coherent series of ideal anthropological types for comparison, the Northland show constructed a fragmented image of nascent globalization, a curious mix of professional performers, Christian neophytes, urban spectators, and modern tourists.[66]

What makes this material even more interesting, however, is the appearance of evidence suggesting that, when it came to the troupe's Inuit contingent, at least, certain signs of their previous travel experiences and professional identities were strategically elided and so well dissimulated as to pass unnoticed. In regard to "the Canadian government's ban on exporting Eskimos," the guidebook goes on to celebrate the presence of the Inuit as a sort of *coup*, claiming, in a display of bravado which was actually quite typical of the recruitment discourse, that the show's organizers had found a way of circumventing it: "Namely, their impresario, Captain Smith, is married to an Eskimo, and one could not very well prohibit the woman, along with their children and next of kin, from following the Captain abroad." The names and ages of the performers are given—the mother is Esther Enutseak, her children are Columbia (nineteen), Peuyok (seven), Denver (one and a half), and "little" Virginia—without any commentary on the American-sounding names. Instead, the performers are further described as Christians, who have been "strongly influenced by Europeans, notably through the Hudson's Bay Company." If such details seem to confirm the notion of cultural displacement and its importance for recruitment, in this case they also serve to contain and conceal a longer, more complicated narrative about native agency.

1.16 "Eskimo Girl," postcard from Hagenbeck's *Tierpark*, ca. 1911–12. The young woman posing for this picture is none other than the Inuit celebrity and entertainer Nancy Columbia. Courtesy of Tierpark Carl Hagenbeck GmbH, Hamburg-Stellingen.

The story of the daughter Columbia, a.k.a. Nancy Columbia, has recently been told in great detail. Born at the 1893 World's Columbian Exposition in Chicago, she was hailed as the "World's Fair Baby" and as the first Eskimo ever born in the United States. It was the beginning of an entire career. Over the next twenty years, Columbia and her family appeared in eight other world's fairs, as well as in a long series of American dime museums, state fairs, amusement parks, and motion pictures. Their impresario in Berlin, the same Captain John C. Smith noted above, was not a "Captain," but rather a proprietor of the "Eskimo Village" in Luna Park at Coney Island. In 1907, he and his wife left Coney Island to run their own business on the traveling circuit, with Esther working not only as a performer but also as the troupe's director, recruiter, and business manager. In the United States, her daughter Columbia was touted as America's most famous Inuit. The troupe's celebrity and professionalism became conditions of their continued employment, including their appearance in Berlin. It is important to stress, however, that their celebrity did not extend as far as Germany. In this context, where the troupe was unknown to the mass public, the performers were billed as typical representatives of "the Eskimo habitat," according to a model of ethnographic representation that had been established several decades earlier. A souvenir postcard from Hagenbeck's *Tierpark* in Stellingen (fig. 1.16), where Columbia and her family also appeared, refers to her as simply "Eskimo girl."[67]

The Northland show and the story of Nancy Columbia brings us back to the beginning of this chapter, to the example of Ella Maria Rasti and the Sami troupe of 1874, which marked the symbolic origin of Hagenbeck's ethnographic enterprise. The trajectory that we have followed, however, is not one of linear development from "natural peoples" to knowing performers "corrupted by European influence," with audiences becoming less discriminating over time, or showmen gradually lowering the bar of authenticity. From the very beginning, Hagenbeck's *Völkerschau* was based on the cultural displacement of native peoples in a global context. Displacement was both a precondition for recruitment and what the ethnographic spectacle needed to camouflage. Picture, if you will, the "Hindu group" of house servants sewing their costumes and learning how to drive elephants in Hagenbeck's menagerie. Imagine the group of migrant agricultural workers from British Columbia being reunited with "traditional" Native American costumes in Germany. Remember, though, that the camouflage model was also complicated by historical issues of assimilation, such as religious conversion, which were often key factors in recruiting. Conversion was a form of cultural displacement that could potentially make it more (not less) difficult to assemble an ethnographic troupe. In this context, theme space did not so much depend on concealing the signs of contact as it revolved around the tension between the act of displacement and the replacement or drafting of individuals into capitalist culture—as exotic commodities, as producers of ethnographic artifacts, as professional entertainers, and as consumers of Western goods and services. Recruitment compounded the larger cultural process of displacement, while creating an exhibition that purported to show "unchanged natural peoples." What performers actually did on display, how they were staged by impresarios, and how they were received by audiences in Europe, raises a different set of questions concerning showmanship, performance, and reception.[68]

CHAPTER 2

THE LIVING HABITAT

Hagenbeck did more than simply gather up "the real thing" and convey it to spectators in Europe. He arranged the various "pieces" of each collection—humans, animals, objects—in order for them to be seen in particular ways, according to existing and innovative principles of visual display. The resulting spectacle was initially called an "anthropological-zoological exhibition" (*anthropologisch-zoologische Ausstellung*). This hyphenated and purposely highfalutin term did not assert the freak-show idea of a biological continuum between humans and animals, as many scholars would seem to assume. Rather, the name denoted a certain approach to exhibition, which was based on the grouping of foreign peoples and exotic animals within the same display space. Hagenbeck's *Völkerschau* was an early and particularly influential form of habitat display, an "ecological" mode that still remains a sort of baseline in museums of natural history. In that context, habitat display generally refers to the idea of exhibiting multiple figures (either wax mannequins or animals preserved by taxidermy) surrounded by appropriate objects and vegetation, arranged in representative scenes, and set against a painted backdrop evoking the special locality in which the specimens are typically found.

Part of a broad movement in the nineteenth century toward contextualized display across several fronts, Hagenbeck's *Völkerschau* reshaped that movement in terms of a *living* habitat. As such, it was paradigmatic.[1] Remarkably, the habitat idea has never been thoroughly analyzed in the context of the *Völkerschau*, even though Hagenbeck was its main proponent. The focus, instead, has been on the show's fascinating but somewhat tangential relationship to scientific knowledge and disciplinary history. Ethnographic performance can obviously be framed in terms of anthropology; entertainers such as Hagenbeck would not have had it otherwise. Such a perspective has also been favored by historians of anthropology and world's fairs. "Too often," as Robert W. Rydell has commented on the historiography of international expositions, "the exhibits by and of Native Americans and colonial people have been subsumed under a broader interest in anthropologists and their involvement with the fairs." As a result, the experiences of native performers at the shows, and their interaction with a diversity of spectators, have mostly been either overlooked or neglected. Anthropological approaches to this material typically elevate the themes of ethnographic authenticity, scientific knowledge, and intellectual authority, at the expense of mass spectatorship, commercial entertainment, and sensual pleasure. The boundaries between science and entertainment always seem to blur in these studies, but ultimately, invariably, science trumps entertainment—and that remains unsaid.[2]

Clearly, Hagenbeck and other showmen traded on the authority of science, and professional scientists profited greatly from the entertainment's existence, but the purpose of trading—indeed, the show's reason to exist—was fundamentally commercial. In this regard, ethnographic performances exemplified a division of labor that Richard Altick, scanning the longer history of combining edification and amusement, has linked to the rise of the public museum in the mid-nineteenth century. For Hagenbeck's shows, the driving force of commercial exhibition was neither science nor education, though both aspects would be highlighted in program brochures, which often included technical-sounding descriptions of each troupe (in terms of ethnicity, region, climate, and so on). Rather, historical discourses of science and education contributed to the production of theme space in this context mainly by encouraging visitors to absorb the scenes around them, to assimilate commercial entertainments not just sensually or physically but also mentally and morally. So, even as I draw on the important archival work that has been done by historians of anthropology, I part company with studies that emphasize the perspective of intellectual elites and prestigious institutions, in order to gain a more nuanced understanding of the *Völkerschau* as a popular entertainment and a key form of nineteenth-century theme space.[3]

The task here is to investigate the production of the *Völkerschau* as a living habitat, with particular focus on core issues of physical presence, shared space, and social interaction. Methodologically, this chapter proceeds from defining the notion of "anthropological-zoological exhibition" and tracing the history of habitat display to investigating more complex themes. These include the interaction of spectators and performers within the themed environment, the surprising (and troubling) potential for social reciprocity, and the related issues of sex, race, gender, and colonial authority. Adding interpretive layer upon layer not only complicates some of our received ideas about the practice of ethnographic exhibition, it also allows us to gain a fresh angle on what is obviously well-trodden ground in the scholarship. Emphasizing the specificity of live shows based on concrete examples helps shed new light on nineteenth-century theme space as a designated area of performance, where the boundaries between the observers and the observed were constantly being tested and negotiated.

"Anthropological-Zoological Exhibitions"

Historians might not believe that Hagenbeck invented the practice of ethnographic performance, but his contemporaries did. For Germans he literally defined it, as the entry for "anthropological exhibitions" in the 1893 edition of a popular German dictionary shows:

> Performances of representative foreign peoples for the satisfaction of visual pleasure and the dissemination of anthropological knowledge. In 1875, Hagenbeck first brought a group of Laplanders with their huts, tools and weapons, and exhibited them in Hamburg, Berlin and Leipzig; they were followed by groups of Nubians, Eskimos, Patagonians, Fuegians, Sinhalese, Hindus, Indians and Cameroonians, some of which were also exhibited in France and England. Following Hagenbeck, others have staged similar shows, such as Buffalo Bill's Wild West, which claimed to depict life in Western North America.[4]

There were numerous reasons for the practice to be defined in this particular way. Between 1875 and 1914, more than three hundred ethnographic troupes appeared in Germany alone. Of these, by the latest count, around one hundred were either produced by or affiliated with Hagenbeck's company. The phenomenal success of his ethnographic enterprise made the showman's name synonymous with an entire genre of nineteenth-century visual culture, one which in Germany encompassed the immensely popular Wild West shows, as well. In fact, the most popular exhibition that Hagenbeck ever produced was the Oglala-Sioux show of 1910, which attracted to its one and only venue in Hamburg more than 1.1 million visitors.[5]

Every troupe, whether it was a family of three or a "caravan" of four hundred people, became part of a larger exhibition that was devoted to representing a particular geographical area or ethnic group. A few of Hagenbeck's troupes consisted of German colonial subjects, but the vast majority of performers were recruited in territories controlled by other colonial powers. Not only people but also ethnographic artifacts and exotic animals were collected for the purpose of mounting a show. In addition, whatever materials or existing structures that could be dismantled and transported to Europe could also be used to furnish the depicted scene. Accessories of many kinds—tools, costumes, ornaments, musical instruments, and cooking utensils—were mobilized to create a convincing expression of foreign space, as were such exotic animals as camels, reindeer, and elephants. At its most elaborate, the built environment achieved epic scale, featuring dozens of huts, shrines, temples, and other structures, spread out across sculpted landscapes stocked with exotic-looking flora and fauna. Whatever the scale—indeed, no matter where a troupe originated—ethnographic exhibitions purported to represent the everyday life of non-Western peoples through a full program of musical performances, ceremonial dances, and dramatic scenes.

These itinerant performances took place in fairgrounds, beer gardens, circuses, velodromes, wax museums, vaudeville houses, exhibition parks, and other settings, but the premiere venues for ethnographic exhibitions in Germany (and throughout Europe, until the last decade of the nineteenth century) were public zoological gardens. The preference for zoos was largely due to their status as institutions of public recreation and edification, the idea being that to appear in this context would in turn confer "respectability" on the troupe by force of association. On another level, the unique combination of garden settings, exotic-looking architecture, and animal collections immediately evoked the "exotic," while appealing directly to the visitor's many senses. Venues were sometimes booked weeks in advance, though they often changed in the course of a tour, depending on how a given troupe fared in local markets. Tour destinations were determined in part by the scale of production as well as by the public's ongoing response, with relatively popular troupes appearing in zoological gardens of major cities and less popular ones searching for audiences at outdoor restaurants in small towns. To maximize profits—the driving concern for entrepreneurs, impresarios, and managers alike—troupes were usually on the road for months, even years, at a time, appearing in as many locations as possible. Aspiring showmen such as Hagenbeck developed marketing strategies that traversed national borders, making frequent appearances in many European capitals including London, Berlin, Paris, Brussels, Copenhagen, Rome, Prague, and Vienna.

Of all the ethnographic shows that Hagenbeck produced between 1874 and 1913, none took place at a world's fair or international exposition. This curious absence helps explain why this aspect of his work is mostly unfamiliar to cultural historians working in the United States, where the world's fairs are widely regarded as the ultimate venue for anthropological exhibition. Nevertheless, it seems to me that Hagenbeck was surprisingly influential in this area as well, even if his relationship to the fairs was an indirect and unacknowledged one. The nature of this relationship can perhaps best be illustrated by a series of troupes that Hagenbeck displayed at the *Jardin d'Acclimatation* in Paris, between 1877 and 1887, and their impact on the *Exposition Universelle* of 1889. It also typifies the bias toward scientific authority that runs throughout the scholarship.[6]

In the literature on world's fairs, the Exposition of 1889 has generally been discussed as marking both a major shift and a defining moment in the exhibition of foreign peoples. To be sure, artifacts, statues, photographs, racial busts, and wax mannequins had been widely used in ethnographic showcases, and the appearance of non-Western peoples—as dignitaries, visitors, chefs, waiters, and laborers—had already been noted at previous exhibitions. Thus, Paul Greenhalgh describes the important shift as one of emphasis: "It was the Paris Exposition of 1889, however, which inaugurated the practice in a more specific sense, whereby colonial peoples were not brought to serve as exotic vendors, waiters and servants, but simply to be looked at." The Paris Exposition created a new standard for subsequent exhibitions. "No subsequent world's fair lacked a variation on this ethnological exhibit," Rydell observes, "and for the better part of the next fifty years, such arrangements of non-white colonials often bore the name 'ethnological villages.'"[7]

What accounts for this shift in emphasis? Greenhalgh explains it in terms of a larger intellectual development, namely, "the rise of anthropology as a discipline in Paris between 1878 and 1889." Anthropology as an informing context is obviously relevant, but its significance as both an agent of change and a framework for explanation has also been overrated. During this period, we are told, anthropologists in Paris began attending a variety of commercial exhibitions. "The most important of these were the ones held at the *Jardin d'Acclimatation*," which was established in 1859 as a center for the study and popularization of botany and zoology. Beginning in 1877, "peoples were brought from all over the world to be displayed alongside the animals," including Nubians, Eskimos, Lapps, Kalmucks, Fuegians, and Sinhalese. Speaking of the first troupe in the series, the so-called Nubians, Girard de Rialle reported to the Anthropological Society:

> The convoy belonged to a foreign merchant whose specialty is furnishing interesting specimens to the zoological gardens of Europe and who is supplied in these countries from which he draws his animals by paying local hunters. This time, instead of leaving them in Africa, he wanted to bring them to Europe, and if we can believe those who say so, he will not be poorly rewarded.

Greenhalgh concludes that "the anthropological community had invented a genre at the *Jardin d'Acclimatation*." Organizers of the 1889 exposition "took note" of these performances, and expanded them "on a grand scale." It needs to be said, however, that the "foreign merchant" who produced this show (and eight others displayed at the *Jardin* during this period) was none other than Carl Hagenbeck. Moreover, not only anthropologists but also commercial spectators attended in unprecedented numbers. In its six-week run, Hagenbeck's 1886 Ceylon show attracted nearly one million visitors, accounting for more than two-thirds of total gate receipts for the *Jardin* that year. If the organizers of the exposition noticed anything about these shows, it was probably their phenomenal popularity and financial success. Hagenbeck helped prepare the ground for native villages at world's fairs by creating a mass public for ethnographic performance in "respectable" venues such as the zoological garden.[8]

In the late nineteenth century, as Neil Harris has noted in his important study of P. T. Barnum (1810–1891), "The road to respectability led through prestigious institutions and their leaders." This was also true, perhaps even more so, for the younger German showman. Witness his close connection to the *Jardin d'Acclimatation* and its director, Geoffroy Saint-Hilaire. It was only after Hagenbeck's repeated success at the *Jardin* that Berlin's Zoological Garden finally opened its gates to his show in 1878. In a further step, Berlin anthropologists began to express interest in the troupes, largely as a result of their recognition by the zoological garden. From their perspective, itinerant troupes offered numerous "specimens" in a controlled setting where scientists could readily take measurements, run experiments, and generate information, without having to travel around the world. Access and availability were especially vital to nineteenth-century German anthropology, with its medical orientation and its focus on the body as an object of knowledge. In exchange, Hagenbeck received what seems to have been an uncommon degree of institutional support, including official affidavits of support from the Museum of Ethnology in Leipzig as well as from the anthropological societies of Berlin and Munich. Institutional endorsements bolstered his public reputation as a respectable ethnographic showman, while enabling him to negotiate German censorship laws on theatrical presentations, if and when they were enforced.[9]

There is another important reason why Hagenbeck sought endorsements from ethnological museums and zoological gardens, and it concerns his particular approach to exhibition, which was fundamentally different from the prevailing modes in each of those institutions. That is, neither the ethnological museum nor the zoological garden had a precedent for implementing habitat displays, and with good reason. Hagenbeck's term of choice, "anthropological-zoological exhibition," was obviously meant to connote "science," infusing the entertainment with an air of prestige, authority, and erudition by invoking not one but two areas of knowledge. When he began producing ethnographic shows, however, such connotations were not yet attached to the idea of habitat display in Germany or anywhere else. On the contrary, as Karen Wonders has shown in another context, it was an unmistakably popular idea. As a curatorial method for exhibiting science, the habitat idea had yet to obtain. For that reason, according to Wonders, it was first implemented not in research museums but in private collections of taxidermy and later, in the 1890s, at museums founded to serve a nonacademic public in particular—namely, the Biological Museum in Sweden and the American Museum of Natural History. In Germany, habitat groups were not endorsed by ethnological museums or by zoological gardens until the early twentieth century, with typology preceding it as the dominant approach in each institution. The director of Berlin's Zoological Garden, Heinrich Bodinus, had initially rejected Hagenbeck's proposals, out of concern that the *Völkerschau* would undermine the zoo's reputation as a scientific institution. When Hagenbeck made his initial foray into habitat display, the idea that would later define the show's scientific format had yet to become scientific. Wonders calls him "the greatest pioneer of naturalistic representation" in Germany, pointing to his innovative methods of animal display first demonstrated in 1895. By that time, Hagenbeck already had twenty years of experience in the context of ethnographic performance.[10]

There is an important connection between museums and ethnographic exhibitions as key forms of nineteenth-century theme space that Wonders has overlooked—that is, the dynamics of physical displacement. By this I mean, above all, the manner of delivering bodies, objects, and spaces to mass audiences, but also the movement of spectators to the spectacle. Alison Griffiths and Mark Sandberg have each emphasized that the actual movement of spectators and collected objects is precisely what distinguishes the museum from the cinema. Unlike that medium, museum-based forms of theme space tend to rely on "shared space," a term that Sandberg uses to emphasize the porosity or overlapping of display space and spectator space. The co-presence of spectators and display objects had the potential for generating both real and uncanny effects. At Skansen and other open-air folk museums, for instance, decoys were sometimes deployed in ways that made it difficult for spectators to distinguish between mannequin bodies and the costumed information guides. Going a step further, visitors in these surround-style museums were led to explore the "inside" of display spaces, having the uncanny effect of blurring the line between mannequins and spectators. This uneasy correspondence was always the most fraught, in-between moment of the folk museums, because it required spectators to adopt a more subtle, more interactive mode than a simple visual subjection of the display. In such instances, there was always the potential for reciprocity to break out, a relationship to the bodies on display that was, perhaps, too close for comfort. The most salient difference here is that the folk museum spectators often had a "genealogical" relationship to the live performers, who in some sense were seen as performing the spectator's own past (assuming a national spectator and not a foreign tourist). The *Völkerschau*, by contrast, ran on a principle of cultural alterity, and the social implications of physical presence were thus more charged. Hagenbeck's notion of anthropological-zoological exhibition had much in common with museum displays, beginning with the choreography of "shared space," but the real and uncanny experience of that space almost certainly had higher stakes for spectators in the actual presence of foreign peoples and living creatures than it did in the "presence" of mannequins or stuffed animals.[11]

In a way, Hagenbeck's brand of habitat display was like no other. Its literal quality of "aliveness" set it apart from the natural history museum's habitat dioramas, the folk museum's genre scenes, and other so-called living pictures. My choice of "habitat" as the key term for contextualization (as distinguished from other possibilities such as "tableau," "immersion," or "scenification") aims to highlight the central issue of both the *Völkerschau* and (later) the *Tierpark*: namely, the grouping together of objects and living beings is in part due to the requirements of keeping alive what is on display. In other words, there is a fundamentally "ecological" principle that the living habitat must adhere to, a need for the display objects to "thrive," which is obviously not crucial to mannequins and museum showcases (or to films, for that matter). Reflecting on the nature of the *Tierpark*, with its various performance spaces, Hagenbeck called it "the opposite of a museum." In the museum context, he asserted, "everything always remains the same, in dead stillness, whereas a fresh, pleasurable, but also merciless vitality roars throughout the *Tierpark*." This powerful sense of aliveness is an important factor that distinguished the *Völkerschau* from other modes of ethnographic display.[12]

The Art of the Habitat

If the term "anthropological-zoological exhibition" is today reminiscent of the freak show, as it is often discussed in the American scholarship, Hagenbeck would have winced at the association. He wanted nothing to do with the antecedents of this tradition of spectacle, from which he claimed to depart. Even as he celebrated his "strong ties" to the fairground culture of an earlier period (by which he meant his father's entertainments), he did everything he could to separate his *Völkerschau* from that milieu and its cultural associations of hoaxing and fraudulence. His was not an art of "humbug," the watchword of P. T. Barnum, who was also one of Hagenbeck's major clients in the animal business.[13]

By 1875, when Hagenbeck made his debut as an ethnographic showman, a powerful fascination with the "real" and the "authentic" had largely superseded the visual culture of artful deception—as the American showman also recognized. Even so, when Barnum organized his own "Ethnological Congress" in 1883, he would exhibit "not only human beings of different races, but also . . . those who possess extraordinary peculiarities, such as giants, dwarfs, singular disfigurements of the person, dexterity in the use of weapons, dancing, singing, juggling, unusual feats of strength or agility, &c." Mocking the authority of world's fairs and anthropological exhibitions, the Ethnological Congress recycled an older genre of fairground display that Barnum helped establish: the freak show with a national affiliation. Although the corporeal and the national were conjoined by Hagenbeck as well, his ethnographic enterprise cannot be equated ipso facto with Barnum's human oddity show. When Barnum presented "The Chinese Giant" or "The Armless Japanese Woman" (shows he also brought to Germany and Austria), physical oddity always trumped national character. Not so in the respectable genre of *Völkerschau*, where the "characteristic" prevailed. At the same time, Barnum's approach to human display—namely, the persistent effort to pass off individual oddities under strategically deceptive and shifting guises—established a set of representational practices against which the "new" show would be distinguished and redefined in positive terms.[14]

Hagenbeck staged non-Western peoples not as individual oddities, but rather in groups as integral parts of a larger imagined whole. In contrast to the American showman, he made a career of exhibiting what he called the "authentic" (*das Echte*). From the outset, Hagenbeck traded in the "typical" and the "characteristic" (as opposed to the extraordinary and the unidentifiable), while at the same time forging a link between these anthropological ideals and his public reputation as a showman. The concept of "type," for example, was implicit in the practice of naming performance troupes according to the most general categories of ethnological group and geographical region. At the same time, historian Sierra Bruckner points out, the commercial use of typologies and other scientific classifications was so loose that their defining characteristics, such as cultural and physical traits, "appear to be random." Ironically, the most stable signifier of ethnographic authenticity was not a scientific category but Hagenbeck's name or brand. By 1880, there was a marked increase in using and even highlighting his name in the titles of exhibitions. To emphasize the supposed link between the showman's corporate identity and his discursive claims is not to conflate the two. The "real" and the "typical" are slippery terms, each of which Hagenbeck deployed—strategically—in order to describe his various troupes, because these terms resonated widely and immediately among spectators. However problematic they may be, whatever audiences may have understood by these terms, they are absolutely necessary to our historical understanding of ethnographic exhibition as a key form of nineteenth-century theme space and of Hagenbeck's brand in particular.[15]

Hagenbeck constructed the "real" and the "typical" in the course of developing a certain approach to ethnographic exhibition, which would ultimately define his contribution to nineteenth-century visual culture. Writing in effect as Hagenbeck's publicist, Heinrich Leutemann framed the idea as a break with tradition. Other exhibitions have "two major flaws," he claimed: "first, they show only the people, that is, without their characteristic surroundings, the dwellings, tools, weapons, domesticated animals, etc. that comprise a unified whole; as a result—and this is the second flaw—it is impossible to see these people in their characteristic activities, using their tools, domesticated animals, etc." By contrast, the argument ran, Hagenbeck's show rectified both problems by mobilizing an uncommon number of production elements, and by arranging them in situ. The 1875 Sami group, for instance, performed a variety of everyday tasks before the public: assembling tents and sleds, ice skating, lassoing reindeer, throwing harpoons, cooking food, nursing a baby. Each of these activities is depicted in Leutemann's illustration (see plate 1), a synchronic summation of Hagenbeck's first *Völkerschau*. His was an art of the habitat.[16]

The idea of the "habitat group" was not original; there were a number of striking precedents. In the late eighteenth century, the amateur naturalist Charles Willson Peale (a painter in his own right) experimented with a similar idea at his popular Philadelphia Museum, a forerunner to the natural history museum in the United States. Similarly, William Bullock created several prototypes at his Egyptian Hall in London. A display called the "Pantherion," for instance, gathered specimens of plants and animals (preserved by taxidermy) from several different continents and arranged them as part of a single scene, to create an imaginary mixed environment. More interestingly, in 1822, he imported to London a Sami family along with several reindeer. Thousands of visitors turned out to see the native performers as they drove a sled around one of the museum's halls. Their canvas tent was assembled against a painted snowy backdrop, with artifacts (snowshoes, tools, weapons, and antlers) mounted on the surrounding walls. Though Hagenbeck was probably unaware of these particular historical precedents, he found a more immediate source in the work of his close friend Leutemann.[17]

An animal painter by training, Leutemann specialized in making "zone pictures," a popular form of geographical illustration, which first emerged in the 1850s when the field of geography encompassed such subfields as anthropology and zoology. In this context, zone pictures aimed to visually render the determining relationship of climate (which here included soil, topography, latitude, etc.) on a given locality and its inhabitants. Based on the much older notion of climatic zones, Leutemann's work concentrated on the interrelationship of humans and animals within a particular habitat, or *Heimat*, the German term being a technical use of the familiar word for "homeland."[18]

The foreword to Leutemann's 1876 geographical atlas, *Zonen-Bilder* (zone pictures), includes a simple but suggestive definition of the genre, written by the geographer and educator Hermann Wagner (who also wrote the explanatory text for the illustrations).

> The following zone paintings (*Zonengemälde*) present to the young reader scenes of animal life from all parts of the world. They begin in Europe, our *Heimat*, then lead him to Asia and Africa, and end with the most recently discovered parts of the globe: America and Australia. The artist unites in each picture a number of the biggest, most important and characteristic animals of each area. In painterly fashion he presents us with scenes from their natural life. These fascinating images depict in equal parts the peaceful family life of the wild animal, its struggle within

the family, its fight against the enemy, and its mastery or hunting by human beings.

Leutemann's image of North Asia (plate 2), for example, "takes us to the northern coast of Siberia," and shows us "the king of the cold zone, the polar bear." The accompanying text extrapolates on the visual details, adding a discursive sense of weight and depth through an excess of information about the average size and range of the depicted animals. Of equal importance, the text elaborates on a fictional story about the interrelationship of humans and animals, which is also suggested by the picture. The use of narrative both visually and textually was a strategy for further engaging young readers by encouraging them to imagine what happens next, so to speak.[19]

Zone pictures were perhaps the most important and certainly the most immediate visual source for Hagenbeck's living habitat. The act of transfer was reciprocal and mutually beneficial, with Hagenbeck supplying the live models, and Leutemann creating illustrations that doubled as advertisements for the shows. Their exchange began as early as 1875, when Leutemann published various images of Lapps to accompany his magazine article, "Nordic Guests" (discussed in chapter 1). Thus, the first images of Hagenbeck's show circulated throughout Germany in the form of zone pictures.[20] As influential sources, they fostered a regional approach as well as a visual emphasis on spatial relations within the depicted scene (see plate 3), which clearly informed both the iconography and the choreography of live performance. The popular format of zone pictures is also important, one which the *Völkerschau* would similarly employ as a technique for soliciting and addressing young audiences in particular. Moreover, if the principle governing the composition of zone pictures is geographical (according to climate, latitude, continent, and region), there is a racial logic to the separation between zones that also informed the selection and succession of different performance troupes.[21]

There are several important differences between the *Völkerschau* and the zone picture, two of which must be emphasized here. First is the lack of overview for wider comparison. For example, in contrast to the illustrated atlas, where a series of zone pictures from around the globe unfolds before the reader's eyes, Hagenbeck presented only one group of people at a time. Whereas the atlas encouraged young readers to move the pages back and forth, oscillating from the particular habitat to a sort of universal overview, there was no equivalent position in the *Völkerschau*. The second difference that must be stressed is the vital role of physical presence, which was a defining feature of nineteenth-century theme space. "What the artist had in mind," Hagenbeck later commented, "was simply a picturesque Nordic scene, which he could only imagine in isolated perfection, complete with humans and animals, against a wintery background wherever possible." In other words, an appropriate emphasis on zone pictures as a visual source fails to acknowledge the insistent materiality and contingency of live performance. What the image could only suggest by pictorial means—that is, the physical presence of foreign peoples and exotic animals—the *Völkerschau*, by contrast, brought directly to the observer. If Hagenbeck's shows delivered "the real thing," they did so not in terms of verisimilitude or *trompe l'oeil*, but rather in terms of tangibility and presence. The distinction is a significant one, not least of all because the concept of verisimilitude implies an order of reading, to which the *Völkerschau* did not adhere. Rather than refer to reality as it existed within a genre (of exhibition, of painting, etc.), the *Völkerschau* sought to bypass representation and refer directly to an external reality, of which it claimed to be a living sample. Long before theme space was theorized in terms of "simulation," it was, literally and figuratively, grounded by the presence of the index in the display space.[22]

In order to create a living habitat (as opposed to a zone picture), a certain degree of instruction, training, and rehearsal was absolutely necessary. Every performance had to be staged and mediated, despite all claims to the contrary. For example, unlike geographical illustrations or museum showcases, in which—theoretically, at least—any animal could be depicted, a *Völkerschau* could integrate only those animals that had already been either trained or domesticated. Some degree of instruction was also, presumably, a necessary condition for the possibility of foregrounding a human presence in the living habitat. In 1880, the director of Basel's Zoological Garden complained in a letter to the impresario Willy Möller that the members of his Nubian Caravan, though "choice" in terms of their physical appearance, lacked "any cohesive training and direction" in how to represent their life and customs. In closing, the zoo director expressed his sincere hope that the troupe's manager, Oscar Stüber, has meanwhile "given the Nubians a bit more background and explained to them their task here in Europe." The upshot is a paradoxical one: Only by coaching them on the local rules of ethnographic performance, only by informing them of their specific roles and obligations, and thus addressing them as performers, could the Nubians be expected to present themselves as non-actors simply "living" in the display space, as they do in their "natural habitat." On this point the impresario and the manager, for their part, also had to be educated.[23]

The issue of performance in this context is a thorny one, but Hagenbeck's living habitat clearly accommodated certain types of overtly staged scenes. These included displays of physical skill and sport, ceremonial rituals, dances, and musical performances, parade-like "caravans" and migration scenes, the saddling and use of domesticated animals, as well as hunting expeditions, fight scenes, and work displays. Significantly, most of these acts necessitated a degree of training, which could also be understood as indigenous, whether it was under the sign of "preparation," "initiation," or "apprenticeship." Each term allowed for a degree of rehearsal and performance, without undermining the supposed authenticity of the spectacle. Choreographed scenes were generally tolerated by the audience so long as they were explicitly coded as tribal reenactments. Some historical spectators were evidently aware of such role-play, and quite satisfied with it. For example, a Berlin newspaper report on the 1880 Labrador show demonstrates a mutual awareness of performance, at the same time giving us a sense of what these performers actually did while they were on display.

> The Eskimos started their show on Sunday in the zoological garden to massive applause from an audience of almost 7,000. The most interesting part of the show is probably the seal hunt. In it, Tobias plays the seal to be hunted, wrapped in furs. As soon as Tareganiak [*sic*] spots him, he drops to the ground, imitating the sound of a seal, crawling towards him. Finally the animal is in firing range, the rifle thunders, the seal is hit, and the hunter jumps up cheering, ties a leash he has brought with him around the body of the shot animal, and trails it to the hut, where wife, kids, and friends await him. Tobias and Tareganiak play their roles with great enthusiasm, and Tobias patiently lets himself be trailed along the ground as the shot seal. The hunt on water is just as interesting.

Since role-play of this kind was generally allowed, it is even more interesting to note what happened later. At the Dresden zoo, the troupe's next stop, the Inuit performers requested to hunt one of the seals in captivity, offering their managers a unique public spectacle in return for fresh seal meat. They even received permission from the zoo's director, Adolf Schoepf, whose son (of the same name) was also the troupe's manager. An urgent letter from Hagenbeck, who was concerned about public relations, put a stop to the plan, temporarily, at least. In his diary entry from 27 November 1880, written in Prague's zoo, the performer Abraham Ulrikab noted that a live seal had been ordered and sent from Holland "for us to eat." There was one condition: "it is only allowed to be stabbed with the seal harpoon" (as opposed to being shot with a rifle). "When I harpooned it with the seal harpoon," Abraham wrote, "everybody clapped their hands greatly like the Eider ducks."[24]

Choreographing authenticity was of course a contradictory task, which called for discursive backup. However much native performers were trained on the job, however much they were perceived to be performing, Hagenbeck would predicate their "authenticity" on the assertion that they were untaught, and therefore perfectly qualified for ethnographic display. In order to situate them as part of a living habitat, Hagenbeck and his team used various techniques for coding performers both discursively and iconographically as living, breathing "signs of themselves." This semiotic maneuver, Kirshenblatt-Gimblett has shown, involves "a suppression of *representation* markers and a foregrounding of *presentation* markers, an avoidance of the suggestion of 'theater' and an attempt to achieve the quality of pure presence, of a slice of life." Leutemann offers a great example in recalling the symbolic origin of Hagenbeck's ethnographic enterprise, the Sami show of 1874.

> There were no actual performances (*regelrechte Vorstellungen*) given. No one was even suggesting as much from the very beginning; nor did these Laplanders, as unaffected natural people (*ungefälschte Naturmenschen*), have so much as a concept of performance. But it was precisely this unprompted activity of theirs that had such an enormous allure for the public. Only the ice skating show and the summer caravan [i.e., the parade-like staging of Sami migration] could be accurately called performances.

Here, once again, Leutemann's official account stands in sharp contrast to his original report. Remember Ella Maria Rasti, the Sami woman who had made such a strong impression on him, precisely because she already had a particular concept of display and demonstrated it quite clearly by soliciting money from the artist, and then holding up various objects for him to draw. The discursive move that Leutemann makes in recasting Rasti and the other members of her troupe as "unaffected natural people" was tantamount to a representational strategy that was usually employed in the performance itself: namely, a refusal of "mimesis" in favor of "presence." Ethnographic exhibition relied on a double gesture, for it required native participants to be competent performers, even as it emphatically disavowed such competence or awareness. Indeed, the authenticity effect of a given show depended on its success at seemingly achieving both of these functions at once. If successful, the dramaturgy of presence seemed all the more convincing.[25]

The living habitat also called for a certain type of display space. "What helped, naturally," Leutemann wrote of the first show, "was the fact that everything appeared in the open air, and not in a circus or in a fairground booth, which had the effect of adding authenticity." Specifically, Hagenbeck added, "the caravan was housed on the spacious lot behind our building, so it took place completely in the open air, without any artificial sets and backdrops." More than just a move out of the booth, the huts and tents that were set up by the performers were recoded and represented as "natural" extensions of the troupe and its way of life (a process of which I will have more to say later). On one level, this move out of the booth and into the open air can be seen as part of a larger discursive strategy for disentangling the practice of human and animal display from its origins in the fairground and its connotations of artifice, deception, and hucksterism. On another level, it is also part of an even broader cultural movement toward outdoor exhibition, spanning world's fairs, sporting events, open-air museums, and many other types of display. Zoological gardens, in particular, were considered to be ideal venues for live ethnographic performance, not only because of their established prestige as cultural institutions, as noted earlier, but also because they offered ample space for outdoor exhibition—as well as the sights, sounds, and smells of far-away places. Large outdoor spaces had other advantages as well. They permitted the building of "natural settings" on a larger and more innovative scale. They also opened up sight lines and allowed for the possibility of having many different focal points, while creating new relationships between spectators and performers.[26]

THE FAMILY UNIT

There were many possible configurations of the habitat group. One of them was the family, particularly in the early shows like the Greenland Inuit of 1877. Representations of family life bolstered the show's claim to exhibiting the everyday, while "naturally" endowing the troupe with an added sense of cohesion. Although the general tendency over time was toward ever-larger groupings, the family can be seen as the original life group, in every sense of the phrase. What makes this idea even more interesting is that the emphasis on observing families appears to have been especially widespread in the German context. Hagenbeck's shows were not simply collections of non-Western families, nor did they present themselves as such. Often, as noted earlier, his agents settled for recruiting "whoever was willing to go," precisely because joining a troupe meant leaving home—indeed, family—for a year, two years, sometimes even longer. As a category of exhibition, however, the family provided a cognitive framework that had the great advantage of being understood by all potential audiences. The family was also a category of late nineteenth-century anthropology. Johann Jakob Bachofen and his American counterpart, Lewis Henry Morgan, theorized about the origins of the family and about such manifestations of families as appeared in matrilinearity and patrilinearity. In claiming to represent the "family life" of non-Western peoples, Hagenbeck traded on a scientific category that was easily recognizable among popular audiences. He also created a cognitive link between the habitat group and the audience that was unique to the context of live entertainment.[27]

The continued effort to exhibit a spectrum of performers in terms of age and gender doubled as a marketing strategy for soliciting a diversity of spectators by appealing to their powers of identification and recognition. It was precisely for this reason that Leutemann stressed the importance of bringing young girls along with the men who usually accompanied the animal shipments and whose mobility was often less restricted. "From the very beginning it was my conviction that women with children, young girls in such groups, significantly multiplied the power of attraction, as anyone with a heart must agree."[28] Such a remark cries out for interpretation. If we imagine a predominately male audience (as other scholars would seem to do), then Leutemann's statement might seem to be aligned with colonial postcards and anthropological photographs, whose status oscillated between scientific evidence and soft pornography.[29] Ironically, however, this is Leutemann's way of acknowledging the preponderance of women, children, and youth in the audience. Of particular importance to the success of Hagenbeck's entertainments were children (and their nannies), because they tended to visit more than once—and then with friends and family members in tow.[30] The high degree of receptivity among young people was also part of the marketing equation. In this regard, if we envision a socially mixed audience, one which relied on paying customers (as opposed to scientists) and especially on women and children, then Leutemann's idea for accumulating spectators assumes new meaning. It also helps explain why it was that child performers were especially popular in ethnographic exhibitions. Viewers could "see" the troupe more clearly if at some level, such as at the level of the family context, the displayed people were visibly somewhat like themselves. Interestingly, a century earlier when natives were brought to Europe (as happened when explorers like Captain Cook or Bougainville brought Tahitians to London and Paris), it was typically a lone young man, much like the individual explorer himself. There, too, the native was transported in such a way that he (it was usually a he) could be "seen" by people able to see exotic difference because of its outwardly similar visible form. Nineteenth-century theme space witnessed the elaboration of this idea, beginning with the shift in focus from the individual to the family.[31]

The role of women and children in the spectacle is also the subject of Paul Meyerheim's wood engraving from 1878, "Eskimos in the Zoological Garden, Berlin," which is based on the troupe that Jacobsen assembled for Hagenbeck in Greenland (fig. 2.1). Usually, spectators and other signs of exhibition were omitted from illustrations, paintings, and woodcuts, for aesthetic as well as marketing purposes, as evidenced by the work of Leutemann. By contrast, this wood-engraved image explicitly depicts a habitat group being displayed and observed in Berlin's zoo. In other words, this is not another zone picture. Rather, it is a genre scene based on the occasion of a *Völkerschau*, and as such it displays a remarkable fascination with the interaction between the troupe and the audience. Though some of the performers here are arranged in situ (Kokkik paddles a kayak in the pond, dogs are arranged around the sled and in the foreground), others are clearly situated vis-à-vis the audience (such as Kojange, standing at center, with one hand in his pocket, the other holding a harpoon), looking and thus relaying the viewer's attention to the right edge of the picture. There, a young Inuit girl (Ane, accompanied by her sister and parents, Maggak and Okabak) receives gifts from a female spectator in the crowd. All eyes are on the exchange. The gifts—a

2.1 "Eskimos in the Zoological Garden, Berlin." Wood engraving by Paul Meyerheim, 1878. Courtesy of Heinz-Georg Klös.

German pretzel and an Oriental fan—are symbolic tokens of familiarity and difference, the currency of exchange at Hagenbeck's *Völkerschau*.

The relay of looks that Meyerheim depicts would seem to confirm Leutemann's emphasis on the pull of sentimentality. Contrary to our received ideas about ethnographic exhibition, there was no taboo against "returning the gaze" of the observer. Participants were not required to turn their gaze inward, as though they were "absorbed" figures in a painted tableau or wax mannequin display, or stage actors behind the invisible "fourth wall." Nor was the reverse gaze necessarily a sign of defiance or resistance to the terms of representation. The *Völkerschau* allowed for ongoing exchange between performers and spectators, while loosely regulating their interaction. As the wood-engraved image suggests (albeit inadvertently), ethnographic exhibitions appealed to the heart as well as to the mind of the spectator. They also appealed to the imagination. From this perspective, Meyerheim's image can be seen as an updated version of a scenario that Susanne Zantop analyzed in her study of precolonial German literature—a fantasy of German benevolence toward colonized peoples. At Hagenbeck's *Völkerschau*, spectators publicly demonstrated their supposed beneficence toward colonized peoples from around the globe, while shoring up their self-image as "superior" colonizers and respectable citizens. In this context, moreover, the family configuration, with its emphasis on women and children, helped accumulate audiences by providing a degree of familiarity while trading on the fantasy of cultural difference. In Hamburg, more than forty thousand people went to see the Inuit show on Easter weekend. It was a family outing, indeed.[32]

2.2 “Animal Caravan.” Illustration by Heinrich Leutemannn, 1876. This image depicting a scene from the African animal trade was based on Hagenbeck’s first Nubian show. Courtesy of Tierpark Carl Hagenbeck GmbH, Hamburg-Stellingen.

CARAVANS

If the family unit was central to the organization of Hagenbeck’s early and relatively small-scale shows, the “caravan” became an omnibus term for groups of virtually any size. It also served to designate various parade-like scenes within a program. First used in 1874, the term described one of the overtly choreographed scenes in the Lapland program: the “summer caravan,” a scene that claimed to dramatize Sami migration. As part of a show’s title, it usually denoted a habitat group consisting of nomadic people. In the wild animal trade, however, “animal caravan” was a term of art for the convoy of wagons, guides, trappers, dealers, and armed native guards that slowly made its way from the colonial interior to the animal holding station, and eventually to a port location, before making the voyage overseas. Hagenbeck staged caravans in every sense of the word.[33]

“Carl Hagenbeck’s Animal Caravan from Nubia,” the first in what would become a series of so-called Nubian shows, offers a fascinating example, because it placed as much emphasis on Hagenbeck’s line of work—the drama and the exoticism of the wild animal trade—as it did on the ethnographic performers (fig. 2.2). The strategic use of the animal dealer's name to identify another type of commodity, that is, an ethnographic entertainment, is discussed in chapter 3. Here it is enough to point out that Hagenbeck's themed environment, the living habitat, is a thoroughly commercialized space. The performers, for their part, were nomadic hunters—in this case, Hamran Arabs—who had earlier worked for Hagenbeck's agent in Kassala. Newspaper advertisements noted their role and coded it in tribal terms: "African animal hunters (Hamrans) have just arrived with the big animal transport," stated one announcement in the Hamburg daily *Correspondent*, indicating that the same group that collected these animals could also be seen at Hagenbeck's menagerie. The same tagline was repeated and elaborated as the caravan made its way across Europe, appearing at the zoological gardens in Düsseldorf and Breslau, at the *Jardin d'Acclimatation* in Paris, and later at the Alexandra Palace in London.[34]

The Nubian Caravan was initially addressed to a specific audience, and situated in relation to an existing form of nineteenth-century theme space: namely, the zoological garden. A leaflet distributed to German viewers was explicit on each point.

> Visitors to our zoological gardens often ask themselves, at the sight of wild and domesticated animals from all parts of the world: "How did these animals get into the hands of men? Who is daring enough to reach his hand out to the masters of the wilderness, and to master in turn the elephant, the rhinoceros, and the lion? Who ventures to bring the captive animals from their distant habitat, to overcome the obstacles that the tremendously bigger, more complicated transport brings with it from deep within the country's interior, and then via steam ship and railroad, all the way to Europe? Who attempts to naturalize the animals to a climate that is in so many ways completely different from their habitat?" The living answers to these questions can be found in:
>
> CARL HAGENBECK'S ANIMAL CARAVAN FROM NUBIA.
>
> The dark brown, well-built, intelligent inhabitants of Nubia, of which we presently find representatives from various tribes before us, are the daring and skilled hunters that captured the wild animals and their young, the very animals that are delivered to representatives of the trade menagerie of Herr Carl Hagenbeck in Hamburg, which in turn, with the help of the same natives, accomplish the costly and laborious task of transporting them to Europe.

By framing the show as a behind-the-scenes look at the process of stocking a zoological garden, and the commercial animal trade on which it was based, Hagenbeck conferred legitimacy upon his main business by virtue of the zoo as an institution,

2.3 "Kalmucks migrating across the Steppe," 1883. Photograph from Carl Hagenbeck, *Von Menschen und Tieren* (1909). Courtesy of Tierpark Carl Hagenbeck GmbH, Hamburg-Stellingen.

while naturalizing his new ethnographic enterprise as a further extension of the animal trade. The symbiotic relationship between the two branches of his business was, literally and figuratively, embodied by the hunters on display. "For the people who are born into this animal-rich landscape," Hagenbeck commented, "hunting is virtually an elemental occupation."[35]

In an interesting turnabout, the Nubian Caravan also fetishized the physical presence of African hunters as an answer back to the "fetish character" (in Marx's terms) of animals in captivity, making visible the labor that the zoo had made invisible and phantasmagoric, for the sake of representing "nature." It is important to note that Hagenbeck makes this move without apparent irony, and without any hint of "deconstructing" the zoo display. He saw exotic animals precisely as commodities, and the caravan as a troupe configuration extended this idea to foreign peoples. It represented at once a living advertisement for the Hagenbeck Company and an ethnographic exhibition in its own right.[36]

The caravan designated a habitat group that was, by definition, on the move. As such it was capable of accommodating a diversity of peoples from regions whose boundaries were geographically imprecise. This included nomadic peoples such as "Hagenbeck's Kalmuck Caravan" of 1883, another troupe assembled in the context of the animal trade, this time in the Volga region of Russia. Twenty-two people (including eight children and two Buddhist priests) were recruited by Hagenbeck's traveler, one Hermann Behnke, who had originally been charged with acquiring a group of Bactrian (two-humped) camels. The ensuing performance included "break-neck riding on half-wild horses," which not only anticipated the emphasis on horse racing in Buffalo Bill's Wild West show but also dramatized and romanticized the itinerant life of nomadic peoples. The culminating attraction, which moved at a markedly slower tempo, was the drama of migration. Hagenbeck described the scene as it unfolded: "They broke camp, dismantled the tents, fastened the individual parts onto horses and camels, and set off on their travels. That is to say, they paraded around a few times in circles, and stopped again at the same spot. The tents were set up and camp life began." While they walked, the men and women "sang a peculiar song," which intrigued at least one reviewer, who transcribed the lyrics and described them as containing "ideas and philosophies of a natural people, which could in fact provide the historian with an endless source of discovery."[37] With its mix of the rowdy and the pastoral, entertainment and education, Hagenbeck's Kalmuck Caravan became his most popular show to date, far surpassing previous attendance records in Paris as well as in Berlin, where more than 93,000 visitors bought tickets for opening day.[38]

WORK DISPLAYS

Over a span of more than thirty years, perhaps the most enduring and malleable form of habitat group was the work display. It began inadvertently with Hagenbeck's very first show. Upon their arrival at each new venue, members of the Sami troupe assembled their wood and canvas tents, and spectators turned out en masse to see them set up, even before the actual show began. A similar phenomenon had been noticed as early as 1867, at the *Exposition Universelle* in Paris, where "visitors . . . were more fascinated by foreign workmen finishing off incomplete pavilions than they were by the pavilions themselves." As these and other examples suggest, the drama of process was not restricted to the temporal framework of a scheduled performance. The sight of native labor outside of the performance context engendered a powerful "authenticity" effect, which also had significant implications for the show per se, not only in the sense that the assembly of huts, tents, or buildings could be seen as unscheduled and therefore unchoreographed, but also—more important—by showing natives in the act of creating their own environment. When participants served double duty as set builders, the spectacle of their labor had the indexical effect of integrating objects and structures into the living habitat, at once emphasizing the materiality of the set and eschewing its status as theatrical or artificial.[39]

Over time, the visual display of nonalienated labor became an integral part of Hagenbeck's *Völkerschau*, as it did later in the context of folk museums and world's fairs. There is some evidence to suggest that work displays became crucial to the popular success of ethnographic troupes generally, no matter what their supposed context of origin. The reified figure of the native artisan obviously drew upon idealized notions of this or that culture, but it was not restricted to any particular region or zone. It is a testament to the generic power of work displays that, in 1899, the director of the "Bisharin Caravan" recruited artisans of different origin because the featured people allegedly "had no industry of their own." By contrast, fine craftsmanship was sometimes recognized (beyond the souvenir's fetish value) as a sign of cultural achievement. Thus, the Nubian Caravan of 1879 was celebrated in the Hamburg press for including not only hunters but also goldsmiths, leather workers, and silk weavers "of exquisite quality." A journalist for the petit-bourgeois newspaper *Reform*, and a frequent commentator on ethnographic shows in Germany, Georg Buchholz expressed his sincere wish that such demonstrations would "make the opinion known, that the Nubians are people capable of culture."[40]

Hagenbeck extrapolated an iconography of native work, which can be seen most clearly through the long series of Sri Lankan exhibitions, the first of which appeared (simultaneous to the Kalmuck Caravan) in 1883. Led by the impresario Johannes Castens, the first "Ceylon" show premiered in Paris and proceeded to the Zoological Garden in Berlin, where it drew more than 90,000 visitors in a single day. So popular was the troupe—which actually comprised a mix of professional and nonprofessional performers from India and Sri Lanka—that Hagenbeck produced at least four more exhibitions on this "theme" between 1884 and 1886, "each one larger and more complete than the one before it."[41]

What this series, like no other, demonstrates is the way in which Hagenbeck's work displays co-opted the circus at the height of its phenomenal popularity. Paradoxical though it may seem, the circus provided a visual model for re-envisioning and refreshing the *Völkerschau* as a living habitat. Leutemann takes credit for this idea, too. "Much earlier," he writes in his biography of Hagenbeck, "in a conversation I had with him about elephants, I mentioned how alluring and educational it would be for once, instead of the usual trained elephants that can only do tricks, to see animals of this kind that could be used for practical work, as I had often read about." Thus, the circus represented, as the fairground had earlier, a negative model of display that the *Völkerschau* would appropriate and re-signify as ethnographic.[42]

What was new and different here, if anything, was the grouping and staging of enormous animals in use.

> Everywhere it went this totally unprecedented group from Ceylon made a sensation. It was a real pleasure for the animal lover to see that noble and powerful animal finally shown as applied to a worthy and practical purpose. To see [elephants] here carrying around big tree trunks, which they did in various ways depending on the circumstances but always with great intelligence, was to gain an idea of just how extraordinarily useful these giants of the animal world can be in the service of men, and thus how important the elephant as a domesticated animal is to its homeland. In this group there were also some little musk oxen, which were harnessed to two-wheel carts, as well as some conjurers and women, but the worker elephants remained by far the greatest attraction. No wonder that Hagenbeck got up the courage to mount another show of the same kind [in 1884]. In so doing he naturally retained the purchased elephants, and sent only the people, the "Sinhalese," back home to recruit others in greater numbers.

That Leutemann so insistently distinguishes the *Völkerschau* from the circus has the reverse effect of calling attention to their affinity, especially in retrospect. According to one scholar, elements of the circus can be found in all of the Sri Lankan shows, with their acrobats, stilt walkers, pole climbers, and trained monkeys. At the same time, the dramatization of work was precisely what set the *Völkerschau* apart from the circus; in this observation Leutemann was correct. Ironically, however, the supposed shift from display value to use value, on which the show's novelty was predicated, meant that the living habitat relied as never before on trained animals and professional performers (such as kornacks). Training might have been anathema to ethnographic exhibition, but it was necessary for the possibility of re-casting living animals and performers as "workers" and re-staging circus tricks as representative scenes of "natural life." If elephants played the leading roles in dramatizations of life in Sri Lanka, their immense presence had the effect of further expanding and naturalizing the space of the living habitat.[43]

THE LIVING VILLAGE

The various groupings—such as families, caravans, work displays—were themselves gathered and rearranged in the idealized native village, a walk-through environment, which also marked the culmination of the habitat idea in the context of human display (fig. 2.4). The village formation encouraged spectators to regard the performers as members of a community (and not just a troupe), bolstering the idea of the *Völkerschau* as "life" by dint of scope and scale. More than just an elaboration of the native encampment, the village evoked a sense of fixity or settlement (as opposed to itinerancy), which complemented the display of nomadic life while extending the show's imaginary geography to represent location and dwelling as well as migration and movement. Interestingly, it is in the Ceylon series, which is usually noted for its obvious affinities to the circus, that there appear the first signs of a full-blown native village. During the 1880s, as this series demonstrates, there was a marked increase in the scale of production—an aggrandizement of the spectacle, which also evokes indirectly a sense of growing competition among showmen. Leutemann referred to this development as "an increase of plentitude," noting the many structures, animals, and performers that were now regularly involved (the 1885 troupe, for example, consisted of at least seventy people). "At that point," he recalled, "a further extension of the massive scale was hardly conceivable."[44]

From the viewpoint of theme space, however, the village was distinguished by more than its hyperbolic scale. The key historical developments can be seen in the arrangement of display elements in relation to one another and in the expanded use of space for performance. A reporter gave the following description of the 1884 Ceylon show: "In the middle of a wide open space there is a large water basin, around which the Sinhalese huts, made of bamboo poles and a roof of dried palm leaves, have been grouped. The spaces between and behind the huts are decorated with palm trees and

2.4 Entrance to the "Sinhalese Village" of Hagenbeck's *Tierpark*, 1908. Courtesy of Tierpark Carl Hagenbeck GmbH, Hamburg-Stellingen.

other large-leafed plants in such a way that the whole indeed strikingly resembles a small, Ceylonese settlement." What makes this arrangement so remarkable, now as then, is the staging of "spaces between and behind" the designated displays, which had the effect of blurring the boundaries between the physical spaces of performance and spectatorship. To elaborate and rearrange the performance space in this way was to enhance its sensory experience, inviting the spectator to physically enter a themed environment that was larger and more encompassing than ever before. The expanded use of space for performance brings us back to the notion that Hagenbeck had moved the practice of human display out of the fairground booth and into the open air. The experience of the native village as an immersive environment for spectators is discussed at length in chapter 3. Here, I focus on its historical origin as a living habitat.[45]

The art of the habitat—its visual economy from the viewpoint of theme space—is perhaps best illustrated by an advertising poster for the 1885 Ceylon show, designed by the Hamburg lithographer Adolph Friedländer (see plate 4). In contrast to Leutemann and his painterly approach, Friedländer not only seems to recognize both the mediated nature of the *Völkerschau* and its construction as a performance; he also explores these qualities through the creative use of his own medium, the graphic image. The poster can thus be seen as an interesting meta-commentary on the "work" of the *Völkerschau* as another type of image-making technology. It further demonstrates the use of space and the role of embodiment that distinguished the living habitat from other modes of ethnographic display.[46]

The title, "Carl Hagenbeck's 1885 Ceylon Expedition," announces the vicarious experience of travel, while referring to the actual mobility on which it depends: that of the objects, bodies, and structures on display. The poster shows a native figure—a snake charmer—standing at the edge of a cracked surface, against a backdrop of palm trees (plate 4). Wrapped around his arms and hanging from his neck is a boa constrictor, its face in close proximity to that of the performer. In one hand, the man holds a flute, in the other a picture, which unfurls before him and extends toward the viewer. The entire composition is framed by what appears to be a kind of wooden border. Looped around the upper-right corner of the frame is a tasseled cord, which "ties" the inset picture to the outer frame (the coils of this cord visually link it to the snake, as well). The created effect is that of a poster-within-a-poster, with the inset picture being physically connected to the exterior one. The interior poster is clearly the more elaborate of the two. Here, before the wider, receding horizon of a lush and mountainous landscape, we see a village with several huts, domesticated animals, and different groups of people. The objects and animals are arranged in use, as integral parts of a representative scene; the human figures in each group are placed in situ and arranged in interacting poses. They are walking, dancing, working, making food, riding animals, and playing music—engaged in the very activities that the *Völkerschau* would claim to present.[47]

Of particular interest here is the rigging or framing device, for it establishes a physical as well as a metonymic link between the performer and the snake in the foreground and the various groupings depicted on the inset poster. The interaction between the different levels of representation unfolds in a series of structural oppositions: part and whole, individual and collective, presence and absence, here and there, "Ceylon" and Ceylon. All of the elements that have been gathered to evoke "Ceylon" (performer, costume, snake, flute, and palm trees) are carefully doubled and redoubled in the interior picture of Ceylon. The nature of the relationship between the two images is emphatically indexical. The performer holds a poster in his hand, and the rigging literally ties it to the outer frame (their borders are also contiguous along two sides). Ceylon, in other words, is precisely what "Hagenbeck's Ceylon Expedition" brings to the public. It is the living habitat (the poster-within-a-poster) that the performer both embodies and presents to his audience. Friedländer's advertisement gestures so confidently toward the show's status as a representation because there is no "illusion" here to be broken. The figures of the living habitat are at once tangible, present, and readily available.

It is one thing to analyze images of ethnographic spectacle by artists such as Friedländer, Meyerheim, or Leutemann. It is another thing to investigate the events to which they refer. Images of spectacle are more than evidence for ethnographic exhibition; they are spectacles of a different kind. When dealing with live, surround-style performances, we need to make some methodological adjustments. For example, it becomes crucial to bear in mind the agency of performers, the participation of spectators, the power dynamics that governed their interaction, and the social relationships between them that nonetheless transpired. The emphatic presence and fullness of nineteenth-century theme space invite us to explore it more in depth as a kind of "contact zone," a term which Mary Louise Pratt has used in order "to foreground the interactive, improvisational dimensions of colonial encounters." In the previous chapter we considered some of the ways in which the long processes of cultural displacement shaped and reshaped the recruitment of performers. The following discussion investigates the transactions between performers and spectators in the context of commercial exhibition.[48]

The Boundaries of Display

The living habitat claimed to represent ethnographic "reality," but what it created in effect was a performance space of intercultural encounter. Just as the group method involved coordinating bodies and objects within a designated area, it also involved testing the boundaries of display. Spectators as well as performers were part of this process. As I have claimed elsewhere, contrary to the received idea of ethnographic exhibition, the co-presence of spectators and performers in shared space created a powerful sense of commonality that competed with the expectation of radical difference. In a sense, close-up encounters were not just permitted, they were arranged. Hagenbeck's *Völkerschau* created a social space, based on a set of assumptions about cultural identity and racial difference, which loosely regulated the behaviors of spectators as well as performers. In so doing, however, it allowed for a surprising degree of casual, unchoreographed interaction. Roving throughout the display area were performers selling exotic souvenirs, *cartes des visites*, and (later) picture postcards. There are various anecdotes of spectators and performers trying to communicate through language, gesture, drawing, writing, and touching. Hagenbeck's show was a social practice of the greatest significance, because it engendered a variety of actual cross-cultural encounters in the context of Wilhelmine Germany. These encounters were always a function of commercial entertainment, where the fundamental premise of cultural superiority and the hierarchical relationship between the observer and the observed would be shaken but never dismantled; that, too, is a fact of shared space. Nowhere do these assumptions become more explicit—and more contentious—than they do at the fence or barrier that often surrounded the space of exhibition.[49]

The spatial border of the display was among the most fascinating signs of nineteenth-century theme space. A rare amateur photograph of Hagenbeck's 1912 Egyptian exhi-

2.5 Female spectators at a "Bedouin" display in Hagenbeck's *Tierpark*, 1912. Courtesy of Tierpark Carl Hagenbeck GmbH, Hamburg-Stellingen.

bition (fig. 2.5), one of the few existing images that depict spectators (who appear to be bourgeois women) as well as performers ("Bedouins"), seems to capture the tension between commonality and difference that organized ethnographic exhibitions in general. Most conspicuous here is the fence around the display, which visualizes the assumed hierarchy of viewers and performers. To a certain extent, the fence can be seen as analogous to the frame of a zone picture or the glass case of a museum display. Each delineates a space for exhibition and, by extension, a space for spectatorship; each device further constitutes the life group as a sight to be seen, while locating the audience in a privileged position vis-à-vis the display. Yet the analogy goes only so far. As a formal barrier, the fence draws even more attention to the alterity of Hagenbeck's *Völkerschau*, its difference as a form of theme space, with its dual emphasis on presence and performance. In practice, the borders of the living habitat were remarkably porous. It was actually possible, under certain conditions, for performers to leave the designated space of exhibition. It was equally possible for spectators to claim an active role, cross the fence, and enter the space of display. Neither scenario was typical, but each of them took place—and did so from the beginning of Hagenbeck's ethnographic enterprise.

The two-way transactions across the borders of display posed a challenge to the construction of alterity that the *Völkerschau* itself exemplified, by transforming the exhibit momentarily into a different entity altogether. Writing in another context, that is, the contemporary phenomenon of environmental theater, performance scholar Richard Schechner has emphasized that "*audience participation takes place precisely at the point where the performance breaks down and becomes a social event.*" Participation and spatial experimentation on this order have "escaped mainstream theater," belonging instead to site-specific performances in the arts, but also, as Schechner observes, to a wide range of theme parks, living museums, and restored villages. In this regard, it is important to explore the key form of nineteenth-century theme space, which preceded and modeled these contemporary entertainments. Participation in the *Völkerschau* marked the point where critics and censors intervened, exercising social control by means of cultural regulation. The lure of participation and thus the stakes of performance were perhaps highest at the fence, where visitors and performers were physically separated, but where they nevertheless met and interacted.[50]

Fences served different and sometimes contradictory functions. On the one side, they suggested a kind of visual mastery over the animals and performers by literally corralling them within a space of display, and framing them as objects of the spectator's gaze. On the other side, however, the living habitat relied for its immersive effects on the spectator's powers of imagination and identification, and from this perspective fences were also obstacles to be surmounted. Fences are thus rarely to be seen in artistic images of Hagenbeck's *Völkerschau* rendered as woodcuts, paintings, illustrations, or lithograph posters, which studiously elided such barriers in order to create the impression of unimpeded viewing. The conspicuous absence of barriers in artistic images can surely be explained in terms of the habitat idea and its implementation. It also evokes the strong desire of visitors to transgress such barriers, as some in fact did. For all the spectators who wanted to be kept apart from foreign peoples, others were unable to hold themselves back. The use of fences varied according to troupe, venue, and audience. Most notably, barriers were used in order to protect the performers from throngs of prying visitors. From the onset, policemen or soldiers were occasionally recruited to enforce these divisions, but even they could not always contain the crowd.[51]

The desire for proximity and some of its effects upon the performer can be shown by an anecdote from Hagenbeck's 1880 Labrador show, a troupe discussed earlier in terms of recruitment. What makes this anecdote so fascinating in the context of exhibition is its particular source and perspective. It comes from the diary of an Inuit named Abraham Ulrikab, the only known account of Hagenbeck's *Völkerschau* written by a native performer. Though the diary is perhaps unique within the set of available evidence, it comments on the give-and-take between performers and spectators that was often the case at Hagenbeck's *Völkerschau*. In this respect, at least, the diary has potential for even greater relevance.[52]

In October-November of 1880, the Labrador troupe appeared in Berlin's zoological garden. One of eight Inuit recruited, Abraham was a Christian neophyte who had been converted and baptized by Moravian missionaries. Among the stated reasons why Abraham decided to join the troupe (noted earlier) was the opportunity to see Europe, to visit other parishes, and to reunite with former "teachers" who had since returned from Labrador to Germany. In Berlin, he and his family received visits from several old "acquaintances" (*Bekannte*)—namely, Brother Elsner, Brother Kern, and Brother Dewitz, who came from around the country in response to Abraham's written request. It was their arrival that prompted Hagenbeck to make a hasty trip from Hamburg to Berlin and demonstrate his concern for the troupe's happiness and comfort; for him, it was clearly an opportunity to boost his reputation in the eyes of missionaries, the show's leading critics in Germany. The Moravian presence also led the zoo's director, Heinrich Bodinus, to grant Abraham and his family permission to attend a service and a dinner that was being held in their honor at the local Hall of Brethren, on 26 October 1880. "That evening the Eskimos did not wear their seal skins but their white communion dress," Brother Dewitz reported. Together with members of the local congregation, they sang songs in German, listened to the church's choir, and heard a sermon in their native tongue, Inuktitut, which was spoken by Brother Kern. This experience of the Inuit family in church and the positive impression that it left on the parishioners became the occasion for further interaction. As Abraham noted in his diary, "the teachers often appeared in our house (in the zoo)," where they ate, prayed, and sang hymns together, "even the women came into our huts and sang along."[53]

Not all visitors were welcomed by the performers. While Abraham and his family warmly received the Moravians in their living space, they were also overwhelmed by throngs of uninvited guests. Abraham records his frustration with being unable to accept more invitations to church or to visit other people's homes, due to the relentless crowds of spectators at the zoo. "We wanted to go, but we were unable, because there were too many people. Yes, it was impossible to go out during the day, before the people, because we were so totally surrounded by them, by such different faces." Throughout his diary, Abraham complains of suffering under the loud noises of the city and the surge of the jostling masses, in particular. He grows weary of signing autographs (it was common practice for spectators to collect signatures as souvenirs and proof of having personally made contact with foreign performers). From the beginning, Abraham complains of curious spectators peeking through every fence, window, and door throughout the day.[54]

The physical and psychological harm that mass audiences sometimes visited upon performers (if inadvertently) is almost palpable in Abraham's diary. So is the hunger for experience and proximity, as the behavior of spectators would seem to suggest. On one occasion, "They came into our enclosure (*Umzäunung*) and everyone wanted to see our kayak, but all at once it [the house] filled up with people, and it became impossible to move." Unable to disperse the crowd, and despite the efforts of soldiers barking orders outside, the troupe's impresarios, Jacobsen and Schoepf, enlisted Abraham's help. "I did what I could," he wrote. "Taking my whip and the Greenland seal harpoon I made myself terrible: One of the gentlemen was like a crier; some quickly shook hands with me as I chased them out; others ran or jumped over the fence.... Ulrike locked our house from the inside and blocked the entrance so that nobody could go in, and those wanting to look in through the windows were pushed away with a piece of wood." In this case, native resistance was mounted not against the terms of representation, but rather against the contingency of spectatorship in shared space.[55]

Here, again, juxtaposing multiple accounts helps demonstrate the complexity of perspective and social interaction that is characteristic of Hagenbeck's version of theme space. In this case, a newspaper story, written after the Labrador troupe's second day in Berlin, begs the question of whether the other participants shared Abraham's particular viewpoint. It also provides further evidence of social and physical contact within the space of performance. For this reason alone it bears repeating:

> Among the curious people visiting the Eskimos on Monday were many children, who tried to communicate with the Eskimos by language and gestures. It was already getting dark, the spectators had left, and the Greenlanders had gone into their huts, as well. Only Tobias, the 21-year-old, not absolutely unhandsome youth sat outside, leaning against a tree. He was surrounded by a group of boys and girls, who joked with him and asked many things. A little boy, maybe 10 years old, with a pretty, smiling face, found the special favor of the northern son, who petted and caressed the clever boy for every comment. Once, he might have touched the boy a little rough; the boy pretended to cry and Tobias jumped up at once, put the boy's head on his chest and covered him with kisses. When the boy looked up again, laughing heartily, Tobias joined him, laughing after a while, and caressed and kissed the boy again. Almost by force the Eskimo had to be separated from the cheerful children, and only after the leader of the group indicated that he [Tobias] will see the children again tomorrow, he said goodbye to his Berlin friends for the day and retreated into the hut.

Written by a Berlin journalist, this sentimental account depicts as quaint the lively interaction between a German child and an Inuit adult. The boundaries of display are effaced here, too, for the entire drama takes place within the display area. Indeed, the story's humor depends on the physical fact of shared space and casual contact. In stark contrast to Abraham's irritation with the crowd, the story of Tobias represents a scene of playful interaction. It also reinforces a major cultural stereotype: that of the child-like native. At the same time, this story about Tobias's open display of fondness for children, and their efforts to communicate with one another, humanizes the performer in ways that challenge the assumption of cultural superiority on which the show, and particularly its use of fences, was based.[56]

Looking back on such episodes, Leutemann would later comment on what he considered to be the predicament of ethnographic exhibition, generally speaking. In so doing, he allows himself a personal observation about the shows, as one who has "stood so near to them from the very beginning." Reminding his reader of the growing scientific interest in performers, he remarks, "one observation must be explicitly stated: the cultural and physical inferiority of the various human races to the Caucasian is in no way so significant as many people still just assume. Even a brief conversation with these people, even if it were mediated by a translator, could prove this point every time." This observation contains not a humanistic critique of the show from an insider's perspective, but an interesting clue as to the show's eventual implosion. Most notably, and perhaps contrary to what one might expect, it did not necessarily depend upon the active resistance of native performers. The lived experience of shared space, which is distinguished by the co-presence of performers and spectators, had several unforeseen effects. For example, in bringing foreign peoples face-to-face with German spectators and thus creating actual (however mediated) social encounters, the *Völkerschau* inadvertently counteracted its anthropological premise that "natural peoples" were absolutely different from "cultural peoples." In its latent challenge to long-held assumptions about human diversity, "even a brief conversation" could have larger implications—for spectators, for performers, and for the commercial success of a particular exhibition.

A different but equally viable outcome of this dialogue was for itinerant performers to grow miserable, angry, homesick, or depressed. Indeed, Leutemann worried that such feelings might be exacerbated by the increased sense of awareness that might also come from sustained interaction with spectators. His conclusion: "These performances have always run smoothly if the audience is kept from conversing with these representatives of foreign peoples. For only in the few instances that such an opportunity for association (*Verkehrsmöglichkeit*) actually developed on the occasion of longer visits did the seeds of discontent sometimes begin to form among these people who have always been harmless from the very beginning." Interaction with spectators had to be minimized if not prohibited, he reasoned, in order to keep performers from resisting their situation of being on display. The logic here is obviously flawed, but the assumption concerning cross-cultural dialogue as a potential threat is nonetheless interesting for what it tells us about the fragility of the *Völkerschau* as a particular type of theme space. Whichever direction it came from—whether from an unforeseen challenge to the spectator's sense of cultural superiority or from the emergence of discontent among the performers—the disruption of Hagenbeck's living habitat was always one conversation away.[57]

Sex, Race, and Colonial Authority

Unlike other forms of nineteenth-century visual culture, the ethnographic exhibition created the exciting and unsettling potential for social reciprocity to break out, even as this tradition of spectacle was based on the cultural assumption of a racial hierarchy. In this regard, the image of spectators hurriedly shaking Abraham's hand before exiting the Inuit's hut is emblematic. According to Thode-Arora, "there emerged among the visitors a strong need and potential to make such contact, as evidenced by the many accounts of spectators unwilling to be separated from performers, the exchange of small presents and expensive gifts, invitations, flirtations, and love relationships." Add to this the penchant for collecting signatures from performers and the increasingly common practice of wandering through living villages, and an even wider range of social interactions comes into view, beyond the usual emphasis on gawking and "returning the gaze." Even Leutemann observed with concern the "opportunity for

2.6 The "Nubian Caravan" of 1876. Photo from Carl Hagenbeck, *Von Tieren und Menschen* (1909). Courtesy of Tierpark Carl Hagenbeck GmbH, Hamburg-Stellingen.

association"—the chance for connection and not just dissonance—that live exhibitions represented. In making this observation, he used a German term, *Verkehrsmöglichkeit*, which is suggestive if not explicit, referring on one level to the possibility of physical contact and specifically sexual intercourse. Privacy was possible to a degree even at a public exhibition, such as the *Völkerschau*, where it became a source of both cultural fascination and anxiety. Thus, anecdotes of midnight liaisons between spectators and performers can be found throughout the Hagenbeck material, suggesting that interracial romance was a minor yet continuous part of the show's appeal. These anecdotes evince certain forces of passionate identification that operated indirectly at the *Völkerschau*, contending with its cultural assumptions and visual stereotypes of racial difference—forces that transgressed and destabilized both the social and physical barriers that were intended to construct distinct spaces of identity. Consequently, anecdotes of encounter also provided critics and censors with some of their most emotionally powerful and effective arguments against the *Völkerschau* as a practice. Both sides of the issue deserve a closer look, because they help draw out the complexities of sex, race, and colonial authority as informing contexts of the ethnographic exhibition in Germany.[58]

The series of Nubian shows that Hagenbeck produced between 1876 and 1879 offers the most famous example, rendering conspicuous the nexus of race, gender, and sexuality that was implicitly embodied in other shows, as well. By all accounts, the Nubian shows were extremely popular among commercial audiences. The first troupe, organized by Bernhard Kohn, drew more than thirty thousand visitors on opening day in Breslau. With the help of various agents, Hagenbeck went on to assemble three more Nubian troupes in as many years. As Leutemann put it, "Germany and surrounding countries were inundated with Nubians for a while." Throughout the many comments that this series of shows elicited, the noted figures are mostly German women and African men. Typical in this regard is one of Hagenbeck's recollections of the first Nubian show: "A young, enormous Hamran hunter, who in spite of his 'tender' age of nineteen years was already six feet tall, caused true devastation in the hearts of European women, and seemed to be not impervious himself to the charms of pale-faced beauties." In this observation Hagenbeck was not alone. Nor was it an isolated incident.[59]

Transactions between spectators and performers figure even more prominently in subsequent shows. Consider, for example, an illustration of the 1878 troupe and its performance in Berlin's zoological garden (fig. 2.7). What most interests me about this image, a composite of scenes from different moments and aspects of a single event, is its plain depiction of social interaction both around and across the boundaries of the display. In one panel (at left), two male performers appear to be signing autographs for members of the crowd; one of the performers reaches over the fence and hands a notebook to a child in the audience. Another panel shows a conversation between

Die Nubier im zoologischen Garten in Berlin. Originalzeichnung von E. Henseler. (S. 186.)

two performers and two spectators (at right), which takes place in the background of a staged "ethnographic" scene. An account of this troupe and its predecessor can be found in the unpublished manuscript of Jacobsen's memoir, which is also worth quoting at length.

> Here I want to mention a phenomenon that we as showmen frequently encountered with southern peoples—namely, the sudden lovesickness that these brown fellows inspired in quite a lot of young girls and also women. It was particularly the years 1877–78, when Hagenbeck's great Nubian troupes came to the big cities in Germany. My colleagues, who traveled with these troupes, told me the most amazing stories about them. At the time, these troupes were in fact the first from the south to appear in Europe, and since one had yet to notice it with other peoples, the women who were struck by this lovesickness were called "Nubian-crazed" ("*Nubiertoll*"). Later, when Indians and especially the Sinhalese came to Europe, one heard similar stories, if not to such a marked degree as with the Nubians. With their lean figures and bronze skin, the barely clothed Nubians excited the young girls most of all. Every day one could see a love-struck little woman stroking and feeling the hand or arm of a brown Adonis for half an hour at a time. It went so far that in the summer of 1878, the troupe was in Berlin's zoological garden, and every black man had found his sweetheart, so to speak, the troupe was preparing to depart, when suddenly the blacks refused to obey, probably goaded by their new girlfriends, and did not want to leave the zoological garden. A group of well-armed policemen had to be summoned, who, with swords and revolvers drawn, separated the pairs, the Nubians being armed with shields and lances, so that the troupe could finally depart Berlin. In Dresden [once again] a few young girls made themselves ready for travel, to accompany the troupe when the Nubians departed. Fortunately, someone informed the parents of one girl, so this little sprout was picked up at the last minute in the train station.[60]

Whether the other girls accompanied the troupe goes unsaid. Since this version of Jacobsen's story was written decades after the fact, it is also worth quoting from an earlier (but no less problematic) source, that of Leutemann, whose account of the 1878 troupe in Berlin gives us a different perspective. Unlike other commentators, Leutemann observes that male spectators and Nubian women were also involved on more than one occasion, beyond the more scandalous visibility of German women and Nubian men flirting and openly associating with one another. Equally interesting is Leutemann's interpretation of the troupe's resonance with mass audiences (a Berlin newspaper reported that more than 86,000 people turned out to see the show on a single day in October). In his words, the troupe

2.7 "The Nubians in Berlin's Zoological Garden." Illustration by E. Henseler. *Über Land und Meer: Allgemeine Illustrirte Zeitung* 41, no. 10 (1878): 189.

> aroused fanatical excitement, especially among the female population—evidence that, when a Berliner learns to 'let go' of his inborn mistrust and apprehension, the excitement can be very significant. Now the male world in Berlin could almost be jealous of the interest that Africa's dark sons inspired in Berlin's women, but the eternal feminine, which was represented on the part of the Nubians this time by one man's sister, who was brought along, justifiably appealed to the men, as well. These Nubians stayed there for several weeks, and they were the talk of the city for just as long.[61]

Members of the German Colonial Society defined the issue quite differently. For them, the so-called Nubian craze offered evidence not that Berliners were actually capable of enjoying themselves (as Leutemann had commented). Instead, they worried that such displays tacitly invited spectators and performers to shed their inhibitions, literally embracing interracial desire and engaging in physical contact. More than a criticism of commercial entertainment, this interpretation became part of a policy statement for the Colonial Society, the largest and most influential organization of the pro-colonial movement in Germany. The objectives of this private organization included lobbying government officials for legislation, promoting colonial expansion and development as well as generating enthusiasm for colonies among an indifferent German public. Until 1900, colonial exhibitions had been integral to its propaganda work at home. In 1896, for example, a private group of industrialists, which included several leaders of the Colonial Society, organized the Colonial Exhibition at the Berlin Trade Exposition. While the exhibition rendered a hegemonic image of African subservience and German superiority in the colonies, the unchoreographed interaction of spectators and performers posed a threat to this vision of colonial authority. The most powerful and enduring memory of the exhibition was that of the strong mutual desire connecting German women and male performers. The show resulted, scandalously, in flirtations, physical contact, even a few marriage contracts. When debates on "mixed marriages" heated up in the German parliament a few years later, one member recalled the 1896 Colonial Exhibition as a public spectacle of "racially unfaithful behavior." Sometimes, as historian Paul Kramer has shown in another context, ethnographic exhibition and colonial propaganda worked at cross-purposes. It is for this reason too that the German Colonial Society decided to intervene in the regulation of public entertainment.[62]

In 1900, a proposal to ban the import of natives from German colonies for the purpose of exhibition was debated by the Society's leaders at their annual convention in Koblenz. Here, the boundaries of display were defined in overtly political terms. "Displays of natives are embarrassing for all of us," said one official. "When they return home, the people bring with them not European culture but rather the very opposite."

"What is the purpose of such displays?" asked another. "The entrepreneurs doubtless have no intention of disseminating ethnological and anthropological knowledge in Europe; their only intention is to earn money. It's purely a slave trade." "When the natives return," another commented, "they are corrupted; they think of themselves as big and important, and no longer stay in their place. Such natives often become good-for-nothings in the colonies. Of course, a few of them shouldn't be counted here, they can be used by the administration as lower employees; but those are only the exceptions." These and other points were integrated into a memorandum, submitted to the German chancellor, calling for federal legislation against the export of natives from German colonies for the sake of public display. In the context of mass entertainment, censorship was an old front of the battle for respectability. Now it became a domestic front of the campaign for German colonies.[63]

Hagenbeck's Nubian Caravans—still memorable, evidently, after more than two decades—were explicitly cited in the memorandum as "the first shows in recent times to arouse general interest." The fact that his troupes had originated from British-controlled territory (Germany had no colonies at the time) was deemed irrelevant. "At these shows, scenes played out in the zoological garden that eye-witnesses recall still today with indignation. The incidents, to which the public on this occasion gave cause, ultimately led to police intervention." While the active role of spectators is acknowledged and even emphasized in places, the proposed legislation targeted colonial entrepreneurs and its rationale focused on the efficacy of colonial authority. Other troupes, further examples, and Germany's recent acquisitions in the South Seas were all cited as evidence of a mounting crisis and as cause for new regulation. The contours of this initiative are worth examining more closely, because they give extraordinary insight into the pro-colonial perspective on a tradition of spectacle that is usually just assumed to have emerged in the service of colonialism. The details are also worth noting because they register, more generally, the social implications of the *Völkerschau* as a type of themed environment.[64]

The memorandum advanced three interrelated lines of argument, each based on a different imperative: to prevent miscegenation and interracial marriage; to maintain a subservient labor force in the colonies; and to prohibit the moral corruption of natives (which was also for the purpose of social control). The first line of argument linked the charged issue of miscegenation to a broader agenda promoting strict racial separation in the colonies—an agenda that later resulted in a series of mandates banning mixed marriages in the German colonies. As early as 1897, the Colonial Society began privately recruiting single women in Germany and sending them to South-West Africa, for the sole purpose of making them sexually available to German men, in an effort to prevent a "colony of half-castes" from developing there. Outlawing the export of colonial subjects to Germany was a corollary to the same agenda.[65]

The second line of argument focused on the earning power of native performers and its latent implications for the colonial economy. Put simply, ethnographic exhibitions paid colonial subjects for "doing nothing at all" (assuming that participants were simply being themselves and not engaged in productive labor as performers). The widespread practice of giving tips to performers only exacerbated the problem. Consequently, the argument went, upon their return to the colonies, natives would either challenge their position as subservient to colonial authority or, worse, refuse to work—and, either way, expect to be paid. Whereas in Canada and in the United States the professionalization of "show Indians" was reluctantly acknowledged and tightly regulated by federal agencies (such as the Bureau of Indian Affairs), members of the pro-colonial movement in Germany privately advocated an interdiction against recruitment, arguing that it "undermined the economic life of whites in the colonies" and its foundation on native labor in specific. Ironically, the practice of recruiting natives, let alone negotiating employment contracts with them, was seen to be bad for business in the colonies.[66]

In a further step, the economic argument underscored the need to control the image of Germany in the eyes of its colonial subjects. At issue here was not the representation of colonial subjects, as one might expect, but rather their individual perceptions of Germany as a wealthy industrialized society. The "consequences" of this experience would be a series of "entirely unjustified and disproportionate demands on the whites, with returning natives grabbing the first chance they have to make propaganda, if the endless stories about existing riches in Germany have not already incited them." In other words, first-hand accounts of German prosperity would only exacerbate the lived experience of radical exploitation and inequality in the colonies, thereby multiplying discontent and raising the threat of challenges to colonial authority.[67]

The third line of argument characterized both exhibitions and audiences as thoughtless proponents of moral corruption, whose effect only spread in the colonies. In this approach, as one scholar has noted, colonial propagandists echoed the criticisms of Christian groups and gave them a new inflection. Both factions sought to prevent the erosion of their respective authority in the colonies; both criticized the shows as prurient and purely commercial; both claimed to be concerned with the physical and moral well-being of natives (the memorandum explicitly mentions alcoholism and alludes to sexual promiscuity); what is more, both emphasized the contributing role of spectators and the negative effects of their exchange with participants. "As regrettable as it is to say," the memorandum continues, "the bad civilizational influence of whites exerted on natives at the shows must nevertheless be declared as a main reason against the latter. Whoever has visited the majority of the shows mentioned earlier cannot have any doubt that the behavior of a considerably large number of whites at these shows has a corrupting influence on the natives." At the same time, as with missionaries, members of the Colonial Society viewed native performers from a paternalistic viewpoint as naïve and therefore susceptible. In the context of public exhibition, this idea only corroborated the need for legislative action. "The natives lack the ability to differentiate between the truly educated from the uneducated spectators, and mistake the behavior of the latter for that of the whole. Necessarily, then, the respect for whites as a whole suffers as a consequence. Generally speaking, the white man is for the natives still the master, who stands high above them, and we must make sure that he stays there, even if it were to require certain measures."[68]

The Colonial Society achieved its stated goal. On 7 May 1901, a federal resolution officially abolished the recruitment and export of German colonial subjects. Similar mandates followed in the individual German territories. Violators were subject to fines and imprisonment, but whether these punishments were ever enforced is unknown. Interestingly, none of these mandates had a tangible effect on Hagenbeck's ethnographic enterprise. If anything, they helped shore up his approach, by banning the practice of other entrepreneurs whose resources were either based in or restricted to the German colonies. The global scope of Hagenbeck's private company, and its undefined and therefore unrestricted relationship to German colonialism, allowed him to continue assembling ethnographic troupes with permission from other colonial powers. The Colonial Society, for its part, continued to organize colonial exhibitions, but it did so within the relatively safe context of the museum, using artifacts, images, and mannequins instead of live performers. Rather than negotiate the agency of performance or the contingency of spectatorship, rather than permit even fleeting moments of potential reciprocity, the Society opted for a more controlled form of theme space, where the construction of meaning and the behavior of spectators could be regulated more thoroughly.[69]

Though the actual effect of the federal resolution is uncertain, its successful passage highlights an interesting tension between divergent yet connected forms of German racism. In its effort to restrict the movement of colonial subjects and shape their perceptions of Germany, to enforce a strict racial divide in exhibitions as well as in the colonies, the Colonial Society asserted a hegemonic notion of absolute difference that (literally) legislated against ethnographic performance and its perceived challenge to colonial authority for the sake of preserving German racial purity and superiority. The central feature of this rhetoric was a set of assumptions about identity, including the notion of colonial subjects as biologically different, morally weak, and culturally inferior. In this view, the agency of performers and their contact with German spectators, particularly women, was anathema.[70]

By contrast, Hagenbeck's approach to ethnographic display emphasized a form of racism that rivaled the assumption of absolute difference and the policy of strict separation, even as it relied for its effect on the spectator's sense of cultural identity and difference. For all its rhetoric of detachment and objectivity, live ethnographic exhibitions represented participants as human beings, rather than as mere objects of display. Some visitors connected and interacted with performers, instead of simply gawking at them. Their interaction points to a more general dynamic on which the show's survival largely depended—namely, a relentless vacillation between physical separation and proximity, cultural chauvinism and curiosity, passionate identification and reassuring difference. Characteristic of this dynamic form of racism is the fence as a porous and contested boundary of display, where racial difference was choreographed as a perceived and more or less enforced divide, but not an insurmountable one. The boundary had to be jointly negotiated by entrepreneurs, spectators, performers, policemen, and others. Their negotiation was momentary, fraught, asymmetrical, and more prone to failure than to success; it was also exhilarating. In this setting, different notions of race circulated and collided in a much more active way than, say, in an ethnological museum. Indeed, the continued popularity of live ethnographic performance—Hagenbeck drew his biggest crowds in the early 1910s—suggests that the show was capable of holding multiple forms of racism as part of its effort to solicit the widest possible audience.

Over time, Hagenbeck's living habitat and its appeal to spectators would change in many ways. Contrary to what one might expect, however, ethnographic exhibition did not become "more colonial" in theme, even with Germany's acquisition of territories. The major development took place on different terms altogether. As we shall see, it followed an arc from constructing "reality" to embracing fantasy, from insisting upon the referential world as the show's primary framework to accepting its status as a fictional universe. Simultaneously, we see a parallel shift in ethnographic display, from an emphatically positivistic mode to an overtly theatrical one, where the contributing roles of spectators, performers, impresarios, and their assistants become acknowledged and appreciated in their own right. As far as spectatorship, this shift represents not simply an escapist flight (from reality, modernity, civilization, and so on), but an active engagement of the physical world on the level of the imagination as well as on the level of the senses. Audience participation in the spectacle only intensified with Hagenbeck's turn to fiction.[71]

CHAPTER THREE

HAGENBECK'S TURN TO FICTION

By the turn of the twentieth century, Carl Hagenbeck had all but withdrawn from the business of human display for reasons that remain unknown. With the death of his father, in 1887, the family-run company was probably reorganized. Carl might have pulled back from the *Völkerschau*, leaving it to his half-brothers, John and Gustav, who already had some experience in recruiting and managing ethnographic troupes. His brother, Wilhelm, presumably took control of "Carl Hagenbeck's International Circus and Menagerie," which was established earlier that year, while Carl refocused on the animal trade. But this hypothetical backstory tells us little if anything about the period from 1890 to 1907, when, rather than produce his own ethnographic shows, as he had earlier, Hagenbeck seems to have mainly financed troupes that were assembled and directed by other entrepreneurs. Toward the end of this period, the construction of his *Tierpark*, a project many years in the making, no doubt engrossed him. And then he returned, dramatically, when the ethnographic exhibition was in its prime, from 1907 to 1913, producing what were certainly the most elaborate shows of his entire career and staging them with great pride at his new *Tierpark* in Stellingen, of which there will be more to say later. First I want to set the scene by discussing the intervening period, which tends to be overlooked. The period is intriguing, because it raises a set of questions about historical change and continuity. Why did Hagenbeck absent himself from the *Völkerschau* business—if, indeed, that is what he did? What then changed or allowed him to return "in grand style," as the later shows are often described?

Perhaps Hagenbeck pulled back, as other scholars have recently speculated, in reaction to increased competition and the mounting public criticism that came with it. After all, the market that he once helped create was now teeming with rival showmen and troupes. Audiences became weary of so much ethnography; anthropologists, though complicit in this development, grew exasperated by the sheer quantity of offerings. And the number of spurious troupes—all agreed—was rising. In 1890, the president of the Berlin Society for Anthropology, Rudolf Virchow, spoke candidly when regretting that "real faith in the reliability of details about tribal affiliation has been utterly shaken, since dependable entrepreneurs such as Herr Carl Hagenbeck have restricted their activity." Rather than risk his good name by becoming associated with bogus entertainments, the hypothesis runs, Hagenbeck sat on the sidelines, sponsoring the troupes of other showmen (assuming they too were "dependable entrepreneurs" and not charlatans), while focusing on the less contentious branches of the larger company.[1]

Around this time, outspoken critics of the *Völkerschau*—and these included members of the police, the church, and the colonial movement—invented a theory of moral decline, the contours of which have been outlined by historian Sierra Bruckner in describing the show's changing cultural associations. To summarize, critics imagined the show's historical transformation through an elaborate series of binary oppositions, in terms of an irreversible slide from science to spectacle, education to entertainment, observation to consumption, rationality to sensuality, authenticity to mimicry, and so on. In order for this model to work, a compatible theory of mass spectatorship was needed. Therefore, the same critics envisioned the audience as undergoing a wide-scale demographic shift: If the first audience was mostly composed of individual male observers from the educated middle classes, it was later overrun by the working-class "crowd," with its decadent and characteristically "female" behaviors. That respectable showmen such as Hagenbeck stepped away from the scene would seem to provide further evidence to support such a theory of moral decline.[2]

To amplify these particular anxieties and privilege the authority of science is somewhat misleading, especially if we want to understand the continued practice of ethnographic exhibition. The trope of decline, however suggestive it might be for a social history of anthropology and its cultural politics, cannot account for the fact that the heyday of ethnographic exhibition was yet to come (and when it did, the broad middle classes were there to participate). Nor can this trope explain the arrival of the Wild West, around 1890, and its collective praise in the German press. In that show—as we shall see—there was hardly a role for science to play, entertainment and commercialism were plain as day, and yet, somehow, the show was deemed respectable by audiences across the board. Their collective voices drowned out even the loudest critics of the *Völkerschau*. If Hagenbeck nearly pulled out of this business due to negative criticism in the press, then positive reviews of the American entertainment gave him several good reasons to reconsider.

The phenomenon of the Wild West in Germany has also led me to reassess Hagenbeck's shows at the turn of the century. In what follows, the guiding assumption is not that representations of the ethnographic became increasingly fictional or "bogus" over time, as if earlier shows were somehow more authentic or less entertaining (they weren't). I want to avoid this sort of authentic/fake assessment that characterizes much of the scholarship. There are other possible frameworks for understanding the ethnographic exhibition—especially around 1900, when the institution was in flux. I offer one of them.

In voicing their enthusiasm for the Wild West, spectators helped redefine the terms of ethnographic exhibition (albeit inadvertently). If science and authenticity were of serious concern to German audiences, then myth and fantasy were far more inspirational. From the viewpoint of nineteenth-century theme space, the Wild West and its enthusiastic reception contributed a major new theme (one that continues to occupy a special place in the German imagination), while creating an affirmative context for the historical peak of ethnographic performance. Hagenbeck continued trading on the authority of science, as one might expect, but in so doing he failed to appreciate the formative power of fantasy and its vital importance to audience involvement. In this miscalculation, he was not alone; it's not as though Buffalo Bill had greater insight into German audiences than Hagenbeck did. What each showman failed to anticipate was precisely the way in which spectators apprehended their shows (literally) in terms of fiction. The story of the Wild West in Germany was, first and foremost, a story of spectatorship and its unexpected consequences for ethnographic performance.

Spectators saw the Wild West in many different and sometimes contradictory ways, but one aspect of the German reception stands out: that is, its ardent embrace of fantasy. Scientists and showmen might have treated Native Americans as bodies of data on the verge of extinction, but popular spectators saw them as living embodiments of figures from the novels of authors such as James Fenimore Cooper and Friedrich Gerstäcker. Indeed, the German reception's organizing logic was one of vivification. To be in the physical presence of actual cowboys and Indians but see in them fictional characters was not to make an ontological error. Most German spectators had no experience of the American West, but they weren't entirely naïve. Nor were showmen or publicists manipulating the audience to this effect; just the opposite, they promoted the idea of historical "reality," not fiction. Rather, to summon "Cooper" and "Gerstäcker" was a way for German spectators to take possession of the American entertainment and make it their own. They did so by means of the one thing that they alone, as spectators, brought to the Wild West—that is, their imagination.

In a way, the act of vivification can also be seen also a step toward future imaginings of the simulacrum and the hyperreal as a copy without an original. It is almost as if the fantasy of "Indians" in the European imagination preceded the ethnographic performances to such an extent that it inverted the causal and logical order of the "real" and its simulation. What makes this inversion even more interesting, however, is that it was very clearly instigated by historical audiences, not by entertainers (who were initially surprised by and unprepared for such a turn of events). In this context, at least, the idea of grafting real actors onto imaginary landscapes first took shape as an effect of spectatorship, not one of representation. Seasoned entertainers such as Cody and Hagenbeck had to stand back from the spectacle, observe the ways in which audiences were addressing it, and make certain adjustments in terms of the production and promotion of future shows.

The dramatic reinterpretation of ethnographic performance as fantasy both drives and anticipates the larger movement of nineteenth-century theme space away from the referential world of "spectacular realities" (to borrow a phrase from Vanessa Schwartz) and toward a diegetic universe of internally related fictional elements proceeding from the imaginary. Thus, the Wild West in Germany helps illuminate a major shift in practice. As much of this material has not been made available in English, exploring it here adds a new chapter to the already voluminous literature on Buffalo Bill within cultural studies, performance studies, and Western history. What makes the German reception so important, for the purpose of my study, is that it helps identify and document a larger transformation in the experience of theme space more generally.[3]

As a historical spectator with a particular interest in the shows, Hagenbeck seems to have taken away two main ideas from the Wild West: first, its unbridled commercialism; second, its (inadvertent) pull on the imagination. My discussion of the first idea proceeds from the assumption that nineteenth-century theme space was already a commercialized space, as evidenced by Hagenbeck's *Völkerschau*. And yet, as the entrepreneur came to recognize, even more could be made of it; there remained a considerable amount of untapped value within the themed environment and the way that spectators interacted with it. This observation helps explain why it was that, even as Hagenbeck pulled back from the *Völkerschau*, he continued to lend his name as well as his money to ethnographic exhibitions that were directed by other showmen. The second idea, the pull of the imagination, was also of course a major aspect of the show's commercialism before the Wild West arrived in Germany. Yet this aspect too would be exploited in new and consequential ways, as evidenced by the shows that Hagenbeck produced toward the end of his career. The present chapter thus begins with the arrival of the Wild West in Germany, and proceeds to explore some of the marketing strategies that Hagenbeck and other showmen used in the years to follow, largely in response to the Wild West's popular reception. It concludes by empha-

Die Bella-Coola-Indianer von der Nordwestküste Amerikas im Zoologischen Garten zu Leipzig: Ein Kannibalentanz.. Originalzeichnung von Fritz Waibler.

3.1 "The Bella Coola Indians from America's Northwest Coast in the Zoological Garden at Leipzig: A Cannibal Dance." The set included a longhouse and two totem poles (each depicted in the background), which the performers reassembled at every stop along the tour. Illustration by Fritz Waibler, in the *Illustrirte Zeitung* (Leipzig), 17 October 1885, 387. Courtesy of the Center for Research Libraries, Chicago.

sizing the role of fantasy within the commercialized space of ethnographic exhibition, as demonstrated by the shows that took place at Hagenbeck's *Tierpark* in Stellingen.

The Wild West in Germany

Carl Hagenbeck's first troupe of Native Americans, the Bella Coola of 1885, was supposed to draw a mass public and simultaneously appeal to an elite group of scientists. With advanced endorsement from the Berlin Anthropological Society and an experienced collector in the field, and with ample resources to finance this private endeavor, Hagenbeck had every reason to believe that he and Jacobsen would make "a huge profit." The resulting troupe was made up of nine Bella Coola performers—all men—

and a collection of more than 1,500 ethnographic artifacts. Jacobsen not only assembled the troupe, but also served as the show's impresario. From September 1885 to July 1886, the troupe visited more than twenty cities, big and small, performing at a diversity of venues. The program consisted almost entirely of music and ceremonial dance numbers, some of which were staged as reenacted scenes from a traditional potlatch. The dances were interspersed with sporting games and magic tricks, all framed by the ethnographic rhetoric of "Indian ways and customs." The program changed several times in the course of the tour, substituting dances and adding a variety of more sensationalized and studiously grotesque numbers—such as the "voluntary immolation of a shaman (magician)"—mainly for the purpose of accumulating customers, but also because the participants grew bored of the original routine.[4]

The Bella Coola show created a sensation within the scientific community, as expected. It directly inspired the work of Franz Boas, a future specialist in Northwest Coast Native American cultures, and Carl Stumpf, the first German ethnomusicologist. Rudolf Virchow hailed the men in the troupe as "different from all American savages so far presented here. By virtue of the deformation of their heads, the peculiar formation of their faces, their quite singular language, their highly developed artisanship, they are immediately rendered conspicuous among the multitude of American native peoples. For this reason they afford one of the most interesting objects for the observation of every thinking human being."[5]

The public saw it otherwise. The crowds in Berlin, for example, were so small that Jacobsen cancelled the show two weeks ahead of schedule, and went directly to Breslau, the tour's next stop. The troupe's bad fortune would not end there. In his diary and private correspondence, Jacobsen complains of low attendance and disappointing profits throughout the year-long tour. "By and large, the public remained rather cool with respect to our performances. Only the scholars thought that this was the most magnificent troupe ever to be shown."[6]

Why did the majority of spectators see it so differently than Virchow and his colleagues did? There are several factors to consider. Leutemann emphasized the absence of women, children, and animals; without them, he reasoned, the Bella Coola "couldn't possibly have the same effect as the other groups." In his view, a living habitat consisting entirely of men never stood a chance. Another factor was competition from a rival troupe, namely, the "Sitting Bull Sioux Indians." Led by the American showman Frank Harvey, the troupe consisted of thirty men, women, and children, a stable of sixteen horses, and a Texas sharpshooter named Happy Jack Sutton. (Despite its name, the show in Germany did not include Sitting Bull, who was at that time touring the United States with Buffalo Bill's Wild West.) With their guns, horses, and feathered headdresses, the cowboys and Indians created a loud, vibrant, and visually potent spectacle. Viewers thrilled to the Sioux, and not to the Bella Coola, which probably explains why Jacobsen took his troupe elsewhere. It also gave rise to another hypothesis: Maybe Hagenbeck had the "wrong Indians." However interesting or "valuable" the troupe might have been for professional scientists, the performers looked "un-Indian" as far as the public was concerned. Rather than defer to scientific authority, spectators in Berlin disagreed with experts and their assessment of the Bella Coola, sometimes loudly. "I'll be hanged if they're real!" shouted one woman in the audience. The reporter who quoted her had this advice for prospective viewers: "If you are not to be disappointed, you must put away all preconceptions, formed perhaps by Cooper, of Indians." Another journalist explained: "Well, they are not those proud, red-skinned figures with cunningly bowed eagle-noses, dark-black, shimmering bushes of hair, and colorful feathers, which school boys reveling in Cooper and *Leatherstocking* like to dream about."[7]

Clearly, viewers brought with them a powerful set of cultural assumptions and fantasies about the larger category of Indians (*Indianer*), which the Bella Coola show, though problematic in other ways, had inadvertently challenged. In a sense, the troupe was "too foreign" to be recognizable. In contrast to their fictive counterparts, ironically, these Indians were "too referential" for spectators to locate. For the majority of viewers, whatever their preconceptions of Indians, the Bella Coola never occurred to them. In bringing the spectacle to the observer, and asserting that move as "authentic," perhaps the *Völkerschau* left too little space for the imagination; the physical presence of the index in the display space might have inadvertently made it difficult for spectators to possess or inhabit the themed environment due to its specific referentiality.

Other scholars have tried to explain the failure of Hagenbeck's first Native American show in terms of cultural clichés and racial stereotypes, the assumption being that the Sioux or Plains Indians, with their horses and feathered headdresses, had already come to stand for all Indians iconographically. By the same logic, American showmen such as Cody and Harvey before him succeeded because they "picked the right Indians at the right time."[8] It is important to stress, however, that, while the mythical image of the Plains Indian certainly set in with the Karl May phenomenon, that didn't take hold until the early 1890s, after a series of Wild West shows had wowed German audiences for several years. In 1885, "Indians" still evoked for German audiences a number of different and sometimes conflicting images. Harvey couldn't have simply "picked the right stereotype," because no single image had yet to dominate (which is one reason why Hagenbeck had assembled a Bella Coola troupe in the first place). It was the Wild West show that crystallized the stereotype of the Plains Indian and its predominance among audiences in Germany, as it had in the United States.[9]

My take on this episode is guided by the invocation of "Cooper" throughout the German reception. The reference might appear to be self-evident, but it needs to be questioned. After all, Plains Indians figure nowhere in Cooper's writings. Another name that was often invoked, usually in the same breath, was that of Friedrich Gerstäcker, the German writer who lived in the United States and positively despised the Sioux (not to mention Cooper). What most interests me here is neither the slippage between cultural associations nor the conflation of tribal affiliations; it's the more potent mix of fact and fiction. While Hagenbeck claimed to deliver "the real thing," spectators faulted the Bella Coola show for its lack of fictive reference points. This is not to say that Harvey's show, for example, was in some way more "literary" than that of Hagenbeck (it certainly was not). Nor does it imply that the Sioux had anything more to do with Cooper and his *Leatherstocking Tales* than had the Bella Coola (they didn't). The point here is one of reception, and its historical implications for our understanding of nineteenth-century theme space. Spectators forged a creative link between the idea of "Cooper" and the physical presence of the Sioux, but not that of the Bella Coola. It was the act of imaginative identification, on the one hand, and the lack of fictional reference points, on the other, that made the crucial difference. A shift was underway in the history of theme space, and spectators led the way.

The English and American Register
Berlin 19th August.

The first Performance on July 23th 1890
Kurfürstendamm, corner Augsburger Strasse (1 Minute from the Zoological Garden).
For the first time in Berlin.
First representation in this city of the only and original
Buffalo Bill's
Wild-West
headed by
Col. W. F. Cody (Buffalo Bill)
formerly scout of the U. S. army on the Indian frontier.
200 Indians,
Cowboys, Scouts, Rangers, Ridders, 200 Animals, Ponies, Burros, Mustangs and Buffaloes.
In an extensive, newly fenced and well timbered park.
On the 23th, 24th, 25th and 26th there will be but one performance daily, commencing at 5 o'clock; ticket office open at 3.30.—Beginning with the 27th there will be two performances a day, at 3 and at 8 o'clock. Ticket office open at 1.30 and 7 respectively.—Evening performances by Electric Lights. Admission 1, 2, 3 and 4 M. Seats for 10,000 people. Covered tribunes. Performances will take place regardless of the weather.—
Notice! This is the identical troup, which has scored such tremendous success in the Paris Exhibition, at London, New York, Rome &c. &c.
Central Office: Unter den Linden 21.

3.2 "For the first time in Berlin." Advertisement for Buffalo Bill's Wild West in *The English and American Register* (Berlin), 19 July 1890. Courtesy of Buffalo Bill Historical Center, Cody, Wyoming; MS6.B5.37.

3.3 "Pictures from Buffalo Bill's Wild West Troupe." Woodcut on paper by P. Krämer. The explanatory caption reads: "1) Buffalo Bill kills and scalps the Sioux chief Yellow Hand. 2) Cowboy in full gallop picking a hat off of the ground. 3) Dance of the medicine man. 4) and 5) Indians attack a settlement. 6) Buffalo Bill shoots glass balls out of the air. 7) Ambush of the Deadwood Stagecoach. 8) Race between a cowboy, a Mexican vaquero, and an Indian. 9) The lassoing, saddling, and riding of wild mustangs, and the buffalo hunt." From *Das Buch für Alle* 5 (1891): 125. Courtesy of the Center for Research Libraries, Chicago.

The arrival of the Wild West in Germany captured the imagination of popular audiences. My signal figure here is of course William F. Cody, a.k.a. Buffalo Bill, and his troupe of more than two hundred cowboys and Indians. "Buffalo Bill's Wild West" show involved a colorful mix of national pageantry (a procession of cowboys, Indians, and army scouts), historical reenactment (scenes from the Indian Wars, such as "Custer's Last Stand"), military display (artillery exercises), sensational melodrama (dramatic narratives of frontier life), and sporting exhibitions (with emphasis on trick shooting and horse racing). In Germany and throughout Europe, this three-hour show followed the same basic pattern: the Pony Express; the attack on the emigrant train; a Virginia quadrille (a country dance) on horseback; "cowboy fun" (horsemanship and lassoing); the attack on the Deadwood coach; Native American dances; and the buffalo hunt.[10] The show began its German tour in Munich on 19 April 1890. Rows of portable bleachers held more than five thousand spectators for daily performances on the Theresienwiese, which was also the traditional site of Oktoberfest. Over a scheduled ten-day visit, the troupe performed before sold-out crowds (even the loges at 4 Marks a piece were full). King Ludwig of Bavaria and his court were guests of honor

Bilder von Buffalo Bill's Wild West-Truppe. Originalzeichnung von P. Krämer. (S. 130)

1. Buffalo Bill tödtet und skalpirt den Siouxhäuptling Gelbhand. 2. Cowboy im vollen Jagen einen Hut von der Erde aufhebend. 3. Tanz des Medicinmannes. 4. und 5. Angriff der Indianer auf eine Ansiedelung. 6. Buffalo Bill schießt Glaskugeln aus der Luft herab. 7. Angriff auf den Deadwood-Postwagen. 8. Rennen zwischen einem Cowboy, einem mexikanischen Vaquero und einem Indianer. 9. Das Einfangen, Satteln und Reiten wilder Mustangs und die Büffeljagd.

on opening day. Hundreds of people camped out overnight to obtain seats. Thousands of people from out of town placed orders via telegraph, to assure themselves of tickets. Thousands more enjoyed "free" seats, with some perched atop nearby buildings and others standing all around the arena's periphery. The Munich show was extended an additional eight days in response to continued demand. The tour then proceeded with shows in Vienna, Dresden, Leipzig, Berlin, Hamburg, Cologne, and Frankfurt am Main, among other cities.[11]

Cody's was not the only Wild West show in Germany at the time; "Doc Carver's Wild America" competed for the same entertainment-seeking public. William F. "Doc" Carver was part of the original troupe, with Cody, when the Wild West show was first created in 1883. Now they were bitter rivals. Unlike Cody, however, Carver had already toured Germany on two previous occasions.[12] In 1890, he returned again, this time trailing Buffalo Bill across Germany, vying with him for spectators—sometimes directly. In Hamburg, for example, they set up camp on opposite sides of the street. Carver had arrived a few days ahead of schedule and thus claimed the prime location on the Heiligengeistfeld (the fairground). He also secured what was then the city's only available battery of portable lights, which allowed for evening performances in addition to the usual afternoon shows. In Hamburg, at least, Cody was left in the dark. When Buffalo Bill's Wild West opened there, on 21 August 1890, the results were reportedly lopsided: "Carver gave two performances and had 80,000 visitors, while Cody gave only one, which was attended by 7,000 persons."[13] If Carver solicited a larger audience on occasion, he did so almost inadvertently. Neither Carver nor Cody anticipated the key to their success in Germany, though both showmen placed their bets on the "reality" of the Wild West that they claimed to represent.

In this regard, it was Cody who seemed to epitomize "real life" in the far West, thanks to his extensive experience as a U.S. Army scout during the Indian Wars, an undaunted rider for the Pony Express, and an equally intrepid buffalo hunter. "Buffalo Bill" was obviously a stage persona and a media personality created with the assistance of professional writers and publicists, but he succeeded in representing himself as a living embodiment of American history. Historical authenticity was the stock-in-trade of Wild West shows, beginning with George Catlin's exhibitions, and had its ethnographic equivalent in Hagenbeck's *Völkerschau*. In the age of scientific positivism, the process of verification and authentication was sometimes crucial to the success of an ethnographic troupe, with native performers being subjected to extensive physical examinations and prominent anthropologists acting as self-appointed cultural regulators. Not so in the Wild West. When Cody's troupe came to Berlin, one reporter asked: "Who would dare question the authenticity of this enterprise?" After all, Cody had assembled a stunning cast of well-known figures, including over the years Sitting Bull, Black Elk, Wild Bill Hickok, and, most important, the celebrated showman himself.

Of course, in Germany and throughout Europe the troupe could not rely on the same degree of familiarity and recognition that it could assume in the United States. Yet the show was advertised in Europe, as in America, as "a historical attraction," promising not only "spectacular scenes and pictures from history," but also "the people who actually experienced them."[14]

The rhetoric of historical authenticity that framed the American show makes the German reception all the more interesting, for it was the fantasy of the Wild West, and not the show's truth claims, that most inspired spectators. This required some adjustment on the part of American showmen. "In Europe," historian Joy Kasson has shown, "the Wild West had to accept—and to learn to trade upon—its own exoticism and its underlying fictionality." Add to this the historical reception in Germany (a context Kasson does not examine) and a broad cultural trend comes into view. In this context, ironically, the Wild West appeared exactly as audiences had imagined it. These cowboys and Indians had to be literally freighted thousands of miles, via train and steamship, for the public to be able to see them here—in the flesh. And yet many spectators took their extraordinary presence as an occasion for reverie (not anthropology), while marveling at the prospect of dreams becoming tangible.[15]

The governing principle of reception in Germany can best be described in terms of "vivification." Other scholars have emphasized the cultural tropes of loss, demise, and preservation that link the shows to museums of the period—tropes that are by now very familiar, particularly in the context of ethnography. To be sure, American showmen invoked theories of imminent loss so as to confer a sense of urgency on their entertainments; critics in the German press pontificated on the romantic idea of "vanishing Indians"; and museum directors lamented the loss of their material culture (which doubled as a self-serving argument for collecting). I want to highlight a different but contemporaneous metaphor, one that gestures more toward life than death, according to the particular "aliveness" of performance. The very idea of vivification in this context at once surprised and delighted viewers, almost as if the practice of spectatorship had become a form of magical thinking. "That these our childhood dreams could one day assume tangible form—who would have ever guessed?"[16]

A passage from a review of Carver's premiere in Hamburg could just as well serve to summarize the nineteenth-century German reception of Wild West shows.

> This performance not only met the public's expectations but far exceeded them. Audiences familiar with the works of Cooper, Gerstäcker, and others who write about Indian life, shall find here embodied everything that the active fantasy ever presented in the liveliest of images: Boldness, skillfulness, primitive vitality and wildness appear before the eyes of the observer in such a colorful succession that one feels pleasantly excited from beginning to end.[17]

To many German spectators, the Wild West seemed to convert fictional characters into living tissue. Rather than preserve the traces of peoples who were supposedly either dead or on the verge of dying, as ethnographic museums and folk museums would claim to do, the shows were seen as giving "life" to figures that never even existed (such as Cooper's Natty Bumppo). The dramatic narratives that played out in the arena were clearly bound up with stories and books that audiences were reading elsewhere (such as the novels of Friedrich Gerstäcker). In Germany, the unintended effect of the Wild West, for all its claims to history and reality, was the vivification of a fictional universe. It was the fictional aspect of the American spectacle, its powerful grip on the German imagination (and not its shared obsession with the "real" and the "authentic") that had profound implications for the future success of Hagenbeck's show, and for the history of theme space more generally.[18]

This aspect of fantasy and its significance for the *Völkerschau* becomes clear under the flickering electric lights of Carver's Wild America.[19] One of the most powerful effects of electric lighting around 1890, as Rosalind Williams has suggested in the context of the world's fair, was that it "nurtured a collective sense of life in a dream world."[20] The dramatic effects of illumination were clearly on display in Hamburg, as well. According to one reviewer, "The evening performances offer the best chance to see a slice of life in the Wild West. When the wild boys on their lively horses ride and jump in the flickering lights of the electric lamps or in the moonlight, images from the stories of Cooper and Gerstäcker take shape before our very eyes. And that's why the evening shows at Carver's Wild America have resonated so deeply with the public." In the Wild West show, electrified lighting was more than instrumental. Within the context of the performance, it was a marker of attraction with tremendous affective force. Instead of interpreting this light as the triumph of science over nature, as a metaphor of progress in glaring contrast to the wild and the primitive on display, German spectators thrilled to it as an integral part of the spectacle. Under starry nights or electric lights, Carver and his troupe oneirically transformed into iridescent objects of fantasy, while their bodies appeared to give physical presence to figures of the imagination. Carver himself learned to emphasize the motion, sparkle, and transformations created by electric lights at dusk. Alluding to the fact that Carver had evening performances in Hamburg, and Cody did not, advertisements playfully asserted the illuminating power of electrified light: "Life on the vast prairies of the far West reveals itself only at sundown." Electricity's way of generating a "fairyland environment," as Williams calls it, "the sense of being not in a distant place, but in a make-believe place," had the effect of enhancing the visceral sense of fantasy that the Wild West already evoked for German spectators. At the same time, the use of electricity also had the very opposite effect, enhancing the idea that the show presented "a slice of life." In Germany, "life on the vast prairie" achieved closure each night with a spectacular display of fireworks. The emergence of artificial light may have disenchanted the night, as Wolfgang Schivelbusch has argued in another context. In the Wild West, however, it sparked the imagination of viewers, transforming the rodeo arena into an electrical prairie radiating, as they saw it, the "primitive energy" of a campfire.[21]

The Wild West inadvertently shone a powerful light on the spectacle and its target audience in ways that many showmen had either overlooked or neglected. To an impresario of the "real," such as Hagenbeck, the idea of appealing directly to the imagination was by no means self-evident. It seemed to contradict the very service that the Wild West and the *Völkerschau* each claimed to provide, which was a convincing impression of travel via the actual movement of the spectacle to the spectator. Yet there it was: the amazing power of fantasy to move spectators emotionally, vicariously. The question for showmen was, obviously, how to harness it.

Inviting spectators to dream and fantasize might not have been Cody's intention, but, like any good entrepreneur, he was constantly seeking new ways of coaxing them to (literally) buy into the themed environment. History offered one way, fantasy another. The two were actually interconnected within the space of performance. That is to say, Buffalo Bill's Wild West offered little in the way of ethnological backup, and its sets were remarkably sparse (especially compared to Hagenbeck's shows), but it was teeming with goods for sale. The Wild West was a thoroughly commodified space where "Buffalo Bill" merchandise was sold at every turn. "Everything from books and sheet music to statuettes and peace pipes were offered and purchased in great quantities. Not all of these items were actually manufactured for the management, but all were promoted with Buffalo Bill's name." To brand his products in such a way was to give them added value, while making them even more attractive to spectators as consumers. Similarly, the use of merchandizing further enhanced the sensorial aspect of the Wild West, and aimed to make the show even more memorable by virtue of the souvenir.[22]

Through the creative use of merchandising, Hagenbeck too would develop a crucial aspect of his ethnographic enterprise and a greater appreciation for the untapped value of his own good name. He did so, in part, by treating the show as an extension of his commercial brand. This development alone deserves some attention, due to the central importance of branding (which is different from advertising) in twentieth-century theme space. Yet it also demonstrates how the practice of branding and merchandising arose in the context of an earlier paradigm.

"Carl Hagenbeck's India"

If Hagenbeck's far-flung network of trappers and agents was crucial to his initial success as a showman, his most valuable assets over the long haul were such intangibles as the name that he made for himself as a showman and the image that he created for his company and his entertainments. As such, the name and the image always had to be managed. This was precisely why, in 1896, Hagenbeck commissioned a new biography by the popular writer Wilhelm Fischer, *Aus dem Leben und Wirken eines interessanten Mannes* (From the Life and Work of an Interesting Man). The ethnographic exhibitions that he sponsored during this period had a similar function, while also insinuating Hagenbeck's name into the very fabric of the display space. It was in the late nineteenth century that theme space became an important extension of commercial branding, and American entertainments set the standard. Hagenbeck would have noticed this development not only in the Wild West shows that came to Germany, but also at the 1893 Chicago world's fair, where several of the ethnographic villages "were sponsored by individual companies, whose names would feature prominently" in the displays. Theme space did not become just another surface for plastering more advertisements. Rather, the brand became the theme.[23]

It is important to emphasize that branding is not the same as advertising, which already occupies a privileged position in visual culture studies. Branding is the larger controlling category (of which advertising is only one small part). The relationship of the ethnographic imaginary to advertising is a topic that has already received much attention. As I contend, however, it was primarily the brand (and secondarily the use of advertising) that shaped the visitor's expectation and experience of theme space in the late nineteenth century. In cultural studies, there is a general temptation to emphasize advertising and simply dismiss branding as meaningless at best and deceptive at worst. According to Baudrillard, "There can be no more impoverished language than this one, laden with referents yet empty of meaning as it is. It is a language of mere *signals*, and 'brand loyalty' can never, therefore, be more than a conditioned reflex of manipulated emotions." This idea of branding as a sort of cavernous language, consisting of signs without referents, also informs the literature on theme space in the twentieth century, where the themed environment is often imagined to be fundamentally void of meaning and therefore either disconnected from the referential world or emblematic of the soulless world in which it was created. Yet this language (however superficial or impoverished it might be) certainly has more to tell us about theme space. I suggest that we expect less of branding to begin with, and explore some of its historical effects instead.[24]

◆ ◆ ◆

John and Gustav Hagenbeck wanted to make a name for themselves as showmen. The initial result was, interestingly, "Carl Hagenbeck's India." Its one and only venue was Berlin, on Kurfürstendamm (near the Savignyplatz train station), where the show took place in the summer of 1898 (see plate 5). The troupe consisted of more than sixty performers, almost all of whom were Tamils from Sri Lanka. With its kornacks and elephants, the India show belonged to a series of "Ceylon" exhibitions that Hagenbeck had organized on a regular basis since 1883. Only this one was managed and directed by his siblings alone, which makes their conspicuous use of his name all the more interesting. Outside of the performance arena, spectators were invited to stroll through an Indian village. On the main street, visitors walked past a series of thatched-roof huts and tilting palm trees, which doubled as street lamps for the evening performances. The "Far East," like the Wild West, revealed itself at night. Zebus pulled rickshaws up and down the streets with visitors in tow. All roads led to "Trishinapoli Square," a central plaza surrounded by plaster-made structures, including "The Golden Cliff Temple," the "Buddha Temple," and a towering monument of the elephant god, Ganesh. There was an Indian Restaurant and an Indian Theater, whose program included contortionists, jugglers, acrobats, *bayadères*, as well as "Mahbool Kahn and Asub Kahn, the Indian wrestlers." At first glance, the program is strongly reminiscent of the variety theater, with its pungent mix of "sensational" acts. In contrast to the variety format, however, all the numbers here revolve around a single, coherent theme, one that is not only sustained for the duration of the show, but also spills out of the theater and extends across the entire showground. The dynamic interaction of variety and unity is everywhere apparent. The Bazaar offered a substantial spread of masks, statues, weapons, pipes, rugs, tables, chairs, and musical instruments—all for sale. Interestingly, however, what unifies this collection, like the larger show, was less its context of foreign origin than its appearance under the sign of Hagenbeck. The theme was unmistakable and everywhere apparent from the moment visitors set foot in the showground, displayed as it was on every table, booth, and structure: "Hagenbeck's Ceylon Tea House," "Carl Hagenbeck's Indian Bazaar," "Drink Hagenbeck's Ceylon Tea!"

If Hagenbeck merely financed the show, as he seems to have done, his name was literally written all over it. In many ways, the *Völkerschau* still belonged to him, perhaps now more than ever before. Like "Buffalo Bill's Wild West," it was "Carl Hagenbeck's India" in every sense of the phrase. His claim to ownership, however, was based not on personal experience (Hagenbeck had never actually been to India), but rather on his public reputation as a reliable purveyor of the "real" and a trustworthy name in the *Völkerschau* business. Over the years, his name obtained cultural meaning for spectators mainly through their past experiences of his entertainments. "Hagenbeck" was more than a figure of the spectator's memory and imagination. It became a way of knowing that not only shaped consumer decision-making, but also shaped the experience of theme space.

In this instance, however, the use of his name was fraught with tension. As children of a second marriage, John and Gustav were not eligible for inheritance when their father died. So, in 1894, they founded an independent export company, "Bros. J. & G. Hagenbeck," with headquarters in Sri Lanka. Later, they traded more aggressively on the family name, styling themselves as the Hagenbeck Bros., a title deliberately reminiscent of the high-class circus, in an effort to bolster their own reputation as showmen. At the turn of the century, though, "Hagenbeck" obtained not because of anything that either John or Gustav had done. Rather, what gave the name purchase was its implied reference to Carl Hagenbeck in particular. Over time, the name became "his." As a brand, it gained currency and was widely circulated independent of the person. Indeed, "Carl Hagenbeck's India" interests me precisely because Carl Hagenbeck wasn't there: The point is not that he had never been to India—it is his absence from the exhibition of India that appeared under his name.[25]

The 1898 India show was a modest enterprise by all accounts. The troupe did not seem especially "foreign" or otherwise extraordinary; ensembles from India and Sri Lanka had visited Berlin many times before. Nor were the sets particularly remarkable in terms of scale, number, or detail; the city had definitely seen more impressive exhibitions. For Berliners, "Carl Hagenbeck's India" was immediately reminiscent of the celebrated "Cairo" section of the Berlin Trade Fair (*Berliner Gewerbe-Ausstellung*), which was in turn an elaborate *Rue du Caire*, a stock feature of world's fairs since 1889. Upon closer inspection, however, "Carl Hagenbeck's India" only resembled "Cairo" if the latter were taken out of context—that is, only if we imagine it without the reassuring presence of civic authorities and imperial patrons, without the surrounding halls of science and industry, without the standard moral justifications of "progress," "education," or "peace among nations." Unlike municipal fairs and international expositions, "Carl Hagenbeck's India" had no official framework whatsoever. Nor was it contained within a larger fair by means of a designated amusement zone (such as Chicago's Midway Plaisance). Nevertheless, the India show was truly striking on at least one account: its aggressive use of branding.[26]

Branding as a practice was not new; it had a history. The key development in the nineteenth century was that the name and image of a product came to serve not only as mnemonic devices or distinguishing features, but also as means of adding economic value to a product (not just symbolic capital). That is the reason why Hagenbeck, and others, learned to trade on his name as a commercial brand. It is also the context in which branding became a salient feature of theme space.[27]

The related notion of "brand image," a recent term that refers to perceptions of a brand as well as to the meaningful associations consumers either have with the brand or hold in memory, is equally suggestive in the context of nineteenth-century visual culture, especially in terms of spectatorship. The point can be made more clearly by contrast with the department store. According to Anne Friedberg, "The 'paradise' of the department store relied on the relation between *looking* and *buying*, and the indirect desire to possess and incorporate through the eye." Yet the reality of that institution—indeed, the historical practice of shopping and its link to spectatorship—was and continues to be mediated by branding as a third, admittedly less dazzling but still powerful term. Then as now, shoppers often look for more than the attention-grabbing display, packaging, or physical features of a product. They also look, sometimes very specifically, for the brand that can distinguish one product from others that are almost identical, by identifying its particular source or maker. From the entrepreneur's perspective, brand image was probably the best single investment that Hagenbeck could have made. For that reason, like any brand image, it had to be protected. If the name or its underlying associations were co-opted by another showman, Hagenbeck stood to lose what was perhaps his most valuable asset.[28]

In the context of ethnographic exhibition, the name helped organize a diversity of offerings in a way that spectators could readily identify and understand. It also announced the troupe's country of origin. In this instance, however, the location was embedded within the brand's name, which in turn had certain implications for the display. Most remarkably, the construction of theme space here was indistinguishable from the promotion and expansion of the brand. Customers paid to visit neither India nor "India," but rather "Carl Hagenbeck's India." Headlining the publicity materials and almost all the signage throughout the showground, the brand name featured more prominently than the context of origin. Branding an entertainment with a name such as "Carl Hagenbeck's India" promised certain benefits to spectators, while establishing an imaginary bond between the audience and the show's sponsor. In addition to an exciting show, it promised such intangibles as quality, reliability, authenticity, and respectability. To project and maintain a strong brand image was to bolster, on a sub-representational level, the entertainment's perceived quality and internal coherence. The themed environment became an increasingly commercialized space, in part due to the strong identification and mutual reinforcement of the brand and the entertainment.

The Hagenbeck brand became a kind of platform on which he and other members of the family could introduce new products, entertainments, and related merchandise. Indeed, one indication of the brand's strength and resilience was the extension of "Hagenbeck," beyond the animal trade and the *Völkerschau*, to other categories like the circus and the zoo or to perishable goods such as tea and tobacco. On the one hand, each extension meant for consumers repeated expressions of the brand and repeated experiences with Hagenbeck's notion of the exotic. On the other hand, "Hagenbeck" carried associations that were not only desirable in other markets, but could also be readily transferred and modified. Theme space became a site for gathering disparate products, arranging them in mutually supporting relationships, and thereby enhancing the memorable as well as the sensory aspects of the environment.

In this instance, the brand's central element was obviously Hagenbeck's name, as it was for Buffalo Bill, but various logos were devised and used strategically, in order to highlight and embellish certain meanings of the brand. The logo for Hagenbeck's Ceylon Tea, which was sold at various stations throughout the India exhibition, offers a case in point (plate 6). The central figure of the tiger embodies and thereby reiterates the particular name of the brand (or at least it does here, for the tagline "Tiger Brand" is not always used on other signs, posters, and figurines—more typical is "Carl Hagenbeck's Ceylon Tea"). On one level, the tiger serves to connote "Ceylon," reinforcing iconographically what was already explicit in the product's name—the tea's exotic source—while giving visual form to a product whose prime attributes are taste and smell. It also reinforces the tea's relationship to the larger "Hagenbeck" brand and its corporate origins in the exotic animal trade. The company's reputation as purveyor of the "real" is both reflected by and extended to a new category. The logo's other main element, the globe or ball, emphasizes a different yet related aspect of the larger enterprise: the worldwide nature of its interests. On another level, the balancing tiger motif itself has been taken from the existing iconography of the circus because of its broad visibility. As a logo for Hagenbeck's tea, it assumes the added function of mediating between the product and consumers by addressing them as the tea cannot, which is to say, as spectators. What is more, like Hagenbeck's International Circus and its various spin-offs, the merchandise sold at Carl Hagenbeck's Indian Bazaar could readily be seen to be consistent not only with the name, the image, and the company behind it, but also with the themed environment in which it was embedded. The products and souvenirs for sale here were not external to the show (they weren't promotional "tie-ins," as in film merchandising today); they were integral components of the themed environment. By appealing directly to the physical senses of the spectator, they mediated the experience of immersion into the themed environment, while extending the brand into the realm of lived experience.[29]

Sensorializing the themed environment in every way—addressing the visitor on the level of touch, taste, and smell in addition to sight and sound—became a strategy for making the experience memorable, not just pleasurable. That was the key to accumulating repeat customers. As Hagenbeck learned early on, parents took their children back to the *Völkerschau* not just to appease them, nor simply for the event itself, but rather to make that shared experience a part of their everyday conversation. With each souvenir, spectators took home with them a physical token of the troupe and, ideally, a happy memory of Hagenbeck's entertainment. If spectators visited the show "in order to have stories to tell" (to repeat a saying quoted earlier), then the showman's task was to make the show both unforgettable and worthy of recounting.[30]

"Carl Hagenbeck's Indian Bazaar," a section of the larger 1898 exhibition, demonstrates the interrelationship of branding and sensory address within the themed envi-

3.4 "Carl Hagenbeck's Indian Bazaar. For Sale—Cigars Made Here by Indians—10 Pfennig a Piece." Unpublished photo from the impresario's private album. Courtesy of Tierpark Carl Hagenbeck GmbH, Hamburg-Stellingen.

ronment. In this context, the work display has been literally framed and embedded in a sales booth, where spectators could purchase among other things "Cigars Made Here by Indians" (see fig. 3.4). The performers, moreover, served double duty as workers and visual attractions. In this photograph, two men sit cross-legged on mats at the rear of the booth, hand-rolling cigars for spectators to see and buy, with encouragement presumably coming from the sales clerks. What this photograph depicts (albeit inadvertently) is a crucial step in the semiotic process of the work display, namely, the transformation of what were previously theatrical props into exotic souvenirs. As Dean MacCannell notes in his now classical study of tourism, "the work display, unlike work itself, *does* open the most closed off areas of industrial society to almost everyone." It makes public (however briefly) the very process that the commodity would conceal. Nevertheless, the very fact that labor is staged, that tourists—in MacCannell's analysis—are incapable of comprehending the meaning of what they see, ultimately renders "inauthentic" not only the work display but also the practice of spectatorship. At Hagenbeck's Indian Bazaar, however, the sanctimonious practice of policing authenticity totally misses the point. It is, above all, "the native touch," the sensual experience of cultural difference, which gives these cigars their unique purchase. In other words, the commodity here mediates a kind of tactile relay between the performers as workers and the spectators as consumers, which, although it does not rule out the possibility of direct contact, the entire display literally enacts as an exchange relation. What it conveys is not simply the idea of consumption but, more important, the fantasy of the commodity. Just as the commodity here mediates the experience of sensual pleasure, so the brand would mediate the experience of cultural difference. The mass-cultural value of Hagenbeck's brand rested on its unmatched ability to accommodate the ethnographic to the fantasy of the commodity. That was its mark of distinction.[31]

The consequences of branding for nineteenth-century theme space become quite clear if we contrast this example with the kind of work displays that were typically offered at Scandinavian folk-ethnographic museums, such as the Nordic Museum in Stockholm, and its open-air extension, Skansen, both founded by Arthur Hazelius. In this context, as Sandberg has shown, "The rural object was imagined to retain a relationship to the hand of an individual maker and to bear the traces of a unique moment of production." This imagined relationship came to bear in the folk museum's version of the work display, where manual labor continued to prevail as a definitive aspect of traditional culture. Having removed the collected object from the context in which it was once used, exacerbating in effect the very loss of native culture that the collecting project would ostensibly mitigate, the museum sought to compensate for that loss by exhibiting the object in situ, as if it were still being used. The folk museum thus circulated artifacts qua images according to a visual economy of preservation and compensation. Through visual display the collected artifact was metaphorically returned to its original owner when placed in the hand of a mannequin, a waxen effigy of the native folk body. Here is the key point of contrast: The fantasy of the commodity was exactly the trend that the late nineteenth-century folk museum tried to counteract with its enshrinement of nonalienated labor and handmade objects. Not so in the ethnographic exhibition. As the booths and tables in Hagenbeck's Indian Bazaar make abundantly clear, unlike the Scandinavian folk museum—and in stark contrast to ethnographic museums and natural history museums across the board—the *Völkerschau* claimed neither to preserve the last traces of a disappearing culture, nor to compensate for its ostensible loss. Rather than imagine a visual economy of scarcity, in the spirit of salvage anthropology, Hagenbeck and his clan openly traded on the commercial fantasy of plentitude, more in the spirit of shopping. Indeed, this emphasis on consumption is precisely what connects Hagenbeck's brand of theme space to the major tradition of theme parks in the twentieth century.[32]

What emerges, by 1900, is a remarkably modern approach to selling the exotic: linking it to a diversity of products; embedding it in a strong brand image; directly appealing to the imagination of consumers; physically surrounding them in a cohesively themed environment; and stimulating all five senses over the duration of the visit. Nowhere was this combined approach developed more fully than it was at Carl Hagenbeck's *Tierpark* in Stellingen. On 7 May 1907, more than ten thousand visitors turned out for the park's official opening. Over the next several years, the crowds grew larger and larger. By the summer of 1914, another seven and a half million people had passed through its gates. It was in this context that Hagenbeck created his own version of the Wild West, while trading on the strength of his brand. Although he was obviously revising a familiar theme, he made it compelling for audiences by inviting them to act out their fantasies of the exotic, to physically enter a realm where dreams, it was said, became tangible.

Enter the Realm of Fantasy

Hagenbeck's *Tierpark* in Stellingen presented itself as a universe of its own, appealing directly to the visitor's imagination. Look at the grand entrance with its art nouveau gate (fig. 3.5). "The colossal, monumental main gate," the first guidebook tells us, "already indicates that a new, strange, exotic world is about to open up before our amazed eyes." The gate itself is doubly monumental, with its group of larger-than-life bronze statues mounted atop gigantic cement pedestals, which mediate between the site and the statuary. As a representational sign, one of the gate's functions is to frame the park's overarching theme. The group depicts an imaginary encounter of figures representing totally different parts of the world. In order to create a sense of visual coherence among them, the figures are arranged in theatrical or interactive poses. An African warrior raises his weapons, strangely contrasting with two polar bears, one with a dead seal under its paw; an Indian warrior—or, as one journalist described it, a figure "totally out of a Cooper novel, it could be Uncas, the hero of our youth"—is rendered beside two lions, posed as if confronting the polar bears. Behind this gate, and framed in the center of the photograph, there appears to rise up from the otherwise flat plains of northern Germany a towering group of craggy rock cliffs. "With a little imagination," wrote Philipp Berges, editor of the daily *Hamburger Fremdenblatt* and the ghostwriter of Hagenbeck's memoir, "one could believe that one has arrived in Gulliver's fantasyland of the Houyhnhnmns." The allusion to *Gulliver's Travels* is perhaps more apposite than the editor intended, ironically referring to a nonreferential place (the utopian land) and to fictional creatures (the rational and virtuous horses) which, in an equally apt reversal, use human beings as humans typically use animals. To pass through this gateway was to enter a realm of fantasy comparable in many ways to the fictional world of a story.[33]

This appeal to the imagination could arguably be construed as addressing the

masses, and yet the opening of the *Tierpark* also marked an upward shift in audiences, even as Hagenbeck continued to solicit the widest possible base. Consider the gathering of prominent guests in the foreground (including journalists, politicians, businessmen, and zoo directors), all bearing witness to the park's grand opening. They remind us that Hagenbeck's enterprise was, in fact, made possible by the support of the broad middle classes, beginning with those who literally invested in it. Their solemn appearance here endows it with a sense of legitimacy, a point that would only be reinforced by the many extended visits of Kaiser Wilhelm II. The park was eminently respectable.[34]

3.5 The enshrinement of fantasy. Opening day at Hagenbeck's *Tierpark* in Stellingen, 7 May 1907. Courtesy of Tierpark Carl Hagenbeck GmbH, Hamburg-Stellingen.

The key venue of ethnographic exhibition in Germany from 1907 to 1914, the *Tierpark* attracted the largest and most prestigious audiences of Hagenbeck's entire career. By gaining more control over the exhibition stage, he completed a process of vertical integration that distinguished him from every other ethnographic showman. What had previously been an itinerant performance found a permanent home in Stell-

3.6 Gateway to "Burma," an ethnographic exhibition at Hagenbeck's *Tierpark* in the summer of 1913. Courtesy of Tierpark Carl Hagenbeck GmbH, Hamburg-Stellingen.

ingen. Here, the show's "reason to exist" was neither debated nor even questioned. Its commercial success allowed him to envision and implement the new park as a viable alternative to the zoological garden. In so doing, something magical happened. Historians of the zoo have widely acknowledged the importance of Hagenbeck's *Tierpark* in terms of zoo design and animal display (as discussed in chapter 4). What has not been recognized—and what amounts, I suggest, to a more radical development—is the liberation from referentiality or, the opening of visual horizons to include imaginary landscapes, which the *Tierpark* also accomplished. By that I mean the way in which it created a fantasyland environment for human and animal display, the sense of entering a magical world, where fictional stories unfold before the eyes, where reality and fantasy seemingly intermingle. The interesting thing is that Hagenbeck managed to hold the line on both issues.

In 1909, Hagenbeck expanded the park's boundary and developed a new area, devoted to ethnographic exhibition. Located across the street from the original park, and connected to it by a footbridge, the new area had its own complex of amenities, buildings, and display spaces (see plate 7). A bird's-eye view of the "Burma" exhibition, from 1913, provides a sense of scale and orientation (fig. 3.6). As visitors approached the bridge, the village's tallest structures—a constellation of gleaming white spires, temples, and pagodas in the photograph—could already be seen rising in the background, building a sense of anticipation and excitement. The name or location of the village was printed in large letters on an arched gateway spanning the bridge. The footbridge led directly to a "Bazaar for ethnographic and zoological curiosities." From there, visitors wandered into the thick of things, with huts and streets leading further, deeper into the village. Work displays lined the streets, each of which doubled as the front for a souvenir stand. There were "woodcutters, silversmiths, ivory carvers, screen makers, cooks, florists, cigar and cigarette-makers, etc." Beyond the village, "Burmese temple ruins" were installed along the edge of a pond (see fig. 3.9). They remained a fixture of the *Tierpark*, and an attraction in their own right, even after the Burma show had ended. The arena was located just to the right of the bridge. In the background, the park's summer restaurant is on the far left; and directly behind the bridge is a large theater for trained animals (*Dressurhalle*). Capable of seating five hundred spectators, the training hall doubled as a make-shift cinema, "Hagenbeck's Kino," where travelogues and safari movies were exhibited on occasion.[35]

IN THE ARENA

Foreign people shows underwent several noteworthy changes at the *Tierpark*. For the first time, as Thode-Arora has suggested, the living village took priority over the regularly scheduled performances. Ownership and control of the exhibition site permitted a shift toward ever-more elaborate staging. Entire villages stretched out across acres of land, encompassing dozens of sets, structures, and artificial landscapes. Yet the village's new priority should not deter us from exploring changes elsewhere in the park, especially in the arena—a large, circular performance space and fenced-in enclosure, with several covered grandstands on one side, not unlike a rodeo. For it is here, in the arena, that we find the tell-tale signs of Hagenbeck's turn to fiction. With the *Tierpark*, he became more than a builder of fantastic landscapes; he also became a kind of storyteller and the creator of a fictional universe. The publication of his memoir, in 1908, eloquently consolidated the public image of Hagenbeck as narrator.[36]

The emergence of narrative in the context of ethnographic exhibition would seem to beg the question of respectability or cultural legitimization. To historians of anthropology, who imagine the *Völkerschau* in terms of spectacle (as opposed to narrative), the very idea of "Hagenbeck's turn to fiction" would presumably confirm the "decline" theory. Here, once again, I take issue with this approach. Alternatively, I would argue that the turn to fiction can be seen as a sign of respectability—and thus, a new bid for the broad middle classes—without the need for scientific authority. His was a strategy for keeping the show commercially viable by embracing its status not as sheer entertainment, but as a fictional dramatic medium. What makes this point so interesting and widely relevant is that, around this time, there were other forms of visual culture, such as the wax museum and the cinema, which had a parallel legitimization accomplished by a turn to fiction. In the context of the cinema, the emergence of narrative around 1907 tends to be discussed in terms of the drive for respectability, the address of individual spectators, the embrace of bourgeois forms (such as the legitimate theater), and the appeal to the middle classes. In short, both institutions—the cinema and the *Völkerschau*—seek to harness the spectator's powers of imagination and identification via narrative, but historians of the cinema and anthropology have interpreted that phenomenon in ways that are diametrically opposed to one another. There were many ways for Hagenbeck to confer legitimacy upon the show, and there was a moment around 1900 when narrative became one of them.[37]

Hagenbeck's turn to fiction was part of a long-term process of narrativization. It involved a series of changes in the textual form of ethnographic performance, which orchestrated the various numbers in the program and subordinated them to the development of a single, coherent storyline. This process began, arguably, with the standardization of the show's variety format. By 1885, to recall an earlier point, "almost all of the performances featured dances, songs, and fight scenes, regardless of the origin of the troupes." The first program brochures, which were also issued around this time, likewise served to identify clearly marked performances in a succession of numbered acts. For example, the brochure for "German Africa: Carl Hagenbeck's Cameroon Expedition," a show organized by the independent entrepreneur Fritz Angerer in 1886, establishes the "Order of Presentations," as follows: "1. Drum Concert. 2. Tschu-Tschu or Fetish Dance. 3. Cont'd. 4. Battle Scene and Dance. 5. Drum Language (known only among the Cameroonians). 6. Canoe Demonstration." Though the program would always entail a variety of sensational acts, the acts themselves became integrated into a more or less continuous sequence of dramatic episodes. The first example of a nascent storyline can be found at the 1895 "East African Village," an indoor show that was sponsored by and nominally "under the directions of Herr Carl Hagenbeck," but organized and managed by one of his animal trappers, Joseph Menges. At the Crystal Palace in London, where the show took place, it featured a blatantly theatrical set, described on the program brochure's cover as "Panoramic Scenery (2,200 feet in length, and averaging 23 feet in height), specially designed and painted by M. Pritchard Barrett" (see fig. 3.7). The use of elaborate stage sets was yet another sign of Hagenbeck's turn to fiction, and one that also accorded well with the show's program. Organized in a sequence of nine scenes, the program established a basic storyline that would later be used for various productions at Hagenbeck's *Tierpark* in Stellingen. Hagenbeck's stories generally dramatized fictional conflicts between warring clans or ethnic groups, which played out in a carefully paced sequence of sensational battle and chase scenes. In melodramatic fashion, they often employed marriage as a device for "restoring peace" and achieving narrative closure by the family reunited. Wedding songs, dances, and

"AFRICA IN LONDON": BEHIND THE SCENES AT THE CRYSTAL PALACE
THE INTERIOR OF THE DARK CONTINENT
DRAWN BY H. LANOS

3.7 "'Africa in London': Behind the Scenes at the Crystal Palace." Illustration by H. Lanos, from *The Graphic* (3 August 1895): 132.

other ceremonial performances followed; a "phantasia" or procession of humans and animals marked what was typically (but not always) a happy ending.[38]

The emergence of narrative was neither instigated by Hagenbeck nor restricted to his *Völkerschau*. By 1890, ethnographic showmen across the board were experimenting with narrative as a nascent continuity system. In a sense, Hagenbeck's ideas for a fictional narrative came straight from the Wild West. His "Oglala-Sioux Indians" of 1910 offers only the most blatant example. As Thode-Arora has noted, the "new" show rehearsed some of the essential components of Buffalo Bill's Wild West—"cowboy fun," the conflict of horse stealing, fight scenes on horseback, ambushes of settlers and the Pony Express, interspersed with dances and races between cowboys and Indians. Only this version takes it a step further, smoothing over the gaps between

3.8 Germans and Native Americans at Hagenbeck's *Tierpark*, Easter weekend, 1910. Courtesy of Tierpark Carl Hagenbeck GmbH, Hamburg-Stellingen.

numbers, and integrating the different attractions into a single, continuous narrative, which is sustained for the duration of the performance.[39]

The 1910 Sioux show was far and away the most popular *Völkerschau* of Hagenbeck's career. If the choice of a Plains Indian show seems over-determined, it is interesting to note that Hagenbeck was initially averse to the idea, "because he feared that the Indians would be too difficult to manage and, due to their knowledge of English, their contact with spectators would become too close." He had to be persuaded. In 1909, Jacobsen invited him to London, where together they watched a Wild West show that was playing at Earl's Court. What Hagenbeck saw there so impressed him that he hired Jacobsen on the spot, and sent him directly to the United States. The resulting troupe consisted of ten cowboys (featuring George W. Everette, a.k.a. "Texas Tex") and forty-two Native Americans from Pine Ridge (see fig. 1.12). Several of the performers had previous experience in traveling shows, including Thomas American Horse, whose father had worked with Buffalo Bill. With its exclusive engagement at Hagenbeck's new *Tierpark* in Stellingen, the show attracted more than 1.1 million visitors over a five-month period. Ticket sales for Easter weekend indicate that adults outnumbered children, three to one.[40]

The main elements of the Sioux exhibition came directly from Buffalo Bill's Wild West, as we can see from the synopsis of the performance that took place in the arena:

> The presentations (*Vorführungen*) offer a picture of the dangerous life of farmers and trappers when the far West was first being settled. A real event frames the presentations—an event which took place in the Black Hills during the early 70s, as the settlers were pressing forward and the Sioux were on the warpath. A band of Indians appears at an isolated farm and, though warmly received, they take the opportunity to steal a horse. Responding to the sound of gunfire, cowboys track and capture the thief. The pony express passes by. At night, out of revenge for the capture of their friends, Indians ambush the stagecoach, attack the farm, and set fire to the lower log cabin. The farmhands are burned alive. Yet the farmer's family, having recaptured the stagecoach, races to the nearest fort, escorted by cowboys, and fighting the redskins all the way.[41]

Significantly, the same plotline would be recycled for other troupes representing different countries of origin. In fact, it had already been used for the Ethiopia show of 1909. There it required only slight modification, substituting the family of settlers with a family of peaceful nomads (the Habr Awal), the Plains Indians with warring desert nomads (Gallas), horses with dromedary camels, and so on. Last, but not least, the famous Deadwood Stagecoach, captured by the Sioux in 1876, and used in Buffalo Bill's reenactment of that event, would be replaced with "Hagenbeck's animal transport," a horse-drawn wagon with cages in tow. In dividing the nomads between good and bad tribes, the Ethiopia show follows the model of Cooper via Karl May, replacing Native Americans with North Africans.[42]

Hagenbeck's version of the Wild West is fascinating for its "post-Buffalo Bill" ethos. In contrast to the Bella Coola, for example, the new show stakes a claim to history, framing the scenes in terms of a "real event" from the 1870s (see plate 8). The narrative program description is augmented by a much longer section on "History," which included entries on the Oglala, the Battle of the Little Bighorn in 1876, the Indian reservation system, Pine Ridge, and the late chief Red Cloud. Continuities between the Indian wars and the troupe's oldest participants are duly noted. At the same time, going a step further than the Wild West shows of 1890, Hagenbeck's *Völkerschau* stakes a claim not only to history, but also to fantasy. At one point, the guidebook refers to the now hackneyed image of Plains Indians, and almost seems to deconstruct it, only to champion that image as precisely what Hagenbeck now has to offer.

> When people speak of Indians, nobody thinks of the numerous tribes in Brazil or in the rest of South America, in Central America or Mexico. They always mean the famous Prairie Indians of legend and history. They are celebrated in countless novels, and they have given rise to a literature as vast as that of knighthood. These stories of knights and Indians, they will be told over and over again to the delight of our youth. The figures of Leatherstocking, Scout, Tecumseh, etc., with their sharp-cut faces, their large hawk's noses, and their characteristic feathered headdresses, these figures are now brought to us and made tangible before our very eyes by this year's *Völkerschau*.

Earlier, such references to imaginative fiction would have been anathema. Remember the Bella Coola. In Hagenbeck's first attempt to exhibit Native Americans, the success of this troupe suffered for lack of fictive referents. The excessive praise that it received from anthropologists only underscored the difference between Hagenbeck's performers and the "Indians" that German audiences had read and dreamed about with great enthusiasm. By contrast, the 1910 Sioux show directly provoked such powerful memories and cultural associations, summoning "Cooper" from the outset, and thereby urging audiences to take possession of the spectacle, as they had earlier, by means of the imagination. The underlying tension between the historical and the fictive aspects of the Wild West shows was one that Hagenbeck would make explicit and exploit.[43]

Rather than criticize this move, journalists who reviewed the show echoed and embellished its use of fictive referents. Listen to one reporter's description of the crowd:

> The pale faces stride past the tents in a state of wonder. Their souls begin to soar when, like dreams from their childhood days, the famous chief of the Mohicans, Chingachgook, the Great Snake, his blood brother Leatherstocking, and the noble Uncas, who longed to take the scalp of the despicable Iroquois chief—all appear, living, before their very eyes. And none of this is imagined, for the copper-colored warriors, Little Wolf and Yellow Thunder, Spotted Weasel and American Horse, and others have actually come from the land where Cooper's novels took place.

This time commentators also referenced the Western novels of Karl May, although there was some irony in this, as one journalist noted with particular relish, for May had recently been "brought before a court and revealed to be a charlatan." Of the many young readers "who felt so congenial" with such fictional characters as Winnetou and Old Shatterhand, some had "perhaps come to the point of no longer believing in the existence of 'real' redskins and cowboys at all. Herr Hagenbeck should be thanked for restoring a bit of that boyish belief, for the Indians camping in the *Tier-*

park are 'authentic' in every respect." Perceptions of authenticity and their cultural associations remained firmly attached to Hagenbeck's shows, even if they were totally unwarranted.[44]

The emergence of characters within a narrative context required even greater choreography and stage management, to be sure, but it also recommended the use of native actors with experience. In this case, the participants had agreed to enact fictional roles that were assigned to them, as stipulated by their employment contracts (one of which is reproduced in this volume as fig. 1.11). Their status as "show Indians" was hardly concealed. In one newspaper report, written from the recruiter's perspective, Jacobsen claims that the only Sioux Indians who were ready to appear as "actors" (*Darsteller*) and willing to endure the hardships of itinerant life could be readily found at Pine Ridge Reservation, which is also the reason why he assembled a troupe there. As we have seen, trained professionals appeared in earlier foreign people shows, and all participants were undoubtedly coached on how to present themselves in terms of audience expectations. The difference was one of degree. It was also one of professionalization, as Jacobsen's comment on the Sioux actors would seem to imply. In the arena, acting also functioned as a kind of continuity device, helping assimilate the various numbers to a narrative through-line. Add to this the fact that between the scheduled arena shows, all performers also appeared as "inhabitants" of the adjacent native village, and we begin to see how the imaginary world of the story extended via acting beyond the arena.[45]

The consequences of this development for a history of theme space are considerable. Above all, the emergence of narrative marked a dramatic shift in practice, from a positivistic mode of ethnographic exhibition to a semiotic and self-consciously performative one. In observing this shift, I do not mean to downplay the performative nature of ethnographic representation in either nineteenth-century anthropology or popular culture more generally. Nor do I have any interest in undercutting my own discussion of performance in Hagenbeck's earlier shows (chapter 2). Rather, what I am suggesting can be described in theoretical terms as a move from museum to diegesis, the latter being the development of an internally consistent fictional space. Hagenbeck faced this transition when the Wild West came to Germany. There, as I have shown, audiences were fascinated by the self-imposed idea that performers could be seen as embodying literary characters—an idea which applied a certain amount of pressure on Hagenbeck to back away from the indexical referent and embrace a fictional one, at the same time.

Ultimately, the *Völkerschau* relinquished neither its claim to authenticity nor its emphasis on physical presence, but its underlying theatricality was brought into the open.[46] In his review of the 1909 Ethiopia exhibition, for instance, Philipp Berges refers to the performance arena as "the highlight of the tour," calling special attention to its stage decoration, and comparing it favorably to that of the legitimate theater: "The furnishing of the showpiece would bring honor on any director." Above all, he gives praise to the performers for their "acting" in the arena. "Many people have discussed the great art of dying on the stage—the art of Sada Yakko or that of Sarah Bernhardt. They could both learn something here. The way the Galla warriors imitate getting shot to death is enough to give one the creeps. They've had plenty of opportunities to see as much in battle, for many of them have actually been to war." What interests me about these comments is not the blatant way in which they served to promote the show. More important, they called attention to the theatrical aspect that had previously been either concealed or soft-pedaled in the context of ethnography, but was now emphasized as an aspect to notice and celebrate.[47]

With the turn to fiction and the shift to more overt performance, with the spread of stories and characters across troupes, the various peoples represented began to lose their referentiality, becoming in a sense interchangeable. The loss of referentiality was controlled, however, by the particular theme or habitat of each show, which always served to naturalize the work of representation and frame the discursive terms of spectatorship. Nevertheless, we begin to discern for the very first time in Hagenbeck's *Völkerschau* a certain gap (however slim) between the body of the actor and what he or she is supposed to represent, between the physical world that is literally brought to the spectator and the diegetic universe that subsists in his or her imagination. The positivistic mode focused attention on a single referent, the body of the native, and that referent by definition led back at once to itself, indexically, and to the particular ethnic group or race it was supposed to stand in for, metonymically. The performance model, by contrast, emphasized the idea of multiple different referents, as determined in part by the viewer. These referents obviously included such categories as tribal affiliations, but they were of minor interest. In this context, the primary referent was not an anthropological type, but a *credible* type of performer. Spectators found the Wild West to be convincing, valuable, and meaningful, even as they recognized its inherent staginess and fictionality. "Whether the Indians actually belong to the tribes named in the program doesn't really matter to us," wrote one reporter concerning Buffalo Bill's troupe of 1890; "they look *wild enough* with their yellow and red-painted faces and bodies, and with their feather dresses. The cowboys look *authentic enough*, too, with their wide-brimmed felt hats and rugged leather pants." Spectators used categories that were sometimes different from those used by anthropologists, and the latter's categories were no more "true" than the former. Imaginative fiction gave popular audiences an equally sophisticated but infinitely more inspiring frame of reference.[48]

The imaginary world of the *Völkerschau* encompassed the story that unfolded in the arena as well as the fictive universe that lay beneath the story. It appeared to exist independent of the spectator, even while the diegesis relied for its existence on the spectator's powers of imagination. The story elaborated in the spectator's mind was based not only on the narrative events that were acted out, scene by scene, but also on the particular fantasies, memories, and associations that allowed the spectator to imagine it. The emotional atmosphere surrounding the story—the pleasure of "sensations," the memory of childhood, the freedom of wild horses, the terror of scalping, the mystery of snake charming, the "primitive vitality" of cowboys and Indians—formed an integral part of this world, even though the diegesis was what created this atmosphere and provoked such individual responses to it. The spectator, in other words, played a crucial role in Hagenbeck's turn to fiction—a role that would need to be developed and controlled in order for him to exploit it, as he would. A shift in audience address was clearly underway, from instilling belief in the spectator (by invoking scientific authority, for example) to encouraging the suspension of disbelief (i.e., inviting a fictional reading). During the arena performance, viewers were implicitly encouraged to hold back, to remain either sitting in one of the grandstands or standing along the fence, and thus maintain a relatively detached and "aestheticized" relationship to the spectacle. At other times, and elsewhere, they were invited to actively participate in the depicted scene—indeed, to become a part of it.

IN THE VILLAGE

In many ways, the village installation can be seen as an extension of the performance arena. For it is here, in the living village, that Hagenbeck takes the performance one step further, elaborating the realm of fantasy to include the spectator in ways that the arena prohibited. This expansion of the diegetic universe was accomplished by various means, including the troupe, the narrative, and the setting. Above all, it was accomplished via the spectator's mobility. The living village had the effect of changing the spectator's relationship to the show and its component parts, strengthening the idea of a fictional universe, while elaborating it as a surround-style environment.

After the arena performance, troupe members paraded to the adjacent village, creating a direct link from one space of performance to another. The very actors that appeared as characters in the arena could now be seen at fixed stations to which they were assigned. Here, emphasis was placed on the relation between the performance and the space in which it took place. Each station was part of a larger network of touristic settings that constituted the native village. In this context, rather than represent fictionalized heroes or villains, as many of them did in the arena, native performers inhabited what were ostensibly their everyday roles. Those who were defined and represented in terms of their high social rank (e.g., tribal leaders) typically occupied the same role wherever they appeared, whereas other members of the troupe had to change roles, a few of them perhaps drastically so (warring nomad in the arena, nut roaster in the village). Generally, though, such discontinuities were downplayed and continuities were highlighted so as to enhance the coherence and global unity of the exhibition.

Spectators, for their part, were impelled to make a similar move from the grandstands into the living village. "In the breaks between performances," one reporter noted with a mix of gusto and bad humor, "you can stroll through the Indian village and pay a visit to Spotted Weasel, Yellow Thunder, Bad Maize Tassel, Eagle Louse (pardon the expression!), and other members of the troupe, even the chief." If Hagenbeck was originally averse to such close encounters, the village openly encouraged them. In contrast to the arena, where spectators were situated as relatively passive observers, the emphasis here shifts to their physical immersion and active participation in the display space. Strolling through the village, spectators practiced a kind of mobile gaze that is less reminiscent of the cinema than it is of the natural history museum, where spectators walk from life group to life group. Film scholar Alison Griffiths has explored this distinction at length, placing emphasis on the actual movement of the museumgoer as well as on tangibility of the display object, two factors that distinguish the experience of the life group from that of the cinematic image. In light of this distinction, the living village allowed for a degree of interaction that went beyond merely spectating, if only for a moment. It was a multi-sensory environment, one in which spectators could do more than just see the life group object or press their noses against the cold glass of a showcase. They could "pay a visit" to the individual performers themselves.[49]

The move from the arena to the village changed the nature of the relationship between the spectator and the performer in two significant ways: First, it resulted in what Schechner calls a flexible and variable focus of attention. "In *multi-focus*, more than one event . . . happens simultaneously, distributed throughout the space. Each independent event competes with the other for the audience's attention. The space is organized so that no spectator can see everything. Spectators move or refocus their attention or select." In contrast to the arena, where "single-focus" dominated, meaning that the entire audience was usually looking in the same direction, the village staged events so that "only a fraction of the audience can see and hear them" at any one time. Rather than absorb a single, overarching statement created by the director or by the exhibition as a whole, spectators were left to assemble their own sense of coherence, engendering many different possible meanings. Second, the move from the arena into the village allowed spectators to physically enter and actually do things within the fictional universe inhabited by performers. At the 1913 Burma exhibition, for instance, spectators could scale and stand on top of temple ruins, to get a view of a "Burmese" ceremony (fig. 3.9). More than just an endorsement of voyeurism, the village setting promoted a full-bodied experience of immersion and participation. In this

3.9 Spectators perch atop temple ruins and watch a "Burmese" ritual, 1913. Courtesy of Tierpark Carl Hagenbeck GmbH, Hamburg-Stellingen.

context, audience participation was solicited in the service of maintaining the fantasy world, and not in the service of deconstructing it.[50]

While the native village encouraged visitors to adopt a more active role than that assumed in the arena, the interaction of spectators and performers was always defined and mediated as an exchange relation. Witness the 1912 Egyptian exhibition, which was evocatively titled, "On the Nile." The village in this exhibition had a sort of open-door policy, which invited potential customers inside to shop, mingle with performers, and join in the display. At one station, visitors could lounge in an "Arabic Café" and drink an "authentic mocha" or take puffs on a water pipe.

> 25. Arabic Café (*Kahwe*). Whoever has a taste for a glass of authentic mocha, prepared oriental style, can obtain this pleasure here. He needs only to take a seat on one of the little benches, built of thin reeds, not unlike a bird cage, and the host will pour him a little bowl (*fingân*) of the thick brown drink. . . . This pleasure is only complete, however, when one smokes one of the pipes hanging on the wall, or tries the nargileh, a water pipe.

3.10 Building 24, "The Weaver," from Hagenbeck's 1912 Egyptian exhibition, "On the Nile." Courtesy of Tierpark Carl Hagenbeck GmbH, Hamburg-Stellingen.

The living village was designed to stimulate all of the senses, including touch, taste, and smell. A visit to station number "11. The Barber" was in order for the more daring visitors, where they were invited not only to watch—"Whoever so wishes may entrust himself to the barber, as well." That some performers doubled as roving salespeople, hawking postcards, brochures, and *cartes des visites* throughout the village, further blurred the boundaries between spectacle and spectator, while emphasizing the distinction between salesperson and customer, instead. Work displays underwent similar transformation and expansion, offering not only goods and attractions, but also a number of services, with an obvious correlation to those of travel and tourism.[51]

Less obvious were the pathways and connections between the arena and the village that were created via narrative. The guidebook itself led from the story to the village; all the reader had to do was literally turn the page. More important, guidebooks helped coordinate the spectator's actual movement through the village, station by station. Hagenbeck numbered every attraction and provided a brief description or photograph of it, much in the manner of Baedecker guides. Each number in the guidebook corresponded to a kind of street address mounted on the exterior of the appropriate building or station. Numerical, narrative, and iconic markers served to give structure and coherence to the entire installation, articulating its sights so that they could be anticipated, imagined, and located. To some extent, then, the function of the guidebook was analogous to that of the plot summary. In the village, however, the spectator could go directly to a particular scene, visit every station in sequential order, or visit them at random.[52]

If the arena recast the variety format as a fictional storyline, the living village reorganized it as an actual location to be explored in the mode of tourism. Instead of undermining the fictional universe, however, the effect was to make the diegesis appear even more substantial, strengthening its ties to geographical space and grounding it in the referential world. Rather than being opposed to one another, the practice of guiding in the village complemented that of storytelling in the arena. Each area presented itself as its own universe, as though it existed independent of the spectator. At the same time, each practice—guiding and storytelling—relied for its effect on the spectator's powers of identification and imagination. Earlier I defined the diegesis, on one level, as the story elaborated within the spectator's mind. This is also the level on which the diegesis encompassed the village. In this context, however, it was the body of the spectator (not that of the actor) that gave continuity to the various scenes by virtue of his or her mobility; the story here was elaborated within the spectator's mind from the multi-sensory impressions left by following the tour's itinerary. If the arena performance can be seen as a story of spectatorship, the village invited spectators to act out their own imaginative stories of exotic adventure.

As spectators moved from the grandstand into the display space, the set itself went from being a background (against which the arena performance took place) to yet another focus of attention. This was especially true of the monumental sets used for the shows at Hagenbeck's *Tierpark*. Unlike other buildings in the village, these structures were made of staff, a mix of hemp and plaster that was commonly employed for ornamental façades on temporary structures such as film and theater sets. The advantage of this material was that it could be molded into virtually any shape. Creating an exotic atmosphere was a particular problem for the *Völkerschau*; it required the spectator to suspend disbelief to a greater extent than the folk museum did, for example, because of its local origins and provincial settings. If the museum relied on relics, the *Völkerschau* made increasing use of building materials such as staff, while encouraging the viewer to use his or her imagination. "On the Nile," for example, featured three-dimensional models of the Cliff Temple of Abu Simbel as well as the Great Sphinx and Pyramids of Giza, all conveniently located in the same place (see fig. 3.11). The hyperbolic scale of these monuments (the Sphinx alone stood more than sixty feet tall) gave the entire *Völkerschau* a greater sense of height and depth, enhancing the spectator's sensation of physical immersion in that world. Shifting focus from the performer to the set had the effect of clearing an imaginary space for the spectator to momentarily occupy and explore. Each structure doubled as a station on the tourist's itinerary. Between performances, one could walk to station number "30. Panorama of Pyramids," or enter number "29. The Cliff Temple of Abu Simbil."

In light of this figure/ground reversal, the spectator's focus shifted to a degree from the body of the performer to the built environment. The difference was even high-

3.11 A monumental set from Hagenbeck's 1912 Egyptian exhibition, "On the Nile." It depicts the Cliff Temple of Abu Simbel, the Great Sphinx, and the Pyramids of Giza. Part of the arena was sand-bagged and filled with water, to suggest a desert well, with "temple ruins" strewn around the edges. The arena's surrounding fence and a long line of spectators are visible at the foot of the temple. Courtesy of Tierpark Carl Hagenbeck GmbH, Hamburg-Stellingen.

lighted in publicity materials such as the guidebook for the Egyptian show. "Though the troupe consists of valuable material," the guidebook tells us, referring to the native performers, "the exhibition would have been relatively plain, hardly raising itself above the level of itinerant shows, if it had been produced in the empty arena. Instead, according to the model worked out by Heinrich Umlauff [the park's artistic director], with the assistance of the engineer (*Bauführer*) Schild and the site foreman (*Polier*) Wagner, a fitting milieu was constructed." Set design, staging, and their respective technicians were acknowledged and even celebrated by publicity materials. More remarkably, however, spectators were encouraged to approach the set as a display object in its own right, worthy of closer scrutiny. Consider the way in which the guidebook introduces "Station 29, The Cliff Temple of Abu Simbil": "At this point, we come to the reproduction (*Nachbildung*) of the façade of this ancient edifice, and now, since it already captured our attention from a distance, we can study it in detail." Rather than direct one's attention away from such a "reproduction," the guidebook goes on to assert the harmonious relationship between imported originals and outright imitations. "The artfully assembled doors and gateways, the delicately made oriel and barred windows, are old originals that were acquired at great expense in order to come as near as possible to reality, and further, in connection with the exact reproductions of the architecture, sculptures, and paintings, in order to render the truest possible copy of an Arab city." The spectator's relationship to the set can also be described as the architectural counterpart to "performance" in the arena, where mythology and reality seemingly intermingled. When it came to the built environment of the set, however, the mobile spectator was encouraged to approach the fictional as "real," and not the other way around. The emphasis lay squarely on the manifestation of tangibility, the embodiment of fantasy; that was the key function of architecture and staging in the context of Hagenbeck's *Tierpark*.[53]

With Hagenbeck's turn to fiction, we see a new sort of imaginary beginning to emerge. We enter a new world, indeed, when the hyperbolic practice of collecting becomes the foundation for a full-blown theme park, with fantasylands composed of elaborate stage-set representations, deployed strategically and spatially for an effect. As the native village made abundantly clear, the effect was one of both sensory immersion and imaginative engagement. In the context of ethnographic exhibition, this sensuous realm of fantasy took shape at Hagenbeck's *Tierpark* in Stellingen. What remains to be shown, however, is the way in which the park both anticipated and modeled new methods of animal display, while creating an imaginative alternative to the nineteenth-century zoological garden.

CHAPTER 4

THE ART OF HAGENBECK'S ZOO

Hagenbeck's *Tierpark* in Stellingen represented an immersive art of tremendous consequence. It helped redefine some of the most basic ways in which spectators both perceived and experienced their relationship to the natural world, while raising their expectations of the themed environment and what it was capable of delivering. Ever since Hagenbeck, for example, zoo-goers en masse have expected to be immersed among living, breathing wild animals in exotic and apparently open settings, which not only simulate the natural world but also sample directly from it. The desire for full-bodied experiences, which give the feeling of plunging into another world, continues to inspire the making of themed environments across the board, from surround-style museum installations and "landscape immersion" zoos to computer-based technologies of virtual reality. This chapter explores the aesthetic dimension of Hagenbeck's *Tierpark*, with particular focus on issues of immersion. In so doing, it also takes us deeper into the nature of theme space as a historical and cultural phenomenon.

By "art" in this context I mean several different things, and throughout my discussion I move deliberately from one meaning to another, inasmuch as their interconnections allow: namely, the *Tierpark* as a form of cultural production; its distinctive concern with aesthetic principles of layout, exhibition, and spectatorship; the human skill and labor (with significant contributions by trained artists) that went into shaping its terrain; the strategic manner in which the park constructed its object of display; and last but not least, the specific relationship between the park and the nineteenth-century panorama as the immersive art *par excellence*. Indeed, the entire *Tierpark* in Stellingen was originally conceived and implemented as a colossal open-air panorama. The significance of this idea has yet to be fully explored by other scholars, perhaps because it is peripheral to a history of the zoo, which is the usual framework for understanding the *Tierpark*. In my view, however, it is the idea of the panorama that leads more incisively and directly to the core of Hagenbeck's project.

A useful point of departure is Oliver Grau's claim in *Virtual Art: From Illusion to Immersion* that immersive experience issues from a particular relationship of spectators to visual images. By immersion he understands the idea of installing the observer within a hermetically sealed, 360-degree "image space," which might refer back to the outside world, but need not do so, and is more inclined to formulate a realm of fantasy, instead. In any case, "the intention is to install an artificial world that renders the image space a totality or at least fills the observer's entire field of vision." Thus, the panorama represents for Grau the key technology of the nineteenth century, whereas experiments in circular cinema and computer art feature prominently in the twentieth century. The technological goal in each instance is "the constitution of presence" or the sensation of being physically located within the depicted scene. At the core of immersion are the visual image's haptic and tactile qualities, which give the impression that it is actually possible to reach out and touch the depicted figures in space.[1]

While I share Grau's interest in immersion and its history as well as his concern with defining its parameters in a meaningful way, I take issue with the basic assumption that immersion is an image-based phenomenon. By this definition, surround-style museum installations, which offer not only objects and mannequins but also original scenic space, such as interiors or entire houses, are categorically excluded (not to mention other modes of immersion in the wider sense of the term, such as reading or listening to music). I also object to the exclusive focus on 360-degree images, which rules out such image-based technologies as dioramas and conventional movie screens, because they create partial views instead of circular pictures. There are many possible ways of achieving immersive effects, and various kinds of immersive experiences. Hagenbeck's entertainments force this point, in part owing to their status as live events. They too relocate the spectator in a strange environment, as Grau defines the immersive experience, but this environment consists of bodies, objects, and spaces from the primary world. What emerges from this material is another form of immersive environment, which is no less paradoxical than that of virtual reality. In the words of Grau, "Unresolvable contradictions have the power to irritate and distress, but they can also mature into full-blown artistic concepts."[2]

There were two interrelated precursors to Hagenbeck's approach, the *Völkerschau* and the panorama. In the first, as we have seen, the *Völkerschau* constructed picturesque views of a particular ethnic group or geographic region, by selecting and (literally) importing representative samples of its peoples and domesticated animals, arranging them in situ, and exhibiting them as a living, breathing habitat group. It also encouraged spectators to adopt a similarly powerful mode of viewing, which encompassed and united all of the display elements—people, animals, plants, artifacts, and buildings—as integral parts of a larger imagined whole. Yet Hagenbeck's *Völkerschau* always involved more than vision and visual display. It was an entertainment space that plunged spectators into a multi-sensory environment, while allowing for various degrees of social interaction with the troupe's performers. This was especially true of the ethnographic villages at Hagenbeck's *Tierpark* in Stellingen. There, visitors roamed the paths and entered various huts, where they listened to non-Western music, smelled the aroma of exotic spices, drank Arabic coffee or Indian tea, and tasted samples of ethnic food. In many ways, they tested the physical boundaries of the display space, and the performers responded in kind. The narrativization of ethnographic performances added yet another dimension, namely, the immersive effects of storytelling, character identification, and imaginative role-play. There is an obvious difference between the idea of being "transported" by imaginative fiction and literally transporting the spectacle to the spectator, but the two modes became linked in the arena, where audiences were invited to imagine the performers as living embodiments of fictional characters, and journalists commented on the quality or plausibility of an actor's performances.

The other significant precursor, as we shall see, was the nineteenth-century panorama. In a series of entrepreneurial moves and conceptual leaps, Hagenbeck appropriated the traditional panorama, that quintessential art of the unframed view, and converted it into the unifying principle of a sprawling, landscaped park. The underlying idea was to create a new and vastly extended form of living habitat, which was also a unique type of panorama: one that was specially designed to accommodate a diversity of wild animals, without the use of cages. The process was one that he had developed and actually patented more than a decade before the *Tierpark* in Stellingen opened to the public. Most of its key techniques—including the extensive use of artificial terrain, the mixing of predators and prey within the same display space, and the innovative system of "open enclosures"—had already been employed in the various traveling panoramas that Hagenbeck exhibited throughout the 1890s. Historians of the *Tierpark* have noted the existence of these prototypes, and framed this material within the context of the zoo—an interpretive move that seems to be justified by the idea that zoos around the world have recently adopted many of the techniques that had already been used in Stellingen. At the time, however (despite all subsequent claims to the contrary), the emergence of Hagenbeck's *Tierpark* was not another zoo story. It was positively inspired by and modeled on the nineteenth-century panorama.

The conceptual relationship among these multifarious endeavors—the park, the panorama, and the ethnographic exhibition—their shared space on a theoretical level, is the visitor's sensory immersion into a living habitat. This relationship is also what makes the *Tierpark* a site of continuity between two different models of theme space, which have traditionally been seen as diametrically opposed to each other: the one being grounded in the ostensible authenticity of objects, the other being driven by the production of synthetic spaces. Their unexpected connection in the *Tierpark* further extends the relevance of this material for a general history of themed environments.

To explore the *Tierpark* as an immersive art, this chapter covers some of the same chronological ground as chapter 3, but with a different topical focus. It begins by establishing Hagenbeck's unique idea of the panorama, by situating it vis-à-vis traditional painted panoramas. The building and layout of the actual park are then discussed as a way of demonstrating how exactly panoramic vision was employed in this context. A discussion of the park's representation of space, its evocative mixing of geographical and fictive referents, highlights some of the phenomenological correspondences with other historical developments, such as the natural history museum and the *Völkerschau*. Further reflection on the visceral experience of the *Tierpark* also helps situate it in relation to amusement parks of the early twentieth century. The tense relationship of the *Tierpark* to the zoological garden will also be addressed, but only after the case for a competing model has been made. Of particular interest is the historical reception of the park by zoo (and theater) directors in Germany, which not only highlights the park's alterity—its pronounced difference from the zoological garden—but also suggests the considerable irony that the zoo-based scholarship has (either eagerly or inadvertently) displaced some of the elements that defined Hagenbeck's contribution.

"The New Panorama"

On entering the building, you are ushered into an ice grotto. Looking out from the covered spectator platform, you see a wild and romantic landscape of craggy, snow-capped icebergs. The landscape emerges from the water below to fill your gaze: floes of ice pile up before you, one on top of the other. On your right and left, walls of pack-ice rise from the ground and recede into the distance. The horizon is framed between them. In the background—you're almost two hundred feet away, so it's not easy to see—there are jagged peaks of ice and snow. You can just make out the contours of a frozen ship, its bow protruding upward like the masses of ice that encase it. There are other people, adults and children, standing around you chattering and pointing fingers at the scene.

The air smells of fish.

You look down a little and scan the water's edge. To the right of the pool, you see two make-shift huts. All around, the pool and its surroundings are teeming with animals: there are literally dozens of seals, cormorants, sea gulls, and Arctic birds of different kinds. Walking among them are three people dressed in sealskin outfits; they appear to be Eskimos. After a while, you see them retreat into the huts.

In the very center of this landscape, there is an opening in the ice and another pool of water. You see a group of polar bears—there are at least ten of them—directly before you. They appear to be roaming about freely, climbing the icebergs, and swimming in the pool of water. There are no bars or fences to separate you from the animals. The people next to you are speculating about how it works when, suddenly, there is a great commotion in the scene before you. The performance is about to begin. This is the setting for a dramatic scene, the habitat for an event.

A woman has emerged from one of the huts, with a bucket in each hand. Left and right, she begins tossing out handfuls of herring, plaice, and shellfish. The seals take notice; their loud barking noises fill the air. The cormorants add their croaking sounds, the gulls their shrieking cries—all are excited by the fish. The entire foreground seems to be in motion, but your attention is drawn to the background, where the polar bears all rise up on their hind legs, as another Eskimo enters the scene. With one loud crack of his whip, he drives them back onto the icebergs. When one of the bears turns his back, you see the man reach out and pat it on the head. On his command, all eleven polar bears descend from the icebergs to form a picturesque group, and hold it momentarily, for you to admire. Another command and the bears stand up, again, this time forming a circle around him. Some of the bears are eating out of his hand, others catching food in their mouths as he throws it to them. He leaves the scene, unscathed. You continue watching as the polar bears spread out again, as the animals in the foreground have already done. Some plop down on the ice, others slide into the water.

It is evening, and the sea is now brilliantly illuminated, the icebergs shimmering in the background. Around you, the sky begins to glow with a halo of shifting colors, an evocative scene of the Northern Lights.[3]

◆ ◆ ◆

In 1896, Hagenbeck received a German patent for an invention called a "Natural-Scientific Panorama" (*Naturwissenschaftliches Panorama*).[4] Just as he was engaged in more aggressive branding of his products, he sought to obtain exclusive rights to a new technique for exhibiting wild animals. The model that he proposed was nominally scientific. Clearly, he continued trading on the authority of science, but he did so in this instance for the sake of winning a patent, and not for selling tickets. The language of the patent application is revealing: It promises to do for wild animal shows what the *Völkerschau* did for human exhibitions. The original plan called for a new and different form of living habitat, one that was capable of accommodating a diversity of exotic animals (including big carnivores or man-eating predators) in the same display space, while at the same time providing audiences with a safe and unimpeded viewing experience. In examining the patent and its various prototypes, we catch a glimpse of the creative process in action. We also gain a fresh perspective on the changing nature of theme space and technology's role in reshaping it. What is perhaps most curious about this process, however, is that Hagenbeck called it a panorama.

Whether you have only a vague sense of what a panorama looked like or you are an expert on nineteenth-century visual culture, you will probably find little if anything about Hagenbeck's design that immediately calls to mind a panorama in the usual sense of the term. His view was something quite unique. So, before we turn to his blueprint for a "new" panorama, we need to look briefly at the history of this medium, to understand how Hagenbeck's model at once differed from and built on other forms of entertainment going by the same name.

First patented in 1787, by the Irishman Robert Barker, the panorama was originally conceived as a vast circular painting to be viewed from a central platform. A special form of architecture was needed to accommodate this unwieldy spectacle, but also to control the light source, the only intruding element from the outside world. Purpose-built rotundas, which allowed daylight to enter from above and led spectators to the viewing platform by means of a tunnel, gave showmen considerable control over the viewing environment and direct influence over the viewer's sensory input. Over time, the panorama's form was frequently revised, inspiring a dizzying number of spin-offs (with evocative names such as the Cyclorama and Maréorama) as well as alternate formats. Among the most notable variants was the giant moving panorama, which used machinery to roll great lengths of canvas past an audience. In subject matter, panoramas and their variants encompassed spectacular views of historical events such as battles, fires, and shipwrecks, but they mostly revolved around the subjects of exotic travel and nature, whether static aerial pictures of individual cities or moving "journeys" over land and sea. Many of these paintings became itinerant exhibits, with multiple copies circulating in cities and fairgrounds throughout Europe and the United States. An "all-encompassing view," the panorama represented more than a convincing form of pictorial illusionism; it also invoked a powerful mode of seeing. This popular medium enjoyed periods of international enthusiasm, from the 1790s to the 1820s, with a revival in the 1880s and '90s. During the latter period, as Vanessa R. Schwartz has argued, there was an identifiable heightening of multi-sensory experience and immersive effects. During this period too, German companies led the way in panorama production, export, and display.[5]

This was also the context in which Hagenbeck envisioned a new type of entertainment that would carry the same name. The basic design had been tweaked and modified many times before, but Hagenbeck put an extraordinary amount of pressure on the panorama as an idea. His was obviously not a painting-in-the-round. At the same time, however, he no doubt sought to benefit from some of the cultural connotations such as "reality" and "immersion" that were already attached to its name. For more than a century, the panorama had captured the imagination of audiences throughout Europe and the United States. It represented an existing and widely understood discourse—by which I mean a grammar, a technique, an institution, a practice, and a way of seeing—that Hagenbeck would appropriate for his own agenda.[6]

The discourse on the panorama was widely appropriated in the nineteenth century and has since been analyzed in many different contexts. The work of cultural historian Wolfgang Schivelbusch, who explores panoramic perception in relation to railway travel, offers a useful example. Schivelbusch describes how the experience of railway travel in the nineteenth century radically transformed the spectatorial relationship between the traveler and the surrounding landscape (by which he means the natural environment as it is perceived). Due to the train's velocity, landscape became detached from the spectator, abstracted, and reshaped as "geographical space," which was constructed as much in the passenger's imagination as it was in the coordinated systems of maps and timetables that a railway network required. In his analysis, Schivelbusch emphasizes the spectator's physical separation from the surrounding environment, and interprets it as a "loss of landscape," with profound implications for our historical understanding of perception. Vision, for example, became framed, mediated by glass, and experienced through the motion of the train. "Panoramic perception, in contrast to traditional perception, no longer belonged to the same space as the perceived objects."[7]

Schivelbusch's analysis of panoramic vision can be extended and complicated by acknowledging that theme space of the period involved actually removing elements from the natural environment, transporting them great distances via railway (and steamship), and reconstructing them as geographical space that spectators could physically enter and explore. If the railway separated the traveler from the space of perception, resulting in a "loss of landscape," theme space compensated for this loss by immersing the spectator in a variety of simulated settings, which were represented as readily available and accessible to the mobile spectator.

This is also the context in which Hagenbeck reinterpreted the idea of panorama, beginning in the mid-1890s. He employed the term in a particular and highly unusual way. By "panorama" he understood a landscaped view that simulated a natural habitat, but did so—and here is the twist—by making the displayed people, animals, objects, etc. all physically present to the spectator's senses. To use the term in this way also implied a further extension of the *Völkerschau* idea, both as a mode of habitat display and as a way of seeing. In this context, as discussed earlier, he had long encouraged spectators to assume a powerful, encompassing view of a foreign culture as situated within a complete environment. The up-gathering force of this vision was seemingly warranted by the production of a unified and (literally) gathered space of display. The wish to bring wild animals into the display space led Hagenbeck to adopt the idea of the panorama and inspired his extraordinary intervention.[8]

It is interesting to note that, shortly before he patented a new process for creating a panorama, Hagenbeck also experimented with dioramic techniques (painted backdrops) as well as with the use of selected plantings and exotic décor in the context of animal training. There, he specialized in assembling and training "mixed-species groups," a type of wild animal show that usually featured an extraordinary combination of predators and prey within the same display space, always in the presence of one or more trainers. The process of teaching members of radically different species to tolerate one another and perform together was painstaking: It involved gradually exposing individual animals to one another, then repeating the process as needed in different combinations and ever-greater numbers. Extremely popular around 1900, mixed groups often appeared in circus and menagerie shows, and they were closely associated with Hagenbeck in particular. In this context, however, the use of natural settings was literally a background issue, of secondary importance to the animal acts at center stage. His early experiments with dioramic backdrops thus took place within an enormous circular cage. Since Hagenbeck's use of natural settings turned out to be so consequential, it is worth pausing to note the difference between this example and the form of cageless display that he would later design and patent as a type of panorama.

Contemporary showmen used various kinds of theatrical settings to stage animals as performers. Whereas traditional motifs included castles, coliseums, and domestic interiors, it became increasingly fashionable around 1900 to decorate training cages with murals of foreign landscapes, especially painted scenes of deserts with sundry pyramids and palm trees. The large outdoor cage, located in the courtyard of Hagenbeck's trade menagerie in Hamburg, offers a case in point. Anticipating Hagenbeck's appearance at the Chicago world's fair, British journalist Raymond Blathwayt paid a visit to the menagerie in 1892 and wrote about his experience of this particular exhibit. Two performances were given in his honor, at which he was allowed to actually enter the cage with Hagenbeck and the trainer Heinrich Mehrmann. "My readers will imagine a great circle carefully railed off from the outside world by iron bars," wrote Blathwayt, but it is the view from inside the cage that interests me here.

> Most cleverly and most artistically this inclosure has been made to resemble the African desert. In the foreground there are planted here and there bushes and a few small palm trees, while in the far off distance there rise, towering to a deep blue tropical sky, grim hoary mountains and sun-stricken rocks. There is thus con-

4.1 "Training of Wild Beasts." A special demonstration by the trainer Heinrich Mehrmann (*right*) for the British journalist Raymond Blathwayt (seated), who visited Hagenbeck (*left*) at his *Tierpark* in Hamburg, ca. 1892. Illustration from "Wild Beasts: How They Are Transported and Trained," *McClure's Magazine* 1, no. 2 (July 1893): 131. University of Washington Libraries, Special Collections, negative no. UW 25807z.

> veyed to the mind an exact impression of the great Nubian deserts, an impression in the force and reality of which is greatly strengthened by the actual appearance of wild beasts themselves, which are lying basking in the heat of the sun or restlessly prowling and growling round the inclosure.[9]

Blathwayt's account only confirms the idea that modern spectators wanted to see wild animals in natural settings—even when the performance featured a series of trained-animal tricks. What makes this account particularly prescient, however, is the fact that the visitor is allowed to go beyond the bars and physically enter the display space. The point can be made more vividly by comparing an illustration of this episode, which elides the bars of the cage and depicts the animals and the spectator in shared space, with Hagenbeck and the trainer at his side (fig. 4.1). The strong impression that this scene made upon the reporter is one that the showman would also seek to create—and enhance—through immersive environments that eschewed cages and simulated habitats, beginning with his design for a new panorama.[10]

PATENT CLAIMS

In his application for a patent, Hagenbeck predicated the novelty of his invention on the fact that the zoological garden and its methods of animal display were now passé, and therefore in need of fresh ideas. "Until today," he argues, zoo animals have typically been kept either inside special houses or behind iron bars. Moreover, zoological gardens have thus far removed animals "from various lands," only to arrange and exhibit them systematically, according to scientific principles. "While the viewer is hereby offered much that is interesting and instructive, the total impression is still relatively primitive, for one might learn about the animals in their character and form, but never gains a clear picture of their ways of life and movement in their natural habitat, as this shall be accomplished by the Natural-Scientific Panorama, which is the object of the present invention." Thus, Hagenbeck begins by citing the zoological garden for egregious abstraction, and offers a type of panorama as a practical, innovative, and characteristically scenic alternative. Here was a way of bypassing the zoo, in order to compete with it on a new level.

Hagenbeck's claim to ownership rested on the idea of the zone picture (developed elsewhere), which he had already co-opted in the context of ethnographic performance. "The new panorama," as defined by the patent, "is essentially characterized by the fact that it presents, on a suitable terrain, one part of a foreign area with the respective creatures (humans and animals) that belong in it." In other words, Hagenbeck's version of the panorama created a kind of zone picture, as the *Völkerschau* had earlier, by the arrangement of living bodies and physical spaces (as opposed to pictorial illusionism). The initial plan was to exhibit groups of humans and animals (the patent refrains from emphasizing one or the other) as belonging to and situated in the particular geographical area from which they originated. As an example, then, the application discusses "part of a polar region," which is also depicted in the accompanying illustration (see fig. 4.2). It is important to underscore that the design was fundamentally interchangeable, *mutatis mutandis*, and not restricted to any one area or zone (non-Western contexts are simply assumed). "If tropical areas are selected for the panorama," the application continues with a different hypothetical example, "then flora will be enlisted for the purpose, in addition to fauna, thereby further enhancing the impression of nature." Thus, the new panorama claimed to display humans and animals, predators and prey, in shared space (Hagenbeck's phrase). Later, it would be reduced to the idea of displaying zoo animals in apparent freedom, but the project was originally formulated in this way: "To keep living humans and animals, particularly wild animals, within a shared space (*innerhalb eines gemeinsamen Raumes*), without the use of windows, bars, fences, or other means that could obstruct the view of the total picture, which at first glance seems hardly possible, is accomplished by the special design of the terrain."[11]

The panorama appealed to Hagenbeck, above all, for its established association with the spectator's immersion in a depicted scene. "By means of artistic painting and sculpture the entire panorama can be completed in such a way that will perfect as much as possible the impression that one finds oneself in the depicted area (*der Eindruck, man befände sich in der vorgeführten Gegend*)." This immersive effect is visually evoked in the patent's accompanying illustration by a spectator who appears to be casually "taking in" the scene, even though there are no apparent physical barriers separating him from the polar bears and Eskimos in the exemplary Arctic scene. With his bowler hat, walking stick, and a camera slung across his chest, the spectator not only wears the trappings of civilization but apparently expects to find a picturesque view (one that he could photograph). Thus, yesterday's zoo-goer is refashioned as a modern tourist, while the animal display, no longer a taxonomic placeholder, becomes a tangible space for the spectator to enter and explore on foot.

Paradoxically, then, the new panorama made no discursive claim to offer an all-encompassing view. On the contrary, it represented only a segment of a larger geographical area, in accordance with the habitat group and its metonymic logic. Like the *Völkerschau* before it, Hagenbeck's panorama relied on selected extracts of the physical world and therefore offered up a partial view ("a slice of life"). To mount an Arctic scene, for example, the patent suggested a rectangular-shaped building, "a suitable terrain which is approximately 25m wide and 60m long." Add to this the use of inward receding walls, as evident from photographs and illustrations of Hagenbeck's panoramas, and the fan-shaped performance space begins to resemble not a panoramic rotunda but a theatrical set.[12]

The task of installing the spectator in a scene that was filled with wild animals required a number of modifications to the panorama's design as well as some extra precautions that were unprecedented in the history of the medium. For example, the *faux terrain* or three-dimensional landscape that was often used in the foreground of panoramas—a practice adopted by panorama makers around 1830—would be expanded from the foreground to encompass the entire display space. With Hagenbeck, in other words, it went from serving as mere transition to functioning as both the setting for a dramatic scene and the stage for a live performance. Typically, the haptic property of *faux terrain* enhanced a pictorial illusion by addressing the viewer's sense of touch and extending it to the image, while helping camouflage the purely visual character of the painting. Oliver Grau has a suggestive way of describing its immersive function in the context of a battle panorama: "It came up close to the spectators, particularly in the section where hand-to-hand combat was depicted, and this strategy of virtually removing boundaries led, or rather pulled, the observer into the depths of the image space." The use of metaphor here should really be marked, but the metaphorical action of "pulling" is nonetheless useful for my purposes, because it helps elicit the radical nature of Hagenbeck's endeavor. In his version of the panorama, *faux terrain* pulled the viewer not toward a two-dimensional image, but toward a large group of living, breathing wild animals.[13]

In a further extension, *faux terrain* would be made not only to rise and fill the viewer's gaze, but also—more important—to sink and fall out of view in certain places. What Hagenbeck proposed was an entire system of physical barriers that would serve in lieu of iron bars by assuming the cage's dual function of containing the animal and protecting the viewer. To quote from the patent, its "implementation would be characterized by the use of interferences (*Hindernisse*) such as trenches, waterfalls, and elevations, in order to prohibit contact between competing kinds of animals, and to create a defense for the people, without disturbing the overall picture." In other words, the sunken barrier known in landscape gardening as the "ha-ha" would be appropriated in the context of the panorama and refunctionalized for creating an unimpeded view of large wild animals. The specific dimensions of these interferences depended on the maximum flight distance of the animal on exhibit, which was calculated and verified by a staff of animal trainers under tightly controlled conditions. "To determine first how high these animals could jump," wrote Hagenbeck, "a stuffed pigeon was tied to a palm branch that was hanging three meters above the ground. The lions, tigers, panthers, and leopards that had been let into the cage soon noticed the pigeon and tried to bring it down." Testing their abilities in the long jump, he added, was already a standard part of the animal training regimen.[14]

Hagenbeck's version of the panorama relied for its effect not only on the use of camouflaged barriers and animal training, but also on a principle of deep staging—a principle that has more in common with the theater and the cinema than it has with the tradition of panoramic painting. The patent calls for a series of receding enclosures, one behind the other, which extend in one direction away from the viewer. Though the patent shows only two enclosures, the *Tierpark* would later accumulate as many as eight within a single view. Take a look at the patent's illustration and the cross-section diagram or legend below it (figs. 4.2 and 4.3). Elevating the spectator on a constructed platform (which is designated as position 1), the new panorama created a sense of spatial unity and depth by shifting the attention from plane to plane, while extending the spectator's vision through multiple enclosures at once. In an Arctic panorama, for example, the viewer would see "a number of seals and arctic birds of diverse kinds" in the foreground (position 2), "Eskimo huts" in the mid-ground (position 3), which concealed the deep trench behind it (position 4, which is almost hidden,

4.2, 4.3 Illustration and cross-section diagram from Hagenbeck's 1896 patent application for a "Natural-Scientific Panorama." Courtesy of Tierpark Carl Hagenbeck GmbH, Hamburg-Stellingen.

Fig. 1.

Fig. 2.

„Naturwissenschaftliches Panorama."

für: Carl Hagenbeck – Hamburg.

G.-M.D. + Pat. D.Ö.U.
E.Fr.A.J.

Gz. Alb. Vitschke.
6. 2. 96. U.

aptly, in a shaded area at the center of the illustration), and a group of live polar bears in the background (position 5). At Hagenbeck's park in Stellingen, the various stage-sets or enclosures would be arranged in ascending fashion, which (literally and figuratively) heightened the sense of entering a living habitat, while drawing the viewer's angle of vision upward and thus deeper into the display space.[15]

ARCTIC EXAMPLES

In the 1890s, Hagenbeck exhibited a variety of itinerant panoramas in cities throughout Germany as well as in Paris, Milan, Chicago, and St. Louis. One of them, the "Arctic Sea Panorama" (*Eismeer-Panorama*), became a major attraction and underwent various incarnations over time. The subject matter was not new. On the contrary, as Russell A. Potter has demonstrated, the Arctic had long been a favorite *topos* of panoramas, offering a seemingly limitless horizon, a strange and mostly unseen world that fascinated Western audiences in the nineteenth century, particularly in the realm of visual culture. In the summer of 1896, around 400,000 visitors paid to see the premiere of Hagenbeck's Arctic Sea Panorama at the Berlin Trade Exhibition. From there, the show went to Hamburg, where it took place on the carnival grounds adjacent to two older rotundas, the "Battle Panorama" and the "High Seas Panorama." The following year Hagenbeck's exhibit traveled to Dresden, Leipzig, Munich, and Vienna, where a live walrus was added to the display. In 1899, an updated version went to Paris, where it was renamed "La vie au Pôle Nord." A stationary version of the Arctic Sea Panorama was one of two main attractions at Hagenbeck's *Tierpark* in Stellingen when it opened in 1907. A slight variation, the "South Pole Panorama," was exhibited in Milan in 1897, and a version of that exhibit too would be added to the park as a stationary panorama in 1911. That very year, Hagenbeck sponsored another "Arctic Sea Panorama" in Berlin, this one designed by his nephew and assistant, Heinrich Umlauff, featuring a group of twenty polar bears, as part of an elaborate *Völkerschau* called the "Northland Exhibition."[16]

Hagenbeck's Arctic Sea Panorama, from 1896, had the same specifications as those that were indicated in the patent. Built by "a large Berlin company," the Arctic landscape "was made out of plaster with asbestos, alum, and other suitable materials, and then painted by the stage painter Moritz Wimmer. It is 60 meters long by 25 meters wide, encompassing in total approximately 3,000 square meters."[17] Behind this landscape, a canvas covering an area of 800 square meters (less than a third the standard size of circular paintings) was stretched across a wooden scaffolding, to create the backdrop. An evocative landscape of snow-capped icebergs, the backdrop was likely painted by Moritz Lehmann, a theater painter and set designer from Vienna who had worked with Hagenbeck before. The painting was located at such a distance from the viewing platform—much farther than conventional panoramas—that a detailed treatment was presumably unnecessary. According to other scholars, "It was simply meant to enclose the panorama at the rear and, in so doing, create a sense of atmosphere as much as it was possible."[18]

As the focus of spectatorial interest moved in this panorama from the production of visual images to the deployment of living bodies, there is some temptation—emanating, perhaps, from our received idea of what a panorama *should* be—to address and evaluate Hagenbeck's version in terms of painted panoramas and find it lacking. A more fruitful approach might be to take the Arctic Sea Panorama on its own terms. To do so, would mean to emphasize the staging of wild animals (think of it as Hagenbeck's equivalent to painting). From this perspective, it becomes more evident that the work of the panoramist was largely administrative and organizational in nature. Hagenbeck himself did not train a single animal on display, nor did he personally trap or collect any of them. As we have seen, the work was done rather by various agents in the field. Hagenbeck, for his part, contracted the labor, including the animal trainers, and supervised the entire production process. This process had a number of stages, which included hunting, trapping, transport, acclimatization, maintenance, and training. Each stage was at once tedious, risky, and highly specialized, involving the sustained effort of many people over a long period of time. The training phase alone took years for some animals. Though nowhere mentioned in the patent (which is restricted to design issues), the painstaking work of selecting, maintaining, and training animals for such a display was paramount to its implementation.

Of particular interest here is the appearance of trainers within the Arctic Sea Panorama as part of its regular performance (see plate 9). As other scholars have recently pointed out, "The presentation of trained-animal groups necessitated the almost constant presence of a trainer within the panorama." The implications of their required presence for habitat display are intriguing. At the Berlin show, for example, the so-called Eskimos were displayed as natural-born trainers, as if their very way of life revolved around feeding the local animals and teaching them to perform tricks. Reviews from Berlin suggest that journalists were much taken by the performance. According to one reporter, the Arctic Sea Panorama included a small "family" of Greenland Inuit, one woman and two men. They wore sealskin outfits and lived in huts that were part of the set. "The food, which they prepare in very primitive kitchen arrangements, on fish oil burners—there is little if any wood in Greenland—mainly consists of meat and fat from creatures of the Arctic Ocean," noted another commentator. "Everything is cooked with fat and fish oil." According to his official publicist, however, Hagenbeck never even planned to employ native performers. Instead, "heavily improvised Eskimos [would] live in the huts and feed the animals."[19]

It helps to recall that the *Völkerschau* began by casting animal handlers as ethnographic performers, offering up "authentic" natives as opposed to ethnic impersonators. The animal panorama reversed that move, replacing native performers with European trainers in costume. A glowing review of the Hamburg show, published in a trade journal for professional entertainers, emphasized that the panorama had three animal trainers "dressed in their original Eskimo costumes, which further heightens the effect." Whether their performance enhanced or detracted from the viewer's experience of the panorama is unclear, but the practice of trainers masquerading as "natives" would not be continued at the *Tierpark* in Stellingen. The use of trainers and trained animals was not a trade secret. Heinrich Bolau, director of Hamburg's Zoological Garden, complimented the show on each point in a review that ran in an illustrated weekly with national circulation. "The animals are exceptionally well trained and obey their keeper's every command, every gesture—a superb accomplishment, indeed," he wrote, "especially for such vicious animals as polar bears." One of these trainers was the young Reuben Castang, who later achieved some notoriety as a wild animal showman in England and the United States. On this occasion, he played the part of an Eskimo and took charge of the polar bear section. According to his biographer, the first time Castang wore his sealskin costume in the enclosure, on opening day in Berlin, one of bears attacked him. "The scent of it had been too much for the animal. He was a seal—food!"[20]

What distinguished this panorama from its many predecessors was the central role of live animals.[21] Advertising posters highlighted the difference: "Everything living!" Beyond pointing to the basic need for Hagenbeck's habitat to thrive, this slogan implied a spectacle that consisted of the sheer number and diversity of living objects. In the late 1890s, as Dittrich and Rieke-Müller have pointed out, the mass trapping of animals allowed for new display forms with ever-larger groupings. In 1896, for example, Hagenbeck bought one hundred and one seals, the most he ever purchased in a single year, the spike in trade being due to his new panorama. Of those received, sixteen seals were in turn sold, thirty-four died either in transit or shortly after their arrival, and the remaining fifty-one would be used over time in the Arctic Sea Panorama. At the Berlin Trade Exhibition, the show began with eleven polar bears, twenty-five seals, and more than fifty "Arctic birds" of different kinds. "No zoological garden has ever exhibited the present far-northern animals in such a considerable number," wrote one commentator. The Arctic Sea Panorama was in fact something of a first: "Never before had Hagenbeck exhibited such large numbers of animals for an extended period of time at his own expense."[22]

The stakes of live display were extremely high, a fact that traveling shows only exacerbated. The continued viability of living, sentient creatures had an unmatched sense of urgency about it, no matter how humane or crassly commercial the motivating forces might have been. Exhibiting and trading in such large quantities, as Hagenbeck did, further increased the difficulty of maintaining individual animals. When the Arctic Sea Panorama began its tour, during the warm summer months of 1896, one of the eleven polar bears and all twenty-five of the seals died in Berlin. Contrary to the show's slogan ("Everything living!"), the losses were so tremendous that Hagenbeck began substituting the animals as they died. Later, he replaced some of the seals with California sea lions—animals that admittedly had no relationship to the Arctic world, but could better withstand the climate and conditions of a tour through the entertainment world.[23]

The inclusion of fauna that did not originate from the Arctic and other instances of species-mixing for aesthetic effect have led some commentators to describe Hagenbeck's panoramas as "unnatural" with minimum commitment to verisimilitude. Yet to treat the panorama as but a thinly disguised circus act is to conflate what were then distinct entertainments. At the Berlin Trade Exhibition, for instance, the Arctic Sea Panorama took place alongside two other Hagenbeck shows. The "Monkey Paradise" combined more than two hundred monkeys in one enormous cage, and staged the entire scene as a fair (a grotesque inversion that is the stock and trade of trained-monkey shows). And the "Zoological Circus," led by Heinrich Mehrmann, was the last vestige of a group that Hagenbeck first exhibited at the 1893 Chicago world's fair. By 1896, the mixed group consisted of polar bears, lions, tigers, panthers, leopards, jaguars, brown bears, and mastiffs. It is telling that reporters in Berlin focused almost exclusively on the panorama. In so doing, they also picked up both on its novelty and, by extension, its distinction from the adjacent shows: namely, the natural setting and cageless display. So did at least one zoo professional, evidently. When the show came to Hamburg, Heinrich Bolau, director of the city's Zoological Garden, positively gushed: "This panorama is probably the very first to be brought to life in this way, by animals that are freely moving about, unfettered. . . . No interfering barriers seem to keep these enormous beasts from the viewers, no bars separate them from us, so that we might believe there is nothing to stop them from paying us an unwanted visit."[24]

The cultural fascination with the Arctic obviously contributed to the appeal of these displays. Historian Vanessa R. Schwartz has argued that panoramas in *fin-de-siècle* Paris served "as visual corollaries of the popular press," depicting the kinds of far-away sights, recent events, and local celebrities that one could readily find in boulevard newspapers, while at the same time rendering them visually apprehensible to mass spectators, thus permitting even greater access and participation to events that might otherwise remain utterly remote.[25] Hagenbeck's Arctic Sea Panorama can also be seen in this light. Specifically, it participated in the media frenzy surrounding the Norwegian explorer Fridtjof Nansen and his extraordinary voyage across the Arctic Ocean. Nansen's story is so captivating that, media hype aside, one can easily imagine why Hagenbeck sought to exploit it. For this Arctic voyage, Nansen designed a new type of ship named the *Fram* ("Forward") that could be carried and not crushed by the polar ice. His plan was to deliberately enclose the ship in the ice and abandon it there, returning via dogsleds and kayaks, while letting the ocean's currents carry it from Siberia back to Spitsbergen. The *Fram* sailed on 24 June 1893. When Hagenbeck's panorama first opened at the Berlin Trade Exhibition, the ship had not been sighted for more than a year. One week later, Nansen and his crew were found by the British explorer Frederick Jackson, and safely returned to Norway. The *Fram* also arrived in one piece. It was major international news when Nansen and his crew sailed it back to port on 9 September 1896. Hagenbeck too was in luck.

When the Arctic Sea Panorama went to Hamburg, where it appeared from October to December of that year, a huge picture of the *Fram* was added to the painted backdrop. It appeared as though Nansen's ship, surrounded by the pack ice, had transported the viewer to this Arctic wonderland (see fig. 4.4). The ship's image was still being used the following year, when the panorama traveled to Dresden, Leipzig, and Munich. By then, the international press was already fascinated by yet another expedition, that of Salomon Andrée, the Swedish explorer who set out for the pole in a hot-air balloon. Journalists in turn began framing Hagenbeck's panorama in terms of these current events. This report ran in the United States:

> The vivid interest in the regions far north, which was so remarkable in days gone by, has recently been stirred anew by the successful efforts of Nansen and Andrée's daring enterprise. In anxious suspense the whole world awaits the time when news from the aeronaut will be received, and our imagination figures up before our eyes a picture of desolate, snow-covered plains, beset with huge and shapeless blocks of ice, and animated with fearful polar bears and inoffensive seals, a scene from the land where so many explorers have succumbed in battle with a great and dreadful foe. But *a more concrete representation than these fancies of our minds* has been set before the interested European. Transplanted, as if by a magician's wand, from regions of perpetual snow into our temperate zone, a scene of arctic life is laid amid the busy life of the great hanseatic town of Hamburg.

On one level, then, the Arctic Sea Panorama was both exhibited and received in terms of sensationalized news in the press, thus giving further evidence in support of Schwartz's thesis. When the show went to Paris, in 1899, though Nansen's voyage was by then old news, the spectator platform there was rebuilt in the shape of a ship's bow and decorated as the *Fram*. In a further addition, the performance now alternated between the usual trained-animal acts, led by the British trainer Willy Judge, and an extensive program of lantern slides depicting episodes from Nansen's voyage.[26]

4.4 "Panorama of Arctic Life and Scenery." Illustration of the Hamburg exhibition, from *Scientific American Supplement*, 11 September 1897 (18098).

On another level, however, Hagenbeck's panorama extended beyond the scope of "spectacular reality" (Schwartz), by providing "a more concrete representation than these fancies of our minds" (to repeat a line quoted above). That is to say, it objectified and vivified a space that existed only in the audience's imagination. For the Arctic represented a fantasyland of awe-inspiring proportions and extreme conditions, a place of wonder and struggle, and thus a conventional setting for representations of Nature as sublime.[27] This space of the imagination is one that Hagenbeck would explore more fully in other traveling panoramas and especially at the *Tierpark* in Stellingen.[28]

The panorama offered more than a medium for representing the "real." As far as Hagenbeck was concerned, it provided more than a slick design for integrating wild animals into the living habitat. It also suggested a means of staging them in fictionalized spaces with an attenuated link to the referential world. Through another series of panoramas, Hagenbeck developed a different yet related theme that would also inform and define his *Tierpark* in Stellingen—namely, the biblical theme of paradise. The whole idea of a new Eden, a space "where cruelty of nature was abolished and peace reigned under the benign influence of culture," was already closely associated with the nineteenth-century zoological garden.[29] Instead of simply invoking this mythological *topos* on the discursive level of association, Hagenbeck went one step further to imagine it as a landscaped scene. His first "Paradise Panorama," with a backdrop painted by Moritz Lehmann, appeared in Milan during the summer of 1897. The following year, a new and expanded version was mounted on the grounds of the Zoological Garden in Berlin. This version carried the more generic title, "Carl Hagenbeck's Animal Panorama." It could be accessed either from within the zoo or (for a higher ticket price) from the adjacent train station.[30] The show included a diversity of animals, more than 150 of them, all apparently within the same display space, set against an idyllic backdrop (another Lehmann painting), with variegated *faux terrain* including "cliffs, caves, green meadows, and forest grounds." Like the Zoological Circus before it, the Animal Panorama featured some thirty predators, including lions, tigers, pumas, leopards, polar bears, and hyenas—but without the large cage. "You ask yourself," wrote one reviewer, "Isn't there any sort of conflict among such diverse animal species? The scene is so peaceful, as it must have been in paradise."[31] The exhibit's design was equivalent to that of the Arctic Sea Panorama. According to Ludwig Heck, then director of Berlin's zoo, "The trench, which separated the back part, with the predators, from the foreground, with the harmless animals, was 4 meters wide and 4 meters deep, and it proved to be safe enough—that is, no predator ever jumped over it."[32]

The paradise panoramas were directly linked to the new *Tierpark* initiative that Hagenbeck launched in 1897. The Swiss artist Urs Eggenschwyler was commissioned to create a promotional advertisement, an illustration of the paradise panorama to be used at the 1898 Berlin show. Its title announced, "Carl Hagenbeck's Zoological Paradise: Zoological Garden of the Future." Indeed, the new panorama posed a direct challenge to the zoo, whose display techniques were deemed outdated. A similar theme would be used at the 1904 world's fair in St. Louis, to promote the new *Tierpark* before a wider international audience. Located on the amusement strip called the Pike, "Carl Hagenbeck's Zoological Paradise" was a semi-circular panorama consisting of three adjacent zones or landscapes—the steppes, the jungle, and the Arctic. Each section was stocked with a mix of animal species, the theme of "paradise" being constituted by the spectacle of their harmonious coexistence within the same display space.[33]

With their emphasis on harmony over habitat, paradise displays might seem at first to militate against the idea of the life group and its referential ties. For some commentators, these panoramas suggest that Hagenbeck simply took the mixed-species group from trained-animal acts, removed it from the circus, and plopped it down in a vaguely naturalistic setting with artificial terrain. It seems to me, however, that the two strategies—referencing the pole, on the one hand, and paradise, on the other—also complemented each other. What constituted paradise was for Hagenbeck the imagined unity of all zones and their animal inhabitants within the park as a coherent whole. The *Tierpark* in Stellingen would encompass a multiplicity of panoramas, each with a different and changing relationship to the natural environment that it claimed to represent. Taken together, they were supposed to evoke visions of earthly paradise. More important, I suggest, they demonstrate an unexpected connection between the referential and the nonreferential, between the naturalistic spaces of habitat display and the utopian dreams of the amusement park. This connection, which is the alignment of two seemingly incompatible models of theme space, demonstrates Hagenbeck's role as a transitional figure, mediating between the supposed authenticity of collected objects and the elaborate simulation of immersive environments. Indeed, the *Tierpark* obtains its historical significance in terms of theme space precisely because it makes this transition so vivid and tangible. The project called for extrapolating the "new" panorama into a full-blown park, creating a vast open-air immersive environment by transforming the rural German landscape into an exotic-themed entertainment space.

Labor, Landscape, and Sculpture

In 1897, Hagenbeck acquired a thirty-five-acre estate in the Prussian town of Stellingen. Located outside and to the north of Hamburg, the area was large enough to accommodate all the branches of his ever-growing business, while providing something that he never found in the city, search though he did for more than a decade: namely, an open space capable of accommodating numerous large enclosures and sweeping exotic vistas. An old potato field lying fallow, the terrain appeared suitable for the purpose, as it was located on a rise, at a higher elevation than the surrounding land, but the access to Hamburg and its port was admittedly poor for Hagenbeck's needs. So he formed a consortium with local investors and, over time, bought up literally every tract of land in a more or less direct line between his property in Stellingen and the city limit of Hamburg, two kilometers away. Their immediate goal was to create a direct connection, a broad cobblestone road for wagon and pedestrian traffic lined on each side

with trees and benches.[34] (When the *Tierpark* opened, in May 1907, people came by foot. Within a few months, however, the road to Hamburg—then called Kaiser Friedrich Strasse—would be outfitted with electric streetcar tracks. Three different lines made scheduled stops at the park's main entrance, offering mass transit to and from various suburbs of Hamburg.) Privately, Hagenbeck went on to acquire all the lots that were immediately adjacent to his estate, which eventually permitted the zoo's expansion to a total of eighty acres.

4.5 The Stellingen estate that Hagenbeck (*standing, at far right*) purchased in 1897. He and his family soon moved into the villa (*pictured here*), to live on the park's grounds. Courtesy of Tierpark Carl Hagenbeck GmbH, Hamburg-Stellingen.

It took more than a year to negotiate so many deals, and the process of acquiring permits and moving the entire operation from Hamburg to Stellingen would add even more preparation time. By the end of 1901, visitors were allowed on the premises. Some of the animals were already being kept there; others would soon be moved from Hamburg to Stellingen. The collection, though somewhat dispersed, was reportedly worth seeing. Charles Peel, the Victorian big-game hunter and travel writer who went there in 1902, described Hagenbeck's collection in his guide to Europe's zoos as containing "the largest stock of live animals in the world. The value of his animals is greater than the value of the animals in any one Zoological Garden in Europe." Visitors could also tour the site of Hagenbeck's new park, as had Peel, and later watch the new terrain take shape. "An enormous task lay before us," wrote Hagenbeck: "To transform a wasteland into a luxury park, a pleasure park with waterfalls and mountain formations, with practical animal shelters and buildings devoted to pure leisure." A team of workers broke ground in October 1902.[35]

From the active modeling of the land, to the planting of tropical flora, to the construction of artificial rockwork, the project at Stellingen called for radical transformation of the local environment. "In order to be able to make changes in the landscape alone, no less than 40,000 cubic meters of earth had to be moved. When the work began, it was a wide, open field with all of six trees on it. A small staff of artists, engineers, architects, landscape gardeners, and laborers set to work, and the place soon resembled a scene from Aladdin's stories of wonder. I saw the work grow and come into being," Hagenbeck enthused, "I saw one plan after another mature and take shape. Little by little, the ideas which I had long kept and fostered (*gehegt*) inside of me began to appear before my very eyes." A reporter, who visited the construction site in spring of 1903, marveled at the "chaotic confusion" of activity surrounding him. "Manual laborers of all branches—masons, carpenters, joiners, mechanics, and others—are scattered by the dozen all over the place." The process of shaping and preparing the ground was still underway. "The vast expanse is covered by a network of field tracks, on whose rails one wagon after the next rolls by, each loaded high with dirt. The excavated earth is thus transported . . . a distance of several hundred of meters, where it is used to form a mountain elevation. There, since much of the dirt is heavy clay, it must be mixed with lighter soil types, in order to make it suitable for cultivation." Planting began shortly thereafter.[36]

When it came to the selection and arrangement of plantings, the task was to create a variegated, wild-looking landscape suggesting a variety of foreign regions according to the individual exhibit. Once mature, the gardens became an attraction in their own right, but their original purpose was to serve in the display of animal life. They did so in various ways: some being common to garden design generally, for example, by framing scenic vistas, and by screening enclosures and potential obtrusions, others being unique to the *Tierpark*, above all, by camouflaging and thus naturalizing the requisite barriers for large wild-animal exhibits. Less obvious was the way in which flora helped open up the possibility for immersive effects by enhancing the viewer's sense of shared space. Like the *faux terrain* in painted panoramas, "it came up close to the spectators" (to borrow a phrase from Oliver Grau), appealing to their sense of touch, while slowly but literally spreading into the display space. Yet the plant life here is perhaps most important for another reason, namely, its role in apparently naturalizing the use of constructed sets that distinguished Hagenbeck's park.[37]

The evocative mix of "tropical" and tropical plants is significant for what it says about the nature of the living habitat in Hagenbeck's new park. On one level, it confirms the habitat's need to thrive. On another level, the strategic mixing of foreign and foreign-looking plants anticipates the function of artificial rockwork and landscaping more generally, which is: to create an exotic mood and a convincing expression of foreign space. Accuracy was beside the point; here, as in the Wild West show, the depicted scene had to look "authentic enough."[38] From the beginning, atmosphere was emphasized over topography. The task was to create an evocative, romantic landscape, which viewers could imagine as a natural environment for what was, practically speaking, an ever-changing diversity of animals on display.

4.6 The main cliff formation under construction, 4 October 1905. When the park first opened, in 1907, the depicted set was called the "High-Mountain Landscape." Courtesy of Tierpark Carl Hagenbeck GmbH, Hamburg-Stellingen.

The key step in the process of making the park was the construction of animal panoramas with artificial rockwork. Here, the painted backdrop of conventional panoramas fell away completely, to be replaced throughout by a rather intricate combination of real and *faux terrain*. In October 1904, Moritz Lehmann and the architect Johannes Wald filed for permission to construct a series of barless enclosures, beginning with what they called a "predators' panorama." Such an unprecedented request was met by local authorities with due concern. The police solicited recommendations from the fire chief, the building inspector, and the district veterinarian—each declared himself to be unqualified for the job. Hagenbeck's long-time clients came to his assistance. Heinrich Bolau, director of Hamburg's Zoological Garden, submitted a positive recommendation based on his experience of the Arctic Sea Panorama in 1896; as did Ludwig Heck, who cited the Animal Panorama of 1898, which appeared in Berlin's zoo. Heck would later criticize the park for its blatant theatricality, as we shall see, but not before his testimony helped clear the way for the construction of the park's main attraction. A building permit was issued within the year.[39]

The central exhibits—stationary panoramas composed of plantings and artificial rockwork—were designed by the Swiss sculptor Urs Eggenschwyler and implemented by a team of local masons. The main cliff formation, or "High-Mountain Landscape," offers only the most conspicuous example. At nearly forty meters high, the grouping was so prominent that visitors could see it from a distance as they approached Stellingen. In this context, the sculptor's raw materials included wood, wire mesh, cement, granite, and paint. The physical shape of each formation was cast as a plaster model. The interior scaffolding was originally made of wood poles and timber, which was built up over a foundation of brick pillars, then covered in wire mesh, coated with cement, and treated finally with a weather-proofing sealant. Thus, the set was bolstered as needed for continued outdoor exhibition. In addition to creating a scenic landscape, the main cliff formation served to conceal animal shelters, service entrances, plumbing and heating pipes, even an electric motor (which powered a waterfall). It also held a pedestrian path with stairs that wound up and around the side of the mountain, leading to an observation deck. There, visitors could gain a bird's-eye view of the park and its surroundings (see fig. 4.7).[40]

In addition to the sculpted terrain, a number of immense granite blocks and boulders, some of them weighing more than two tons each, were integrated into some of the sets. The rocks had been reclaimed from old seawalls in Hamburg's port. From there, they were transported to Stellingen and placed in certain exhibits by a group of worker elephants and their Sri Lankan drivers, who were also professional *Völkerschau* performers (fig. 4.8). Some of these blocks were presumably used in the new, stationary version of the Arctic Sea Panorama, where they would be integrated with the artificial rockwork, and coated with white paint, to resemble mounds of pack ice (fig. 4.9). This mix of actual, artificial, and reclaimed rockwork typified the composite nature of Hagenbeck's sets. The diversity of materials also gives some indication of the labor and the many workers that were necessary for the zoo's construction—the traces of which would mostly be camouflaged before opening day.[41]

By contrast, the work of individual artists such as Eggenschwyler was touted in press releases, newspapers interviews, and commemorative brochures. Indeed, the

4.7 View from atop the main cliff formation, ca. 1906. The main gate, still under construction, is at far left. Running diagonally from left to right is the road that was built to link Stellingen and Hamburg, which is just visible on the horizon. Courtesy of Tierpark Carl Hagenbeck GmbH, Hamburg-Stellingen.

4.8 Worker elephants and their drivers haul boulders through the park, ca. 1903–5. Photo courtesy of Tierpark Carl Hagenbeck GmbH, Hamburg-Stellingen.

conspicuous role of artists was announced to visitors, from the moment of their arrival, by the park's grand entrance (see fig. 3.5). As noted in the first guidebook, the theater painter Lehmann designed the gate's stage-like composition, and the individual

4.9 Painting the icebergs, shortly before opening day. Courtesy of Tierpark Carl Hagenbeck GmbH, Hamburg-Stellingen.

figures were created by two young sculptors—the animals by Josef Franz Pallenberg, who trained in Cologne, and the native warriors by Rudolf Franke, who studied with the eminent sculptor Reinhold Begas at the Berlin Academy. The guidebook even describes plans for an (unrealized) sculpture garden, which would link the gate to the zoo's main restaurant: a magnificent promenade to be "lined on both sides with individuals and groupings of outstanding animal and ethnographic types, giving artists an opportunity to display and sell their work." Promoting the work of artists was obviously a self-serving strategy, claiming for the park an explicitly cultural pedigree, while identifying Hagenbeck as a patron of the arts. On another level, however, and even though the sculpture garden was never realized, the central role of sculptors could be felt throughout the entire park.[42]

Other scholars have noted the involvement of artists and architects in the park's construction as a general point of interest, without applying analytical pressure or considering the implications of this observation. Yet the role of sculptors in the park is fascinating, because it brings out the sculptural dimension of theme space that would be further elaborated in the twentieth century (via theme parks and film sets, for example). While theme space is arguably more dynamic and ephemeral than sculpture, they share a certain relationship to physical space that needs to be highlighted. That is to say, in a manner that is analogous to sculpture, the *Tierpark* occupied a site, it took up physical space, it moved earth around, and it changed the local environment. Instead of merely opening up a vista for the spectator to look at, the *Tierpark* literally carved out a space for spectators to enter with their bodies. The exhibits were thus immersive and tactile in ways that distinguished the park from the nineteenth-century zoological garden—and linked it, suggestively, to other immersive environments. The *Tierpark* and its signal exhibits artistically embodied a physical and haptic space that was, at the same time, a fantasyland of exotic adventure for visitors to explore with their senses as well as with their imagination.[43]

The Park as "Panorama"

Originally, Hagenbeck's *Tierpark* in Stellingen was also known by another name: *Das Panorama*. The term in this context had several different uses and meanings. In the narrowest sense, it designated individual exhibits such as the "Arctic Sea Panorama," a stationary version of the traveling show already discussed at length. In the widest sense, it referred to the park as a whole. Initially, moreover, the park was identified, received, and celebrated as such in the press. "Hagenbeck calls the entire place his panorama," a reporter noted in 1906, "and he claims with justified pride that there isn't another one like it in the world." Other scholars have written about some of the zoo exhibits as panoramas in the narrowest sense, without situating them within the larger history of panoramic art. Conversely, the only historian of the panorama to mention Hagenbeck's work, Stephan Oettermann, cites the itinerant version of the Arctic Sea Panorama, but the fullest expression of Hagenbeck's idea—his interesting notion of the park as panorama—has gone unobserved. The *Tierpark* represents a forgotten contribution to the history of panoramic art. At the same time, however, it also made a major and enduring contribution to the history of theme space and immersive environments by pushing the idea of the panorama beyond its conventional (and characteristically unseen) boundaries.[44]

The image of the park as panorama is perhaps best illustrated by the maps and guidebooks that were sold to visitors at the entrance of the park. The self-guided tour (in German, *Rundgang*) of the park, which is described at length in the main section of the guidebook, begins with a sweeping description of "The Panorama." In this usage, "panorama" refers to the park in its entirety and also to a way of seeing it as such, a mode of vision that embraces the park's grounds and its many attractions as one. Positioning the newcomer before the first exhibit (number 1 on the corresponding map, see plate 10), the guidebook surveys the scene:

> a magnificent panorama unrolls before our eyes, one which, in its idea as well as in its execution, deserves to be called an artwork of the highest order—Hagenbeck's Animal Paradise—one which gathers the earth of all zones and regions, together with their characteristic animal inhabitants, and brings them to living representation, all in one place. To the right, first, the great pond with its tropical and subtropical Aquatic Birds; immediately behind them, in a great clearing, the colorful lot of Hay Eaters which live in all longitudes and latitudes of the entire earth; and behind them, in turn, the Lion's Ravine, with its numerous inhabitants, while mighty vultures perch in cliff caves above. Rising in the background, the steep cliff walls of the High-Mountain Ridge, on whose dizzying heights ibex and wild sheep perform the daring art of climbing with the greatest of ease. To the left, the Northern Landscape with the Arctic Sea Panorama brings to a close this delightful animal paradise.[45]

What begins as a simple analogy (the park as painting, as artwork, as moving panorama that "unrolls before our eyes") leads directly to the related notion of the panorama as a form of synthesis: a gathering of things from across an area too vast to be perceived at once. Although this use of the term is more commonly found in newspapers and literature, where it is used metaphorically, here it is meant quite literally. Unlike other entertainments going by the name panorama, the *Tierpark* actually takes living things from disparate places, physically brings them to the observer, and arranges them to be seen. Its overarching claim to aesthetic value rests on the fact of physical presence and on the particular way in which the natural world has been collected, organized, and displayed as one. Hagenbeck's special use of the panorama—as the basic unit of display, as a way of seeing the entire park, as a mode of synthesizing the many zones of the earth, all at the same time—was noticed at the time by members of the scientific establishment, including the director of Frankfurt's zoo, Kurt Priemel, who also identified its innovation. "What is new," he admitted, as part of a larger argument that Hagenbeck's *Tierpark* should not be confused with a zoological garden, "is the combination of many different more or less naturalistic enclosures to form a single, unified panorama."[46]

Indeed, the entire park can be accurately described as an outdoor super-panorama, combining multiple smaller panoramic exhibits that were spatially arranged in relationship to one another. The most complex section of the larger panorama was the cascading series of open-air exhibits located in the center of the park (plate 10, numbers 1 through 10 and number 34), which culminated visually in the main cliff structure, the "High-Mountain Ridge." A hyperbolic exercise in deep-staging—and thus, a further extension of Hagenbeck's patent idea—each enclosure at once framed and appeared as a constituent part of the enclosure that was behind and raised above it, creating the impression of a single, expanding view, whose continuity effect was enhanced by the strategic use of elevation, rockwork, and gardening. "In the same way," the guidebook continues, "the many winding paths *through* the panorama are arranged so that they and the audience remain hidden from sight, without disturbing the overall picture of the panorama." The *Tierpark* created a unique type of panoramic space that viewers could physically enter and traverse, allowing for closer looks at some of its component parts as well as for wider vistas of the surrounding area. There was no regular oscillation between overview and scene, but there was unprecedented emphasis on having multiple, spatially distinct vantage points (as opposed to the single, centralized viewing platform of an orthodox indoor panorama), with special emphasis on designing unexpected views by means of rockwork as well as landscaping. As we have seen, there were peaks, dens, and winding pathways; there were tunnels and trails leading spectators into the *faux terrain*; and there were various perches, high above, where spectators could take in a wider view. Similarly, the entire park could be regarded as one enormous panorama, or as a series of interrelated exhibits, or as a set of individual attractions, depending on one's approach. Allowing the animals to be seen from various levels and distances enhanced the visitor's sense of being immersed in the larger panorama, which was the park in its entirety, while providing ample opportunities to experience a diversity of animal behaviors.[47]

At the same time, however, there was an interesting difference between the park as panorama and its nineteenth-century namesake. Unlike the painted panorama, which was a hermetically sealed space devoted to maintaining a pictorial illusion of reality, Hagenbeck's *Tierpark* invited the viewer—at certain strategic locations throughout the park—to look away from the exhibits and notice the difference between representation and reality. Indeed, this bifurcated view is emphasized from the very beginning, in the guidebook's description of the park's strange terrain as it appears from outside of the main gate. "In the background," that is, on the other side of the gate, and simultaneously framed by it, "gigantic cliff structures rise up from the park's welcoming landscape, and give the park a foreign quality also in terms of scenery, so that the park in its entirety conjures up the impression of a high-mountain oasis in the middle of the surrounding, uniform, north German flatland." As the tour continues, the perspective is occasionally turned around, and the audience is invited to scan the horizon of this north German flatland from an elevated position within the park. Rather than conceal every glimpse of the outside world, as a painted panorama would do, the park created a number of vistas and observation decks whose function was to frame and thereby emphasize a spectacle of adjacent and contrasting spaces. At various points along the self-guided tour, visitors were invited to climb stairs that wound up into the rockwork, ascend to viewing platforms within the *faux terrain*, high above the animals, and admire the scenic beauty of such juxtapositions between the strange landscape

4.10 "Paradise." This photo from ca. 1908 shows a receding series of outdoor panoramas leading up to the "High-Mountain Landscape." Courtesy of Tierpark Carl Hagenbeck GmbH, Hamburg-Stellingen.

on the inside of the park and the more familiar surroundings outside of it. Where else in the history of panoramic art were spectators encouraged to compare and contrast the depicted space with the surrounding environment?[48]

Here was a panorama that displayed a surprisingly ambivalent relationship to the referential world. On the one side, the *Tierpark* emphasized its separateness from reality, comparing itself to fantasylands of imaginative fiction (such as *Gulliver's Travels*), even presenting itself as a unique sort of diegetic universe, which the spectator could actually enter and explore. On the other side, the park also highlighted certain visible connections to the surrounding countryside, almost as if to smooth over the physical boundary that marked the park's outer edge. What emerges from this material, however, is not so much an internal contradiction as the interesting impossibility of separateness in the context of open-air displays and park-like settings, where spectators had extraordinary mobility and the power exerted by the panoramist over the audience was relatively limited (as compared to the situation in a rotunda, where the panoramist had tremendous active control over the viewer's sensory input). This is not to suggest that Hagenbeck fostered a critical awareness of the difference between representation and reality—that, in revising the panorama as a medium, the park also increased the spectator's critical distance from what was on exhibit. On the contrary, the *Tierpark* asked its visitors to willingly suspend their disbelief and explore a space of possibility or impossibility, which just as easily conflated reality and fantasy as it pointed to their spectacularized juxtaposition.

The theme of "paradise" offers a good example. After all, the first guidebook identified the grounds not only as "The Panorama," but also, more specifically, as "Hagenbeck's Animal Paradise." The entire park, in other words, could be seen as the stationary version of the paradise panoramas that Hagenbeck took to Milan, Berlin, and St. Louis. In using this conceit, he and his publicists also invoked the tradition of the great botanical gardens of the sixteenth and seventeenth centuries. These gardens, as John Prest has shown, were interpreted by their contemporaries in the context of a re-creation of earthly paradise. If Eden could not be discovered East or West, then it would be re-created by means of collecting, gathering together specimens of plants from around the world, and cultivating them in one place. The form the botanical garden took was that of an encyclopedia, a "book" laid out in pages. The focus on plants and the exclusion of animals was significant, according to Prest. "The ideal of peace among animals," though one of Eden's most striking features, "has remained the preserve of poets and visionaries." In other words, "it was always much easier to think in terms of recreating the vegetable side of the original Garden of Eden, than it was to think of the animal."[49]

The recovery of Eden was also a context in which Hagenbeck and his contemporaries interpreted the *Tierpark*, when it first opened in 1907. One commentator compared it to Lucas Cranach's well-known painting of *Adam and Eve*. Others described the park as a second Creation. "The Lord God is known to have closed the Garden of Eden to the public forever, but Herr Carl Hagenbeck created it anew. Today, from a zoological viewpoint, we no longer need envy Adam and Eve." As I have suggested, the notion of paradise was not at odds with the geographical zone or habitat; on the contrary, it represented the up-gathering vision of all zones as one. Whereas individual exhibits referenced the geographical world (however generally), the park as a whole referred back, if you will, to the original habitat. Here, once again, there were multiple frames of reference, whose priority depended upon the viewing positions that visitors chose to occupy as they strolled throughout the park.[50]

The Treatment of Place

Such emollient visions of paradise have, understandably, led some historians to question Hagenbeck's commitment to scenic realism, arguing that, when it comes to geography, at least, the *Tierpark* cannot be seen as a blueprint for zoos of the twentieth century. The paradise theme in particular has been singled out and interpreted as undercutting the idea of the *Tierpark* as a forerunner of the "habitat zoo," which remains an important baseline for practice in the early twenty-first century. In the words of one scholar, "Zoos have not seen their task as that of exhibiting animals in fantasy landscapes since the opening of the *Tierpark* in Stellingen." It is important to add, however, that the same observation could also be made of the *Tierpark* itself. In many ways, the park's treatment of place changed over time, and what was "there" in the beginning was anything but fixed or permanent. However, to dismiss the emergence of fantasy as aberrant within a normative history of zoo design is to miss the larger point. Theme space was designed to accommodate a diversity of spaces, real and imagined, and spectators were encouraged to explore them all. Indeed, the *Tierpark* created many different places within a single place, according to its existing diversity of offerings or merchandise (much as Disneyland would later). As a result, it developed a remarkably loose and malleable relationship to geography. The park was built on shifting ground. Its original openness to imaginary horizons distinguished the *Tierpark* from zoological gardens and aligned it more closely with the kind of "creative geography" that was being pioneered in the cinema and would later inform the Disney theme parks, as well.[51]

The selection of settings for the park's central exhibits was primarily governed by a principle of visual potency. In 1905, for example, construction on the main exhibits had just begun when Hagenbeck's new assistant and the park's resident biologist, Alexander Sokolowsky, proposed the idea of adding a mud-flat enclosure, whose purpose would be to educate spectators about the biological diversity of species and behaviors particular to such an environment. Hagenbeck demurred. Though the suggestion was consonant with the habitat idea, a mud-flat enclosure would hardly draw a crowd. In the creation of natural settings, moreover, the chief concern was not specific referentiality. The "Northland Landscape" admittedly had "penguins from the South Pole." At the same time, however mixed or inaccurate the exhibits might have been, they maintained the idea that the animals on exhibit trailed their referential ties behind them. For example, in the "Hay Eaters" (*Heufresser*) enclosure, the 1907 guidebook points out that "a truly international society of hay and grass-eating hoofed animals has been thrown together," including (at the time of printing) specimens from Africa, Borneo, Corsica, Europe, India, Peru, Sardinia, Sumatra, and Tibet. Even a fantasy space such as "paradise" was referential on some level—a point that this list of represented continents and nation-states makes abundantly clear.[52]

ZOOGEOGRAPHY

Historians have rightly emphasized the terms "habitat" and "geography" in the context of Hagenbeck's park, but interpreted them—erroneously, I think—within the context of zoological gardens. This approach works backward from zoos built later in the twentieth century, zoos that were explicitly planned and organized around specific habitats or continents (often citing Hagenbeck as forerunner of this approach), and seeks to find continuities with the original park in Stellingen. The technical term for this discussion is zoogeography (*Tiergeographie*) or, the study of the origins and interrelations of animal groups as they are distributed around the entire globe. Its basic category is the region (*Gebiet*) or zone, a theoretical entity that is created around the distribution of different species. Zoos that are built on this scientific principle tend to have exhibits representing specific regions, populated with animals that are characteristic of each. Historians refer to this practice both when they claim that Hagenbeck pointed the way to zoogeography and when they dispute that thesis. For example, according to Lothar Dittrich and Annelore Rieke-Müller, Hagenbeck's landscapes "were not committed to strict zoogeographical viewpoints." Elizabeth Hanson offers a similar corrective. "Although Hagenbeck's park, in retrospect, has been labeled a harbinger of zoogeographically organized zoos," she writes, "it was not planned as such."[53] I join these scholars in emphasizing the significance of geography, and I agree with them on one point: namely, Hagenbeck improvised and experimented with exhibit designs. But I object to a history that situates the park within a teleology of the zoo. The inspiring ideas and organizing principles of the *Tierpark* were already available to Hagenbeck at the time, albeit in a different context.

By 1907, the idea of zoogeography had yet to make inroads in zoological gardens, but it had been firmly established in natural history collections and geographical atlases. In that context, the key source was Alfred Russel Wallace's study, *The Geographical Distribution of Animals* (Die geographische Verbreitung der Thiere, 1876). In addition to serving as a veritable handbook for zoogeographic collections, it established a visual iconography and compositional principles for zoological illustration, as evidenced by the work of the German draftsman Johann Baptist Zwecker. The illustrations in this volume show idyllic scenes featuring groups of different animals, each characteristic of the region, and set within a "natural" yet equally representative landscape (see fig. 4.11). If this example seems familiar, it is because the mode of illustration that zoogeography promoted was directly related to what the animal painter Heinrich Leutemann called "zone pictures," which in turn provided the pictorial basis for Hagenbeck's "living habitat" (as shown in chapter 2).

The link between Hagenbeck's work and the natural history museum is perhaps even more striking. In the German context of such museums, we find a wide-scale preference for open displays—groups of objects and figures that are not behind glass—and *faux terrain*, as Susanne Köstering has recently demonstrated. Hagenbeck might have been oblivious to the specific tenets of zoogeography, as other scholars have suggested, but he probably visited some of these museums, such as the one in Hamburg-

4.11 "Characteristic Animals of East Africa." Illustration by the German artist J. B. Zwecker, plate 4 of Alfred Russel Wallace, *The Geographical Distribution of Animals*, vol. 1 (New York: Harper and Brothers, 1876).

PLATE IV.

CHARACTERISTIC ANIMALS OF EAST AFRICA.

Altona (est. 1901), where the concept of zoogeography was visually demonstrated and described in terms of "life pictures" (*Lebensbilder*). Even a cursory glance at zoogeographical groups from natural history museums of the period confirms that Hagenbeck's park was part of a broad, ongoing movement in the late nineteenth century. As I have argued, Hagenbeck made *the* major contribution to the German practice of habitat display, by introducing his ethnographic exhibition in 1874. The park in Stellingen created a series of living zone pictures, with a new and variable focus on wildlife, and distributed them spatially throughout the park.[54]

The key figure here is Hagenbeck's first scientific assistant, Alexander Sokolowsky. As a boy, growing up in Hamburg, he was an avid collector of "creatures" and thus a frequent customer of Umlauff's *Weltmuseum* and Christiane Hagenbeck's exotic bird shop; he visited Carl Hagenbeck's menagerie so many times that Hagenbeck stopped charging him an entrance fee. Sokolowsky began studying zoology at the University of Jena with Ernst Haeckel, where, inspired by his mentor, he also honed his skills in zoological illustration and painting. Continuing his studies at the Berlin University, he worked with the zoologist Karl Möbius, director of the Zoological Museum, where Sokolowsky also worked in one of the collections.[55] For two and a half years, he served as an unpaid assistant to Ludwig Heck at Berlin's Zoological Garden. In 1904, when he was overlooked for a new paid position, he returned to his home town of Hamburg. In Sokolowsky's return, Hagenbeck saw an opportunity: Here was yet another experienced museum person cast off by an official Berlin cultural institution, in a situation comparable to that of Jacobsen, the amateur collector who had once worked for the Royal Museum of Ethnology. Even better, Sokolowsky was highly educated and experienced in scientific writing as well as in museum work.[56]

Sokolowsky's duties at the park were various and not restricted to zoology. Actually, they were quite similar to the duties that the animal painter, Leutemann, had once performed as Hagenbeck's first adviser. Above all, Sokolowsky became Hagenbeck's mouthpiece in the press, a sort of zoological publicist, charged with shaping the park's scientific and popular perception. He probably assisted in designing particular exhibits during the final stages of construction, as well. In each of these ways, he framed Hagenbeck's work in terms of both art and science, as Leutemann had earlier in the context of ethnography. Sokolowsky even drew upon the same visual model as his predecessor—the zone picture.

His first statement as Hagenbeck's new publicity man was published in 1905, while the park was still under construction. In it, Sokolowsky offers a two-tiered rationale for abandoning the zoological garden as a model and embracing Hagenbeck's *Tierpark*, instead. The two levels of his argumentation are, logically, science and art. On one level, he describes both Hagenbeck's itinerant Arctic panoramas of the 1890s and the new exhibits at Stellingen as "zoogeographical zone pictures." The park might not have been planned in terms of zoogeography, but it was explicitly described as such by Hagenbeck's publicist from the start. In so doing, Sokolowsky represents the *Tierpark* and its method of displaying wild animals as accomplishing for the zoological garden the biological turn that had already taken place in the natural sciences, and he explicitly compares the park to the natural history museums in Berlin and Hamburg. On another level, that of art, he shrewdly appeals to public criticism of zoological gardens, giving voice to the popular preference for seeing animals in natural settings (as opposed to cages), and thus ratcheting up the pressure on zoo directors such as Heck. "Art has a special interest in the keeping of wild animals in an environment that is as free as possible, one which corresponds as closely as possible to their native habitat." At stake here is the very cultural status of the zoological garden, which Sokolowsky openly challenges. "Instead of building stylistically correct stone palaces, the value of such rational housing being dubious if the animals are supposed to thrive, from now on the task would be to construct grotto-like enclosures and dwelling spaces, whose total composition must be taken as much as possible from the animal's natural habitat."[57]

In providing Hagenbeck with discursive backup, Sokolowsky offered a variety of arguments that, in retrospect, highlight the park's circularity. Its full-scale representations of natural settings were based on existing images of representative habitats, drawn from geographical handbooks, natural history museums, landscape gardens, even mythical iconography, and integrated with Hagenbeck's version of the panorama and panoramic vision. As a new form of living habitat, the *Tierpark* also drew upon the *Völkerschau*, which in turn was based on the zone picture, and so on. Such representational circularity, though dizzying, is useful nevertheless because it creates a context for understanding the role of habitat display in the park, without having to make (or refute) a teleological argument about zoo history.

GEOGRAPHICAL ALIGNMENT

Over time, the park would take steps to ground its animal displays more firmly in geography by adding new exhibits and modifying old ones. Never again would it claim to depict paradise or other mythological *topoi*. When the "South Pole Panorama," for example, opened in 1911, the guidebook emphasized the exhibit's devotion to authenticity in at least three ways: by means of technology, imagery, and affiliation.

> The designs for the South Pole Panorama were made by Mr. Heinrich Umlauff, using motifs from the wealth of photographic material brought home from South Georgia [an island in the South Atlantic Ocean, near the Antarctic Peninsula] by the latest expedition of the Hagenbeck Company. These photographs, highly inter-

esting sceneries and recordings of the animal life in these far-flung regions, will also be projected by a sciopticon in the cliff tunnel that we go through as we exit, and they can be viewed for a small fee.

The use of visual media—namely, the sciopticon, a form of magic-lantern projection—is interesting in this context, because it provides a degree of technological support or infrastructure for the construction of open enclosures, not unlike the pipes and scaffolding beneath the larger display. At the same time, the lantern slides redouble the exhibit's claim to authenticity, while continuing in the aesthetic tradition of set design. That this particular set was designed by Umlauff, owner of a local ethnographic museum and artistic director of the *Völkerschau* area of Hagenbeck's park, was highlighted by the latest issue of the guidebook, much as Eggenschwyler and other artists were featured in the first brochures.[58]

The push toward geographical organization and authenticity extended beyond this one exhibit, as illustrated by the blueprint for "Carl Hagenbeck's *Tierpark* in Berlin," a high-profile campaign launched in 1911. Rather than simply reproduce the panoramic design of Stellingen, the plan called for organizing the new site and its exhibits according to continents. The project would be abandoned, however, shortly before Hagenbeck's death. Perhaps the most significant evidence, then, is the emergence of the "Africa Panorama" in Stellingen. In this case, there was no new planning or construction involved. Rather, the transformation was semiotic in nature. No later than 1927, the "Hoofed-Animal or Hay Eaters" enclosure was simply renamed the "African Steppes," with the animals now coming from that continent exclusively, and the larger series of nested panoramas to which this enclosure belongs has since become known as the "Africa Panorama." The rezoning project would be overseen by Hagenbeck's eldest son, Heinrich, who went on to become a first-rate designer whose expertise was sought after by zoos in the United States and around the world.[59]

While there is solid evidence of geographical realignment, the historical point here is one of divergence and multiplicity. Later, under new management, the park would aspire to become a respectable zoological garden. Initially, however, it tested the limits of its enclosure and self-sufficiency, developing its aesthetic potential as both a park and a panorama (as opposed to a garden-variety zoo). Hagenbeck's park was originally a complex of geographical and imaginary places, which visitors were invited to visit and explore in a variety of ways. It sought to encompass everything from Eden to the South Pole in the same field of vision. Whereas animal displays in the zoological garden referred to taxonomic systems and found meaning in scientific discourses, at Hagenbeck's park they referred to places of origin. They also carried meaning within themselves.

Hagenbeck's park distinguished itself from nineteenth-century zoological gardens not simply by its interest in geographical space, but also by its coordinated effort to create an imaginary universe that visitors could inhabit (albeit momentarily) in the presence of wild animals. Open enclosures and natural settings invited the free play of the spectator's imagination. That is what made these exhibits so attractive at the time, and that is what gave them staying power. The park's artful combination of physical bodies and fantasy spaces was singularly alluring. To offer such divergent spaces, to permit such experiences of adventure, and to do so by combining live animals with the latest display technologies, was to create an exciting alternative to the zoological garden, while at the same time expanding the zoological imagination and immersing the spectator's mind and body in a mythical world of exotic adventure.

The Amusement Park Sublime

In terms of its offerings and the kinds of visceral experiences that it promised, Hagenbeck's park had more in common with amusement parks such as those at Coney Island than it had with zoological gardens from the period. With its stated devotion to "pure leisure" and its operative mode of controlled risk, the *Tierpark* also harkened back to Vauxhall Gardens and earlier pleasure parks, but the link to Coney Island was direct and contemporaneous. Beginning in 1894, Hagenbeck sponsored a series of trained-animal acts first at Manhattan Beach and later at Luna Park.[60] As different versions of the mixed-species group, these shows complemented one another in terms of tone. One of them, "Carl Hagenbeck's Animal Kindergarten," was a so-called happy family show, with the youngest trained animals playing together in the most unlikely of groups. Another was "Hagenbeck's Wild Animal Show," a cabinet piece of gentle training—it originally featured the trainers and groups from the Chicago world's fair—whose advertising, however, lured customers by subverting the ethos of that method, reverting back to the older iconography of man-eating predators and death-defying trainers, instead (see plate 11). By all accounts, it was a popular and profitable show, giving some indication as to its staying power at Coney. "To say that the performances were thrilling and sensational but half expresses it," according to one reviewer. "They had all of those qualities, and then went beyond anything that one can imagine before seeing them."[61]

When Luna Park first opened, in 1903, "Hagenbeck's Trained Animals" had a prime location on Surf Avenue, in an area called the Court of Honor. There, it was billed as one of "Thirty-Nine Supreme, Stupendous, Spectacular, Sensational Shows! By day a Paradise—at night Arcadia!" Flanked by such attractions as A Trip to the North Pole, The Dragon's Gorge, The Streets of Delhi, Shoot the Chutes, Twenty Thousand Leagues under the Sea, a Chinese Theater, the Helter Skelter bamboo slide, and The Eskimo Village (where Nancy Columbia and her family worked), Hagenbeck's Wild Animal Show contributed to the park's overarching aspirations: its original emphasis on theatricality and participation, its profusion of exotic attractions, its insistent otherworldliness, and its related appeal to visitors' imaginations.

The *Tierpark* in Stellingen would initially follow in the tradition of the enclosed amusement park, operating on a similar dynamic of pleasurable relaxation and wild adventure. This dynamic is significant because it marks a further distinction of the *Tierpark* from the zoological garden. In that context, the practice of spectatorship tended to vacillate between knowledge (as demonstrated by the taxonomic systems of arrangement and display) and leisure (as grounded in the use of landscape gardening to link the various buildings). Even when the *Tierpark* made claims to science and education—through the mouthpiece of Sokolowsky, for example—these claims did not serve to organize the historical experience of spectatorship. What moved spectators to visit the park, and what moved them within the park, as they circulated among its various exhibits, was the alternating promise of sensory immersion and imaginary adventure. Much of this genealogy would be eschewed after Hagenbeck's death, when the park was effectively reinvented as a zoo. Yet its role in the culture of modern amusements becomes even more evident if we look at the ways in which Hagenbeck's park invited visitors to experience and interact with the displays, the full-bodied mode of spectatorship that the park at once created and regulated to some degree.[62]

THE THRILLS OF SPECTATORSHIP

At the "Northern Landscape," for example, visitors who paid an extra fee of 10 Pfennig could enter "a wide, roomy tunnel," and climb a stairway that led to an elevated viewing platform called the "Northern Plateau." From this perspective, which was located directly above the Arctic Sea Panorama, viewers could look down, directly below them, and see the seals and polar bears from above, or they could look outward, along a horizontal axis, extending their gaze over the surrounding park. Here was another instance of the oscillation between scene and overview that was a central feature of spectatorship in Hagenbeck's park. (In plate 12, for example, several people are visible just below the massive rock at the top of the exhibit; the entrance to the mountain was located on a path that led around the exhibit and behind it, to the left.) In this instance, however, it is reasonable to assume that most people who paid extra wanted more than another point of view; they wanted a ride. From the platform, that is, spectators had the option of either walking back down the stairway or descending what one reporter called "a Canadian tobogganing slide," a steep-looking chute that extended from the top of the rockwork to the main path below. Built into the side of the artificial rockwork or ice floes of the Northern Landscape, the slide rapidly funneled spectators through a walled passage between the polar bears, on the one side, and the caribou, on the other. There were other stations throughout the park where animals (including camels, llamas, zebras, elephants, ostriches, and giant tortoises) doubled as rides for children, in particular. The toboggan slide is interesting, however, not only because it was made for adults as well as for children, but also—more important—because it was literally an in-built part of the original panorama's design and implementation. An integral piece of the park's theme space, it demonstrates a striking parallel to the physical jostling of bodies and hurtling through space that is more typically associated with amusement parks of this period.[63]

Perhaps the park's greatest sensation could be had at the edge of the open enclosure. This was especially true of the Predators' Ravine (or *Raubtierschlucht*, as it was called in German). As its name suggests, the exhibit originally assembled a mixed group of big cats—lions and tigers—in the same space of display. In order for the different species to coexist within a relatively small area, some degree of training was absolutely necessary. (Even so, this arrangement would not last for long, due to fighting among the different species, resulting in the removal of the tigers and the renaming of the exhibit as, simply, the "Lions' Ravine.") There is an intimation of the need for training in a flattering review, published shortly before the park's official opening, in which a British journalist noted of this exhibit: "It is only right to add, perhaps, that all these beasts are tamed animals; that is to say, they are accustomed to the presence of their keeper, who can move freely in and out among them." Generally speaking, however, visitors were not informed of this idea. Instead, signs and guidebooks focused their attention elsewhere.[64]

At the Predators' Ravine, and throughout the park, the thrills of spectatorship played out along the threshold of display as an effect of shared space (see fig. 4.12). A 1906 newspaper advertisement highlighted, "In the Predators' Ravine there are currently 12 lions and 3 tigers in freedom, without bars, separated from the public only by a moat that is 8 meters wide and 5 meters deep." While the mixing of lions and tigers was highly unusual from the perspective of the zoological garden, spectators focused rather on the moat's exact dimensions, which immediately became a source of fascination and anxiety. *Yes, but is that wide enough? How can you be sure? Exactly how far can a full-grown tiger jump? What about the lions? Has one of them ever tried to jump the moat? And what happened then?* As soon as the park opened to the public, "Visitors asked so many questions about this ditch, which is hidden from their view by a narrow strip of garden, that the proprietor has now erected a turnstile, and for a small fee one can pass right to its edge at one corner of the den," wrote one reporter. "The distance from the animals' side of the ditch to the public footpath," he added, "is 30 feet." This policy was also explained in the first guidebook. Turnstiles, safety regulations, posted warning signs—all these devices probably had a double effect, heightening the sense of excitement by calling attention to the potential hazards, creating

4.12 "The Predators' Ravine." Photo from the first *Guide through Carl Hagenbeck's Tierpark in Stellingen* (1907), 5. Courtesy of Tierpark Carl Hagenbeck GmbH, Hamburg-Stellingen.

a certain waiting period and thus a sense of anticipation, while at the same time manipulating the conditions of spectatorship.[65]

Perhaps for this reason advertising posters sometimes resorted to an iconography of violence, exploiting the visitor's fear of a potential attack by sensationalizing it as a melodramatic scene (see, e.g., plate 13). At the open enclosure, fear—whether felt or feigned—was the emotional counterpoint to the panoramic vista and the more placid experience of scenic beauty. What permitted the park to be thrilling, it seems, was the controlled modulation of distance and proximity, risk and safety, destabilization and reassurance. This modulation, which is the deliberate evocation of two simultaneous and contradictory impulses, came to bear directly on the experience of spectatorship, by forcing viewers to decide which stance to take at any given moment, and thus further implicating them in the spectacle and in the emotions it evoked.

For even momentary loss of power or control to seem attractive as an experience, the park had to provide visitors with ample reassurance of their safety. This was certainly one effect of building secure, level walkways around the exhibits. Providing visitors with exact distances of particular trenches and the jumping capabilities of the animals on display was another technique, but one that also had the opposite effect of suggesting false danger. Hagenbeck was obviously cognizant of how visitors responded to the novelty of open enclosures. The thrill of a potential brush with danger stimulated palpable feelings of discomfort and excitement at the same time. In his memoir, he reassured audiences that, despite appearances, the open enclosure actually provided greater security than cages ever did. Designing immersive environments that transformed visual curiosity into spine-tickling thrills, while assuring visitors of their safety again and again, placed Hagenbeck squarely in the laboratory of sensations where nineteenth-century theme space was reinvented for the twentieth century.[66]

The experience of spectatorship at the park, its peculiar intensity or craving to thrill, involved exploring this seemingly precarious threshold. With the divide between visitors and animals concealed from view, with the barrier refashioned as shared space and covered by vegetation, some visitors first examined the boundary, the trench itself, in order to see if they were indeed safe. Others willingly suspended their disbelief. Indeed, the trenches and their effects on historical spectators were absolutely central to the park's reception. Writing for a popular family magazine, Albert G. Krüger described his experience of ascending from the first exhibit to the High-Mountain Ridge, searching the entire way for a secret barrier, with a mix of apprehension, curiosity, and frustration.

> Completely open and unsecured, one elevation, one terrace gives way to the next. . . . Anxiously, I entered the deeper lying paths which led into the maze of cliffs, to find out how [the enclosure] was secured. But here too, there was still no barrier, no caging. I only saw a trench. . . . Only a trench! And yet, not one of the predators has so far made the short leap to nearby prey. The ingenious design affords the animals freedom in every direction—except to get a running start. And where is the magic in that, if the predators can't even make an attempt to jump?[67]

At Hagenbeck's park, in comparison to his traveling panoramas, the display space was moved closer to the viewer for an effect and made relatively shallow for security's sake. Broad and shallow staging within the enclosure pushed the "action" to the foreground, in closer proximity to the audience, but simultaneously restricted one axis of the animal's range of movement. Predators could pace endlessly back and forth (parallel to the path), but they were restricted in their movement from background to foreground, just in case one of them were to actually give it a go. For Krüger, who was evidently thrilled by the prospect of cageless display, shallow staging at once inspired a fantasy of wildness unbound and dispelled its potentially violent reality. The "magic in that," which this spectator either failed to see or found disappointing, was a modern form of enchantment via the production of special effects.

The sensory excitement that spectators felt or found lacking can be accurately described in terms of the sublime. In the words of one visitor: "When you approach the Lions' Ravine, surrounded and vaulted by majestic cliffs, you experience the feeling as though you were walking in the desert and happened upon a brood of lions, and, since you know that you are safe, and you enjoy this sensation as purely aesthetic." To emphasize the sublime is to explore the park as an imaginary terrain in search of its strong appeal to the emotions. Historically, the capacity of the depicted scene to evoke strong emotional feelings such as terror has been regarded as characteristic of higher forms of landscape painting. Here, as in painting, the sublime experience relies for its effect on the viewer's situation. "The position of being both spectator and potential victim/participant is crucial to the full experience," according to art historian Malcolm Andrews. "It is a matter of being taken as close to disaster as is compatible with still retaining the sense that one is not actually in danger ('the brink of Destruction'); it is both destabilizing and reassuring, the two feelings in dynamic tension." The security of that position is necessary so as to be able to enjoy such a feeling as terror, to take pleasure from the contemplation of a situation that could not actually harm the spectator, except in the imagination. If this aspect of the painterly image can indeed be thrilling (and theorists of the sublime seem to agree on this point), then Hagenbeck upped the ante by choreographing an aesthetic experience of living, breathing wild animals. It is one thing to see a depiction of another person in a risky situation, however convincing or awesome it may appear; it is quite another thing for a spectator to think (even fear) that he or she might actually be in physical danger.[68]

First-time visitors were particularly susceptible to the park's immersive effects. Perhaps the most famous instance was Thomas Alva Edison's visit on 27 September 1911. "Edison walked around a group of trees, to suddenly confront a lion face-to-face, with nothing, apparently, to separate them. It scared the daylights out of the old inventor." To be caught by surprise, to experience the momentary feeling of having inadvertently trespassed—that was the park's most potent and visceral effect. When the display space was successfully naturalized as shared or overlapping with that of the viewer, it delivered a kind of shock, a bodily response that registered the momentary collapse of the presupposed gulf between the wild and the civilized. The unexpected proximity to danger had a sensational effect in both senses of the phrase. Witness Edison's astonishment. One could certainly argue, however, that the open enclosure was a type of a novelty act, a one-off sensation, producing an initial shock in first-time visitors, but probably seldom took repeat customers by surprise. The novelty argument would help explain Hagenbeck's ceaseless quest for new animals, entertainments, combinations, and enhancements, as an effort to keep audiences coming back for more. At the same time, it is also worth recalling the parallel to the *Völkerschau*, and the role of the fence as a fascinating sign. In that context (which is to say, elsewhere in the *Tierpark*), a sur-

4.13 *Diplodocus carnegiei*. The sculptor Josef Pallenberg (*in a smock, standing on the scaffold at far left*) and his assistants create a statue for the "Primeval Landscape," ca. 1909. Courtesy of Tierpark Carl Hagenbeck GmbH, Hamburg-Stellingen.

prising diversity of spectator relations developed along and across the borders of the display. There were many possible thrills of spectatorship, not one. In designing the *Tierpark*, Hagenbeck went even further to construct a diversity of places for viewing, which in turn allowed for an even broader spectrum of involvement and detachment. The *Völkerschau* reminds us that the porosity of display space and viewer space was a central—and enduring—characteristic of nineteenth-century theme space, which continued to issue in new and different forms.[69]

MONSTERS AND MACHINES

The relentless search for different themes and thrills can be suggested by comparing two examples—a classic juxtaposition of the primitive and the modern. In the first instance, between 1908 and 1909, Hagenbeck added a "Primeval Landscape" (*Urweltlandschaft*), or dinosaur group, which was located on the eastern section of the park, an area mainly devoted to ethnographic exhibition. It featured neither fossils nor mounted skeletons but rather large-scale sculptures (see, e.g., fig. 4.13), created by Josef Pallenberg (who also designed the animal statuary for the park's main gate).

4.14 Jurassic Park. A section of the "Primeval Landscape." Photo from Friedrich Knauer, *Der zoologische Garten: Entwicklungsgang, Anlage und Betrieb unserer Tiergärten* (1914; Leipzig: Theodor Thomas, n.d.), 166.

Here was another sculpted landscape, expanding the park's imaginary terrain in yet another direction. According to one paleontologist, "What we have here is a group of sauropods, distinguished by their fantastic forms and above all by their truly fabulous proportions, which is why they are called dinosaurs or terror-saurians (*Schreckensaurier*)." To suggest their enormous weight, several of the figures are partly submerged in a marsh or pond, behind them a family of horned dinosaurs (fig. 4.14). Some of the more spectacular figures (not pictured here) included a towering Iguanodon, a twenty-two-meter Diplodocus, and an "Allosaurus feeding on the remains of a Brontosaurus." Thus, Hagenbeck's park became one of the few early precedents to what Stephen Jay Gould has called "dinomania."[70]

My second example belongs to the "modern," but it is perhaps even more surprising than that of the primeval. In 1913, the Hagenbeck Company entered into a financial agreement with the Hugo Haase Company of Hannover. The plan was to build an "American-style" enclosed amusement park adjacent to the *Völkerschau* area of the *Tierpark*, and connected to it by a wide, tree-lined promenade. It would be called the "H. H. Park" (pronounced "ha-ha," as in, amusing). Like Hagenbeck's park, it was a private commercial enterprise that aimed to attract the widest possible audience. Hamburg already had its own Luna Park (which was named after the more successful amusement park at Coney Island). In 1911, the Haase Company also operated six rides (which was more than many amusement parks had in the United States) at the carnival grounds in Hamburg. Part of an aggressive campaign against Luna Park, Haase combined efforts with Hagenbeck, forming a complex of two parks, which could be visited for the price of a single ticket: 50 Pfennig for adults, 25 Pfennig for children (with a 20 Pfennig discount on evenings and Sundays). The addition of an amusement park exemplified Hagenbeck's promotion of the *Tierpark* as more than a zoo, which is to say, its status as a space of tourism, commerce, entertainment, and adventure. The H. H. Park opened in May 1914, a few months before the outbreak of war.[71]

A carousel manufacturer and amusement-park tycoon, Haase developed at least seventeen different mechanical rides, all of which were on display in Stellingen. The H. H. Park, like other amusement parks around 1900, specialized in physically bracing rides, which also represented exoticized forms of everyday modes of transportation. They played on cultural anxieties as well as pleasures surrounding the mechanical, in particular. Invoking the sublime without saying as much, historian John F. Kasson has written of Coney Island: "Riders could enjoy their own momentary fright and disorientation because they knew it would turn to comic relief; they could engage in what appeared dangerous adventure because ultimately they believed in its safety."[72] What linked such rides at H. H. Park to Hagenbeck's exhibits was, broadly, the theme of fantasy and adventure. There was the "Iron Sea" (*Eiserne See*), in which men and women rode in two-seater cars on a track made of flexible metal. The undulating motion of the metal floor propelled the cars forward, as passengers steered from side to side. A mechanical water slide descended a steep incline "at racing speed," from a height of thirty-three meters, with spectators lining the rails and watching as boats sailed past (fig. 4.15). A scenic railway (*Gebirgsbahn*) and a sky ride (*Seilbahn*) each brought passengers to the top of an artificial peak, where a Mountain Restaurant had seating for five hundred people. For the return ride, one could choose between a toboggan (*Rodelbahn*), built for speed, which took but a few seconds to reach the ground; or, a mechanical gondola (*Kahnfahrt*), built for couples, which wound its way for twenty minutes through a series of tunnels and grottos. On the ground, the "Upper Bavaria" restaurant had seating for five thousand. The largest building was an exhibition hall that accommodated fifteen thousand visitors. The sceneries ranged from the "Swiss Alps" to the "North Pole," but they also included numerous "grotesque motifs" reminiscent of Coney's Luna Park. At night, the H. H. Park "radiated in a sea of light, offering a fairy-like view." Six towers, twenty meters high, were each illuminated with "thousands of tiny light bulbs" and "automatically alternating colored lights." Beyond the many rides and spectacles, there were also games of skill and chance, such as the "'Living Shooting Gallery,' which gives the passionate hunter a chance to shoot at predators of all kinds, which appear on film."[73]

The *Tierpark* and the amusement park corresponded in many ways. Active participation in the spectacle and physical sensations of risky adventure under controlled conditions were attractions of both parks, allowing for transitions and continuities between them. For their part, visitors brought with them certain practices of spectatorship and consumption, as they roamed among the various rides and exhibits, concession stands and native villages, gift shops and game booths, walking from one park to the next. Up and down the promenade, which separated and linked the two parks,

4.15 The "Water Slide and Mountain Restaurant" were among the main attractions of the H. H. Park in Stellingen, 1914. Photo courtesy of Tierpark Carl Hagenbeck GmbH, Hamburg-Stellingen.

there were multiple points of intersection, including theatrical settings, immersive environments, exoticized views, spectacular lighting, and cutting-edge technology. A similar dynamic also powered the two parks, oscillating as they did between active, intense amusements that physically involved patrons, and leisurely pleasures of panoramic views and scenic rides. Of equal importance, each park radiated the distinctive sense of entering a special realm, one that was decidedly apart from the surrounding world, yet strategically referring back to it on occasion. Each created a space of possibility or impossibility, where incompatible spaces were represented and juxtaposed. The main elements that linked the *Tierpark* and the amusement park—the modulation of safety and danger, the vacillation between sensory immersion and imaginary adventure, the merger of incompatible spaces in one physical place—were critical elements of theme space at large.

The Alterity of the *Tierpark*

The alterity of the *Tierpark*—its difference from the nineteenth-century zoological garden—was conspicuous and fascinating to early audiences. It was also a source of controversy. News of the park spread far and wide, as images of its grand panoramas were broadcast across Europe and the United States via newspapers and illustrated magazines. Journalists waxed lyrical. Zoo directors took notice. Writing for an audience of scientists, administrators, and other zoo professionals in Germany, one commentator reviewed the new park with a mix of astonishment and perplexity.

> Elevated as it is and built out of artificial rock, the animal paradise in Stellingen has only a few animal houses. From a single point, the viewer sees all of the animals romping about in apparent freedom. The illusion becomes even more convincing as one goes to other places around this enormous park. When the visitor roams across the wide plateau, strolls past a rushing little river, and a Japanese island, with its characteristic vegetation, suddenly comes into view, he believes for a moment that he has been conveyed to an exotic world, which is really and truly present. When he stands before the Predators' Ravine and sees these kings of the desert freely moving about, or views with astonishment the sea lions and giant walruses writhing around in the North Pole Panorama, he has the sense that he is seeing something extraordinary.

Throughout the article, it is almost as if the writer has to contain his enthusiasm on account of his readers, some of whom had already publicly criticized the *Tierpark* for various reasons. Nodding to their complaints, the reporter acknowledges that "perhaps something theatrical lies in the entire presentation, something showman-like, which totally departs from the way of a zoological garden. But when you leave Stellingen, after visiting the *Völkerschau* arena, the native village, and the ostrich farm, you have seen something extraordinary, gigantic. The fullness of objects, the overwhelming of the masses—it all makes an extraordinary impression on the observer." And so he concluded in a way that might have discomfited members of the scientific establishment: "A totally new kind of zoological institution, Hagenbeck's enterprise has secured a place for itself in the history of animal keeping."[74]

Indeed, the *Tierpark* contradicted some of the most characteristic features of the zoological garden. In contrast to almost every major zoo that was built in the nineteenth century, beginning with the London Zoo at Regent's Park, the *Tierpark* was neither founded by a zoological society nor based on scientific principles. Nor did it share the same yearning for objectivity and rationality that most zoological institutions displayed with pride. Its collections were not organized systematically. Rather than represent reality in the static form of taxonomy, it encouraged visitors to imagine "what if" in the dynamic form of an immersive environment. Its featured displays situated wild animals not in abstract iron cages but in barless enclosures that had been shaped to resemble natural settings, and arranged in panoramic fashion. There were also some interesting continuities with the zoological garden. For example, Hagenbeck's park followed in the tradition of the *Jardin des Plantes* in Paris—especially insofar as it combined a picturesque garden with landscaped settings, winding paths, and exotic animals in a large collection. Like the *Jardin*, Hagenbeck's park aspired to be a place of recreation. It too made certain scientific and pedagogical claims. But the similarities end there. Unlike the *Jardin*, Hagenbeck's park did not originate as a botanical garden, nor did it requisition animals from a royal menagerie. Its landscapes were not organized around buildings or cages, as they were in Paris. Nor was the park officially dedicated to the service of the nation. The contrast is worth extending a bit further. Unlike most of the zoological gardens built in Germany during the nineteenth century—and more zoos were established here than anywhere else in this period—the *Tierpark* was neither a civic institution nor a joint-stock organization. It was a private venture, owned by Hagenbeck alone, one that allowed him to experiment in ways that directors of public zoological gardens could not.[75]

The *Tierpark* was uniquely self-sufficient in terms of financing, organization, and infrastructure, the implications of which are difficult to overstate. For one thing, it gave Hagenbeck exceptionally wide latitude in designing the park and in experimenting with new technologies of animal management and exhibition. Add to this the fact that he was very familiar with the prevailing techniques—in the course of his career he visited nearly all of the major circuses, menageries, and zoological gardens—and it becomes easy to recognize that, on this terrain, in stark contrast to that of ethnographic exhibition, he had little if any need for outside authority. "If there is one individual able to speak with authority on how a zoological garden should be built and conducted," wrote one commentator in *Scientific American*, "it is Mr. Carl Hagenbeck of Hamburg."[76] Self-sufficiency further permitted him to focus almost exclusively on spectators and other customers. Unlike zoo directors, he was not beholden in any way to shareholders, civic organizations, or scientific societies. Not surprisingly, then, Hagenbeck's corporate vision differed from that of public zoological gardens. In the zoological context, for example, there was an almost obsessive concern with self-justification in terms of higher objectives such as progress, science, education, civilization, and conservation. While Hagenbeck personally believed in these cultural ideals, the sole reason for the park's existence was commerce. The *Tierpark* was devoted not to the popularization of scientific knowledge but rather to the circulation of products and consumers.

CIRCULATION

Whoever visited the *Tierpark* for the first time needed a certain degree of orientation. Anticipating as much, the first souvenir guidebook began with a series of "Orienting Observations," informing visitors of what to expect and, ideally, how to proceed. "The guide through Hagenbeck's *Tierpark* makes no attempt to be a zoological guidebook, which informs and teaches visitors about the abundant animal world living here. It is much rather a simple, straightforward guide *to* the individual attractions that are widely distributed throughout the *Tierpark*." Instead of reciting facts about animals, the booklet concerned itself with the movement of visitors through the park, from one attraction to the next, encouraging them to follow a designated main route (with exhibit numbers and directional arrows), to prevent over-crowding and to keep people from "running into each other." The recommended itinerary was thus designed for a pleasurable mode of circulation, offering "the shortest possible route" through the park "with minimal repetition." It maximized the flow of traffic, while framing certain views, leading visitors past concessions, screening out the sight of other patrons at certain places, and elsewhere creating places of social gathering. In practice, visitors were neither prodded nor corralled, and it is reasonable to assume that many people followed their own interests and agendas. At a minimum, the guidebook helped make the park legible and comprehensible, enabling spectators to easily identify and locate any one of its many attractions, while pursuing their own interests.[77]

At the same time, however, the expected need for orientation remains significant, especially in terms of the park's unique layout. The point can be made by comparison with the leading model of zoological organization and display in the nineteenth century—the London Zoo in Regent's Park. There, visitors followed signs from one building to the next, where animals were arranged in taxonomic groupings, with pedagogical labels on the exhibits, in accordance with the scientific principles on which the zoo was originally based. The taxonomic mode was expressed architecturally, by the interrelationship of buildings throughout the grounds, and by the interrelationship of cages within a particular house. Landscape gardening had an important role in this context, too—creating transitions between buildings, permitting what the spectator has learned to "sink in," allowing for momentary relaxation, and generating anticipation for what has yet to be seen—but its role was subordinated to the taxonomic system that governed the organization of buildings and cages. At Hagenbeck's park, by contrast, "the systematic relationship of animals has also been avoided in the arrangement of different enclosures and buildings. In order to maintain the design's park-like character, they have been spread out far apart from one another, just as the housing and the grouping of the animals have been arranged not in terms of kinship but more in view of their natural habitats and ways of life." In promoting the ideas of "natural habitats" and "ways of life" as viable alternatives to taxonomic organization, the guidebook not only anticipates some confusion on the part of veteran zoo-goers, but also provides them with a rationale for change. Hagenbeck's *Tierpark* radically altered the conventional relationship among spectators, guidebooks, and exhibits.[78]

This new relationship can perhaps best be defined in terms of circulation. On every level, the park's organization was defined by the bottom-line logic of the trade menagerie. Like the many paths that wound throughout the park, the exhibits were arranged for circulation: that of commodities. Every animal on display here was also (literally) for sale. Soon after one was purchased, it would be replaced by another—possibly a member of an unrelated species or even an animal from a totally different part of the world. The economic fact of high turnover alone ruled out the idea of displaying animals in terms of fixed scientific categories. Instead of trying to create full sets of each genus, as some zoological gardens did (a practice that is often compared to stamp collecting), the aim here was to continue meeting the demands of particular buyers while at the same time representing animals in a way that would be alluring to mass spectators.

The *Tierpark* incorporated modern forms of accumulation and display, which were more in line with an emerging consumer culture than they were with the rigid frameworks of understanding and containment that structured the zoological garden. Here, once again, is the guidebook from 1907:

> The usual zoological lessons in such catalogs must necessarily be omitted here, because the park's animal stock—in keeping with the status of the Carl Hagenbeck Company as an animal emporium—is constantly changing. The animals are ever coming and going. Where a Norwegian lynx or a Siberian wild sheep is kept today, there a Russian wolf or an Arabian ibex might be standing tomorrow. Yet this *constant change in stock* has the great advantage of offering the public as well as the zoologist *always something new*.

Commercial operations were thus presented as benefits in terms of spectatorship, and visitors took notice. "The whole park offers not just an ordinary kind of zoological garden," wrote one commentator; "it is the immense storehouse in which the global Hagenbeck firm stocks its living goods."[79]

CONTROVERSY

Even before it opened to the public, Hagenbeck's *Tierpark* in Stellingen was seen and discussed as being *opposed* to a zoological garden. Here was an exhilarating alternative to the buildings and cages of that institution, with their obtrusive bars, scientific labels, and taxonomic organization. It seemed to be in a class all its own. One reporter called it "a facility that is totally unique, but one that will appeal to imitation if only in smaller measure. It is not, as one might think, a zoological garden; no term other than '*Tierpark*' can be used, if one would accurately describe it." For the scientific establishment, however, Hagenbeck's phenomenal success became a reason for concern. By 1909, a scant two years after the *Tierpark* opened, Hamburg's Zoological Garden found itself in dire straits due to low attendance, lobbying the city for additional subven-

4.16 The crowd at Hagenbeck's *Tierpark*, ca. 1909. Courtesy of Tierpark Carl Hagenbeck GmbH, Hamburg-Stellingen.

tions, yet reluctant to purchase new animals from its main supplier—namely, Hagenbeck. It was in this context that some of the most senior zoo directors in Germany launched a series of public attacks against Hagenbeck in newspapers, magazines, and trade journals, seeking to reframe the popular discussion along conventional zoological lines. The main points of this debate are worth mentioning, not only because they give a sense of the park's German reception (albeit from a very "interested" perspective), but also because they help bring out the perceived alterity of the *Tierpark*. Indeed, zoo directors insisted upon its difference as an institution.[80]

The terms of debate were established by Ernst Schäff, director of Hannover's Zoological Garden. Although he acknowledged that the use of "containers corresponding to natural conditions in the wild" were "without a doubt theoretically desirable," Schäff maintained (against all evidence to the contrary) that open enclosures were "practically unfeasible." Hagenbeck's success, he averred, was entirely based on extravagant advertising, which in effect bamboozled spectators. Part of a more elaborate argument in favor of taxonomic organization, he questioned the park's "scientific value," and simply dismissed it "from a didactic perspective." Thus, Schäff voiced his strong support for the Hamburg Zoological Garden as a scientific and educational institute, stressing that Hagenbeck's park was merely a "trade and show-enterprise in grand style."[81]

All of these terms were used and reused by a number of other zoo directors, each with a different emphasis and rhetorical pitch. For example, Ludwig Heck (Berlin), who had earlier helped Hagenbeck obtain a building permit in Stellingen, now accused him of having used publicity not only as "propaganda" for the new *Tierpark*, but also as "an aggressive jab" at zoological gardens that "aimed to turn the public opinion against them." Given the opportunity to reply, Hagenbeck wrote in the same newspaper, "It never occurred to me to conduct aggressive 'propaganda' against zoological gardens, whose directors are all my clients and good friends." Besides, he concluded, "The *Tierpark* in Stellingen is a self-sufficient enterprise and it has no interest in competing with any garden in the world." Zoo directors had a different take on this issue. Kurt Priemel (Frankfurt) acknowledged the park's distinctive character, which he located precisely in its panoramic design, but he did so as a way of arguing for its absolute difference. Speaking on behalf of his colleagues, Priemel concluded: "We are convinced that the *Tierpark* will continue to exert a significant power of attraction for the broad public even after its novelty has faded. . . . But we hope that in time others will come to understand that the organizing principle of this enterprise can never ever be exemplary for zoological gardens. Both kinds of animal exhibition have their place, but they have little if anything to do with one another, and they cannot be compared."[82]

In 1909, the idea that zoological gardens around the world would later co-opt this model was by no means self-evident. On the contrary, Germany's leading zoo directors made a public show of rejecting it. To assert the alterity of Hagenbeck's *Tierpark* was a discursive strategy for framing and containing it. Indeed, the zoo directors involved in this controversy went on to organize an international boycott against Hagenbeck as an animal dealer. Its success was one reason why Hagenbeck, in an effort to survive the boycott by creating new sources of revenue, added such things as dinosaurs and mechanical rides in the first place—moves which not only exacerbated the tension between the *Tierpark* and the zoo, but also strengthened its connection to the amusement park, in particular.

"THE HAGENBECK REVOLUTION"

Today, a century later, the making of the *Tierpark* is widely understood as heralding a major shift in zoo design and animal exhibition. It is often described in shorthand as the "Hagenbeck revolution." In the twentieth century, zoos throughout Europe, Asia, and the United States adopted various elements from Stellingen, as noted by historians, planners, and administrators alike. Throughout the literature, the *Tierpark* has appeared in many different and sometimes contradictory forms, but almost always in hyperbolic terms of originality, and invariably as a kind of zoo. Indeed, it has been called the first "modern" zoo, the first zoo to use barless enclosures, the first zoo to advocate humane training, the first zoo to display animals in natural settings, the first zoo to emphasize "acclimatization," the first zoo to suggest that animals might be "better off" in captivity than they are in the outside world, the first zoo to organize exhibits nonsystematically (according to either habitats or geographical zones), the first zoo to display animals in large social groups, the first zoo to feature mixed-species exhibits, the first zoo to add amusement-park rides—and the first zoo to combine a number of these elements. As this list of proverbial "firsts" is meant to suggest, the use of this trope is unsettling in terms of teleology, but it is also indicative. The same elements that once made the *Tierpark* so problematic for zoo directors would later make it seem prescient for historians. Nigel Rothfels' study, *Savages and Beasts: The Birth of the Modern Zoo*, tacitly endorses this framework. Hagenbeck's *Tierpark*, curiously, has gone from being the antithesis of the zoological garden to its apotheosis.[83]

In a further step, since the 1920s, the park and its directors (all Hagenbeck's descendants) have effectively reinforced this sort of historical back-reading in two interrelated ways: first, by cultivating a strong awareness of the park's extraordinary history and broadcasting a certain image of it to visitors; second, by aspiring for international recognition as a legitimate zoological garden, instead of exploring the park's potential to create an imaginative alternative to that institution, as Hagenbeck had earlier. The park's drive for legitimacy was followed by a programmatic shift from hunting, collecting, and trading animals to an ethos of protection and conservation, which was completely in tune with zoos of the twentieth century. Over time, then, the park's sense of alterity has been inadvertently diminished not only by historians, but also by the historical process that they ostensibly seek to chronicle and understand. While zoos around the world were being designed and renovated in the mold of Stellingen, as if to corroborate this idea of a Hagenbeck revolution, the original park underwent its own transformation, becoming more and more of a conventional zoological garden. If the cultural function of the zoo itself was to mitigate alterity, to represent otherness in a way such that it became domesticated, then zoo directors and historians have also enacted this idea by transforming Hagenbeck's *Tierpark* into a garden-variety zoo.

HAGENBECK'S CONTRIBUTION

The controversy of 1909 presented for the first time a coherent assessment of Hagenbeck's *Tierpark* from the perspective of the zoological establishment. In the same year, Alfred Freiherr von Berger—poet, playwright, director of the famous Burgtheater in

Vienna, and professor of philosophy and aesthetics at the university there—published an extraordinary essay on the *Tierpark* that interpreted it from a different angle altogether. He had visited the park during his tenure as director of the Deutsches Schauspielhaus in Hamburg. Drawing on this experience as well as on the discourse of philosophical aesthetics, von Berger developed an original reading of the park's visual form, its layout, even its "cultural" significance. The *Tierpark* might be noted among zoo professionals for its innovative methods of animal keeping and acclimatization, he acknowledged, "but what strikes the layman as even more significant is the bold subjectivity of its composition. One immediately senses that an artistic person here attempted, within the framework of a functioning park, to concentrate his peculiar view of the world into a colossal symbolic painting, admittedly, not in colors on a flat canvas, but rather, as befits a man of action, in three-dimensional space, in stone and water, in flesh and blood." Von Berger saw the *Tierpark* through the aspect of realism in the arts.

> In approximately the same period that produced the realistic milieu drama in literature, and gave scenic art the impetus to embody with painterly force the living spaces of people depicted on stage, Hagenbeck reformed the menagerie business in a similar way, probably without being influenced by the ideas or objectives of modern theater. He showed the public animals not as it has previously been done, disconnected from their natural environment, in cages and bare enclosures, but rather surrounded them with a landscape resembling their habitat.

Visiting the park was for him analogous to viewing a genre scene in painting or on stage. "The observer is given the illusion of stumbling upon the life of animals who feel oblivious to being watched. To accomplish this," he continued, "Hagenbeck removed the famous 'fourth wall,' which on the animal stage, whose actors are lions and tigers, was understandably maintained at least in the form of iron bars, and replaced them with a moat that is invisible to the public." Von Berger was perhaps alone in emphasizing and discussing the aesthetic dimension of the *Tierpark*, taking it seriously as a work of art comparable to other, more familiar forms of visual culture. His analysis is so free of the usual language of zoo criticism, which is entirely beholden to the zoo as an institution, that it demands consideration. At the same time, as this chapter has demonstrated, Hagenbeck's contribution was much more provocative—and much more concrete—than the notion of realism is able to convey.[84]

The *Tierpark* involved more than just creating the illusion of a natural world, and covering up the seams. What characterized the park, historically speaking, was its unique combination of panoramic vision and physical presence in the service of creating a fantasy world of exotic adventure. This combination was also a strategy for immersing visitors in the depicted environment, while at the same time implicating them in the imaginative side of the experience. To emphasize the park's creative interpretation of the panorama and its productive antagonism to the nineteenth-century zoological garden, as I have done, is to resituate the *Tierpark* in its historical context. It was a new and exceptionally vibrant entertainment zone, where multiple and divergent genealogies of theme space intersected, the results of which were neither restricted to nor determined by the zoo's trajectory.

The point can be developed even further by exploring the interconnection of the park and the cinema. Hagenbeck's animals and ethnographic troupes offered a variety of interesting subjects for newsreels, travelogues, and wildlife films—some of which were also exhibited at the *Tierpark*. With its artificial terrain, landscaped views, and native villages, the park itself became an appealing site to early German filmmakers and studio executives—especially during World War I, when foreign travel was strictly forbidden, and fiction films set in an exotic milieu were thus in high demand. As film historian Tom Gunning has suggested, "The relation between films and the emergence of the great amusement parks, such as Coney Island, at the turn of the century provides rich ground for rethinking the roots of early cinema." In Germany, there is probably no richer ground—and certainly none more neglected—than Hagenbeck's *Tierpark*. The relevance of this material is far-reaching. It invites us to consider the origins of filmic diegesis as another type of themed environment, while exploring the afterlife of nineteenth-century theme space from the viewpoint of early cinema.[85]

CHAPTER FIVE

THE PARK AND THE CINEMA

On 20 June 1908, Kaiser Wilhelm II visited Hagenbeck's *Tierpark* in Stellingen for the very first time. "Good morning, comrades!" he said to Hagenbeck and his sons, who greeted the German Emperor at the park's main gate. "I already know your zoo from the cinema, but my brother *ordered* me to see it in person, so now show me what you've got here!" What I find intriguing about this mundane and presumptuous comment is the idea that one could "know [Hagenbeck's] zoo from the cinema." Of course, the Kaiser meant it literally, referring to newsreel footage of the park's grand opening. Metaphorically, however, it is an interesting turn of phrase. In this sense, the idea of knowing the park from the cinema suggests that there was an identifiable connection between the two institutions, which in fact there was. Opening day at Hagenbeck's *Tierpark* also marked the beginning of an exceptionally rich and dynamic exchange with the cinema. The ever-changing stock of exotic animals and entertainments that distinguished the park from the zoological garden also supplied more than ample material for a range of nonfiction films, including panoramic views of the park, trained-animal acts, ethnographic performances, and "tours" of native villages. For historians of early cinema, this sort of crossover on the level of nonfiction will come as no surprise, even if the Hagenbeck material is totally unfamiliar. What is extraordinary, however, is that the *Tierpark* also provided both a visual model and a physical site for producing a diversity of feature films, from safari adventure films to erotic melodramas.[1]

This chapter explores some of the unexpected connections between nineteenth-century theme space and filmic diegesis. The park and the cinema shared, above all, a mutual interest in creating fantasy worlds out of actual objects, bodies, and spaces, and in presenting each world as a complete, self-contained environment. The medium of film constructs space differently than the park's living habitats. In the films to be considered here, for example, staging wild animals in natural settings usually required the use of multiple camera set-ups and numerous takes; in some instances, it called for access to various locations, actors with acrobatic skills, and custom-built cages. Double exposure was certainly another possible strategy, but one that was not employed by any of these particular films, because it very often lacked a felt sense of tension between the actors and the animals. In other ways, however, filmic mediation could actually enhance the reality effect that the habitat displays created. For example, the impression of seeing live animals in simulated landscapes became even more convincing by flattening the perspective and bathing the entire scene in light, which gave it an added sense of internal coherence. Moreover, wildlife films created a visual experience of nature that some spectators might have preferred to that of the *Tierpark*, because it constructed a highly edited and rapidly paced event, which eliminated any dull moments in favor of emphasizing visually arresting or emotionally exciting ones. At the same time, however, it needs to be stressed that filmic diegesis relies for its immersive effect on the relative disembodiment of the spectator, who must vicariously leave his or her physical space (a seat) in the theater, so as to enter a fictional one, which is only "present" by virtue of technological recording and projection. Visitors to the *Tierpark*, by contrast, physically entered and moved throughout a space of live performance that was highly responsive to their actual presence in it. Bearing in mind such differences and their various effects, I contend that the cinema represents a themed environment with strong ties to its nineteenth-century predecessor, especially in regard to diegetic space.[2]

What follows is an investigation into the origins of filmic diegesis, concentrating on three different but interrelated levels of its construction: namely, the image, the set, and the studio. I begin with the image, because it constitutes that sample of the larger story world that appears before the spectator. By the same token, the cinematic image invites the spectator to mentally extrapolate from the figures, objects, and spaces on screen to a larger fictional universe, which is partly an invention of the viewer's imagination. Pre-filmic stages of production such as the set and the studio constitute even stronger, more explicit connections—but they do so ironically, by dismantling the park and its existing collections, and rearranging them in new ways. Nineteenth-century theme space was a model to be revisited and revised. What comes across on every level—image, set, and studio—is the cinema's fascination with an earlier model of theme space as well as with its visual topoi. Throughout this chapter there is a considerable amount of unpublished archival material to be presented for the very first time in English. The goal, however, is to reexamine the original idea of theme space through a new and different lens.

The Image as Shared Space

With the invention of film, it has often been suggested, the visual representation of wild animals underwent radical transformation. An early expression of this idea appears in Joseph Delmont's book, *Wild Animals on the Films* (1925): "Film made it necessary to present the predator in a totally different way than on stage or in the circus. The animals should be shown in the forest, in the jungle, or on the steppe, in absolute freedom and pristine wildness." Indeed, the romantic ideal of "unspoiled nature," and the related effort to conceal any signs of a human setting in rehearsing this ideal, is a central characteristic of wildlife films, as historian Gregg Mitman has shown. In his view, this ideal is also the legacy of wildlife films for theme parks, such as Disney's Animal Kingdom. As we have seen, however, the penchant for seeing living, breathing animals in natural settings and in apparent freedom was not new; nor was it unique to cinematic mediation. In fact, the paradoxical liberation of animals in film is closely related to the "open enclosures" or animal panoramas in Hagenbeck's *Tierpark*. Wildlife films and theme parks have a longer history and a more complex relationship than film-specific accounts are able to suggest.[3]

Their history begins, significantly, with the emergence of safari films. Between 1907 and 1908, Ole Olsen, founder of Nordisk, the first Scandinavian production company, purchased from Hagenbeck a variety of large predators for a series of three fake safari films: namely, *Polar Bear Hunt* (*Isbjørnejagt*, 1907), *The Lion Hunt* (*Løvejagten*, 1907), and *Bear Hunting in Russia* (*Bjørnejagt i Rusland*, 1908).[4] Though set in such far-flung locations as the Arctic Ocean, the African jungle, and the Russian steppe, the films in this series were not records (or reenactments) of historical expeditions led by well-known sportsmen or scientists. They were simulated safaris, in every sense of the phrase. Though fictional, the Nordisk productions were not exceptional; most safari films involve what Derek Bousé describes as "a good deal of staging, acting, dramatic storytelling, and fabricating of events." Nevertheless, all the films in this series made a strong and, on some level, undeniable claim to authenticity—that is, all of the animals that Olsen acquired from Hagenbeck were literally shot and killed before the camera. Unlike the living habitat, which needed the bodies on display to thrive, photography and film allowed for the continued visibility of animals in spite of—and in this case precisely because of—their death. Even so, as we shall see, the park and the cinema had much to offer each other.[5]

In a certain sense, the safari film would do for the cinema what the *Tierpark* did for the zoo. What makes this analogy so suggestive is the film genre's overriding concern with staging humans and animals not just in natural settings, but also—more interestingly—in shared space. The desired effect is clearly illustrated by a poster advertisement for the German release of *Polar Bear Hunt* (see plate 14). Designed by the Hamburg lithographer Adolph Friedländer (who also created advertisements for Hagenbeck's entertainments), the poster indicates that more than one polar bear was used, as were other animals—seals, sea lions, and walruses—conjuring a more abundant and expansive sense of the Arctic as a natural habitat than the film's title would seem to suggest. The aesthetic concern with visual openness and shared space is common to all three Nordisk productions. Of the films in this series, however, the most important was *The Lion Hunt*. It was also the most notorious. Animal rights activists in Copenhagen tried without success to block this production on cruelty charges. Ultimately, however, the controversy became a source of free advertising for Nordisk not only at home but also abroad. The film sold 256 copies, making it the company's biggest commercial success to date, with a vast majority of the copies going to foreign distributors. By all accounts, *The Lion Hunt* put Nordisk on the map of world cinema.[6]

For historians of early silent film, *The Lion Hunt* remains something of a curiosity due to its seemingly prescient use of montage—that is, parallel editing—as a strategy for constructing the hunt. The consensus seems to be that the editing in this case represents not an emergent formal system based on the relationship between shots, but a fortuitous effect of another issue, one which is usually explained in terms of a problem-solution model. "Olsen and Larsen were faced with the problem of making the space of the lions appear as contiguous with that of the hunters, and of having other African animals in the film while not having to transport them to Elleore. The solution they hit upon, commonplace today, was unheard of in 1907." Alternatively, Danish historian Marguerite Engberg, who interviewed Larsen shortly before his death, proposed a narrative or story-based explanation. By her account, "Larsen had no conception of the significance of editing in *Løvejagten*, but simply said that they had to photograph and edit the film that way in order to get the story across and give the impression of a real hunt." It seems to me, however, that what passes for nascent cross-cutting or narrative integration in film-specific accounts can also be understood as a significant form of crossover between the cinema and the living habitat. Seen from the "outside" perspective of theme space, the film obtains new meaning.[7]

The crossover from nineteenth-century theme space can be seen already in preproduction. To begin with, Olsen rented a flat, sandy island named Elleore, in the midle of a fjord (which is really more of an inlet) near Copenhagen. The private island offered a controlled environment for filmmaking, which was readily accessible to the city, but visually unimpeded by it. The off-shore location also provided a sufficient buffer from animal-rights protesters who had already sought to disrupt the shoot. From the *Tierpark* in Stellingen, Olsen purchased (what Hagenbeck described in his account book as) "two defective male lions" for a total of 3,000 Marks. With the animals en route to Copenhagen, Olsen and his team planted dozens of improvised palm trees around the island. Assisting him was Viggo Larsen, a former army officer who not only served as

5.1 “Africa” on the island of Elleore, near Copenhagen. *The Lion Hunt* (Nordisk, 1907; dir. Viggo Larsen), production still. Courtesy of the Stills & Posters Archive at the Danish Film Institute, Copenhagen.

the film’s director, but also performed as a hunter in each of the three safari films. To bolster the film’s image of “Africa,” they recruited a black man named William Thomson, who was actually a recent immigrant from a Danish colony in the Caribbean, to play the role of native servant. The action was filmed by three different cameras—two of them posted atop a purpose-built wooden shed, another in a boat offshore. The head cameraman was Axel Graatkjaer (who went on to become a major cinematographer in Weimar Germany). All of them were protected by a group of non-commissioned Army officers crouching in bushes and standing behind the cameras with rifles loaded and ready. Once the filming on Elleore had been completed, the company visited a local forest as well as the Copenhagen Zoo, where they “back-filmed” a number of scenes whose purpose was to fill the celluloid jungle with flora and fauna, giving it a greater sense of plentitude than the sandy little island had allowed.[8]

The resulting film constructs a diegetic space that is strongly reminiscent of a living habitat display. It begins with an expository passage, identifying the hunters and their native servant, locating them in an exotic-looking landscape, and creating a sense of the larger world in which the story is set. The emphasis here is on the wonder of the natural world and its revelation through the camera, the stock-in-trade of wildlife films. A Danish program brochure from 1907 provides a useful description.

> Two hunters, followed by their servant, a Negro, have broken camp in order to hunt for lions. . . . Though they follow only one goal, the lion, they allow themselves to admire Nature's wonders along the way, stopping occasionally to examine the jungle's splendor and the abundance of strange animals. There lies the lazy hippopotamus down by the riverbank; there monkeys scamper about in a labyrinth of vines. Look: they catch one! (The little fellow is not too happy to be touched by white hands.) There stands the ostrich, sniffing the air, on the lookout; there is the llama, shy and frightened.

Initially, we see the hunters kneel down and scan the surrounding area, which has the important effect of foregrounding the origin, the control, and the authority of viewing. As the hunters look around them, they look and point repeatedly into off-screen space, and the film begins to alternate between images of the hunters and images of exotic fauna presented as inhabiting a jungle. Cut-in shots of wildlife direct our attention to the environment as a source of visual pleasure. The film's spatial relations, however, are clearly organized around human figures, as demonstrated by the repeated returns to the hunters, the implication being that these figures—and, by extension, we as spectators—are surrounded by animals in the jungle. Each of the depicted animals is thus mediated by a human presence; we see them through the eyes of the hunters. The world that is available to their senses is what the spectator is invited to imagine. Consider the fact that the animals up to this point in the film are actually located in multiple different cages at the Copenhagen Zoo, and the effort to construct a coherent diegetic space becomes even more striking. Throughout this passage, all traces of the zoo are carefully screened out by positioning the camera either above or between the bars of the various cages. Much as Hagenbeck used trenches and moats to achieve a sense of shared space, Olsen and Larsen enlist recording, framing, and camera positioning to bypass the cage, while promoting an experience of sensory immersion in the depicted scene.[9]

5.2 "There lies the lazy hippopotamus down by the riverbank." *The Lion Hunt* (Nordisk, 1907; dir. Viggo Larsen), frame enlargement. Courtesy of the Stills & Posters Archive at the Danish Film Institute, Copenhagen.

The Lion Hunt simulates an African landscape and presents it as a complete

5.3 "[T]here monkeys scamper about in a labyrinth of vines. Look: they catch one!" *The Lion Hunt* (Nordisk, 1907; dir. Viggo Larsen), frame enlargement. Courtesy of the Stills & Posters Archive at the Danish Film Institute, Copenhagen.

environment, not only by means of camerawork, but also through the coordination of the bodies on screen. The rapid movement of figures in and out of the frame creates an expectation that space lies not only outside of the frame but also "before" and "after" it (an expectation which is later reinforced by the linear trajectory of the hunt). At this point, it must be emphasized that the centrifugal movement of characters out of the frame relies for its diegetic effect on the porosity of the frame as a kind of border. If the analogy to cageless display comes to mind once again, then a caveat is necessary: In contrast to the *Tierpark*, where the actual movement of animals and spectators is restricted along the threshold of the exhibit, the limits of the cinematic image are easily crossed by the bodies that appear on screen. At one point, a hunter exits the frame at left and returns a moment later carrying a small monkey in his arms. Staging the apparent ease of physical movement and access on screen becomes a strategy for emphasizing and reinforcing the viewer's impression of spatial coherence by means of choreography, rather than merely suggesting it by the associative use of editing.[10]

The emphasis shifts abruptly when the lions are released from their unseen cages, and the actual hunt begins. "A roar splits the silence of the tropical night: The hunters wake up, seize their guns and shoot. They are quite close to the lion, and the picture shows how one hunter fires on the king of beasts at dangerously close range. . . . A moment later, we see the one hunter, victorious, standing next to the lion's body." A

5.4 Shooting "Lion No. 2." A contentious scene from *The Lion Hunt* (Nordisk, 1907; dir. Viggo Larsen), frame enlargement. Courtesy of the Stills & Posters Archive at the Danish Film Institute, Copenhagen.

version of the chase structure, the hunt is contrived around a visual pattern of repetition and alternation, which is then doubled. An intertitle puts it bluntly: "On the trail of lion No. 2 . . ." Following this, we see a hunter (Larsen) enter the frame from the right and set up for another shot, but he does so directly in front of the camera, blocking the spectator's view of the lion that is now reeling in shallow water. The actor, apparently, became so absorbed by the act of shooting that he forgot momentarily where the film camera was located. As if prompted from off-screen, the hunter stands up, moves two steps to the left, and readies himself once again (see fig. 5.4). The whole point of staging and redirecting this sort of movement across the horizontal axis of the frame is to create the effect of a single sustained view, in which the hunter and the lion appear in shared space at the very moment when the animal is to be literally shot and killed.[11]

Close textual analysis of *The Lion Hunt* suggests that film historians have placed too much emphasis on the novelty of montage at the expense of its interrelationship with other cinematic elements. In a sense, the entire film works to eschew montage in favor of staging within the individual shot. Significantly, the hunters and the animals are brought into the same image space without the use of either editing or trick photography. The key move takes place three different times, at every dramatic highpoint: when the hunters encounter the monkey, and again with each of the lions. Olsen even makes it explicit that this effect, which he singles out in a promotional letter to an American distributor, is the extraordinary one: "The hunter is in the picture while the lions are shot—a point which makes the piece still more interesting." Rather than tout the innovative use of editing (the fact that it goes unmentioned here supports the idea that he was unaware of its novelty), Olsen emphasizes the choreography of bodies, their tense interaction, and the physical fact of shared space.[12]

The argument about frame space can perhaps best be summarized by borrowing a few terms from the French critic André Bazin and his influential theory of realism. In his view, the cinema is essentially a form of art based in recording, for which preexisting objects and spaces are absolutely necessary. The cinema comes into its own, he avers, by revealing the world as it "really" is. Instead of emphasizing the formative power of editing, Bazin fetishizes the "objective" quality of the camera's lens, the indexical quality of the photographic image, and the spatial integrity of the cinematic frame. His well-known preference for depth of field offers only the most obvious example. Throughout his writings, Bazin privileges techniques of *mise-en-scène* (i.e., what gets placed or appears before the camera) as opposed to those of montage (or editing). "When the essence of a scene demands the simultaneous presence of two or more factors in the action," he contends, "montage is ruled out." For instance, "it is inconceivable that the famous seal-hunt in *Nanook* should not show us hunter, hold, and seal all in the same shot. It is simply a question of respect for the spatial unity of an event at the moment when to split it up would change it from something real to something imaginary." We needn't accept the theoretical opposition between *mise-en-scène* and montage in order to comprehend the key point as it pertains to early wildlife films. In this case, Olsen and Larsen made fortuitous use of editing even as they emphasized the spatial proximity of hunters and animals within the individual frame. The filmmakers never swerve from their plan to kill the lions, but their fundamental need for the preexisting world, and their insistence on choreographing humans and animals in shared space, at once draws on an earlier model of theme space and demonstrates its continuation by other means.[13]

◆ ◆ ◆

Here we can pause to link the spectacle of animal death back to the living habitat. For all its emphasis on vitality and presence, Hagenbeck's *Tierpark* also carved out a space where such kill shots were, in fact, permitted under certain conditions—namely, when motion pictures were involved. Two examples stand out as most relevant: one in terms of film production, the other in terms of exhibition. The first example comes from an early German melodrama or circus film, titled *Die lebende Brücke* (*The Living Bridge*, Komet, 1912; dir. Friedrich Müller), whose interesting distinction was duly noted in the trade press. "The *Tierpark* and its inhabitants have already provided occasion for various film recordings," wrote one reporter, referring to the making of nonfiction films in particular. "Now, for the very first time, Herr Direktor Hagenbeck has also proven to be a practical sponsor and collaborator in the production of cinematic dramas." In light of the cinema's many opponents in Germany, the cooperation of such a respected figure was publicized as a tacit show of support for the larger film industry. The writer thus concludes by thanking Hagenbeck for "generously making his *Tierpark*, personnel, animals, props, etc., available for a cinema drama."[14]

The Living Bridge unfolds in a series of risky confrontations between humans and animals, all set in the milieu of a traveling circus and menagerie. First, the menagerie owner's wife walks a tightrope over a group of sixteen lions below her—a scene that is staged in the famous Predator's Ravine. Later, she rescues her daughter from an escaped bear, by actually shooting and killing it before the camera. "The highly dramatic plot among other things made it necessary for the film to show the killing of a bear," to quote the same reporter. "Herr Hagenbeck selected a grown Malaysian bear that had spent eight years in captivity, and was avoided by all of the keepers, even the most courageous ones, due to his exceptionally dangerous behavior. Since this predator also mounted the mightiest resistance against all efforts to train him, the director of the *Tierpark* decided to sacrifice this useless eater for the success of the cinema drama, even if he was a magnificent showpiece for the public due to his gigantic body size." The spectacularized killing of a captive animal brought Hagenbeck and *The Living Bridge* into the orbit of a wide-ranging German debate about the cinema's social and aesthetic value. Nevertheless, while cinema reformers criticized Hagenbeck for collaborating in the production of what they called "trash films" (*Schundfilme*), the censor in Berlin let the kill shot stand.[15]

The second example pertains to the exhibition of wildlife films at the park, which took place in a makeshift movie house known as "Hagenbeck's *Kino*." Though planned for some time, the cinema opened in the summer of 1913, contemporaneous to the elaborate Burma show, adding to and thereby extending the park's network of attractions, as the amusement park would later. Films were screened in the former animal-training hall, adjacent to the native village (see fig. 5.5). In its first year of operation, Hagenbeck's *Kino* accounted for one-third of the park's total revenue. The overarching program had a thematic focus, which was made explicit by a sign posted above the main entrance: "Living Pictures from the Hunting and Animal World." In 1913, the

program included various films by celebrity sportsmen such as the German Robert Schumann and the American Paul J. Rainey. In particular, it was *Paul J. Rainey's African Hunt* (released in Germany as *Jagd auf Löwen* or, Hunt for Lions) that probably accounted for most of the park's movie receipts that year. Writing of its reception in the United States, Bousé links the phenomenal success of this film to its rapid pacing, to its extraordinary use of pack dogs for hunting, and to the film's hyperbolic display of animal death. "Accounts vary of the actual death toll: Rainey may have killed 27 lions in 35 days, or 9 lions in 35 minutes, or both, and a total of 74 lions on the entire trip." Whereas circus films and melodramas such as *The Living Bridge* amassed "sensations," early safari films such as *Rainey's African Hunt* piled up the bodies. In each case, however, the park made a space for the spectacle of animal death, so long as it appeared at a certain remove from the visitor, framed and contained within context of film.[16]

5.5 "Hagenbeck's *Kino*: Living Pictures from the Hunting and Animal World." Kaiser Wilhelm II and his entourage are depicted here, exiting the cinema. In the foreground are two performers from the "Burma" troupe of 1913. Courtesy of Tierpark Carl Hagenbeck GmbH, Hamburg-Stellingen.

The opening of Hagenbeck's *Kino* inspired various members of the park's personnel to try their hand at filmmaking. Whereas earlier some of Hagenbeck's trappers became *Völkerschau* recruiters and impresarios, later they began second careers in the film industry. Around 1913, trapper Christoph Schulz accepted an offer to travel and film with the famous hunter Schumann in the German colony of East Africa. Several different wildlife films were the result of their expedition, one of which, *Aus der afrikanischen Wildnis* (From the African Jungle, 1914), was made specifically for exhibition at Hagenbeck's *Kino*. By this time, however, there were many different interlopers between the park and the cinema. Most significant among them were not the celebrated trappers-cum-filmmakers, but the people whose responsibility it was to decorate the park and its living habitats, some of whom around this time also went to work in the film industry.[17]

5.6 "In Hagenbeck's *Kino* (training hall building): Presentation of the famous film by Paul Rainey, *Hunt for Lions*." Advertisement poster from 1913. Courtesy of Tierpark Carl Hagenbeck GmbH, Hamburg-Stellingen.

The Set as Collection

The connection between the park and the cinema is perhaps strongest in regard to set design. This is particularly true of the late 1910s, a period when the film set became a spectacle in its own right. During this period new film genres took shape, the very names of which announced the set's new-found importance, whether they emphasized the hyperbolic scale of production, such as the "monumental film" (e.g., *Cabiria*, Italy, 1914; dir. Giovanni Pastrone) and the "historical epic" (*Intolerance*, U.S., 1916; dir. D. W. Griffith), or flaunted the lavish use of props, costumes, and furnishings, such as the German *Ausstattungsfilm* or "décor film" (*Passion*, Germany, 1919; dir. Ernst Lubitsch). The last category was also used, significantly, in marketing the many different feature films that were made at Hagenbeck's *Tierpark*. What most interests me about these films in particular is what they suggest about the origins of set decoration (*Ausstattung*), and its implications for our historical understanding of filmic diegesis as a new type of themed environment, more generally.[18]

There was a moment in early German cinema when the cultural practice of set decoration relied on the availability of existing collections. All of the film sets to be examined here are not merely reminiscent of Hagenbeck's *Tierpark*. They were literally once part of it. The

334 335 336 337 338 339 340 342 341 343 344 345 346 347 348

Tafel XVII. 334—348.

very sceneries and props that Hagenbeck had employed for the purpose of creating a series of living habitats would occasionally be co-opted by filmmakers and put to new use. What is more, some of the very personnel who shaped the park and its displays found that their skills were also highly desirable in the burgeoning German film industry.[19]

The key figure in this regard is Hagenbeck's own nephew and set decorator, Heinrich Umlauff (1868–1925). Before the film industry turned him into a property man, Umlauff worked for several decades in the museum business. Founded by his father in 1868, the J. F. G. Umlauff Natural-Goods Store and Museum (*Naturalien-Handlung und Museum*) was actually a commercial trade house that retailed everything from pickled insects to Asian art. As a young man, Heinrich and his brother, Johannes (1874–1951), each worked as curators and honed their skills in taxidermy. Together, they created some of the very first "life group" museum displays in Germany. Heinrich went on to develop a particular emphasis on ethnographic objects and scenes, whereas Johannes focused on zoological specimens. Their close relationship to Carl Hagenbeck (J. F. G. Umlauff married Hagenbeck's oldest sister Caroline in 1863) became crucial to the museum's development. In the late 1860s, the museum occupied space in the same building as Hagenbeck's trade menagerie in St. Pauli. When the senior Umlauff died in 1889, Hagenbeck helped run the museum until Heinrich was ready to take over as its director, which he did in 1894. By this time, Umlauff had already gained an international reputation as a major dealer in ethnographic artifacts, with such notable clients as Chicago's Field Museum and the American Museum of Natural History. He sold individual objects and entire collections not only from his storefront in Hamburg but also through richly illustrated mail-order catalogs (see, e.g., fig. 5.7). Eventually, the Umlauff Museum became an important source of "primitive art" for young German artists including Ernst Ludwig Kirchner. By the same token, and more important for Heinrich Umlauff, he also supplied Hagenbeck's many ethnographic troupes with whatever they needed in terms of props, costumes, and furnishings.[20]

5.7 Samples from *The Ceylon Collection of the Museum Umlauff, Hamburg*. Catalog No. 113 (Hamburg: Friedländer, 1900), sales catalogue. The objects in this collection were assembled by John Hagenbeck and imported to Germany in 1899, along with a troupe of ethnographic performers. Some of these artifacts were used by the performers as part of the "native industry" displays at John and Gustav Hagenbeck's "Ceylon Exhibition" (1900) before the collection went to auction.

Around 1907, Umlauff became head of "artistic direction" (*künstlerische Oberleitung*) at Hagenbeck's *Tierpark* in Stellingen, where he helped design panoramas as well as ethnographic exhibitions. In this capacity, he was credited with directing some of the most elaborate spectacles Hagenbeck ever produced, including the Oglala-Sioux show of 1910 and the Egyptian exhibition of 1912. The enormous architectural motifs of the latter show—the Sphinx, the pyramids, and the Cliff Temple of Abu Simbel—established Umlauff's reputation as an accomplished designer of monumental sets (see fig. 3.11). These and other examples of his work were celebrated in souvenir guidebooks and newspaper reviews at a time when film architects (such as Robert A. Dietrich, who in 1913 designed the "Arabian Street" at Deutsche Bioscop's studio in Babelsberg) were regarded as little more than carpenters, receiving no bill-

5.8 On the set of *Peer Gynt* (Richard Oswald-Film, 1918; dir. Viktor Barnowsky). Scenes from the "Arabic Quarter" were filmed at Hagenbeck's *Tierpark* in 1917. Among those pictured here are Heinrich Umlauff (*far left, smoking a water pipe*) and beside him Erich Pommer, the famous German film producer and founder of Decla Film Company. Copyright: Museum für Völkerkunde, Hamburg.

ing whatsoever in film credits or program brochures. In short, Umlauff's expertise and resourcefulness augured well for his future success in the film industry. At the *Tierpark* he demonstrated exceptional ability in the creative mixing of collections and reproductions, choreographing museum objects and ethnographic performers within simulated exotic landscapes and native villages. Moreover, as director of an "ethnographic museum," he offered not only a wealth of exotic paraphernalia but also a sense of cultural authority.

In 1917, Umlauff launched a new career in the film industry. One important context for his move was the popular craze among German audiences for "Indian" films and other exotic subjects, as evidenced by the phenomenal success of *The Maharaja's Favorite Wife* (*Maharadjahens yndlingshustru*, Nordisk, 1917; dir. Robert Dinesen). The Danish production created such a stir in wartime Germany that critics dubbed it "Maharaja mania." Between 1917 and 1925, three sequels, a spoof, a re-make of the original, and countless other "India" films would appear in Germany and Denmark. Umlauff was hired to decorate the sets and provide costumes for two exotic melodramas, which were part of this cycle, each produced by the Decla Film Company and directed by Otto Rippert—namely, *The Foreigner: A Strange Story from Tibet* (*Der Fremde: Eine seltsame Geschichte aus Tibet*, 1917) and *The Princess of Travankore: An Indian Love Story* (*Die Königstochter von Travankore: Ein indisches Liebesdrama*, 1917). Both of these films were shot at Decla's studios at Weißensee, on the outskirts of Berlin.

A third production, an adaptation of Henrik Ibsen's drama, *Peer Gynt* (Richard Oswald-Film, 1918; dir. Viktor Barnowsky), marked Umlauff's return from Berlin to Hamburg. Part of the drama (act one) takes place in Morocco, in the Sahara desert, and in Cairo. Rather than create another "Arabic Quarter" in Berlin, Umlauff brought his new colleagues to Hagenbeck's *Tierpark* in Stellingen, where a collection of outdoor sets, organized around a similar theme, was readily available in the form of an ethnographic village. The sceneries, which Umlauff had designed and built, could also be adapted for the purpose of filmmaking. To top it off, two different ethnographic troupes happened to be performing there, at the same time: "an outstanding troupe of Bedouin riders and a large Sudanese Caravan."[21] Umlauff lured the production of *Peer Gynt* to Stellingen with a standing collection of outdoor sets and sceneries, and a ready-made cast of professional foreign actors, whose costumes (and horses) had already been coordinated with the settings. More important, perhaps, it was this production that captured the attention of other producers such as Erich Pommer, who (along with the acclaimed cameraman Carl Hoffmann) visited the set of *Peer Gynt* while touring Hagenbeck's *Tierpark* and assessing its potential as a site for other large-scale film productions (see fig. 5.8).

Between 1917 and 1921, at least seven different production companies made films at Hagenbeck's *Tierpark*. The films included: *Peer Gynt* (Richard Oswald-Film, 1918; dir. Viktor Barnowsky); *Sadja* (Ring-Film, 1918; dir. Adolf Gärtner); *Eyes of Jade* (*Die Augen von Yade*, Hella-Moja-Film, 1918; dir. Iwa Raffay); *The Love of the Bayadère* (*Die Liebe der Bajadere*, Argus-Film, 1918; dir. Svend Gade, who also wrote the script for *The Maharaja's Favorite Wife*); *Death and Love* (*Der Tod und die Liebe*, Vera-Filmwerke, 1919; dir. Paul Otto); *Harakiri* (Decla, 1919; dir. Fritz Lang); *The Golden Sea*, part one of

5.9 An interior set decorated by Heinrich Umlauff, from *The Golden Sea* (part one of *The Spiders*, Decla, 1919; dir. Fritz Lang), production still. The exotic objects strewn about the room—Buddha statues, Sri Lankan masks, South Sea woodcuts, Oriental rugs, and tribal weapons—could also be found in the Umlauff Museum and its sales catalogs (cf. fig. 5.7). Bundesarchiv-Filmarchiv Berlin, Sign. 5984.

The Spiders (*Der goldene See*, part one of *Die Spinnen*, Decla, 1919; dir. Fritz Lang); *The Prey of the Furies* (*Die Beute der Erinnyen*, Sächsischer Kunstfilm, 1921; dir. Otto Rippert); and *Ebb and Flow* (*Ebbe und Flut*, Vera-Filmwerke, 1921; dir. Martin Hartwig). Significantly, none of these films has a story set in Hagenbeck's *Tierpark* (or in a zoo, for that matter); all of them take place in foreign locations, which is precisely why they were made there in the first place.[22] As one reporter put it, "The great cliff formations, which dreamily emerge from winding ponds among rich arrangements of trees and bushes, were practically made as background and scenery to give living pictures the fidelity to nature that they require." Indeed, with only minor adjustments, the park's various settings could be revised to anchor any number of generic scenes that took place in "Egypt" (*Peer Gynt*), in "Japan" (*Eyes of Jade* and *Harakiri*), in "India" (*Sadja, Death and Love*), "China" (*The Prey of the Furies*), or on "an island in the South Seas" (*Ebb and Flow*). For each production, it was Umlauff's job to supply the necessary props and costumes from his private warehouse and to supervise both the conversion of existing sets and the construction of new ones. For example, *The Love of the Bayadère*, which takes place in India, called for the addition of a "massive entrance to a cliff temple, a pretty little temple pavilion, a runic grove, a colossal staircase rising up to a temple, and a massive tower," all of which had to be either built or grafted onto existing structures.[23]

Of all these films, *Eyes of Jade* made the most creative and sustained use of the park as a themed environment in its own right. A version of the "Madame Butterfly" story, the film recycles numerous motifs from the park as it stood—including gardens, pathways, cliff formations, and of course the "Japanese Island," with its representative flora, statuary, and architecture. In the words of one commentator, who visited the set when the film was in production, "A miniature Japan has been constructed in Stellingen near Hamburg. Delicate tea houses, winding waterfalls, in whose reflection Japanese foliage sways back and forth—in short, a wonderful Kino-Japan filled with the aura of authenticity has settled outside of the old hanseatic city." Two production stills from *Eyes of Jade* demonstrate this transformation more vividly on the level of concrete example. The first image (fig. 5.10) shows the young Norwegian diplomat, Kay Nordhong (Henri Peters-Arnolds) and his Japanese lover, Moi Fa Loi (played by Takka Takka, a Japanese-German actress who lived and worked in Berlin). The park's leafy gardens and artificial rockwork appear in the background; flower-blossom trees figure prominently in the right foreground. This particular image, which was also used as a publicity photo, recalls deliberately the composition of Japanese woodcuts—a stylistic move that Fritz Lang would explore further in *Harakiri*, another version of "Madame Butterfly" that would be filmed there a few weeks later. If the *Tierpark* was created under an aesthetic impulse, as I have claimed, it also seems to have moved the filmmakers who came to work there.[24]

5.10 Vertical framing revises the park's gardens, ponds, and cliffs to evoke Japan, recalling the composition of a Japanese woodcut. From *Eyes of Jade* (Hella-Moja-Film, 1918; dir. Iwa Raffay), production still. Bundesarchiv-Filmarchiv Berlin, Sign. 24336.

The second image (fig. 5.11) shows how the creative process of recycling the park's exotic motifs is taken one step further. From the very beginning of the film, the park's great cliff formations serve to evoke "Japanese mountains," and some of the animal panoramas are reframed so as to signify ocean shores and inlets. In this particular scene, Moi Fa Loi retreats to "the Grotto of the Children's Spirits"—a former seal and walrus exhibit—where she mourns the death of her son. She paddles a canoe through an archway in the cliffs,

5.11 Ma Fa Loi (played by the Japanese-German actress, Takka Takka) sits and meditates in "the Grotto of the Children's Spirits." From *Eyes of Jade* (Hella-Moja-Film, 1918; dir. Iwa Raffay), production still. Bundesarchiv-Filmarchiv Berlin, Sign. 24336.

ascends a rocky bank, and seats herself there in the lotus position amidst a collection of vases, statutes, shrines, and other memorial objects.[25]

A similar combination of elements appears in Fritz Lang's *The Golden Sea*, but the effect is remarkably different. For this production, one of the park's animal panoramas was used to stand for a remote South American setting. In the "rock caverns" (*Felsenkammern*) underneath "the ancient Incan City of Ruins," the vases and statues strewn about are coded as accursed objects bringing death to those who would possess them (fig. 5.12). A high-angle shot helps screen out blatant signs of the *Tierpark*, while recycling one of its premiere displays. In this case, an outdoor panorama becomes a subterranean space (one of many to be found in Lang's films). Here, too, the conspicuous arrangement of vases, shrines, statues, and other exotic-looking objects suggests a choreography of objects that is perhaps more commonly associated with museum-based displays. The absence of animals and the knowledge that these spaces are Hagenbeck's vaunted panoramas make the deployment of objects all the more striking. As the cavern scene would seem to suggest, filming the exotic sceneries at Hagenbeck's *Tierpark* did not merely have a denotative function; it was meant to dazzle the audience.[26]

Umlauff played an important role in the development of set decoration as a collection-based practice, but he was not alone. The work of his younger brother,

5.12 "Gold! Gold!" *The Spiders*, Part One: *The Golden Sea* (Decla, 1919; dir. Fritz Lang), publicity still. Bundesarchiv-Filmarchiv Berlin, Sign. 5984.

Johannes, helps round out the picture. In 1912, after a long-standing dispute between the siblings, the collections of the original family museum were divided between them: Heinrich retained ownership of the J. F. G. Umlauff Company, its building, and its extensive collections of ethnological artifacts; Johannes took the zoological specimens to form the basis for his own store across town. After that time Johannes competed against his brother directly, and he continued to do so when German director Joe May hired him to work as a property man at the May Film City in Woltersdorf, near Berlin. There, Johannes Umlauff helped decorate some of the monumental sets for what would become two of the period's best-known exotic adventure films—namely, *Mistress of the World* (*Die Herrin der Welt*, 1919) and *The Indian Tombstone* (*Das indische Grabmal*, 1921). Without access to his family's ethnographic collections, however, he necessarily had to find another source from which to rent huge quantities of all the necessary props, costumes, and furnishings. Thus, in preparation for *The Indian Tombstone*, he

5.13 Spotlight on the museum artifact—on loan. Also pictured here is Irene Rowland (Mia May) in *The Indian Tombstone* (*Das indische Grabmal*, May-Film, 1921; dir. Joe May), frame enlargement. Courtesy of the Deutsche Kinemathek, Berlin.

went to the Museum of Biology, Ethnography, and Trade (*Museum für Natur-, Völker- und Handelskunde*), which is today known simply as the Overseas Museum (*Übersee-museum*), in the city of Bremen, where he procured among other things:

> A train-wagon full of Indian mats, palm leaves, hemp ropes, coconuts, a thousand bundles of bananas with stems; two wagons of bamboo poles, which were needed to build huts; from the . . . museum I took the whole collection of Chinese paraphernalia. . . . For the Buddhist scene I had an entire Chinese temple with interior Buddha statues, holy vessels, big candelabras, silk blankets and flags; for places to sit in this room, there were marble tables, chairs, and stools. . . . I had but three days to pack everything into three train wagons. As I took my leave from [the museum's director] Professor [Hugo] Schauinsland and his colleagues, I paid a rental fee of 10,000 Marks; the material was insured against any damage for 250,000 Marks.[27]

The example of Johannes Umlauff provides further evidence of the film set as an extraordinary form of collection, only here on a "monumental" scale. What distinguishes this evidence, however, is the fact that Johannes Umlauff would receive almost no credit for his work on the set. The work of his brother, by contrast, was widely

5.14 Umlauff built this Japanese-style house on the pedestrian path, which winds around the park's main cliff formation (the cliff's base is visible in the background). Pictured here are the film's protagonists, O-Take-San (Lil Dagover) and Olaf J. Andersen (Niels Prien). From *Harakiri* (Decla, 1919; dir. Fritz Lang), publicity still. Bundesarchiv-Filmarchiv Berlin, Sign. 33559.

noted, reviewed, and celebrated in the press. Heinrich Umlauff earned considerable recognition for his services, as his name was flaunted in publicity materials, which in turn made his work even more conspicuous. As spectators read in the film's opening credits of *The Golden Sea*, "The exotic structures and props were supplied by the ethnographic museum of Heinrich Umlauff, Hamburg."[28]

What Umlauff delivered, ultimately, and what production companies such as Decla sought by association with him, was more than an inventory of authentic-looking objects. He also provided a certain amount of "cultural capital" (to borrow a term from Pierre Bordieu), which attached to the films in which his name and his objects appeared. In the different taglines on these productions, Umlauff's name, role, and affiliation are literally advertised up front, through advertising paraphernalia and opening film credits, so that audiences were made aware of his contribution and urged to appreciate its significance. In each case, his business is identified as a "museum," and not a warehouse or curio shop, with strong implications that he also possesses a degree of scientific expertise and authority. To quote an advertisement for *Harakiri*: "Under the exemplary direction of Fritz Lang, at whose side stood Heinrich Umlauff, with his experiences in the field of ethnography, as adviser, Decla has set a new standard in cinematography. The J. F. G. Umlauff Museum made available its entire Japanese collection. There are Japanese buildings, entire Japanese streets, the *Yoshiwara* in Nippon (Nagasaki), the typical Japanese houses of bamboo, the diversity of Japanese flora and fauna. In short, this film conveys to us an attractive, faithful image of Japan" (see fig. 5.14).[29] Spectators were thus invited to imagine the hand of the collector delivering objects from his museum, placing them on the set, and arranging them before the camera. The Berlin critic Karl Figdor spoke for others when he marveled at the film's "truly authentic Umlauff interiors (*wirklich echte Umlauffsche Interieure*)."[30] A further contrast makes the emphasis placed on Umlauff even more apparent. The very films that highlight his involvement refrain from even mentioning that they were filmed at Hagenbeck's *Tierpark* in Stellingen.[31]

The implications of this precious material are intriguing, for what it suggests is not the fundamental creation of a new space (the façade set) but the recycling of existing objects and spaces, which are put to different use. It is a thorny problem to realize that much of this distinction gets conflated in the final image, so that the authenticity claims in these films rely on discursive, non-visual, and extra-filmic evidence (such as publicity material). It seems to me, however, that this elision makes the attempt at recycling all the more interesting, for so much history lies in these spaces and such great effort went into acquiring these objects in the first place. Fritz Lang and other directors were evidently intrigued by the idea, and it had a live function in the movie-making practice at the time. Why was that so? After all, it would seem to defy the very logic of designing for the cinema. "The main problem during set construction," as French designer Léon Barsacq has suggested, "is how to reconcile authenticity of appearance with [the] great mobility of the elements of the set. It would be just as unreasonable to employ real gold ingots for a scene in a film as to build the wall of a set with real blocks of granite." And yet this is essentially what Umlauff was hired to do—much as he had done earlier, in the context of the *Völkerschau*. At the time he joined the film industry, the issue of authenticity remained a salient one, and so did the practice of collecting. Theme space had long been defined for mass audiences by the choreography of collected objects and bodies, and it is this model that film companies in turn would appropriate and revise. The material basis that linked these forms of theme space, which was the physical displacement of the spectacle to the observer, provided a usable platform for the film set as a type of built environment.[32]

The Park as Film Studio

The first scholars to explore the film studio registered its debt to nineteenth-century visual culture in the very language that they used to describe what it was that they were seeing. For example, in her 1913 dissertation "On the Sociology of the Cinema," Emilie Altenloh coined the term "museum parks" (in German, *Museumparks*) for what was then the totally new phenomenon of assembling large, outdoor film sets. Since only a portion of her dissertation is available in English (i.e., her important survey of Mannheim audiences, the very first study of historical spectators), her descriptive walking tour of an unnamed studio back-lot, which comes from a different section of the dissertation, bears repeating. Rather than travel in search of locations, Altenloh wrote, the latest strategy was

> to gather together various motifs through the addition of parks, in which all possible sceneries stand beside one another. We begin, for example, from an old castle, which originally reigned supreme over this entire area. Directly adjacent to it we see a half-completed new building, and a bit farther down we enter the courtyard of a country farmhouse. Chickens, ducks, geese, dogs, and even two bears live their lives here as actors. The house is connected to "the jungle," with a river flowing through it, and ten steps beyond that we come to a garage, which contains the cinema's most important component part: namely, the automobile. From a modern streetcar we step immediately into medieval Rothenburg, with its steep roofs and narrow lanes.

Reading this description, it is easy to imagine why the term "museum park" should have occurred to her. The very aspects that Altenloh highlights—fragmentation, displacement, artifice, juxtaposition—would later be emphasized by Siegfried Kracauer in his well-known 1926 essay, "Calico-World: The UFA City in Neubabelsberg." If the studio back-lot was a peripheral site of film production when Altenloh wrote her dissertation, it was absolutely central by the time that Kracauer visited Germany's most famous studio near Berlin. Nevertheless, he still compares it to a museum, a zoological garden, and a wildlife preserve. "Greenhouses complete the collection." In comparison to other forms of collection, however, Kracauer imagines the film studio as enacting an even more radical process of transformation and mixing: "the things that rendezvous here do not belong to reality. They are copies and distortions that have been ripped out of time and jumbled together. They stand motionless, full of meaning from the front, while from the rear they are just empty nothingness." The film studio thus combines the natural and the artificial, the collected and the constructed, in ways that suggest both its inheritance from an earlier model of theme space, and its transformation of this model, at the same time. In Kracauer's analysis, the film studio amassed the remnants of physical reality for the sole purpose of converting them into a lighted and dazzling surface. It is against this backdrop of the studio set that Hagenbeck's *Tierpark* also needs to be seen.[33]

In 1919, the Deutsche Éclair (Decla) Film Company signed exclusive, multi-year agreements with Umlauff's museum and Hagenbeck's *Tierpark*. Though never fully realized, the plan was not simply to rent space within the *Tierpark*, but to transform it into a completely different entity: a modern studio complex. The park would be integrated, dissolved, and renamed "The Decla Film City in Hamburg-Stellingen." Just as zoological gardens around the world began experimenting with selected ideas from Hagenbeck's innovative model, the *Tierpark* faced conversion into a film studio. By studio I mean the physical and institutional infrastructure for film production, including stages, back-lots, buildings, and facilities. I also mean a site where diegetic elements (sets, props, costumes, and so on) are assembled, stored, and arranged in time and space. In a sense, the film studio's very reason to exist was a diegetic one; it was fundamentally devoted to the creation of imaginary story worlds. In this case, significantly, it originated as a collection of collections. The plan for the Decla Film City can indeed be read as a blueprint for re-making nineteenth-century theme space along cinematic lines. It provides exact details for the production of synthetic spaces out of existing collections of objects, bodies, and sets that, until very recently, were integral elements of a functioning park. Just as Hagenbeck had converted the panorama into a new type of living habitat, the film company would radically transform the park into a new type of themed environment.[34]

The fact that Decla's proposal was accepted might surprise some readers, and rightly so. The very idea would seem to contradict the phenomenal popularity of Hagenbeck's *Tierpark*. In the years leading up to the war, the park attracted on average more than one million visitors per year. It was definitely a place that was meant to be revised, again and again, to generate repeat spectators. And yet, however mutable and provisional the park might have been, it was certainly never destined to become a film studio. Hagenbeck and his employees often collaborated with filmmakers, as I have shown, but the idea that the entire park might one day be sold to a film company was by no means self-evident. Nor does it seem obvious in retrospect.[35]

There were three major factors contributing to the park's transformation into a film studio: Hagenbeck's death, the outbreak of war, and the burgeoning German film industry. Carl Hagenbeck died on 14 April 1913; he was sixty-eight years old. Over the last few years of his life, he accumulated a huge amount of debt, which he bequeathed to his sons, Heinrich and Lorenz. Since 1909, his animal business suffered tremendous financial losses because of the boycott of German zoo directors, whose efforts only intensified when Hagenbeck launched a public campaign to build a new *Tier-*

park in Berlin. This mountain of debt was the financial backdrop for such spectacular projects as the dinosaur habitat, the movie house, and the Hugo Haase amusement park. By adding such attractions, Hagenbeck sought to increase revenue from gate receipts, and thereby compensate for at least some of his losses in the animal trade. It was also against this backdrop that he transformed his privately owned business into a family company and named his sons as co-owners. In so doing, Hagenbeck hoped to circumvent the boycott, which was aimed at him personally, by installing his sons as the company's new front men, without actually relinquishing control over the animal business or the larger firm. The plan, however, failed. Upon his death, Hagenbeck had accumulated so much debt that the family's lawyer advised Lorenz and Heinrich to refuse their inheritance (they did not). In 1914, the older son Heinrich was drafted by the military, returning in 1918. During the interim, John Hagenbeck co-directed the park with his nephew Lorenz, though the latter was frequently absent from Hamburg, touring with the Carl Hagenbeck Circus through neutral Sweden. As another scholar has shown, it was the circus, and not the trade menagerie, that kept the company solvent during the war.[36]

The most significant factor contributing to the park's transformation was probably Germany's prolonged engagement in the war. By October 1914, Germany's international maritime trade had already come to a standstill, with dire consequences for an exotic animal business. "The firm of Hagenbeck has on its hands scores of wild animals with no market for them," the *New York Times* reported. "Hagenbeck is left in the lurch with 75 full-grown lions, 45 tigers, 70 trained polar bears, 100 hyenas, and 67 elephants, besides five caravans [i.e., ethnographic troupes], which ought to be on their way home to Africa, India, or wherever their homes may be, with their horses, camels &c. All these men and beasts must be housed and fed."[37] The sea blockade, which some historians have described as the most potent weapon in the Allied arsenal, resulted in severe food shortages (especially of meat) and a nation-wide policy of enforced rations (including a prohibition on feeding bread and grain to animals). Germany's livestock would soon be depleted by as much as eighty percent, and show animals presumably fared worse. At Hagenbeck's park, the entire collection of seals, sea lions, and walruses became the first to die of malnutrition. In 1918, the lions and tigers succumbed to food poisoning. Still other animals, inadvertently fed the same diseased meat, would be put out of their misery. Though the park was not totally depleted as a result of the war, it suffered tremendous losses. The living habitat no longer thrived; its demise seemed imminent.[38]

The situation grew even worse after the war. By May 1919, when Decla was negotiating with Umlauff, the war had formally ended, but the sea blockade was still enforced and would remain so for another two months. In fact, during the first year of the armistice, the range and scope of the blockade was extended to include new areas and greater restrictions on food imports in particular. As a result, widespread starvation and food rationing continued throughout the year. The Hamburg economy was hit particularly hard by these additional measures, as fishing in the Baltic Sea was banned for the first time, as were fish imports from Scandinavian countries. To regain the opportunity to import food, Germany was required to surrender its merchant marine, which it did in July 1919, followed by the best of its rolling stock (thousands of train engines and wagons). The closure of shipping lanes had long prevented Hagenbeck's *Tierpark* from restocking, which was logistically impossible during the war. After the war, hyperinflation and astronomical exchange rates prohibited German dealers from paying freight charges to foreign shipping lines. Companies from Allied countries seized the opportunity to take over markets that had been dominated for years by German dealers. Prospects for recovery in the animal trade were bleak.[39]

The film industry, by contrast, was flourishing in postwar Germany. Its consolidation was a direct result of Germany's wartime isolation and the urgent need for self-sufficiency. Theaters, distributors, and production companies multiplied as never before. This trend continued, momentarily, in the war's immediate aftermath. In a 1919 report titled "Film-Founding Fever!" the Berlin critic Fritz Olimsky exclaimed, "Not a day goes by without the founding of a new film company." In Hamburg, for instance, three film studios, twenty theaters, and almost as many production companies were established between 1914 and 1919. In Olimsky's view: "The astounding rise of the Hamburg film industry can be traced back to the stranglehold on German overseas trade, which left hanseatic merchants casting about for new spheres of influence."[40]

John Hagenbeck offers a particularly relevant example. In 1918, he quit his post as acting director of the *Tierpark* and established the John Hagenbeck Film Company in Berlin. A scant year later, without having produced a single film, he opened a second office in Hamburg. Here, the company produced its first feature, *Darwin* (1919; dir. Fritz Bernhardt), an exoticized version of the sexual "enlightenment films" (*Aufklärungsfilme*) that swamped the German market after the war. This one transformed Darwin's principle of sexual selection into an erotic melodrama set in a tropical jungle. Johannes Umlauff supplied the costumes, props, and tribal paraphernalia. Between 1919 and 1924, the John Hagenbeck Film Company produced fourteen features and nine short animations. The emergence of this small production company offers only one case of Germany's "film-founding fever," but it is one that exemplifies the role of hanseatic merchants and of the Hagenbeck clan in particular.[41]

The massive infusion of capital into the Hamburg film industry lured major companies from Berlin to create subsidiaries there, which brings us back to Decla and its takeover of the *Tierpark*. Founded by Erich Pommer, Decla emerged from the war a relatively strong company, having produced some of Germany's most artistically interesting films to date. Crucially, however, it "lacked a modern, technically well-equipped studio." As Pommer explained, "The Decla studios in Weißensee [near Berlin], which were being used until now, had become too small and outdated." Through its merger with the Bioscop Film Company, Decla would later gain access to the facilities at Neubabelsberg, the quintessential studio of the German cinema past and present. Prior to this, however, Pommer tried a rather different approach, one which aimed to literally capitalize on the company's various wartime productions in Hamburg. Historically, Decla had placed great emphasis on the appearance of its props, costumes, and settings, as evidenced by the use of Umlauff's museum and Hagenbeck's *Tierpark*. The proposed strategy was to monopolize these resources, and at the same time acquire some much-needed space for internal expansion and future development.[42]

The park's transformation into a film studio is clearly spelled out by the terms of each agreement. According to the first contract, signed on 9 May 1919, Decla gained exclusive access to the "entire museum as well as to Umlauff's own rich experience in the field of ethnology; [. . .] it also gives Decla exclusive rights to his extensive exotic collections." In one fell swoop, the museum became a prop department (*Filmfundus*), and Umlauff its manager. By acquiring his collections of artifacts, costumes, and furniture, which were diverse enough to accommodate a broad spectrum of exotic subjects, and deep enough to supply multiple productions at the same time, the film company locked in a reliable independent supplier with a public reputation for quality and "authenticity." The first contract set the terms for the Hagenbeck agreement, which Umlauff also helped negotiate. As the Berlin trade journal *Lichtbildbühne* reported, on 11 October 1919, "Decla is creating a second center of activity in Hamburg. The company has obtained exclusive rights from Hagenbeck in Stellingen to shoot films there on the largest scale; the agreement gives Decla the opportunity to build enormous mountain scenes, waterways, city buildings, etc." The *Tierpark* had a proven track record as an imaginary space that spectators found convincing in person. Its uncanny ability to stand in for other places, real and imagined, became a resource that the company would co-opt in the context of film production. This "multi-year agreement" further stipulated that "all of the park's collections and motifs will be made available to Decla." Finally, it was reported that "a Decla subsidiary will build a modern studio with all the latest technology as well as a big film city on a 16,000 square-meter [15-acre] lot adjacent to the *Tierpark*." Among the planned studio buildings were indoor stages, photographic laboratories, and cutting rooms. The combined agreements were in keeping with Decla's projected image as a first-rate company on the ascent.[43]

The strategy, then, was to merge the various resources of the museum and the park and convert them as needed to form the necessary physical and institutional infrastructure for film production. The plan's centerpiece was the *Tierpark*. On the most basic level, the park and its grounds provided a range of facilities, including gas, water, and electric utilities. It also offered ready access to a major port city, with

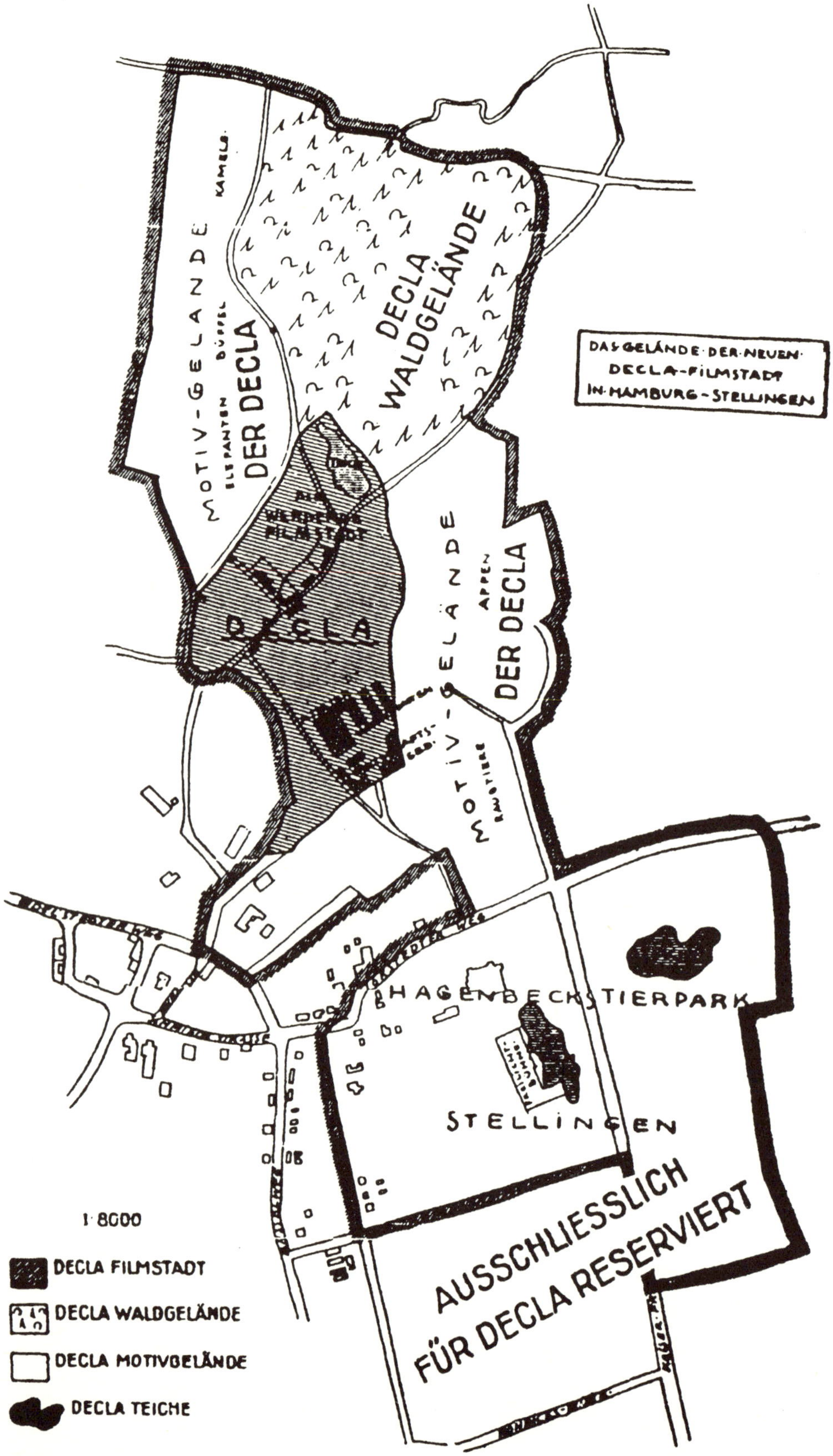

DAS GELÄNDE DER NEUEN DECLA-FILMSTADT IN HAMBURG-STELLINGEN
MOTIV-GELÄNDE DER DECLA
DECLA WALDGELÄNDE
DECLA
MOTIV-GELÄNDE DER DECLA
HAGENBECKS TIERPARK
STELLINGEN
AUSSCHLIESSLICH FÜR DECLA RESERVIERT
1:8000
DECLA FILMSTADT
DECLA WALDGELÄNDE
DECLA MOTIVGELÄNDE
DECLA TEICHE

an expanding network of transportation and communication lines (roads, streetcars, railways, steamships, telegraphs, and telephones) already in place. Stellingen made a reasonable choice as far as location, too. In his important production manual, translated from the original Danish into German as *Der Film: seine Mittel, seine Ziele* (The Film: Its Means and Aims, 1919), the most comprehensive account of the film studio to date, director Urban Gad claimed that when it came to choosing a studio's location, the decisive factors were access and availability. "The terrain must be situated where it has easy connections to a city, so that people and things can be transported as rapidly as possible. And since there is nothing on God's great earth that is not essential to a film studio, it must preferably be located near a big city, because there one finds the best possibilities for procurement." In a sense, Decla planned to streamline the process even further by acquiring entire collections that had already been assembled and by hiring various specialists to manage them. For all these reasons—infrastructure, location, access, and availability—the *Tierpark* in Stellingen was ideal for the future site of a new film city.[44]

Decla's plan called not only for the acquisition of existing spaces and collections but also—more important—for their radical transformation. In this regard, it helps to recall that the *Tierpark* was originally conceived as a kind of super-panorama for mobile spectators to explore. Decla, by contrast, envisioned reshaping the grounds, dismantling the living habitats, and reallocating the remaining collections. For example, selected animals (elephants, buffalos, camels, monkeys, and carnivores are indicated on the diagram) would be moved to one of several "motif grounds," or back-lots, where they would be stored, and not displayed, until their presence was needed (however briefly) for future use on any number of possible sets. Until now, the park's collections were basically identical to its display spaces. Its conversion into a film city necessitated that the park's collections be divided from their spaces of display for the very first time. As indicated above, the agreement also called for the construction of new outdoor sets that were not, however, designed to accommodate live animals over time. Nor were they built for the continued presence of roving visitors. Rather, the entire park was to be reorganized and realigned according to the principles governing film production on what was then the largest scale.

The proposal for the Decla Film City represents more than the genealogical blueprint of a modern studio complex: It diagrams explicitly some of the steps in a process of redesigning historical forms of theme space, for the purpose of creating new forms of theme space that are specific to the film medium. It further offers a unique view of the studio city's foundation (both literally and metaphorically) on older, collection-based forms of theme space. What is so fascinating about the Decla Film City is that these very institutions had a previous existence as an actual *Tierpark* and a functioning museum. In contrast to world-famous studio cities such as Babelsberg or Universal

5.15 "The grounds of the new Decla Film City in Hamburg-Stellingen." The legend indicates (*from top to bottom*): studio buildings, forest grounds, motif grounds, and ponds. Map from "Die Expansion der 'Decla,'" *Lichtbildbühne* (11 October 1919): 24.

City, this one did not merely compare with or poach from earlier forms of collection; it literally acquired and built on them. In so doing, it also makes explicit both the infrastructure and the impulse for collecting that lies half-hidden beneath the grounds of the film studio more generally.[45]

A collection of collections, the Decla Film City synthesizes the different aspects of filmic diegesis that have been emphasized and examined here: namely, the image, the set, and the studio. The conceptual relationship that emerges from this synthesis is one of interconnection between different models of theme space. The making of synthetic spectacles such as film space and imaginative worlds such as filmic diegesis was not so much opposed to as based on nineteenth-century theme space, which relied for its effect on the choreography of material objects, bodies, and spaces. In other words, the Decla Film City remains salient, even though it was never completed, because it demonstrates so vividly the combination of collection and simulation that resides at the core of nineteenth-century theme space, and takes this combination as a model for later developments.

✦ ✦ ✦

Less than one year into the project, Decla abandoned its film city in Hamburg-Stellingen. Yet another series of mergers and acquisitions brought with it unrestricted access to Neubabelsberg, Germany's largest and most famous studio complex, located just outside of Berlin. Consequently, it was reported in the trade press, Hagenbeck's park became "available to other film companies, as well." Several more features were made there by other companies, some of which made elaborate use of the park's grounds. By then, however, Hagenbeck's *Tierpark* had officially folded, and its future as an institution was uncertain.[46]

On 3 October 1920, Hagenbeck's *Tierpark* closed its gates to the public. In a press release issued shortly before this event, the company gave a detailed list of more than two-thousand animals that had died there since 1914, including seventy-four lions, sixty-eight ostriches, fifty snakes, forty bears, twenty-eight camels, one hundred and sixty baboons, and one thousand turtles. The few surviving animals were sold at rock-bottom prices to various clients in Allied countries. The American showman John Ringling, Barnum's successor, purchased the greater part of this emaciated collection and had it shipped to New York. According to the *New York Times*,

> After seeing scores of its most valuable animals perish of hunger because Germany's drastic wartime food regulations precluded their getting enough to eat, after losing scores of others because lack of coal caused them to freeze to death, the Hagenbeck firm has given up, for the time being at least, the struggle to keep in

> business. And, in view of the fact that Germany's loss of colonies and merchant marine makes it difficult for the firm to meet competition from other countries, there is a possibility that Stellingen may remain closed permanently and the name of Hagenbeck, for years renowned throughout the universe, become only a memory.[47]

The actual conditions there were probably worse than this report would make it seem, but the park did not shut its gates forever. Heinrich and Lorenz Hagenbeck created trade companies in The Hague and New York City, securing investments from foreign banks and reestablishing some of their father's international partnerships. Though the park remained closed to the public for nearly four years, it continued to serve as a depot for animals traded by the Hagenbeck subsidiaries abroad. Only by relocating its capital, and investing it abroad, would the park survive Germany's postwar economic crisis. On 24 May 1924, the year in which a new currency was introduced to stabilize the German economy, Hagenbeck's *Tierpark* in Stellingen re-opened its gates to visitors. What they found there, however, was that the simulated landscape had changed over time: the prolonged absence of animals and visitors allowed the few remaining groundskeepers to focus on the gardens as never before.

If the name Hagenbeck no longer resonates throughout the universe, it is also more than just a memory. Even today, we are surrounded by forms of theme space and immersive environments that bear the imprint of his legacy.

CONCLUSION

THE FUTURE OF NINETEENTH-CENTURY THEME SPACE

This book ends with a discussion of the park and the cinema, because their intersection represents at once the continuation and the transformation of theme space in the twentieth century and beyond. Many commentators have suggested in passing, as if it were self-evident, that the "birth" of the cinema also marked the "death" of Hagenbeck's entertainments, particularly that of the ethnographic exhibition. This idea will be immediately familiar to historians of visual culture, because it is a basic trope of the discourse on "pre-cinematic" entertainments more generally. If Hagenbeck worried about film's implications for the future success of his ethnographic enterprise, it is interesting to note that he added a make-shift cinema at the very point where the ethnographic village met the performance arena. At this juncture, the new medium of film represented not the metaphorical death of the living habitat but the continued vivification of exotic fantasies through the aspect of a new (cinematic) imaginary—witness the many fiction films that were made at Hagenbeck's *Tierpark*, or Decla's bid for the park and its collections. Conversely, however, the fact that Decla pulled up stakes in Hamburg and the fact that the *Tierpark* re-opened a few years later invite us to imagine a genealogy of theme space whose various historical forms are divergent but not disconnected. The enduring fascination with being in the living presence of wild animals and foreign peoples, as evidenced by contemporary zoos, museums, resorts, and tourist attractions, only confirms the continued visibility of nineteenth-century theme space in a global media environment that consists of more than simulacra.

This book concentrates on Hagenbeck and his multifarious endeavors because together they gave shape to a performance-based model of theme space that was later imitated worldwide. Other figures organized folk-ethnographic displays, native villages, and Wild West shows, but none had the kind of access to networks of collecting that Hagenbeck had, because of his work in the international animal trade, which also permitted him to assemble more ethnographic troupes than any other showman of the period. More important, as I have argued, his approach to habitat display was paradigmatic. The *Völkerschau* purported to exhibit "characteristic types" of non-Western peoples from a particular climatic zone or geographical region, surrounded by representative flora and fauna as well as by ethnographic artifacts and structures. His was a living habitat based on the physical presence of wild animals and foreign peoples in the midst of European spectators. For this type of spectacle to remain viable over time, the bodies on display had to thrive, a fact that further distinguished Hagenbeck's work from other types of habitat display, such as zone pictures and museum dioramas.

Collecting for ethnographic troupes entailed a complex series of negotiations among various social agents—including performers, recruiters, interpreters, missionaries, administrators, impresarios, entrepreneurs, scientists, artists, publicists, and spectators—with a range of different and often conflicting agendas. An awareness of this complexity is crucial, if we want to explore the cultural context of recruitment and display. It also allows us to gain a more nuanced (if necessarily limited) historical understanding of what motivated people to join a troupe in the first place. There is more than ample evidence of wide-scale displacement and native self-determination, which clearly undermines the showman's usual claim that performers were essentially "unchanged natural peoples." Similarly, a consideration of newspaper accounts both promoting and reviewing some of the earliest troupes poses a direct challenge to our received idea of the audience as naïve.

Historical spectators' awareness that troupe members were human beings, and not ideal anthropological types, was directly linked to the porosity of display space and viewing space, and the various ways in which performers and spectators rehearsed and revised different scenarios of cross-cultural encounter within the context of live entertainment. If the physical fact of shared space created a sensation of immersion in a strange world, it also introduced the more unsettling potential for reciprocity. The interaction between spectators and performers emerged as an unforeseen effect of the ethnographic shows that undermined their racist tenor and invoked a theme of shared humanity. This theme and its social implications were evidently troubling enough to raise concerns among outspoken religious critics, social conservatives, and pro-colonial propagandists. And yet, the longer trajectory of ethnographic exhibition is defined by increasing spectator participation and multisensory involvement in the spectacle.

Thus, Hagenbeck's later shows offer strong and hitherto neglected evidence of a larger transformation in theme space, from an expectation of "authenticity" and documentation to a willing acceptance of performance and simulation. If the idea of theme space originated in gathered scenes of actual objects and bodies, then how did it become transformed into something so different, so—synthetic? In this context, the relevant transformation first manifested, significantly, not in the cinema but in earlier forms of collection and display. The unexpected emergence of a fictional universe from the origins of ethnographic display was largely an effect of spectatorship, as evidenced by the German reception of the Wild West show. Through the imposition of fantasy, audiences sought to possess and command the spectacle, leaving showmen to respond by embracing (even prompting) the idea of the spectator's imaginative engagement. The professionalization of native performers, such as Hersi Egeh Gorseh and Nancy Columbia, added to this development, while bolstering the impression of respectability that the show needed in order to be widely marketable. Native participants were recruited to play identifiable roles within what was now explicitly described as a "show." Most important, the space of ethnographic display was reconstituted as a diegetic space, where dramatic stories unfolded before the audience—stories that relied for their effect on the spectator's powers of imagination and identification. The fictional story world of the arena spilled over into the ethnographic village and beyond. Whereas "villagers" and spectators shuttled back and forth between the two sites, enacting the very crossover that took place on the level of performance, souvenir guidebooks and program brochures provided discursive backup for this idea of an expansive imaginary world.

A coherent space apart, the *Tierpark* distinguished itself from the outside world by invoking the idea of a diegetic universe. In stark contrast to the zoological garden, but directly related to the nineteenth-century panorama, the *Tierpark* created a multisensory environment for visitors to enter and explore as a parallel world. This surround-style and full-bodied approach to display is also why Hagenbeck called the entire park a "panorama." For their part, visitors were urged to adopt a panoramic mode of viewing and to immerse themselves in the depicted scenes by envisioning them as unbounded. The creation of fantasy landscapes, such as the "Predators' Ravine," was always the most fraught aspect of the park, because it required the spectator's suspension of disbelief in order to enjoy an exhibit, as one might enjoy a work of imaginative fiction—only Hagenbeck's raw materials were alive, tangible, and physically present. If themed environments, such as open-air museums and amusement parks, were commonly located at the edge of a city, the *Tierpark* represented a liminal space like no other: It paralleled the natural world, creating an imaginary space that offered an alluring alternative to reality, while at the same time claiming to represent the physical world by virtue of the living bodies on display.

In a further step, this book explored the cinema's fascination with nineteenth-century theme space and its continuation by other means. Filmic diegesis was literally built on existing collections and immersive environments, even as it dismantled these collections and redeployed these environments according to a cinematic logic of detachment, seriality, and duplication. The fictional universe of the cinema has a history, and it is deeply embedded in other cultural practices of collection and display. In excavating this history we find a dense composite of "real" and synthetic spaces, the layered traces of simulated worlds—and a world of simulation—that underwent change over time.

◆ ◆ ◆

"The world is now too small for the animal trade." Hagenbeck issued this blunt statement in an 1887 letter to his friend Leutemann. By the age of forty-three, the world-famous animal dealer was busy organizing some of the largest shipments of elephants ever sent to the United States, when he commented on the looming obsolescence of his business, which depended for its survival on the relative abundance of precious resources. Whether this observation implied self-criticism is doubtful. If Hagenbeck anticipated a shift from an era of collecting to one of conservation, he continued in the former practice for the rest of his career. Wide-scale collecting projects such as his would obviously be challenged by the growing scarcity of natural resources due to rapid industrialization, colonial exploitation, and capitalist expansion—the very forces that had provided the impetus for Hagenbeck's enterprise. As Kirshenblatt-Gimblett so eloquently observes, "Exhibition is instrumental in the foreclosing of what is shown." If the German showman can be seen to represent the alterity of nineteenth-century theme space, its historical allegiance to the physical world, and its respective technologies of circulation, then the arc of his entertainments also points to the future of theme space in new technologies of virtual reality and transportation. Indeed, their interconnection is precisely what appears in retrospect under the sign of "Hagenbeck."[1]

A longer trajectory thus arises out of the paradoxical terrain of nineteenth-century theme space. As the world seems to shrink because of the continued transformation of time and space, we change our object of interest as well as our mode of interacting with it, from collected spaces to synthetic ones. At the same time, our immersion into virtual reality—our heightened awareness of the new media environment—also increases our need to respond to the physical world, precisely because we are changing it so radically. As with Hagenbeck and his contemporaries, we keep upping the ante and exploring the consequences as well as the possibilities in terms of theme space. It's a small world, after all.[2]

NOTES

Introduction ✦ Under the Sign of Hagenbeck

1 Neil Harris, "Expository Expositions: Preparing for the Theme Parks," in *Designing Disney's Theme Parks: The Architecture of Reassurance*, ed. Karal Ann Marling (Paris: Flammarion, 1997), 19–27.

2 August Heinrich Kober, "Carl Hagenbeck 1844–1913," in *Die Großen Deutschen: Neue Deutsche Biographie*, ed. Willy Andreas and Wilhelm von Scholz (Berlin: Propyläen, 1936), 4: 301. Similar riffs on the showman's name appear in Ludwig Zukowsky, *Carl Hagenbeck's Reich: Ein deutsches Tierparadies* (Berlin: Volksverband der Bücherfreunde Wegweiser-Verlag, 1929), 8; Carl Zuckmayer, "Hamburg, Hafen, Hagenbeck," *Arche Noah* 1 (1949): 3; Lothar Dittrich and Annelore Rieke-Müller's *Carl Hagenbeck (1844–1913): Tierhandel und Schaustellungen im Deutschen Kaiserreich* (Frankfurt am Main: Peter Lang, 1998), 1, 236. The latter is also the most reliable and comprehensive secondary source on Hagenbeck and his company.

3 Michel Foucault, "Of Other Spaces," *Diacritics* 16, no. 1 (spring 1986): 25.

4 One exception is Scott Bukatman's essay, "There's Always Tomorrowland: Disney and the Hypercinematic Experience," *October* 57 (1991): 55–78. Greil Marcus, "Forty Years of Overstatement: Criticism and the Disney Theme Parks," in *Designing Disney's Theme Parks: The Architecture of Reassurance*, ed. Karal Ann Marling (Paris: Flammarion, 1997), 201–7. On the communications literature, see Susan G. Davis in *Spectacular Nature: Corporate Culture and the Sea World Experience*

(Berkeley: University of California Press, 1997), 3–5. The preferred terms in German are: *Themenwelt* ("theme world"), *Erlebniswelt* ("experience world"), and *Erlebnisraum* ("experience space"), in addition to transliterations such as *Themenpark* or English words such as "theming" and "themed environment." See Susan Ingram and Markus Reisenleiter, eds., *Placing History: Themed Environments, Urban Consumption and the Public Entertainment Sphere / Orte und ihre Geschichte(n): Themenwelten, urbaner Konsum und Freizeitöffentlichkeit* (Vienna: Turia + Kant, 2003).

5 Jean Baudrillard, *Simulations*, trans. Paul Foss, Paul Patton, and Philip Beitchman (New York: Semiotext[e], 1983), 25. Michael Sorkin, "See You in Disneyland," in *Variations on a Theme Park: The New American City and the End of Public Space*, ed. Michael Sorkin (New York: Hill and Wang, 1992), 208. See also the title essay in Umberto Eco's *Travels in Hyperreality: Essays*, trans. William Weaver (San Diego: Harcourt Brace Jovanovich, 1986), 3–58; Sharon Zukin, *Landscapes of Power: From Detroit to Disneyworld* (Berkeley: University of California Press, 1991); Stephen M. Fjellman, *Vinyl Leaves: Walt Disney World and America* (Boulder, CO: Westview Press, 1992); Mark Gottdiener, *The Theming of America: Dreams, Visions, and Commercial Spaces* (Boulder, CO: Westview Press, 1997).

6 Celebrations of theme space echo through architectural studies such as *Learning from Las Vegas*, by Robert Venturi, Denise Scott Brown, and Steven Izenour (Cambridge, MA: MIT Press, 1972), and *Animated Architecture*, ed. Derek Walker (New York: St. Martin's Press, 1982), as well as through the scholarship on "post-tourism." On Disney parks and postmodern theory, see Alan Bryman, *Disney and His Worlds* (London: Routledge, 1995), 161–83.

7 See Ed Cohen, "The 'Hyperreal' vs. the 'Really Real': If European Intellectuals Stop Making Sense of American Culture Can We Still Dance?" *Cultural Studies* 3, no. 1 (1989): 25–37; Neville Wakefield, *Postmodernism: The Twilight of the Real* (London: Pluto Press, 1990), 98–115; Janet Ward, *Weimar Surfaces: Urban Visual Culture in 1920s Germany* (Berkeley: University of California Press, 2001), 1–43.

8 Mark B. Sandberg, *Living Pictures, Missing Persons: Mannequins, Museums, and Modernity* (Princeton: Princeton University Press, 2003). Cf. Anne Friedberg, *Window Shopping: Cinema and the Postmodern* (Berkeley: University of California Press, 1993).

9 On the museum's version of "liveness," see Sandberg, *Living Pictures, Missing Persons*, 8–10; and Jane Desmond, "Displaying Death, Animating Life: Changing Fictions of 'Liveness' from Taxidermy to Animatronics," in *Representing Animals*, ed. Nigel Rothfels (Bloomington: Indiana University Press, 2002), 159–79.

10 The saying usually goes, "When one makes a journey, then he has something to tell about" (*Wenn einer eine Reise tut, dann kann er was erzählen*). The "travel"

quotation appears in a review of "Dr. Carver's Wild-Amerika," *Hamburger Nachrichten* (7 September 1890), morn. ed.

11 The "polar bear" quotation appears in *Ein Rückblick*, a souvenir brochure created for the grand opening of Hagenbeck's *Tierpark* in Stellingen (Hamburg, 1907), 2 (Tierpark Carl Hagenbeck, Hamburg-Stellingen; hereafter abbreviated as TCH). The 1856 advertisement is reproduced in *Hagenbeck: Ein zoologisches Paradies: Hundert Jahre Tierpark in Stellingen*, by Matthias Gretzschel, Klaus Gille, and Michael Zapf (Hamburg: Carl Hagenbeck, 2007), 18. The "never hesitated" quotation appears in the commissioned biography by Heinrich Leutemann, *Lebensbeschreibung des Thierhändlers Carl Hagenbeck* (Hamburg: Hagenbeck, 1887), 13. On the fairground experience in nineteenth-century Hamburg, see Carl Thinius, *Damals in St. Pauli: Lust und Freude in der Vorstadt* (Hamburg: Christians, 1975). On traveling menageries, see Annelore Rieke-Müller and Lothar Dittrich, *Unterwegs mit wilden Tieren: Wandermenagerien zwischen Belehrung und Kommerz 1750–1850* (Marburg: Basilisken-Presse, 1999).

12 Typical of firms established in the mid-nineteenth century, the Hagenbeck Company relied for its key personnel on family members. For an annotated family tree, see Erna Mohr, "Das Geschlecht Hagenbeck," *Der Zoologische Garten*, N. F., 21, no. 1 (1954): 2–9.

13 For a vivid account of this network, see H. M. von Kadich, "Gastliche Tage bei Karl Hagenbeck," *Der Zoologische Garten* 64, no. 2 (February 1903): 39–40. The "entire world" quotation appears in Carl Hagenbeck, *Von Tieren und Menschen: Erlebnisse und Erfahrungen von Carl Hagenbeck* (1908; Berlin-Charlottenburg: Vita Deutsches Verlagshaus, 1909), 136; original emphasis. Though widely available, the abridged English version, *Beasts and Men: Being Carl Hagenbeck's Experience for Half a Century among Wild Animals*, trans. Hugh S. R. Elliott and A.[rthur] G.[ordon] Thacker, with an introduction by P. Chalmers Mitchell (London: Longmans, Green, and Co., 1909), is so loose and different from the original as to be unhelpful for the purposes of this study. Unless otherwise indicated, all translations are my own.

14 The "commander" quotation appears in Kadich, "Gastliche Tage," 88; see also C. J. Cornish, "The Moltke of Menagerie Owners," *English Illustrated Magazine* 14 (October 1895): 82–88. The "world conquerors" quotation appears in Otto Neumann-Hofer, "Karl Hagenbeck und sein Tierparadies," *Daheim: Ein deutsches Familienblatt und Illustrationen* no. 23 (6 March 1909): 11. For "monopoly" claims, see Kadich, "Gastliche Tage," 38, 88; Harold J. Shepstone, "The Trade in Wild Animals," *Scientific American* 88, no. 20 (16 May 1903): 376–78; Charles F. Brownell, "Marketing Wild Animals," in *Leslie's Monthly Magazine* 60, no. 3 (July 1905): 287–95.

15 James Clifford, *Routes: Travel and Translation in the Late Twentieth Century* (Cambridge, MA: Harvard University Press, 1997); Elizabeth Hanson, *Animal Attractions: Nature on Display in American Zoos* (Princeton: Princeton University Press, 2002), 9; Carla Yanni, *Nature's Museums: Victorian Science and the Architecture of Display* (London: Athlone Press, 1999), 8–11. Cf. Timothy Mitchell, *Colonizing Egypt* (Cambridge: Cambridge University Press, 1988); Annie E. Coombes, *Reinventing Africa: Museums, Material Culture and Popular Imagination in Late Victorian and Edwardian England* (New Haven: Yale University Press, 1994); Tony Bennett, *The Birth of the Museum: History, Theory, Politics* (London: Routledge, 1995); Coco Fusco, "The Other History of Intercultural Performance," in *English is Broken Here: Notes on Cultural Fusion in the Americas* (New York: The New Press, 1995), 37–63.

1 ✦ The Business of Collecting

1 Heinrich Leutemann, "Nordische Gäste," *Die Gartenlaube* 75 (1875): 742–44, here 742.

2 Leutemann, *Lebensbeschreibung*, 49; Carl Hagenbeck, *Von Tieren und Menschen*, 82.

3 All quotations appear in Leutemann, "Nordische Gäste," 742.

4 All quotations appear in Leutemann, "Nordische Gäste," 742–44.

5 Hagenbeck is quoted in Leutemann, *Lebensbeschreibung*, 50.

6 Leutemann, *Lebensbeschreibung*, 48; Walter Benjamin, "The Work of Art in the Age of Mechanical Reproduction," in *Illuminations*, ed. Hannah Arendt, trans. Harry Zohn (New York: Schocken, 1969), 223.

7 An important effort to mine the archive for half-hidden traces of native performance is *Bontoc Eulogy* (1995), a pseudo-documentary film by Marlon Fuentes. In a postmodern gesture, Fuentes constructs a fictional native character (the director's "grandfather"), who supposedly lived in the Philippine Village at the 1904 St. Louis world's fair. The film asks what it was like to be displayed at the fair as a way of exploring contemporary questions of Filipino-American identity, cultural memory, and displacement.

8 Increased speed of shipping meant that capital was less tied up in transit—a weighty benefit for an entrepreneur such as Hagenbeck, whose "goods" cost a great deal in relation to their survival. In addition to British and other foreign shipping lines, he generally used Norddeutschen Lloyd, which gave him special discount rates, HAPAG for his American routes, and Woermann for shipments to and from the German colonies in Africa. Hagenbeck and his travelers also relied heavily on private charters and independent entrepreneurs, especially in order

to reach more remote areas not served by commercial lines. See on this point Adrian Jacobsen, *Die weiße Grenze: Abenteuer eines alten Seebären rund um den Polarkreis*, ed. Albrecht Janssen (Leipzig: Brockhaus, 1931), 61. The "expansion" quotation appears in Leutemann, *Lebensbeschreibung*, 75.

9 I here borrow the title of Ellen Velvin's account of the wild animal trade, *From Jungle to Zoo* (London: S. Paul & Co., 1914).

10 In a sense, Hagenbeck took his first step toward vertical integration within the animal trade, where he had already bypassed indigenous middlemen and replaced them with European agents, as part of an effort to increase control over both the supply and the selection of exotic animals. In a further step, as Nigel Rothfels has noted, "later Hagenbeck catchers, such as John Hagenbeck and Christoph Schulz, took over the catching process as well, albeit relying on the substantial labor of local peoples." Nigel Rothfels, *Savages and Beasts: The Birth of the Modern Zoo* (Baltimore: The Johns Hopkins University Press, 2002), 52.

11 The "impulse" quotation appears in Carl Hagenbeck, *Von Tieren und Menschen*, 80. The first instance of this account, as told by Hagenbeck, can be found in Wilhelm Fischer, *Aus dem Leben und Wirken eines interressanten Mannes* (Hamburg: Baumann, 1896), 24.

12 I take issue with the argument of Dittrich and Rieke-Müller, who reject Hagenbeck's account because the animal market collapsed after and not prior to his initial foray into human exhibition (*Carl Hagenbeck*, 31–34, 144n127). Rather than dismiss Hagenbeck's account as unreliable, it should instead be understood within the context of the larger phenomenon of the Great Depression, its various surges or aftershocks, and its historical perception by Hagenbeck and his contemporaries. See David S. Landes, *The Unbound Prometheus: Technological Change and Industrial Development in Western Europe from 1750 to the Present*, 2nd ed. (1969; Cambridge: Cambridge University Press, 2003), 231–6; Eric Hobsbawm, *The Age of Capital, 1848–1875* (1975; New York: Vintage, 1996), 29–47, and *The Age of Empire 1875–1914* (New York: Vintage, 1987), 34–46; David Blackbourn, *The Long Nineteenth Century: A History of Germany, 1780–1918* (New York: Oxford University Press, 1998), 190–91. On shipping, see Daniel R. Headrick, *The Tentacles of Progress: Technology Transfer in the Age of Imperialism, 1850–1940* (New York: Oxford University Press, 1988).

13 Hobsbawm, *Age of Empire*, 62–67; Eric Wolf, *Europe and the People without History* (Berkeley: University of California Press, 1982), 310–53; and Daniel R. Headrick, *The Tools of Empire: Technology and European Imperialism in the Nineteenth Century* (New York: Oxford University Press, 1981).

14 Other markets of the live animal trade were tied to the proliferation of menageries, trained-animal shows, pet shops, hunting parks, colonial armies, and scien-

tific laboratories. Hagenbeck sold animals to any and all of them. On Hagenbeck as animal trader, see esp. Dittrich and Rieke-Müller, *Carl Hagenbeck*, 13–144. The "constellation" quotation appears in Carl Hagenbeck, *Von Tieren und Menschen*, 83.

15 The business of animal trapping changed over time, and Hagenbeck was a major proponent of its professionalization. On Lorenzo Casanova, see "Casanova und Hagenbeck," *Die Gartenlaube*, no. 3 (1869): 42–47; Leutemann, *Lebensbeschreibung*, 15–16, 20–22; Carl Hagenbeck, *Von Tieren und Menschen*, 54–69; Dittrich and Rieke-Müller, *Carl Hagenbeck*, 18–25. For short biographical notes on Hagenbeck's recruiters, see Hilke Thode-Arora, *Für fünfzig Pfennig um die Welt: Die Hagenbeckschen Völkerschauen* (Frankfurt am Main: Campus, 1989), 40–58. For a discussion of his animal catchers in English, see Rothfels, *Savages and Beasts*, 44–80. Frank Buck's comment on "every German consul" is quoted in Hanson, *Animal Attractions*, 78.

16 Josef Menges, "Bemerkungen über den deutschen Thierhandel von Nord-Ost-Afrika," *Der Zoologische Garten* 17 (1876): 229–36, here 232. Menges might have been a newcomer to the animal business, but he was already very familiar with the region and its changing economy. From 1874 to 1876, he had assisted Charles George Gordon, governor of Sudan's Equatoria province, in mapping the upper Nile River and establishing along it a line of trading stations. Though Menges probably soft-pedaled the hazards of this occupation in order to attract new business, his description is corroborated by a rare first-hand account by a British sportsman who visited the station in the winter of 1875, when Kohn was in charge. See Arthur B. R. Myers, *Life with the Hamran Arabs* (London: Smith, Elder, 1876), 43–44, 55, 303–4.

17 Carl Hagenbeck, *Von Tieren und Menschen*, 83, 84. Hadidje returned with the 1878 caravan for another European tour, and it is doubtful that she was alone in this. She might have also taken part in one or both of the intervening and subsequent Nubian shows. See Emil Dominik, "Die Nubier im zoologischen Garten Berlins," *Über Land und Meer* 41 (1878): 186–87, with an illustration of Hadidje on 189.

18 Previously, Hagenbeck had no need for representation in the United States because his business partner in England, Charles Rice, also covered the American market. Rice died in 1879. The "circuitous route" quotation appears in Carl Hagenbeck, *Von Tieren und Menschen*, 90. On the competition with Reiche, see Dittrich and Rieke-Müller, *Carl Hagenbeck*, 65–71. On the role of European dealers (including Reiche, Hagenbeck, and others) in the United States, see Richard W. Flint, "American Showmen and European Dealers: Commerce in Wild Animals in Nineteenth-Century America," in *New Worlds, New Animals: From Menagerie to Zoological Park in the Nineteenth Century*, ed. R. J. Hoage and William A. Deiss

(Baltimore: The Johns Hopkins University Press, 1996), 97–108; and Hanson, *Animal Attractions,* 79.

19 During the 1880s, Indian and Sri Lankan teahouses became stock features of British expositions. See Paul Greenhalgh, *Ephemeral Vistas: The Expositions Universelles, Great Exhibitions and World's Fairs, 1851–1939* (Manchester: Manchester University Press, 1988), 85. The parallel with Hagenbeck is obvious, but the context in which he exploited this interest, and extended it to the continent, was specific to the animal trade. On Kohn's death, see Fischer, *Aus dem Leben und Wirken,* 23. The "African animal trade" and "globetrotter" quotations appear in Carl Hagenbeck, *Von Tieren und Menschen,* 91; the "human exhibitions" comment is on 93. On the elephant exports, see Dittrich and Rieke-Müller, *Carl Hagenbeck,* 37, 43. In 1895, Menges organized "Carl Hagenbeck's East African Village and Great Display," which appeared at the Crystal Palace in Sydenham. See *East African Village and Great Display by the Natives of Somaliland under Direction of Herr Carl Hagenbeck* (London, 1895), TCH.

20 Here I must note that I requested official permission to use the Jacobsen Collection at Hamburg's ethnographic museum (Hamburgisches Museum für Völkerkunde) four times in as many years and was repeatedly denied access, each time for a different reason. Thus, my discussion of Jacobsen here relies on published primary and secondary sources. As for Jacobsen's unpublished correspondence papers, I am at the mercy of what other scholars, who did have access to the Jacobsen Collection, chose to either note or quote for the purposes of their own research agendas. In particular, historian of folklore Hilke Thode-Arora has been pivotal in compiling information about Hagenbeck's ethnographic enterprise. Her work is foundational in the sense that it is first-tier research, with special access to the Hamburg museum. The present study, by contrast, is driven by ideas and theoretical concerns to a degree that Thode-Arora's work is not. Jacobsen's "two regrets" are quoted in Thode-Arora, *Für fünfzig Pfennig,* 54.

21 Jacobsen, *Die weiße Grenze,* 26; cf. Johan Adrian Jacobsen, *Alaskan Voyage 1881–1883: An Expedition to the Northwest Coast of America,* trans. Erna Gunther from the German text of Adrian Woldt (1884; Chicago: University of Chicago Press, 1977), 220. The best available essay on Jacobsen is "Johan Adrian Jacobsen Brings Treasures from Alaska," by Ann Fienup-Riordan, in *Yup'ik Elders at the Ethnologisches Museum Berlin: Fieldwork Turned on Its Head,* with Yup'ik transl. by Marie Meade and German trans. by Sonja Lührmann, Anja Karlson, and Adelaid Pauls (Seattle: University of Washington Press, 2005), 3–34.

22 Jacobsen's statement to the Danish interior minister is quoted in Fienup-Riordan, "Johan Adrian Jacobsen Brings Treasures from Alaska," 3. Details on the Copenhagen negotiations including the terms of agreement are available in Heinrich

Leutemann, "Die Eskimos in Deutschland," *Daheim* 14, no. 28 (1878): n. pag.; Jacobsen, *Die weiße Grenze*, 27–28; Thode-Arora, *Für fünfzig Pfennig*, 68–69. The business of collecting foreign peoples was regulated, not unlike other forms of international trade. Collectors were required to get official permission from colonial authorities in order to bring a troupe to Europe. To that end, collectors had to negotiate employment contracts with the performers, as Jacobsen did with the Greenland Inuit in 1877; in some cases, security bonds or other monetary guarantees for due payment of salary and safe return had to be posted in advance of the troupe's departure for Europe. Policies varied widely and changed over time. In 1901, for instance, Germany banned the import and public display of German colonial subjects. I discuss this development at length in chapter 2. Permissions from other colonial powers abruptly terminated in 1914, with the outbreak of war. See Hilke Thode-Arora, "'Charakteristische Gestalten des Volkslebens': Die Hagenbeckschen Südasien-, Orient- und Afrika-Völkerschauen," in *Fremde Erfahrungen: Asiaten und Afrikaner in Deutschland, Österreich und in der Schweiz bis 1945*, ed. Gerhard Höpp (Berlin: Verlag das Arabische Buch, 1996), 109–34, here 114.

23 The "savages" quotation appears in Leutemann, "Eskimos in Deutschland." Details on the Inuit's protest and immunization appear in Thode-Arora, *Für fünfzig Pfennig*, 70. The quotations from Jacobsen's autobiography appear in *Alaskan Voyage*, 220, 221; cf. Jacobsen, *Die weiße Grenze*, 39–40. On the ethnological collection, see Hilke Thode-Arora, "Indianer und Inuit in Europa: Völkerschauen," in *Indianer 1858–1928: Photographische Reisen von Alaska bis Feuerland*, ed. Eva König (Heidelberg: Edition Braus, 2002), 69–73.

24 On the troupe's alleged wealth, see Carl Hagenbeck, *Von Tieren und Menschen*, 89; Jacobsen, *Die weiße Grenze*, 43–44; Thode-Arora, *Für fünfzig Pfennig*, 158.

25 The quotations concerning the Jacobshaven episode appear in M. Hoffmann, *Beiträge über Leben und Treiben der Eskimos in Labrador und Grönland: Aus dem Tagebuch des Herrn Carl Hagenbeck in Hamburg mit dem Schiffe "Eisbär" nach Grönland entsandten Herrn J. A. Jacobsen* (Berlin: M. Hoffmann, 1880), 9, 5, 12.

26 The "graves" quotation appears in Jacobsen, *Alaskan Voyage*, 223. Hoffmann's program includes an illustration of "The First Excavation," i.e., grave robbery (14). On the provision of "food and supplies," see Hoffmann, *Beiträge über Leben und Treiben der Eskimos*, 16. For a detailed account of the 1880 Inuit troupe, see Hilke Thode-Arora, "Das Eskimo-Tagebuch von 1880: Eine Völkerschau aus der Sicht eines Teilnehmers," *Kea: Zeitschrift für Kulturwissenschaften* 2 (1991): 87–115; in English, Hartmut Lutz, ed. and head trans., *The Diary of Abraham Ulrikab: Text and Context* (Ottawa: University of Ottawa Press, 2005).

27 The "mothering" quotation appears in Leutemann, *Lebensbeschreibung*, 53.

28 Jacobsen's unpublished diary is quoted in Thode-Arora, "Das Eskimo-Tagebuch," 106; and in Lutz, *The Diary of Abraham Ulrikab*, xxiv.

29 Details concerning the medical care of performers appear in John George Hagenbeck, *Mit Indiens Fahrendem Volk* (Berlin: Scherl, 1932), 15–16, 104–106. On the opposite end of the spectrum, the American showman, R. A. Cunningham, boasted in his publicity materials of literally kidnapping natives and exhibiting troupes until every participant died. In the 1880s, Cunningham worked as an agent for P. T. Barnum and independently brought several troupes to Germany, where he also occasionally worked for Hagenbeck. For more on Cunningham, see Thode-Arora, *Für fünfzig Pfennig*, 41–42, 59, 63. Brother Dewitz is quoted in Lutz, *The Diary of Abraham Ulrikab*, 34.

30 This was not an isolated incident. See Leutemann, *Lebensbeschreibung*, 61–65; in English, see Rothfels, *Savages and Beasts*, 96–97.

31 The "Bastian" quotation appears in Fienup-Riordan, "Johan Adrian Jacobsen Brings Treasures from Alaska," 4. On Jacobsen's collections for Berlin's museum, see Peter Bolz and Hans-Ulrich Sanner, *Native American Art: The Collections of the Ethnological Museum Berlin* (Seattle: University of Washington Press, 1999). Studies of museum collecting in which Jacobsen figures prominently include Douglas Cole, *Captured Heritage: The Scramble for Northwest Coast Artifacts* (Seattle: University of Washington Press, 1985); H. Glenn Penny, *Objects of Culture: Ethnology and Ethnographic Museums in Imperial Germany* (Chapel Hill: University of North Carolina Press, 2002).

32 The Bastian quotation appears in the untitled preface to Nørgaard's *The North-West Coast of America: Being the Results of Recent Ethnological Researches from the Collections of the Royal Museums at Berlin, Published by the Directors of the Ethnological Department, Translated from the German* (New York: Mead, 1883).

33 For a detailed account of his museum expeditions, see Fienup-Riordan, "Johan Adrian Jacobsen Brings Treasures from Alaska," 3–35; the "lightning speed" quotation appears on 33. For Jacobsen's grab-and-run method, see esp. 6–8; on grave robbing and stealing, see 7, 11, 15–16, 18, 19. On negotiating with families, see John George Hagenbeck, *Mit Indiens Fahrendem Volk*, 9–10.

34 Jacobsen's comment on his "position at the museum" is quoted in Fienup-Riordan, "Johan Adrian Jacobsen Brings Treasures from Alaska," 26.

35 The "good-bye" quotation appears in Jacobsen, *Alaskan Voyage*, 78. For an account of the Koskimo episode written in English, see Cole, *Captured Heritage*, 62–63.

36 The selection criteria quotation appears in Thode-Arora, "'Charakteristische Gestalten,'" 114–15; see also Thode-Arora, *Für fünfzig Pfennig*, 59–67.

37 Jacobsen also probably used photographs to help pitch his ideas to Hagenbeck

and later sell his collected objects back in Europe. On Jacobsen and photography, see Wiebke Ahrndt, *Rote Wolke, Blaues Pferd: Bilder aus dem Leben der Sioux* (Hamburg: Christians Verlag and Hamburgisches Museum für Völkerkunde, 1997), 35–46; Eva König, "Johan Adrian Jacobsen: Impresario und Sammler (1853–1947)," in *Indianer 1858–1928: Photographische Reise von Alaska bis Feuerland*, ed. Eva König (Heidelberg: Edition Braus, 2002), 31–35, here 35. Jacobsen's description of "Indian dances" is quoted in Fienup-Riordan, "Johan Adrian Jacobsen Brings Treasures from Alaska," 8.

38 Hagenbeck's initial reply is quoted in Fienup-Riordan, "Johan Adrian Jacobsen Brings Treasures from Alaska," 8. The instructions are in Carl Hagenbeck, letter to Johan Adrian Jacobsen, 5 January 1882 (TCH).

39 The "glaring contrast" quotation appears in Leutemann, *Lebensbeschreibung*, 51.

40 The "essence" quotation appears in Elizabeth Edwards, editor's Introduction to *Anthropology and Photography, 1860–1920* (New Haven: Yale University Press, 1992), 7. On Dammann, see Elizabeth Edwards, "Photographic 'Types': The Pursuit of Method," *Visual Anthropology* 3 (1990): 249–54; the quotation appears on 254. The John Hagenbeck quotation appears in his *Fünfundzwanzig Jahre Ceylon: Erlebnisse und Abenteuer im Tropenparadies*, ed. Viktor Ottmann (Dresden: Verlag Deutsches Buchwerkstätten, 1922), 49.

41 The performers' names and ages appear in Thode-Arora, *Für fünfzig Pfennig*, 72. Jacobsen's comment on "family life" is quoted in Thode-Arora, "Indianer und Inuit in Europa," 69.

42 The Bisharin Caravan appeared in Vienna, Basel, and Frankfurt. The quotations from Willy Möller can be found in *Die Bischaris*, program brochure (1899), 3, 7 (TCH). For more on Möller, see Thode-Arora, *Für fünfzig Pfennig*, 55.

43 There are at least three different accounts of the 1885 trip, as detailed by Wolfgang Haberland in "Nine Bella Coolas in Germany," *Indians and Europe: An Interdisciplinary Collection of Essays*, ed. Christian Feest (Aachen: Edition Herodot, Rader Verlag, 1987), 337–74, and further in "'Diese Indianer sind falsch': Neun Bella Coola im Deutschen Reich 1885–86," *Archiv für Völkerkunde* 42 (1988): 3–65. Yet another (dubious) account is given by local historian Cliff Kopas, in *Bella Coola* (Vancouver: Mitchell Press, 1970), 234–36. The "direction" quotation appears in Cole, *Captured Heritage*, 68. On Victoria as a center of native trade and labor, see Jacobsen, *Alaskan Voyage*, 5. By one estimate, as many as six thousand Native Americans were headed for the hop fields of Washington that summer, "an astonishing one quarter of the Aboriginal population of British Columbia took part in the migration." Quoted in Paige Raibmon, *Authentic Indians: Episodes of Encounter from the Late-Nineteenth-Century Northwest Coast* (Durham, NC: Duke University Press, 2005), 79.

44 Compared to hop-picking, these wages were low, but presumably the idea of

performing seemed preferable to working in the fields. According to Raibmon, pickers struggled to earn one dollar a day (*Authentic Indians,* 79–80). For a transcription of the contract in the English original, see Haberland, "'Diese Indianer sind falsch,'" 56–57. A copy of the contract is available at TCH. On the professionalization of "show Indians" in Canada and the United States, see L. G. Moses, *Wild West Shows and the Images of American Indians, 1883–1933* (Albuquerque: University of New Mexico Press, 1996), 137–38.

45 Writing in the early 1930s, John George Hagenbeck describes a network of "trusted people" extending from Ceylon to Madras, comprised of native agents who scouted local talent, and a base camp in Colombo, where recruits were sent, paperwork for employment and international travel was processed, food and equipment was gathered, and other preparations were made for the journey to Europe (*Mit Indiens Fahrendem Volk,* 8). The "already accustomed" quotation appears in Anne Dreesbach, *Gezähmte Wilde: Die Zurschaustellung "exotischer" Menschen in Deutschland 1870–1940* (Frankfurt am Main: Campus, 2005), 65.

46 The guest list for this promotional event included Prince Hohenlohe-Schillingsfürst (son of Chlodwig Karl Viktor, the former German chancellor), the mayor of Danzig, the director of Schickau Shipyards, and representatives of the Hamburg-Amerika Shipping Line, as detailed by the same reporter in "Die Aethiopier bei Hagenbeck," *Hamburger Echo*, 16 May 1909, 1st ed.

47 The "monopoly" and "relationship" quotations appear in Thode-Arora, "'Charakteristische Gestaltn,'" 125–26. Here it should be added that Gorseh spoke German and sent his son to school with the Hagenbeck children. In 1905, he also played a key role in delivering for Hagenbeck one thousand dromedary camels to German colonial troops in South-West Africa—Hagenbeck's grim contribution to German genocide against the Herero people (Thode-Arora, *Für fünfzig Pfennig*, 161–62). Further instances of native entrepreneurialism are detailed in Sierra Ann Bruckner, "The Tingle-Tangle of Modernity: Popular Anthropology and the Cultural Politics of Identity in Imperial Germany" (Ph.D. diss., University of Iowa, 1999), 326–40.

48 By this time, Hagenbeck was one of the world's most famous showmen, with the ethnographic troupes being a major part of his legacy—and his new *Tierpark* in Stellingen, having just opened, created much international interest. Thus, in addition to his instructions for Jacobsen, Hagenbeck enclosed five copies of his autobiography, twelve photo albums, and several sets of picture postcards, in order to create a sense of prestige around this endeavor, assuming that this idea would be attractive (albeit for different reasons) to government agents as well as to prospective recruits. Carl Hagenbeck, "Instructions for Mr. Adrian Jacobsen for his voyage to South Dakota, U.S.A.," 5 January 1910 (TCH). For a detailed account

of this recruiting trip, see Wolfgang Haberland, "Adrian Jacobsen on Pine Ridge Reservation, 1910," in *European Review of Native American Studies* 1, no. 1 (1988): 11–15.

49 The companies are listed in Haberland, "Adrian Jacobsen," 11.

50 Everette had worked at John Hagenbeck's "Ceylon Village" at the 1908 Colonial Exhibition in London (Thode-Arora, *Für fünfzig Pfennig*, 42). The "American Horse" quotation appears in Ahrndt, *Rote Wolke, Blaues Pferd*, 43. The "wig" quotation appears in Haberland, "Adrian Jacobsen," 12. Excerpts from Jacobsen's diary of 1910, which support these points about selection and compromise, can be found in Hilke Thode-Arora, "Die Hagenbeckschen Völkerschauen: Indianer Nordamerikas in Europa," in *Indianer Nordamerikas: Kunst und Mythos*, ed. Patricia Rochard (Mainz: Schmidt, 1993), 80–87, here 84.

51 Three of the 1910 contracts are available at TCH. Following instructions by the U.S. Indian Superintendent in Pine Ridge, child performers—and there were several in the troupe—earned no wages, but their necessary expenses (food, clothing, lodging, transportation, medical care) were covered by Hagenbeck. At issue here, presumably, were child-labor laws in the U.S. (Thode-Arora, *Für fünfzig Pfennig*, 79).

52 Barbara Kirshenblatt-Gimblett, *Destination Culture: Tourism, Museums, and Heritage* (Berkeley: University of California Press, 1998), 18; on Hagenbeck, see 42.

53 Shortly after the Bella Coola troupe's return to British Columbia, in 1886, Franz Boas encountered two of the former participants (much to their surprise) in Victoria. A few years later, he met four other members of the same troupe, who were working in a cannery there (Thode-Arora, *Für fünfzig Pfennig*, 159). This period also marked the beginning of permanent white settlement in Bella Coola, including missionaries and a full-time trader. In 1894, a colony of Norwegian immigrants was established in Bella Coola, partly as a result of Fillip Jacobsen's continued work in the area as surveyor, trader, and collector (Kopas, *Bella Coola*, 237, 241–91). The "contact" quotation appears in Thode-Arora, "'Charakteristische Gestalten,'" 115. Long passages of the article by Maria Cronau are transcribed in Haberland, "'Diese Indianer sind falsch,'" 50–53.

54 All quotations come from Leutemann, *Lebensbeschreibung*, 55.

55 Saloni Mathur, "Living Ethnological Exhibits: The Case of 1886," *Cultural Anthropology* 15, no. 4 (November 2000): 492–524; here, 511. It is important to note that Mathur analyzes an extremely unusual case, in which many of the performers were actually prisoners in an Indian jail, who learned their "trades" as inmates, and were brought to London by the warden himself (ibid., 507). Even in this case, social marginalization within Indian society created the context for "participation."

56 All quotations appear in Leutemann, *Lebensbeschreibung*, 55. The role of Wilhelm Hagenbeck is noted by Dittrich and Rieke-Müller in *Carl Hagenbeck*, 156.

57 Contrary to Leutemann's claim, Hagenbeck would in fact assume troupes from agents he had not commissioned, such as the Patagonian troupe of 1881, which was brought to him without advance notice by a man named Captain Schweers. All quotations here come from Leutemann, *Lebensbeschreibung*, 55–57. Contemporary newspaper reports indicate that the performers were not Hindu but predominately Muslim, with the exception of one Buddhist; see on this point Miriam Ferdinand, "'Völkerschauen' in Hamburg im Spiegel der Lokalpresse während des Kaiserreichs (1875–1917)," master's thesis, Universität Hamburg, 2004, 58; a copy is available at TCH.

58 Kirshenblatt-Gimblett, *Destination Culture*, 162. See also Barbara Kirshenblatt-Gimblett, "The Ethnographic Burlesque," *TDR: The Drama Review* 42, no. 2 (summer 1998): 177.

59 On the Greenland troupe, see Leutemann, "Eskimos in Deutschland." Tom Henry is quoted in Kopas, *Bella Coola*, 235.

60 The number of parishes given by Jacobsen is quoted in Lutz, *The Diary of Abraham Ulrikab,* xviv; see also Hoffmann, *Beiträge über Leben und Treiben der Eskimos,* 12. The "compulsion" quotation appears in Stephen Loring's informative essay, "In Torngak's Realm: The Nineteenth-Century Photography of Moravian Missionaries in Labrador," in *Imaging the Arctic*, ed. Jonathan C. H. King and Henrietta Lidchi (Seattle: University of Washington Press, 1998), 207–20; here, 207. Here it should be added that the Moravians only initiated a new period of contact. In the two centuries prior to their arrival, as Loring has noted, the Inuit "gained considerable experience in dealing with Europeans, and had acquired a strong desire for European manufactured products and raw materials" (ibid., 209).

61 On the Christian/pagan dichotomy, see Loring, ibid., 209, 212–15. Brother Kretschmer is quoted in Thode-Arora, "Das Eskimo-Tagebuch," 90; see Lutz, *The Diary of Abraham Ulrikab,* 6. Jacobsen is quoted in ibid., xviii. The *Frankfurter Nachrichten* critique is quoted in ibid., 47. On the Moravian trading monopoly, see Loring, "In Torngak's Realm," 207–8, 212.

62 Letter from Brother Kretschmer to Brother Connor, 20 August 1880, quoted in Thode-Arora, "Das Eskimo-Tagebuch," 90; see Lutz, *The Diary of Abraham Ulrikab,* 11–12. Jacobsen observed a similar practice on his 1877 trip to Greenland: namely, Inuit women serving as housemaids and nannies in the homes of Danish colonial officers (*Die weiße Grenze*, 35–36).

63 Vine Deloria Jr. has stressed the opportunity to learn about the larger world as a major reason for joining an itinerant show such as Buffalo Bill's Wild West. See Vine Deloria Jr., "The Indians," in *Buffalo Bill and the Wild West*, by The Brooklyn Museum, Museum of Art at the Carnegie Institute, and the Buffalo Bill Historical Center (Brooklyn: Brooklyn Museum, 1981), 45–56. The "desire" quotation

appears in Thode-Arora, "Das Eskimo-Tagebuch," 90; cf. Lutz, *The Diary of Abraham Ulrikab,* 6–10.

64 Missionary societies wanted ethnographic exhibitions to showcase dramatic contrasts between Christianized and "heathen" natives, thereby demonstrating the successful efforts of the church abroad. Each of these points featured prominently in church-sponsored ethnographic exhibitions. On the ambivalent role of missionaries, see Balthasar Staehlin, *Völkerschauen im Zoologischen Garten Basel 1879–1935* (Basel: Basler Afrika Bibliographien, 1993), 122–31; Bruckner, "Tingle-Tangle," 390–403; Ulrich van der Heyden, "Südafrikanische 'Berliner': Die Kolonial- und Transvaal-Ausstellung in Berlin und die Haltung der deutschen Missionsgesellschaften zur Präsentation fremder Menschen und Kulturen," in *Fremde Erfahrungen: Asiaten und Afrikaner in Deutschland, Österreich und in der Schweiz bis 1945,* ed. Gerhard Höpp (Berlin: Das Arabische Buch, 1996), 135–56. The "neophytes" quotation appears in Lutz, *The Diary of Abraham Ulrikab,* xxii; for supporting evidence, see 8. Brother Kretschmer's comment on the "the baptized and the heathen" appears on 12.

65 The preference of Christianized Inuit for wearing European clothing is discussed at length in the program brochure—the probable source for the reporter's ironic commentary (Hoffmann, *Beiträge über Leben und Treiben der Eskimos,* 18–21). The "national costume" and "wild Eskimos" quotations appear in Lutz, *The Diary of Abraham Ulrikab,* 48, 50. For translated excerpts of Virchow's 1880 report, first published in the *Zeitschrift für Ethnologie*, see Lutz, *The Diary of Abraham Ulrikab,* 57–62.

66 All quotations appear in the guidebook and program brochure, *Ausstellung Nordland: Führer durch die Ausstellung: Lappländer, Samojeden, Eskimos, Schweden*, with text by Johannes Flemming (n. pub. [1911]), 30, 32, 13 (TCH).

67 Quotations and details from the Berlin show appear in *Ausstellung Nordland: Führer*, 19, 29. For an account of the Inuit troupe, see Jim Zwick, *Inuit Entertainers in the United States: From the Chicago World's Fair through the Birth of Hollywood* (West Conshohocken, PA: Infinity Publishing, 2006). Although it is not mentioned in Zwick's detailed chronology, the Berlin show fits into the troupe's schedule: During the summer of 1911, they performed at the "Festival of Empire" in London, after which they "possibly [went] on a broader tour of Europe," returning to the United States in the spring of 1912 (ibid., 120–21). Nancy Columbia also served as "cover girl" for *Ausstellung Nordland: Rundgang durch die Ausstellung*, a guidebook to Hagenbeck's 1911 show in Berlin. This image, which is a cropped version of figure 1.16, was probably first printed for the Jamestown Exposition in Virginia, where she and her family performed in the summer of 1907 (cf. Zwick, *Inuit Entertainers,* 90).

68 This tension between cultural displacement and assimilation also helps explain the striking number of newspaper reports of off-duty ethnographic performers shopping for Western clothes and attending the theater in major European cities. See, e.g., "Indianer in der Stadt," *Münchener Nachrichten*, 25 April 1890; "Die Indianer im Gärtnerplatzthater und im Orpheum," *Münchener Bote*, 30 April 1890; both clippings from the William Frederick Cody / Buffalo Bill Papers, WH 72, Western History Collection, The Denver Public Library.

2 ✦ The Living Habitat

1 The shows had various German designations. For example, Leutemann referred to them as *Völker-Schaustellungen* (foreign people displays), using *Gruppen* (groups) and *Truppen* (troupes) for short. Hagenbeck employed each of these terms as well as *Karawane* (caravans), a word that was often used in the titles of shows. Over time, the short form, *Völkerschau* (foreign peoples show), and its plural, *Völkerschauen*, became the favored terms for advertising paraphernalia. They have also dominated in the scholarship since Alfred Lehmann's essay, "Zeitgenössische Bilder der ersten Völkerschauen," in *Von fremden Völkern und Kulturen: Hans Plische zum 65. Geburtstag*, ed. Werner Lang, Walter Nippold, and Günther Spannaus (Düsseldorf: Droste, 1955), 31–44.

2 Anthropological approaches include recent work by Sierra A. Bruckner, "Spectacles of (Human) Nature: Commercial Ethnography between Leisure, Learning, and *Schaulust*," in *Worldly Provincialism: German Anthropology in the Age of Empire*, ed. H. Glenn Penny and Matti Bunzl (Ann Arbor: University of Michigan Press, 2003), 127–55; and by Andrew Zimmerman, *Anthropology and Antihumanism in Imperial Germany* (Chicago: University of Chicago Press, 2001), 15–37. A similar framework prevails in the film literature. See, e.g., Fatimah Tobing Rony, *The Third Eye: Race, Cinema, and Ethnographic Spectacle* (Durham, NC: Duke University Press, 1996), 21–43; Assenka Oksiloff, *Picturing the Primitive: Visual Culture, Ethnography, and Early German Cinema* (New York: Palgrave, 2001); and Alison Griffiths, *Wondrous Difference: Cinema, Anthropology, and Turn-of-the-Century Visual Culture* (New York: Columbia University Press, 2002). I too emphasize a scientific perspective in my article on early ethnomusicology, "The Sound of Evolution," *Modernism/modernity* 10, no. 2 (April 2003): 297–325. The quotation is from Robert W. Rydell, "The Literature of International Expositions," in *The Book of the Fairs: Materials about World's Fairs, 1834–1916, in the Smithsonian Institution Libraries* (Chicago: American Library Association, 1992), 30.

3 Writing of the London entertainment industry, Altick explains the rise of the public museum in the mid-nineteenth century as a division of labor resulting from the

confrontation between amusement and instruction. Recognizing that commercial showmen would not supply uplift (despite all claims to the contrary), the state "assumed responsibility for the instructional side of the exhibition business as part of its larger, reluctant acceptance of responsibility for providing schools and teachers for the masses." Richard D. Altick, *The Shows of London* (Cambridge, MA: Harvard University Press, 1978), 4.

4 The entry for "Ausstellungen, anthropologische" appears in *Meyers Konversations-Lexikon*, 5th ed. (Leipzig: Bibliographisches Institut, 1893), 2:217. Cf. Stefan Goldmann, "Wilde in Europa: Aspekte und Orte ihrer Zurschaustellung," in *Wir und die Wilden: Einblicke in eine kannibalische Beziehung*, ed. Thomas Theye (Reinbek: Rowohlt, 1984), 243–69; Thode-Arora, *Für fünfzig Pfennig*, 19–22; Staehlin, *Völkerschauen*, 21–34; Rothfels, *Savages and Beasts*, 86–87.

5 After Hagenbeck died in 1913, his relatives occasionally mounted ethnographic shows. A partial list of shows from 1875 to 1930 is available in Thode-Arora, *Für fünfzig Pfennig*, 168–72. Bruckner lists more than one hundred shows by various organizers in "Tingle-Tangle," 473–506. Dreesbach gives the highest figure, namely, four hundred between 1875 and 1940, but there seem to be discrepancies among her various ways of calculating it, and for obvious reasons she does not provide a list of troupes (cf. *Gezähmte Wilde*, 11, 79, 111).

6 The absence of Hagenbeck's *Völkerschau* at a world's fair has yet to be explained, presumably for lack of evidence, but three general factors deserve consideration: First, Germany never hosted a world's fair during Hagenbeck's lifetime. In this context, unofficial, traveling exhibitions such as his remained the dominant practice. Second, by the time ethnographic performances featured prominently at world's fairs held elsewhere, beginning in 1889, Hagenbeck had momentarily pulled back from the *Völkerschau* business (as discussed in chapter 3). Third, when Hagenbeck exhibited at American world's fairs, in 1893 and 1904, he did so as a way of promoting his animal business in the United States, where the circus was at its peak and a number of new zoos were either in planning or under construction. See Ortwin Pelc, "Hagenbeck auf den Weltausstellungen in Chicago (1893) und St. Louis (1904)," *Zeitschrift des Vereins für Hamburgische Geschichte* 86 (2000): 89–113.

7 Greenhalgh, *Ephemeral Vistas*, 85. Rydell, "Literature of International Expositions," 4. The living ethnological displays at the 1889 Paris exposition became in turn a model for organizers of the 1893 world's fair in Chicago. Robert W. Rydell, *All the World's a Fair: Visions of Empire at American International Expositions, 1876–1916* (Chicago: University of Chicago Press, 1984), 55–58.

8 The 1889 Paris exposition introduced a colonial city, where nearly two hundred Africans and Asians were installed in various simulated villages representing mostly (but not exclusively) the French colonies. All quotations appear in Green-

halgh, *Ephemeral Vistas*, 86, 87. Gate receipts are cited in William H. Schneider, *An Empire for the Masses: The French Popular Image of Africa, 1870–1900* (Westport, CT: Greenwood Press, 1982), 130. Schneider likewise treats the shows as "French," even though some of the primary sources that he uses, including the *Bulletin de la Société de l'acclimatation*, made Hagenbeck's role explicit. Nevertheless, Schneider is correct to emphasize that Exposition organizers sought to harness the show's potential for official purposes such as advertising French colonialism and shaping popular attitudes toward it (ibid., 141). Cf. Carl Hagenbeck, *Von Tieren und Menschen*, 79, 89, 428.

9 The "respectability" quotation appears in Neil Harris, *Humbug: The Art of P. T. Barnum* (Chicago: University of Chicago Press, 1973), 173. On the belated interest of German anthropologists, see Leutemann, *Lebensbeschreibung*, 54. The role of anthropologists as mass-cultural gatekeepers tends to be overstated by historians of anthropology; see, e.g., Zimmerman, *Anthropology and Antihumanism*, 18–20. The public exhibition of itinerant troupes was subject to the same commercial laws as popular lecturers, vaudeville houses, and second-rate theaters. In order to exhibit and conduct business, impresarios had necessarily to demonstrate their shows were "guided by a higher interest of art or science." Quoted in Wolfgang Jansen, *Das Varieté: Die glanzvolle Geschichte einer unterhaltenden Kunst* (Berlin: Edition Hentrich, 1990), 68. For a fascinating look at the bureaucratic regulation of ethnographic shows, including excerpts from police records, see Dreesbach, *Gezähmte Wilde*, 227–45. Copies of the Berlin, Leipzig, and Munich endorsements are available at TCH.

10 Karen Wonders, *Habitat Dioramas: Illusions of Wilderness in Museums of Natural History*, Acta Universitatis Upsaliensis, Figura Nova Series 25 (Uppsala: Almqvist and Wiksell, 1993), 10, 119, 41. On life groups in the American Museum of Natural History, see esp. Griffiths, *Wondrous Difference*, 3–45; in the Smithsonian, see Curtis M. Hinsley, Jr., *Savages and Scientists: The Smithsonian Institution and the Development of American Anthropology 1846–1910* (Washington, DC: Smithsonian Institution Press, 1981), 108–9. In her recent study of natural history museums in Germany, Susanne Köstering responds to Wonders by arguing that, whereas Scandinavian and (later) American museums were partial to depicting "an open, natural landscape" (hence their particular preference for the diorama), German museums preferred "a closed, protected environment" for display. Though out-of-museum displays exceed the scope of Köstering's study, the Hagenbeck material contradicts this part of her thesis and offers a leading example of open-air habitat display in the German context and beyond. Köstering's quotations appear in *Natur zum Anschauen: Das Naturkundemuseum des deutschen Kaiserreichs 1871–1914* (Cologne: Böhlau, 2003), 173. For more on the life-group debate in German

museology, see Britta Lange, *Echt, unecht, lebensecht: Menschenbilder im Umlauf* (Berlin: Kadmos, 2006), 128–53.

11 See Griffiths, *Wondrous Difference,* 40; and Sandberg, *Living Pictures, Missing Persons,* 10. On the folk-museum spectator, see ibid., 208–16.

12 Carl Hagenbeck, *Von Tieren und Menschen,* 452.

13 On the American emphasis on "freak shows," see Dreesbach, *Gezähmte Wilde,* 323–26. The "strong ties" quotation appears in Carl Hagenbeck, *Von Tieren und Menschen,* 20. On Barnum, see Harris, *Humbug: The Art of P. T. Barnum*; and James W. Cook, *The Arts of Deception: Playing with Fraud in the Age of Barnum* (Cambridge, MA: Harvard University Press, 2001).

14 See Vanessa R. Schwartz, *Spectacular Realities: Early Mass Culture in* Fin-de-Siècle *Paris* (Berkeley: University of California Press, 1998). The "peculiarities" quotation appears in P. T. Barnum, *Selected Letters of P. T. Barnum,* ed. A. H. Saxon (New York: Columbia University Press, 1983), 226. On "The Ethnological Congress," see Bluford Adams, *E Pluribus Barnum: The Great Showman and the Making of U.S. Popular Culture* (Minneapolis: University of Minnesota, 1997), 175–85. On freak shows, see Leslie Fiedler, *Freaks: Myths and Images of the Secret Self* (New York: Simon & Schuster, 1978); Robert Bogdan, *Freak Show: Presenting Human Oddities for Amusement and Profit* (Chicago: University of Chicago Press, 1988); Rosemarie Garland Thomson, ed., *Freakery: Cultural Spectacles of the Extraordinary Body* (New York: New York University Press, 1996).

15 Bruckner, "Tingle-Tangle," 347–48. Here it must be added that the invocation of typologies, however loose or random it may have been, was further undermined by the historical practice of naming individual performers—especially in program brochures, but also in newspaper articles. What emerges, then, is a paradoxical relationship between the discursive construction of difference according to "type," and its partial undercutting by signs of individual identity.

16 The *Völkerschau* involved spectators in a process of authentication, but it had no equivalent to the central role of epistemological uncertainty in Barnum's human oddity shows such as the notorious "What Is It?" Nor did Hagenbeck use publicity, as had Barnum, in order to spread confusion and promote indeterminacy as a way of soliciting curious viewers. See James W. Cook, "Of Men, Missing Links, and Nondescripts: The Strange Career of P. T. Barnum's 'What is It?' Exhibition," in *Freakery*, ed. Rosemarie Garland Thomson, 139–57. The "two flaws" quotation appears in Leutemann, "Eskimos in Deutschland."

17 On Peale, see Edward P. Alexander, *Museum Masters: Their Museums and Their Influence* (Nashville, TN: American Association for State and Local History, 1983), 45–77. On Bullock, see Altick, *The Shows of London,* 235–52, 273–75. Since 1863, Leutemann made annual visits to Hagenbeck's menagerie, in search of live exotic

animals as models for his drawing. He was loosely affiliated with the Leipzig artist Emil Schmidt. Mostly, he worked on commission as an illustrator of newspapers, magazines, and popular books (including travelogues, adventure novels, and fairy tale collections). On Leutemann's contribution to the history of zoological illustration, see Claus Nissen, *Die zoologische Buchillustration: Ihre Bibliographie und Geschichte* (Stuttgart: Anton Hiersemann, 1966), 1: 252–53.

18 The technical usage of *Heimat* was widely circulated through a standard reference work for German museums of natural history, namely, Alfred Russel Wallace's *The Geographical Distribution of Animals* (New York: Harper and Brothers, 1876), trans. A. B. Meyer as *Die geographische Verbreitung der Thiere* (Dresden: Zahn, 1876). Both versions include zone pictures by the German draftsman Johann Baptist Zwecker. Prior to this publication, Zwecker was known for illustrating travelogues by Samuel Baker and David Livingstone, among others, in addition to numerous children's books. For examples of zone pictures in Hagenbeck's advertising paraphernalia, see Hoffmann, *Beiträge über Leben und Treiben der Eskimos*, frontispiece, 7, 19.

19 Hermann Wagner, foreword to *Zonen-Bilder: Nach Aquarellen von Heinrich Leutemann, mit erklärenden Schilderungen für die Jugend von Hermann Wagner* (Stuttgart: Julius Hoffmann, 1876), n. pag.

20 See also Heinrich Leutemann, *Leutemann's Bilder aus dem Völkerleben mit erläuterndem Text von Prof. Dr. Alfred Kirchhoff* (Fürth: Löwensohn, 1888), n. pag. This project was initiated by Kirchhoff, director of the Geographical Institute at the University of Halle, where he had already studied several of Hagenbeck's troupes (see, e.g., Alfred Kirchhoff, "Die Nubier in Halle," *Mittheilungen des Vereins für Erdkunde zu Halle* [1879]: 49–64). Several of the depicted figures in this album were based on recognizable performers from Hagenbeck's itinerant troupes. Thode-Arora first noted this resemblance (*Für fünfzig Pfennig*, 149–50), and Rothfels identified another example (*Savages and Beasts*, 120).

21 The selection of cultural themes or troupes and their change over time was keyed in part to the different (weather- and entertainment-related) seasons in Germany, with people from "cold zones" usually being exhibited during the winter, and people from "hot zones" during the summer. On race and climate, see esp. Mark Harrison, *Climates and Constitutions: Health, Race, Environment and British Imperialism in India, 1600–1850* (New Dehli; New York: Oxford University Press, 1999); and esp. Dror Wahrman, *The Making of the Modern Self: Identity and Culture in Eighteenth-Century England* (New Haven: Yale University Press, 2004), 83–126.

22 The "picturesque" quotation appears in Carl Hagenbeck, *Von Tieren und Menschen*, 80.

23 The need for domesticated animals is stressed by Dittrich and Rieke-Müller, *Carl*

Hagenbeck, 148. The director of Basel's zoo is quoted in Staehlin, *Völkerschauen*, 70.

24 For an account of "mock hunts" at the 1877 Greenland Inuit show, see Jacobsen, *Die weiße Grenze*, 42–45. The entire Berlin review of the 1880 Labrador show, first published in the 18 October issue of the *Norddeutsche Allgemeine Zeitung*, is translated and reprinted in Lutz, *The Diary of Abraham Ulrikab*, 14; Hagenbeck's letter opposing the hunt of a zoo animal is quoted in Fienup-Riordan, "Johan Adrian Jacobsen Brings Treasures from Alaska," 4; the "seal harpoon" quotations appears in Lutz, *The Diary of Abraham Ulrikab*, 44, 52. Here it should be noted that William F. Cody ("Buffalo Bill") would later simulate buffalo hunting as part of his Wild West show.

25 Kirshenblatt-Gimblett, *Destination Culture*, 55, 74 (original emphasis); Leutemann, *Lebensbeschreibung*, 49; cf. Carl Hagenbeck, *Von Tieren und Menschen*, 81. On the dramatics of "presence" versus "mimesis," see Richard Schechner, *Between Theater and Anthropology* (Philadelphia: University of Pennsylvania Press, 1985), 83–84.

26 The move from indoor to outdoor exhibition spaces has also been emphasized by historians of world's fairs with regard to architecture. The Paris *Exposition Universelle* of 1867, organized by Frédéric Le Play, is often cited as the first time that a park was created primarily for exhibiting model homes outside of (and on this occasion separate from) the official exhibition halls. On the push toward outdoor display in other contexts, see Alexander, *Museum Masters*, 239–75; Edward N. Kaufmann, "The Architectural Museum from World's Fair to Restoration Village," *Assemblage* 9 (June 1989): 21–39; Martin Wörner, *Vergnügung und Belehrung: Volkskultur auf den Weltausstellungen 1851–1900* (Münster: Waxmann, 1999), 49–57. The "open air" quotation appears in Leutemann, *Lebensbeschreibung*, 49. The "spacious lot" quotation appears in Carl Hagenbeck, *Von Tieren und Menschen*, 81.

27 See Johann Jakob Bachofen, *Das Mutterrecht*, ed. Hans-Jürgen Heinrichs (1861; Frankfurt am Main: Suhrkamp, 1975); Lewis Henry Morgan, *Systems of Consanguinity and Affinity of the Human Family*, Smithsonian Contributions to Knowledge 218 (Washington, DC: Smithsonian Institution, 1871). The "animal family" was also advocated as the basic unit of zoological museum display by Germany's leading taxidermist, Philipp Leopold Martin, in *Die Praxis der Naturgeschichte* (Weimar: Voigt, 1870), 2:69.

28 Leutemann offers a pertinent detail concerning the gender division of Hagenbeck's second Nubian Exhibition (1877), whose troupe included fifteen men and one woman. "I had a rather heated argument with [Hagenbeck's agent] old Kohn . . . because he adamantly claimed that the Egyptian government prohibited him from recruiting Nubian women. My doubts about that claim were confirmed

when women and girls later came over" as members of other troupes (*Lebensbeschreibung*, 55). Buffalo Bill's Wild West show, by contrast, traded mostly on the spectacle of masculine virility, with exceptions confined to a few sharpshooters such as Annie Oakley, whose gender difference in this arena was precisely the point. Native American women appeared in Wild West shows beginning in 1889. See Sarah Wood Clark, *Beautiful Daring Western Girls: Women of the Wild West Shows* (Cody, WY: Buffalo Bill Historical Center, 1985).

29 See, e.g., Malek Alloula, *The Colonial Harem*, trans. Myrna Godzich and Wlad Godzich (Minneapolis: University of Minnesota Press, 1986); and more recently Zimmerman, *Anthropology and Antihumanism*, 174–77.

30 The younger the viewers, it seems, the more intrusive they were. In the very first entry of his diary from 1880, the Inuit performer Abraham Ulrikab had this to say about the audience: "It is not beautiful in Berlin, because so many trees and people make it impossible, indeed, because so many children come" (quoted in Thode-Arora, "Das Eskimo-Tagebuch," 92).

31 I thank Miriam Kahn for this insight in reference to figures such as Omai, the Polynesian who was brought to London by Captain Cook in 1774.

32 An equally suggestive image depicting a similar exchange in Berlin, this one illustrated by Heinrich Leutemann, can be found in the supplement to *Daheim* 14, no. 28 (1878). For more on Paul Meyerheim and other modern German animal painters, see Kai Artinger, *Von der Tierbude zum Turm der Blauen Pferde: Die künstlerische Wahrnehmung der wilden Tiere im Zeitalter der zoologischen Gärten* (Berlin: Reimer, 1995). On the "benevolence" fantasy, see Susanne Zantop, *Colonial Fantasies: Conquest, Family, and Nation in Precolonial Germany, 1770–1870* (Durham, NC: Duke University Press, 1997), 7–8. The attendance figure appears in Thode-Arora, *Für fünfzig Pfennig*, 168.

33 The German term *Karawane* probably resonated in different ways, evoking at once images of itinerant performers (or *fahrend Volk*), nomadic tribes (*wandernde Völker*), including so-called gypsies (*Zigeuner*), and animal transports (*Tiertransporte* or *Tierkarawane*). The "summer caravan" quotation appears in Leutemann, *Lebensbeschreibung*, 49.

34 The "Hamrans" quotation appears in "Carl Hagenbeck's Handelsmenagerie und Thierpark," advertisement, *Hamburgischer Correspondent* (25 June 1876), 8. An updated advertisement with the same title, announcing the arrival of more natives and animals, appeared the following day on page 8.

35 The pamphlet was probably written for the Düsseldorf show, the very first time that a Hagenbeck troupe appeared in a public zoological garden, as noted in chapter 1. The excerpt is quoted in Thode-Arora, "'Charakteristische Gestalten,'" 109–10; original emphasis. Other translated passages from this pamphlet appear

in Rothfels, *Savages and Beasts*, 53–55. The "animal-rich" quotation appears in Carl Hagenbeck, *Von Tieren und Menschen*, 143.

36 See Karl Marx, "The Fetishism of the Commodity and Its Secret," in *Capital* (London: Verso, 1976), 1:163–77; Emily Apter and William Pietz, eds., *Fetishism as Cultural Discourse* (Ithaca: Cornell University Press, 1993).

37 The "break-neck" quotation appears in Leutemann, *Lebensbeschreibung*, 67; the description of the migration scene is from Carl Hagenbeck, *Von Tieren und Menschen*, 95; the "historian" quotation appears in G. S., "Eine Kalmückenkarawane in Deutschland," *Illustrirte Zeitung* (8 September 1883): 213.

38 These performers seem to have taken special pleasure in the tour experience. Two letters addressed to Hagenbeck, each from the leader of the 1883 troupe and translated into German, are available at TCH. The first thanks Hagenbeck for "ordering your representative to show us attractions such as the cathedral in Strasbourg," adding "special thanks to Hermann Behnke, who cared for us like a mother." A follow-up letter from 30 October 1883, titled "Dankschreiben des kalmückschen Fürsten" (Letter of Thanks from the Kalmuck Prince), confirms that they safely arrived home and were paid in full. The Prince closes by asking Hagenbeck to "write often" with information about future tours and promises to "write again soon." The following year, Hagenbeck organized another troupe, which might have included some of the same performers. It is described by Friedrich von Hellwald, in "Die Kalmücken," *Die Gartenlaube* 32, no. 39 (1884): 644–45. The 1884 program is transcribed in Dreesbach, *Gezähmte Wilde*, 177. For more on each troupe (including names of all participants), see Arash Bormanshinov, "Kalmyks in Europe in the Nineteenth Century," *Mongolian Studies* 11 (1988): 5–24.

39 The spectacle of set-up would be anticipated and publicized in local newspapers, a practice that began in the mid-1870s and continued into the 1910s. See, e.g., Leutemann, "Eskimos in Deutschland"; and the announcement for Hagenbeck's "Burma" show in *Hamburger Fremdenblatt*, 3 May 1913. The "pavilions" quotation appears in Greenhalgh, *Ephemeral Vistas*, 85.

40 Cultural juxtaposition remains the logic of display at living history museums such as Plimoth Plantation in Massachusetts or Colonial Williamsburg in Virginia. The preference is to show preindustrial, craft-oriented work processes, to make visible what capitalism has effaced and thereby rendered mysterious. In its emphasis on cultural performance and juxtaposition, the living-history version of the folk museum is yet another heir to the *Völkerschau*. On living-history museums, see Kirshenblatt-Gimblett, *Destination Culture*, 189–200; and Schechner, *Between Theater and Anthropology*, 80–98. In the context of world's fairs, see Bennett, *The Birth of the Museum*, 81–82. For a discussion of the Bisharin Caravan, see chapter 1; the "no industry" quotation appears in Möller, *Die Bischaris*, 7.

The "exquisite quality" and "capable of culture" quotations appear in Ferdinand, "'Völkerschauen' in Hamburg," 43.

41 Leutemann, *Lebensbeschreibung*, 66. Here it should be noted that Joseph Menges, one of the animal trappers Hagenbeck sent to Sri Lanka in 1882, independently organized and financed a "Ceylonese" show that same year. John Hagenbeck and his son John George Hagenbeck later specialized in exhibiting people from India and Sri Lanka, mounting at least another ten shows between 1887 and 1927.

42 In 1887, the animal dealer made his own foray into the circus business with "Carl Hagenbeck's International Circus and Sinhalese Caravan." The very elephants and performers that formed the Ceylon show of the previous year could be reorganized as a circus. After a series of disasters, including an elephant stampede in Munich that left several spectators dead in 1888, the Sri Lankan group detached from the circus and toured France and Belgium as a *Völkerschau* once again, now under the direction of Eduard Gehring (Thode-Arora, *Für fünfzig Pfennig*, 171). For an account of Hagenbeck's circus before it was disbanded and sold, see Leutemann, *Lebensbeschreibung*, 78–80; the "alluring" quotation appears on 65.

43 Leutemann, *Lebensbeschreibung*, 65. On the ubiquity of circus elements, see Staehlin, *Völkerschauen*, 62–65.

44 Leutemann, *Lebensbeschreibung*, 65–66.

45 L. Beckmann, "Die Hagenbeck'schen Singhalesen," *Die Gartenlaube* 32, no. 34 (1884): 564–66; here, 564. See also Fritz von Schirp, "Die Hagenbeck'sche Singhalesenkarawane," *Illustrirte Zeitung* (3 October 1885): 338.

46 Friedländer's dazzling work can be found in Ruth Malhotra, *Manege frei: Artisten- und Circusplakate von Adolph Friedländer* (Dortmund: Harenberg, 1979); *Menschen, Tiere, Sensationen: Zirkusplakate 1880–1930*, ed. Carl-Albrecht Haenlein and Wolfgang Till (Hannover: Kestner-Gesellschaft, 1978); and *Plakate 1880–1914*, ed. Viktoria Schmidt-Linsenhoff, Kurt Wettengl, and Almut Junker, Kleine Schriften des Historischen Museums Frankfurt 29 (Frankfurt am Main: Pippert + Koch, 1986).

47 The actual 1885 performance featured "various groups, which constantly circled the enclosure, so that there was always something for the audience to see" (Staehlin, *Völkerschauen,* 63). This innovative format, whose effect was to maximize the space for performance, is also visualized by the composition of the interior poster.

48 Marie Louise Pratt, *Imperial Eyes: Travel Writing and Transculturation* (London and New York: Routledge, 1992), 6–7. For a model study of museums as contact zones see Clifford, *Routes,* 188–219.

49 Consider, for example, the following comment in a review of an untitled Native American troupe that performed in Frankfurt's zoological garden in May 1879: "In the breaks [between performances], the foreign guests happily converse with

the public, mostly with the help of sign language, as only one of them speaks English" ("Die Indianer im Zoologischen Garten," *Frankfurter Journal*, 9 May 1879). In a further example, Jacobsen recalls that the Greenland performer named Okabak wrote Inuktitut messages on the back of *cartes des visites*, and gave them to spectators in exchange for money. It appears that Okabak enjoyed undermining the impresario's posture of cultural authority, writing messages that were meant to frustrate Jacobsen, who was unable to translate them for curious spectators (*Die weiße Grenze*, 41). On the vacillation between identification and difference, see my "From the Exotic to the Everyday: The Ethnographic Exhibition in Germany," in *The Nineteenth-Century Visual Culture Reader*, ed. Vanessa R. Schwartz and Jeannene M. Przyblyski (New York: Routledge, 2004), 323–24.

50 Richard Schechner, *Environmental Theater*, new and exp. ed. (New York: Applause, 1994), 40 (original italics), xiv–xv.

51 Among the most extraordinary acts of participation was that of the poet and bohemian Peter Altenberg, who, in summer 1896, frequented the "Ashanti Village" at the Vienna Zoo, where he regularly entered the display space and mingled with the performers. In so doing, he added his own self-consciously choreographed performance—an early example of what Barbara Kirshenblatt-Gimblett calls (to quote the title of her 1998 essay) "The Ethnographic Burlesque." See Peter Altenberg, *Ashantee* (Berlin: Fischer, 1897); Werner Michael Schwarz, *Anthropologische Spektakel: Zur Schaustellung "exotischer" Menschen, Wien 1870–1910* (Vienna: Turia + Kant, 2001), 187–98; Andrew Barker and Leo A. Lensing, *Peter Altenberg: Rezept die Welt zu sehen* (Vienna: Braumüller, 1995), 77–85.

52 A word of caution: All of the quotations from Abraham are third-hand at best. His twelve-page hand-written diary was first translated from the original Inuktitut into German by the Moravian missionary Georg Kretschmer. The original is lost. The most extensive selection of German passages can be found in Thode-Arora, "Das Eskimo-Tagebuch von 1880." A full English translation of the diary, along with translated correspondence and newsletters from the Moravian Archives, is readily available in Lutz, *The Diary of Abraham Ulrikab*. All English translations here are my own, based on Thode-Arora, with exception of those passages that are only available in Lutz.

53 The "communion dress" quotation appears in Lutz, *The Diary of Abraham Ulrikab*, 39. The "house" quotation appears in Thode-Arora, "Das Eskimo-Tagebuch," 93. The parenthetical explanation, "(in the zoo)," was probably added by Brother Kretschmer, who translated the original into German. Abraham's entry on the church service appears in Lutz, *The Diary of Abraham Ulrikab*, 18–21.

54 The "different faces" quotation appears in Thode-Arora, "Das Eskimo-Tagebuch," 93.

55 The “enclosure” quotation is in Thode-Arora, “Das Eskimo-Tagebuch,” 96–97; see also Lutz, *The Diary of Abraham Ulrikab*, 39–42.

56 The story of Tobias comes from an untitled article, first published in the 21 October 1880 issue of the *Norddeutsche Allgemeine Zeitung* (morn. ed.), trans. and reprinted in Lutz, *The Diary of Abraham Ulrikab*, 15.

57 Leutemann, *Lebensbeschreibung*, 69.

58 Thode-Arora, “‘Charakteristische Gestalten,’” 126.

59 The “inundated” quotation appears in Leutemann, *Lebensbeschreibung*, 68. For the “charms” quotation, see Carl Hagenbeck, *Von Tieren und Menschen*, 84.

60 Jacobsen’s memoir is quoted in Thode-Arora, *Für fünfzig Pfennig*, 117–18; further examples of erotic liaisons are given on 118–19. See also Staehlin, *Völkerschauen*, 89–91; Haberland, “Nine Bella Coolas,” 362, 365; Kopas, *Bella Coola*, 236; Dreesbach, *Gezähmte Wilde*, 170–73.

61 The attendance number is quoted in Dominik, “Die Nubier,” 186. The “fanatical excitement” quotation appears in Leutemann, *Lebensbeschreibung*, 57–58.

62 For an introduction to the German Colonial Society, see Helmuth Stoecker, “The Annexations of 1884–1885,” in *German Imperialism in Africa: From the Beginnings until the Second World War*, ed. Helmuth Stoecker, trans. Bernd Zöllner (London: Hurst; Atlantic Highlands, NJ: Humanities Press International, 1986), 21–38, here 23–24. For more, see Richard Victor Pierard, “The German Colonial Society, 1882–1914,” Ph.D. diss., State University of Iowa, 1964; and the in-house history by Erich Prager, *Die deutsche Kolonialgesellschaft, 1882–1907* (Berlin: Reimer, 1908). On the 1896 Colonial Exhibition, see Bruckner, “Tingle-Tangle,” 134–222; and Roland Richter, “Die erste deutsche Kolonial-Ausstellung 1896: Der ‘Amtliche Bericht’ in historischer Perspektive,” in *Kolonialausstellungen: Begegnungen mit Afrika?* ed. Robert Debusmann and János Riesz (Frankfurt am Main: IKO-Verlag für Interkulturelle Kommunikation, 1995), 25–42. The “behavior” quotation appears in Kathrin Roller, “‘Wir sind Deutsche, wir sind Weiße und wollen Weiße bleiben’: Reichstagsdebatten über koloniale ‘Rassenmischung,’” in *Kolonialmetropole Berlin: Eine Spurensuche*, ed. Ulrich van der Heyden and Joachim Zeller (Berlin: Berlin-Edition, 2002), 73–79, here, 78–79. On the disconnect between empire and exhibition, see Paul Kramer, “Making Concessions: Race and Empire Revisited at the Philippine Exposition, St. Louis, 1901–1905,” *Radical History Review* 73 (1999): 74–114.

63 These quotations from a business meeting of the German Colonial Society appear in “Antrag I der Abteilung Metz gegen die Ausfuhr von Eingeborenen aus den deutschen Kolonien zum Zwecke der Schaustellung,” *Deutsche Kolonialzeitung* 17, no. 28 (12 July 1900): 329–30.

64 The “incidents” are cited in the memorandum (*Denkschrift*), which was titled “Zur

Frage der Ausfuhr von Eingeborenen aus den deutschen Kolonien zum Zwecke der Schaustellung," submitted on behalf of the Colonial Society by Rear Admiral D. Strauch to the German chancellor Chlodwig zu Hohenlohe-Schillingsfürst, and first published in the Society's official organ, *Deutsche Kolonialzeitung* 17, no. 44 (1 November 1900): 500; continued in no. 45 (8 November 1900): 511, 513; and no. 46 (15 November 1900): 520. See also Prager, *Die deutsche Kolonialgesellschaft,* 144.

65 The "colony of half-castes" quotation appears in Helmuth Stoecker, "German Empire in Africa before 1914: General Questions," in *German Imperialism in Africa: From the Beginnings until the Second World War*, ed. Helmuth Stoecker, trans. Bernd Zöllner (London: Hurst; Atlantic Highlands, NJ: Humanities Press International, 1986), 185–229; here 211. On sending German women to South-West Africa, see Pierard, *German Colonial Society*, 204, 264–65; Lora Wildenthal, *German Women for Empire, 1884–1945* (Durham, NC: Duke University Press, 2001), 90–91.

66 Such arguments did not go unopposed. To give only one example, the socialist leader August Bebel criticized the mentality of colonial entrepreneurs, who viewed African peoples as "an inferior race against whom anything is allowed, the only limit being that of one's own personal interest." As a result, colonial subjects are "required to work inhuman hours and are treated without the slightest regard for their physical or material well-being." Quoted in Stoecker, "The German Empire in Africa before 1914," 210. The "doing nothing" quotation appears in Strauch, "Zur Frage der Ausfuhr," 513; the "economic life" quotation on 520.

67 Ibid., 520.

68 On parallels between colonialists and missionaries, see Bruckner, "Tingle-Tangle," 375–410. The "bad civilizational influence" and "uneducated" quotations both appear in Strauch, "Zur Frage der Ausfuhr," 520.

69 Adoption of the proposed ban was announced in "Zur Eingeborenenfrage," *Deutsche Kolonialzeitung* 18 (25 May 1901): 203. As Bruckner notes, some impresarios circumvented the law, and a few entrepreneurs, such as native impresario J. C. Bruce of the "Togo Company," were officially granted exceptions ("Tingle-Tangle," 379, 420–23). For a detailed account of the various colonial mandates, see Harald Sippel, "Rassismus, Protektionismus oder Humanität? Die gesetzlichen Verbote der Anwerbung von 'Eingeborenen' zu Schaustellungszwecken in den deutschen Kolonien," in *Kolonialausstellungen: Begegnungen mit Afrika?* ed. Robert Debusmann and János Riesz (Frankfurt am Main: IKO-Verlag für Interkulturelle Kommunikation, 1995), 43–64. On the colonial museum, see Joachim Zeller, "'Das Interesse an der Kolonialpolitik fördern und heben': Das Deutsche Kolonialmuseum in Berlin," in *Kolonialmetropole Berlin: Eine Spurensuche*, ed. Ulrich van der Heyden and Joachim Zeller (Berlin: Berlin-Edition, 2002), 142–49.

70 It is interesting to note that the Colonial Society's arguments would later be rehearsed in Nazi Germany as arguments for shutting down the "German Africa Show" (*Deutsche Afrika-Schau*), a colonial exhibition first organized by the native impresario J. C. Bruce (former director of a troupe called the "Togo Company") and later co-opted by the Nazi state. Opponents of the show emphasized its failure to advance a hegemonic view of German racial superiority and the related tendency to promote inappropriate mixing among spectators and performers. According to one Nazi official, such performances "should serve to increase the distance between African *Neger* and our German *Volk*, not to deaden the feeling for that distance." See Elisa von Joeden-Forgey, "Race Power in Postcolonial Germany: The German Africa Show and the National Socialist State, 1935–1940," in *Germany's Colonial Pasts*, ed. Eric Ames, Marcia Klotz, and Lora Wildenthal (Lincoln: University of Nebraska Press, 2005), 167–88; here, 180.

71 In other words, ethnographic performance did not follow the same trajectory that historian David M. Ciarlo has mapped out for racial imagery in German print advertising, from the use of vaguely exotic to specifically colonial iconography. Cf. David M. Ciarlo "Rasse konsumieren: Von der exotischen zur kolonialen Imagination in der Bildreklame des Wilhelminischen Kaiserreichs," in *Phantasiereiche: Zur Kulturgeschichte des deutschen Kolonialismus*, ed. Birthe Kundrus (Frankfurt am Main: Campus, 2003), 135–79.

3 ✦ Hagenbeck's Turn to Fiction

1 As evidence of increased competition around 1900, Dreesbach notes, at least one hundred and fifty shows were mounted in the last quarter of the century, followed by another 150 shows between 1900 and 1914 (*Gezähmte Wilde*, 111). The "dependable" quotation appears in an untitled report in *Verhandlungen der Berliner Gesellschaft für Anthropologie, Ethnologie und Urgeschichte* 22 (1890): 589. For speculation on Hagenbeck's withdrawal, see Dittrich and Rieke-Müller, *Carl Hagenbeck*, 166–67.

2 Bruckner, "Spectacles of (Human) Nature, 129–30, 140–44, 148–54." Here I would add that the "decline" model is a powerful trope of the historical discourse on popular culture more generally. Architectural historian Wolfgang Friebe offers a useful example concerning world's fairs. Of the 1900 *Exposition Universelle* in Paris, he writes: "The public was no longer interested in machines and technology; what they came for was to be entertained by spectacles involving water, light, illusions, and traveling in all its forms. It was no longer those thirsty for knowledge who streamed through the portals of such exhibitions, but those eager for diversion. . . . This exhibition made clear the fact that the original inspiration for

such exhibitions had, morally speaking, fallen by the wayside." Wolfgang Friebe, *Buildings of the World Exhibitions*, trans. Jenny Vowles and Paul Roper (Leipzig: Edition Leipzig, 1985), 133. Cf. Greenhalgh, *Ephemeral Vistas*, 86–87; Rosalind H. Williams, *Dream Worlds: Mass Consumption in Late Nineteenth-Century France* (Berkeley: University of California Press, 1982), 59.

3 The first and only collection of visual materials on the Wild West in Germany is the exhibition catalog, *I Like America: Fictions of the Wild West*, ed. Pamela Kort and Max Hollein (Munich: Prestel, 2006). A portion of this chapter appears in the catalog as "Seeing the Imaginary: On the Popular Reception of Wild West Shows in Germany, 1885–1910" (213–29).

4 The "profit" quotation appears in Carl Hagenbeck, letter to Johan Adrian Jacobsen, 5 January 1882 (TCH). Schedule and program details appear in Haberland, "Diese Indianer sind falsch," 15, 17–35.

5 The "savages" quotation appears in Haberland, "Nine Bella Coola Indians," 359. On Stumpf's encounter with the Bella Coola, see my "The Sound of Evolution."

6 Quoted in Haberland, "Nine Bella Coolas," 358.

7 Leutemann, *Lebensbeschreibung*, 67. On Harvey's troupe, see "Die Sioux-Indianer," *Hamburger Fremdenblatt*, 20 November 1885; and "Hanseatisches Panopticum," *Hamburger Fremdenblatt*, 29 November 1885, 1st supplement. In a move reminiscent of George Catlin's early nineteenth-century Indian gallery shows, the live performance of Harvey's troupe was supplemented by a collection of illustrations by the well-known German artist and traveler, Rudolf Cronau. For a partial list of Native American troupes in Germany, see Katinka Kocks, *Indianer im Kaiserreich: Völkerschauen und Wild West Shows zwischen 1880 und 1914* (Gerolzhofen: Oettermann, 2004), 86–89. For the "wrong Indians" thesis, see Haberland, "Nine Bella Coolas," 361–62. The "hanged" and "disappointed" comments are quoted in Cole, *Captured Heritage*, 71. The "preconceptions" review is quoted in Thode-Arora, "Indianer Nordamerikas in Europa," 82.

8 The "right Indians" quotation appears in Robert E. Bieder, "Marketing the American Indian in Europe: Context, Commodification and Reception," in *Cultural Transmissions and Receptions: American Mass Culture in Europe*, ed. Rob Kroes, Robert W. Rydell, and Doeko F. J. Bosscher (Amsterdam: VU University Press, 1993), 23.

9 Historians of the Wild West often point to Karl May, the popular German writer of Western novels, in order to explain why the show met with greater enthusiasm in Germany than it did elsewhere in Europe. See, e.g., Joseph G. Rosa and Robin May, *Buffalo Bill and His Wild West: A Pictorial Biography* (Lawrence: University Press of Kansas, 1989), 146–47; Rudolf Conrad, "Mutual Fascination: Indians in Dresden and Leipzig," in *Indians and Europe: An Interdisciplinary Collection of*

Essays, ed. Christian F. Feest (Aachen: Rader, 1987), 455–73; Paul Reddin, *Wild West Shows* (Urbana: University of Illinois Press, 1999), 111. Cf. Jeffrey L. Sammons, "Nineteenth-Century German Representations of Indians from Experience," in *Germans and Indians: Fantasies, Encounters, Projections*, ed. Colin G. Calloway, Gerd Gemünden, and Susanne Zantop (Lincoln: University of Nebraska Press, 2002), 185–93. On the stereotype of the Plains Indian in the United States, see Sarah J. Blackstone, *Buckskins, Bullets, and Business: A History of Buffalo Bill's Wild West* (New York: Greenwood Press, 1986), 131.

10 All of the main elements are noted in "Buffalo Bill's Wild-Amerika," *Illustrirte Zeitung* (12 July 1890): 41, and illustrated by Albert Richter on 46–47. The show's program and its establishment are detailed by Don Russell in *The Wild West: A History of the Wild West Shows* (Fort Worth, TX: Amon Carter Museum of Western Art, 1970), 33–35. Due to the extensive material on Buffalo Bill's Wild West, I have restricted my analysis to its German reception. On Cody and his show more generally, see Don Russell, *The Lives and Legends of Buffalo Bill* (Norman: University of Oklahoma Press, 1960); Joy Kasson, *Buffalo Bill's Wild West: Celebrity, Memory, and Popular History* (New York: Hill and Wang, 2000), 41–55; and Louis S. Warren, *Buffalo Bill's America: William Cody and the Wild West Show* (New York: Knopf, 2005).

11 In 1891, Buffalo Bill's troupe returned to Germany, appearing in other, mostly smaller cities. Details on the Munich show come from "Buffalo Bill," *Münchener Fremdenblatt*, 20 April 1890; "Buffalo Bills Wild West," *Münchener Fremdenblatt*, 21 April 1890; "Buffalo Bills 'Wilder Westen,'" *Münchener neuste Nachrichten*, 21 April 1890; "Die amerikanische Arena," *Münchener Fremdenblatt*, 22 April 1890; "Indianer in der Stadt," *Münchener Nachrichten*, 25 April 1890; *Münchener Bote*, 26 April 1890. For a description of the Munich program, see "Buffalo Bills Wild West," *Münchener Fremdenblatt*, 21 April 1890. All sources here come from the William Fredrick Cody / Buffalo Bill Papers, WH72, Western History Collection, of The Denver Public Library (hereafter cited as DPL).

12 See Raymond W. Thorp, *Spirit Gun of the West: The Story of Doc W. F. Carver* (Glendale, CA: Arthur H. Clark, 1957), 116, 119–22, 180; Signor Saltarino, *Fahrend Volk: Abnormitäten, Kuriositäten und interessante Vertreter der wandernden Künstlerwelt* (Leipzig: Weber, 1895), 89–92.

13 "Cowboys Painting Hamburg," *San Francisco Examiner*, 28 August 1890, available in MS 6, William F. Cody Collection, Series VI: E, W. F. "Doc" Carver scrapbook, microfilm roll 1 (BBHC; hereafter abbreviated as BBHC-Carver).

14 On Catlin as forerunner to Buffalo Bill, see Reddin, *Wild West Shows*, 1–52. The "who would dare" quotation appears in "Wild-West," *Freisinnige Zeitung*, 24 July

1890 (BBHC-Cody). The "historical attraction" quotation comes from a June 1890 advertisement in an unnamed Dresden newspaper (BBHC-Cody). Extended historical claims are made in "Buffalo Bill's Wild West Journal," a German-language supplement to the *Berliner Tageblatt*, 22 July 1890; and in Wilhelm Wyl, "Der 'Wilde Westen' in Berlin," *Berliner Tageblatt*, 23 July 1890 (both in BBHC-Cody).

15 Kasson, *Buffalo Bill's Wild West*, 84.

16 "Buffalo Bill's Wild West," *Münchener Tageblatt*, 21 April 1890 (DPL).

17 "Dr. Carver's Wild-Amerika," *Hamburger Nachrichten*, 22 August 1890, 2nd supplement. Similar statements can be found in "Biographisches über Buffalo Bill," *Allgemeine Zeitung* (Munich), 15 April 1890 (DPL); "Buffalo Bill und seine Karawane," *Münchener Tageblatt*, 17 April 1890 (DPL); an untitled Munich review in the *Augsburger Abendzeitung*, 27 April 1890 (DPL); "Buffalo Bills Wild West in Dresden," *Meitzener Tageblatt*, 3 June 1890 (BBHC-Cody); an untitled article on the Dresden premiere, in *Anzeiger und Tageblatt* (Freiberg), 1 June 1890 (BBHC-Cody); "Buffalo Bills Wild West-Truppe," Hannover *Presse*, 3 July 1890 (BBHC-Cody); "'Wild-West' in Berlin," Berlin *Lokal-Anzeiger*, 24 July 1890 (BBHC-Cody).

18 Sociologist Karl Markus Kreis has noted that Wild West shows in Germany made cowboys and Indians widely available for imaginative role-play. The vivification idea would seem to strengthen his hypothesis. See "Indians Playing, Indians Praying: Native Americans in Wild West Shows and Catholic Missions," in *Germans and Indians: Fantasies, Encounters, Projections*, ed. Colin G. Calloway, Gerd Gemünden, and Susanne Zantop (Lincoln: University of Nebraska Press, 2002), 195–212. For historical sources, see "Indianer-Spielen," *Tageblatt* (Dresden), 4 June 1890 (DPL); and "Die Wirkungen der Vorstellungen Buffalo Bill's," *Nachrichten* (Leipzig), 22 June 1890 (BBHC-Cody).

19 By 1890 the Wild West had become a new outdoor evening entertainment, part of the electric landscape that was just taking shape in Hamburg as it was in cities throughout Europe and the United States. Both electric lighting and the Wild West had their origins in the theater, and both became significant cultural practices in the late nineteenth century. Like the Wild West, electrified light had an unmistakably kinetic energy. It didn't just illuminate things in the nocturnal city, as other scholars have brilliantly shown; it created new sights to be seen. See esp. David E. Nye, *Electrifying America: Social Meanings of a New Technology, 1880–1914* (Cambridge, MA: The MIT Press, 1990); and Joachim Schlör, *Nights in the Big City: Paris, Berlin, London 1840–1930*, trans. Pierre Gottfried Imhof and Dafydd Rees Roberts (London: Reaktion Books, 1998).

20 Williams, *Dream Worlds*, 85.

21 The "slice of life" quotation appears in "Dr. Carver's Wild-Amerika," *Hamburger Nachrichten*, 7 September 1890, morn. ed. The advertisement for "Carver's Wild-

Amerika" appears in *Hamburger Fremdenblatt*, 26 August 1890, 2nd supplement. Williams, *Dream Worlds*, 84. Wolfgang Schivelbusch, *Disenchanted Night: The Industrialization of Light in the Nineteenth Century*, trans. Angela Davies (Berkeley: University of California Press, 1995).

22 Blackstone, *Buckskins, Bullets, and Business*, 42.

23 Greenhalgh, *Ephemeral Vistas*, 105.

24 On the ethnographic imaginary in advertising, see esp. Thomas Richards, *The Commodity Culture of Victorian England: Advertising and Spectacle, 1851–1914* (Stanford, CA: Stanford University Press, 1990), 119–67; Anne McClintock, *Imperial Leather: Race, Gender and Sexuality in the Colonial Contest* (New York: Routledge, 1995), 207–31; and Jeffrey Steele, "Reduced to Images: American Indians in Nineteenth-Century Advertising," in *Dressing in Feathers: The Construction of the Indian in American Popular Culture*, ed. S. Elizabeth Bird (Boulder, CO: Westview Press, 1996), 45–64. The quotation appears in Jean Baudrillard, *The System of Objects*, trans. James Benedict (London: Verso, 1996), 191–92; original emphasis.

25 After Carl Hagenbeck's death in 1913, the name obtained new value, and its use for commercial purposes has at times been contested within the family. Today, his name and its connotations continue to shape the corporate identity of the *Tierpark*, its family tradition, and its exceptionally strong sense of history. Most recently, the local significance of "Hagenbeck" was cited as central to the park's successful campaign to earn protection as an official cultural monument (*Kulturdenkmal*) of the city of Hamburg. In order to secure financing for the future, the park has integrated itself into a burgeoning heritage industry.

26 On the Cairo exhibition in Berlin, see Paul Lindenberg, *Pracht-Album photographischer Aufnahmen der Berliner Gewerbe-Ausstellung 1896* (Berlin: Werner, 1896). Ceylonese and Indian teahouses also appeared in British exhibitions since the early 1880s (see Mathur, "Living Ethnological Exhibits").

27 See Peter H. Farquhar, "Managing Brand Equity," *Marketing Research* (September 1989): 24–33; Kevin Lane Keller, *Strategic Brand Management: Building, Measuring, and Managing Brand Equity* (Upper Saddle River, NJ: Prentice Hall, 1998); Naomi Klein, *No Logo*, 1st rev. ed. (New York: Picador, 2002).

28 Witness the illegal use of his name in the "Hagenbeck-Wallace Circus," which made its American debut in 1907, unbeknownst to the German entrepreneur. For details, see George L. Chindahl, *A History of the Circus in America* (Caldwell, ID: Caxton Printers, 1959), 126–28; Fred D. Pfening, Jr., "How Wallace Bought Hagenbeck," *Bandwagon* (July–August 1964): 12; Charles Philip Fox and Tom Parkinson, *The Circus in America* (Waukesha, WI: Country Beautiful, 1969), 95. The quotation appears in Friedberg, *Window Shopping*, 42.

29 Hagenbeck's Ceylon Tea would also be sold by John and Gustav Hagenbeck at

their 1902 India show. *Gebr. Hagenbeck's Indische Carawane: Die Malabaren*, program brochure, TCH.

30 Showmen even suggested the role of memory to spectators. See, e.g., *Gebrüder J. & G. Hagenbeck's Indische Völkerschaften*, program brochure, 1904 (Hamburg: Adolph Friedländer, n.d.), 8 (TCH).

31 Dean MacCannell, *The Tourist: A New Theory of the Leisure Class* (1976; Berkeley: University of California, 1999), 62.

32 Sandberg, *Living Pictures, Missing Persons,* 188. One could argue that the example of cigars or perishable goods forces the consumption argument in a way that museum accessions might not. Yet consider some of the other items that Hagenbeck sold to spectators. These included rugs, mats, pots, necklaces, ornaments, musical instruments, and wood carvings (e.g., masks, figurines, totem poles, even full-sized kayaks). All of these items were made and demonstrated within the context of ethnographic exhibition, and any of them could find their way into museum collections (as some in fact did). Generally, performers kept the money that they received for such objects, and Hagenbeck profited from the "interest" that these sales added to the show.

33 The gate description appears in the guidebook, *Führer durch Carl Hagenbeck's Tierpark, Stellingen*, with text by Nikolaus Schiller-Tietz (1st ed.; Hamburg: Verlag von Carl Hagenbecks Tierpark, 1907), x (TCH). All citations to *Führer* (1907) refer to this edition, unless otherwise indicated. For the "Uncas" quotation, see "Hagenbecks Tierpark," *Hamburger Echo*, 7 May 1907, 2d ed. For "Gulliver" and other literary allusions, see Philipp Berges, "Hagenbecks Neuschöpfungen: Eröffnung der Völkerschau Aethiopien," *Hamburger Fremdenblatt*, 16 May 1909, clipping from the Staatsarchiv Hamburg (hereafter abbreviated SAH), A902 "Hagenbecks Tierpark." On the role of Berges, see Haug von Kuenheim, *Carl Hagenbeck* (Hamburg: Ellert & Richter, 2007), 148, 192–93.

34 For a partial guest list, see "Die Eröffnung von Hagenbecks Tierparadies," *Hamburger Nachrichten*, 7 May 1907, eve. ed.

35 The Bazaar is first mentioned in the guidebook of 1911, the same year in which a "Japanese Shopping Pavilion" was installed on the other side of the bridge, so that the bridge was now flanked by gift and souvenir shops (TCH). By 1914, a "Gift Shop" was added, kitty-corner to the Bazaar, at the edge of the village. The list of native artisans comes from an advertisement for "Völkerschau: Birma," *Hamburger Fremdenblatt*, 11 May 1913, morn. ed. The idea of an enduring space for ethnographic exhibition became a model for imitation, as evidenced by the 1912 plan for the (unrealized) "Ethnological Garden" in Berlin. It called for elaborating the *Völkerschau* into a fixed-site theme park, featuring a complex of national pavilions (organized by continent), ethnographic villages, curio shops, and theme

restaurants, as well as a large cinema theater and an outdoor arena with a retractable roof. An investment portfolio, titled *Ethnologischer Garten: Internationale Völkerschau*, can be found in *Acta betreffend verschiedenen Angelegenheiten der ethnologischen Abteilung*, Vol. 18. 1.8.1911 bis 31.8.1912, Pars III.c (Museum für Völkerkunde Berlin).

36 The scholarship on Disney theme parks claims that narrativization is what defines theme space and distinguishes it from the amusement rides and parks of 1900, but the example of Hagenbeck helps recover its longer history. See, e.g., Beth Dunlop, *Building a Dream: The Art of Disney Architecture* (New York: Harry N. Abrams, 1996); Karal Ann Marling, "Imagineering the Disney Theme Parks," in *Designing Disney's Theme Parks: The Architecture of Reassurance*, ed. Karal Ann Marling (Paris: Flammarion, 1997), 29–176; Deborah Philips, "Narrativised Spaces: The Functions of Story in the Theme Park," in *Leisure/Tourism Geographies: Practices and Geographical Knowledge*, ed. David Crouch (London: Routledge, 1999), 91–108. Thode-Arora prioritizes the village in "'Charakteristische Gestaltn,'" 126.

37 On narrative as a form of legitimatization in the wax museum, see Sandberg, *Living Pictures, Missing Persons*, 73. In the context of early cinema, see Charles Musser, "Moving Towards Fictional Narratives: Story Films Become the Dominant Product, 1903–1904," in *The Silent Cinema Reader*, ed. Lee Grieveson and Peter Krämer (London and New York: Routledge, 2004), 87–102; Tom Gunning, "Weaving a Narrative: Style and Economic Background in Griffith's Biograph Films," in *Early Cinema: Space, Frame, Narrative*, ed. Thomas Elsaesser (London: BFI Publishing, 1990), 336–47; and Tom Gunning, "From the Opium Den to the Theatre of Morality: Moral Discourse and the Film Process in Early American Cinema," in *The Silent Cinema Reader*, 145–54.

38 The "fight scenes" quotation appears in Thode-Arora, *Für fünfzig Pfennig*, 107. The program for German Africa comes from *Deutsch-Afrika: Carl Hagenbeck's Kamerun-Expedition* (Munich: Verlag von Fritz Angerer, 1886), 16 (TCH). Details about the "Panoramic Scenery" and the storyline of the 1895 show can be found in the program brochure, *East African Village* (TCH), as well as in "Somaliland at Sydenham," *The Graphic* (3 August 1895): 139.

39 Cf. Ernst Pinkert's Egyptian Exhibition and Bedouin Caravan of 1890, which was basically an "Arabian" version of the Wild West with its diverse mix of pageantry, equestrian stunts ("Egyptian Buffalo Riders"), and even a dramatic ambush scene. *Aegyptische Ausstellung und Beduinen-Karawane*, program brochure, dir. Ernst Pinkert (24 May 1890) (TCH). Thode-Arora, *Für fünfzig Pfennig*, 110.

40 The exact figures are as follows: 83,155 adults and 25,815 children, for a total of 108,970 visitors on Easter weekend. "Pfingsten in Hagenbecks Tierpark in Stellingen," *Hamburger Nachrichten*, 18 May 1910. The "too close" quotation appears in

Thode-Arora, *Für fünfzig Pfennig*, 76. A collection of posters and postcards from the show is readily available in Kort and Hollein, *I Like America,* 209–11.

41 *Sioux-Indianer: Carl Hagenbeck's Tierpark, Stellingen, 1910*, with text by Johannes Flemming (Hamburg: Carly, 1910), 5 (TCH).

42 A vehicle of imaginary identification, the animal transport invites spectators to envision themselves on safari with Hagenbeck. That an animal trapper appeared as a figure in the arena further reinforced the association of the spectacle with its sponsor. See *Völkerschau Aethiopien*, with text by Johannes Flemming (Hamburg: Adolph Friedländer, 1909), 3–4 (TCH).

43 In emphasizing Hagenbeck's debt to Buffalo Bill, I take issue with the argument presented in Schwarz, *Anthropologische Spektakel*, 207–22. The "numerous tribes" quotation appears in *Sioux-Indianer*, 9.

44 The "pale faces" review is quoted in Thode-Arora, "Die Hagenbeckschen Völkerschauen," 85; other passages from the same review are readily available in Thode-Arora, *Für fünfzig Pfennig*, 1–3. The May commentary appears in "Wild-West bei Hagenbeck," *Hamburger Nachrichten*, 16 April 1910.

45 Jacobsen is quoted in Ferdinand, "'Völkerschauen' in Hamburg," 56.

46 The cover for the guidebook for Hagenbeck's "Bedouins" subtly evokes the theater by design: A colorful cloth wrap—an ethnographic artifact from the show—serves at once as "stage," "proscenium," and "theater curtain," by the way in which it appears to be folded and visually arranged. The show's title, date, and location ("*Völkerschau* 1912—Bedouins—Carl Hagenbeck's *Tierpark*, Stellingen") are all framed in the solid-black center of the design—on stage, as it were. A color reproduction is available in Ortwin Pelc and Matthias Gretzschel, *Hagenbeck: Tiere, Menschen, Sensationen* (Hamburg: Hamburger Abendblatt, Axel Springer Verlag, 1998), 45.

47 Berges, "Hagenbecks Neuschöpfungen."

48 "Buffalo Bills Wilder Westen," Tharandt and Mohorn *Anzeiger*, 3 June 1890 (BBHC-Cody); emphasis added.

49 The "breaks" quotation appears in "Sioux-Indianer bei Hagenbeck." For the village-museum analogy, see Griffiths, *Wondrous Difference*, 38–43.

50 Schechner, *Between Theater and Anthropology,* xxxvii.

51 The "Arabic Café" and "Barber" quotations appear in the guidebook, *Am Nil: Bunte Bilder aus Egypten dem Wunderlande der Pyramide: Völkerschau 1912, Carl Hagenbeck's Tierpark, Stellingen*, with text by Johannes Flemming (Hamburg: Carly, 1912), 18, 26 (TCH). On performers as salespeople, see Thode-Arora, *Für fünfzig Pfennig*, 114; and Rhonda Garelick, "*Bayadères*, *Stéréorama*, and *Vahat-Loukoum*: Technological Realism in the Age of Empire," in *Spectacles of Realism: Gender, Body, Genre*, ed. Margaret Cohen and Christopher Prendergast (Minneapolis: University of Minnesota Press, 1995), 294–319, here 310.

52 One journalist stressed these different possibilities in a review of the Somali exhibition, which was organized for the park's grand opening. See "Hagenbecks Tierpark," *Hamburger Echo*, 7 May 1907, 2d ed.

53 For a relevant discussion of the predilection for Egyptian settings in early cinema, see Antonia Lant, "The Curse of the Pharaoh, or How Cinema Contracted Egyptomania," *October* 59 (Winter 1992): 87–112. The "Umlauff" quotation appears in *Am Nil*, 5. The guidebook (*Am Nil*) further notes that "The Sphinx and Pyramids were carried out by Franz Gruber & Co.," specialists in theater decoration for "Hamburg's largest stages as well as for court theaters and other first-rate stages both domestic and international" (32). The Cliff Temple description appears on 27. The "oriel" quotation appears on 13–14.

4 ✦ The Art of Hagenbeck's Zoo

1 Oliver Grau, *Virtual Art: From Illusion to Immersion*, trans. Gloria Custance (Cambridge, MA: The MIT Press, 2003), 13, 14; on haptic space, see 126.

2 Ibid., 15.

3 This evocation draws on multiple different spectator accounts: "Hagenbeck auf der Berliner Gewerbe-Ausstellung," *Hamburger Correspondent*, 11 June 1896, eve. ed., 1; Karl Russ, "Hagenbecks Eismeer-Panorama auf der Berliner Gewerbeausstellung," *Über Land und Meer: Deutsche Illustrirte Zeitung* 76, no. 42 (October 1896): 679, and its accompanying illustration by the famous animal painter Wilhelm Kuhnert on 672–73; "Carl Hagenbeck's Eismeer-Panorama," *Der Kurier* 6, no. 53 (31 October 1896): 974–75; and Max Hartung, "Die Sächsisch-Thüringische Industrie- und Gewerbe-Ausstellung in Leipzig," *Die Gartenlaube* (1897): 316–20, here, 320; Heinrich Bolau, "Karl Hagenbeck's Eismeer-Panorama," *Illustrirte Zeitung* 108, no. 2793 (9 January 1897): 57–59. For a translated version of the last article, see "Hagenbeck's Panorama of a Northern Sea," in *Scientific American Supplement*, 11 September 1897, p. 18098–99.

4 The name "Natural-Scientific Panorama" would not be used for any of the traveling panoramas that he exhibited, which were titled according to either the particular "habitat" on display (e.g., "Carl Hagenbeck's Polar Panorama") or the category of animals generally (as in, "Carl Hagenbeck's Animal Panorama").

5 On the history of the traditional panorama, see Heinz Buddemeier, *Panorama, Diorama, Photographie: Entstehung und Wirkung neuer Medien im 19. Jahrhundert* (Munich: Wilhelm Fink, 1970); Altick, *The Shows of London*, 128–210; Ralph Hyde, *Panoramania! The Art and Entertainment of the 'All-Embracing' View* (London: Trefoil, 1988); Marie-Louise von Plessen, *Sehsucht: Das Panorama als Massenunterhaltung des 19. Jahrhunderts* (Basel and Frankfurt am Main: Stroemfeld/Roter

Stern, 1993); Stephan Oettermann, *The Panorama: History of a Mass Medium*, trans. Deborah Lucas Schneider (New York: Zone Books, 1997); Bernard Comment, *The Panorama* (London: Reaktion Books, 1999). On panoramas in Germany, see Helmut Börsch-Supan, "Die Anfänge des Panoramas in Deutschland," in *"Sind Briten hier?" Relations between British and Continental Art, 1680–1880*, ed. Zentralinstitut für Kunstgeschichte in München (Munich: Fink, 1981), 161–80; Stephan Oettermann, "Die Reise mit den Augen: 'Oramas' in Deutschland," in Plessen, *Sehsucht*, 42–51; and chapter 4 of Oettermann, *The Panorama*, "The Panorama in Germany."

6 Living animals had been occasionally used in panoramas with three-dimensional foregrounds. In such instances, however, animals merely served as living accoutrements, bolstering the "reality effect" of the painting, which continued to define the panorama's subject. Interestingly, Hagenbeck reverses the historical relationship of art and reality that was typical of panoramas: Art would here be used to put the finishing touches on the physical world, and not the other way around. Cf. Dolf Sternberger, "Panorama of the 19th Century," trans. Joachim Neugroschel, *October* 4 (fall 1987): 3–20; here, 5–8.

7 Wolfgang Schivelbusch, *The Railway Journey: The Industrialization of Time and Space in the Nineteenth Century* (Berkeley: University of California Press, 1986), 53, 55, 64. For explorations of panoramic vision in other contexts, see Walter Benjamin, "Paris, Capital of the Nineteenth Century," in *Reflections: Essays, Aphorisms, Autobiographical Writings*, ed. Peter Demetz, trans. Edmund Jephcott (New York: Schocken Books, 1986), 146–62; Margaret Cohen, "Panoramic Literature and the Invention of Everyday Genres," in *Cinema and the Invention of Everyday Life*, ed. Leo Charney and Vanessa R. Schwartz (Berkeley: University of California Press, 1995), 227–52; and Alison Griffiths, "'Shivers Down Your Spine': Panoramas and the Origins of the Cinematic Reenactment," *Screen* 44, no. 1 (spring 2003): 1–37.

8 Bruckner has even characterized Hagenbeck's *Völkerschau* as a "panoramic ethnographic landscape" (as opposed to a freak show or a colonial exhibition), citing the *Tierpark* in Stellingen as evidence ("Tingle-Tangle," 274). The upshot is accurate, but the approach is misleading: It back-reads the *Tierpark* discourse onto the *Völkerschau*, which Hagenbeck developed much earlier, while conflating the historical notion of habitat display with the idea of panoramic vision.

9 The "great circle" quotation appears in Raymond Blathwayt, "Wild Beasts: How They Are Transported and Trained," *McClure's Magazine* 1, no. 2 (July 1893): 130–31, here 130. The "inclosure" quotation is from Raymond Blathwayt, "Hunting the Beasts: Karl Hagenbeck Tells of His Exploits in Foreign Jungles," *Detroit Journal* 6 May 1893; reprinted the next day in *Chicago Post*, *Toledo Commercial*, and *Los Angeles Times* (all clippings from TCH). For an "inside" account written from a

trainer's perspective, see Hernann [*sic*] Boger, "Training Wild Beasts," *The Independent* 55, no. 2865 (29 October 1903): 2551–57.

10 An itinerant version of this giant encaged diorama was also shown in London, as part of the 1895 "East African Village and Great Somali Display," which took place at the Crystal Palace. The diorama was painted by Moritz Lehmann. The British naturalist and popular writer, C. J. Cornish, who interviewed Hagenbeck on the scene, heralded it as "a specimen page of the 'Zoo of the Future'" ("The Moltke of Menagerie Owners," 84). It is must also be noted that the ethnographic performance here also took place before a vast "Panoramic Scenery," which was painted by M. Pritchard Barrett (see fig. 3.9). The following year, as we shall see, Hagenbeck would hire Lehmann to paint the backdrop for his very first "Arctic Sea Panorama," a traveling panorama that premiered in Berlin. If the *Völkerschau* in London did not inspire Hagenbeck's idea for an animal panorama, it certainly gave him and Lehmann a common point of reference.

11 "Naturwissenschaftliches Panorama," certificate no. 91492, filed at the H. & W. Pataky patent bureau (Berlin) for Carl Hagenbeck on 6 February 1896 (TCH). All patent quotations refer to this source.

12 All quotations come from "Naturwissenschaftliches Panorama."

13 The quotation is from Grau, *Virtual Art*, 106. For more on *faux terrain* in panoramas, see ibid., 44, 58, 84n127.

14 The name "ha-ha," according to Horace Walpole, comes from the sense of astonishment that "common people" expressed "at finding all of a sudden an unperceived check to their walk." Quoted in Christopher Thacker, *The History of Gardens* (Berkeley: University of California Press, 1979), 183. The "pigeon test" quotation is from Carl Hagenbeck, *Von Tieren und Menschen*, 384.

15 Quotation from "Naturwissenschaftliches Panorama."

16 Russell A. Potter, "Arctic Spectacles: Visions of the North in Panoramas, 1820–1874," in *The North in Film: Papers Presented at "Visions of the North, Voices of the North," Northern Culture Conference*, ed. A. W. Plumstead (North Bay, Ont.: Nipissing University, 1999), 9–36. On contemporaneous German fantasies of the Arctic, see David Thomas Murphy, *German Exploration of the Polar World: A History, 1870–1940* (Lincoln: University of Nebraska Press, 2002).

17 Russ, "Hagenbecks Eismeer-Panorama," 672.

18 Quotation from Dittrich and Rieke-Müller, *Carl Hagenbeck*, 184.

19 The "constant presence" quotation appears in Dittrich and Rieke-Müller, *Carl Hagenbeck*, 192. The "family" remark can be found in Russ, "Hagenbecks Eismeer-Panorama," 672. For the "food" quotation, see "Hagenbeck auf der Berliner Gewerbe-Ausstellung." The "improvised Eskimos" quotation appears in Fischer, *Aus dem Leben und Wirken*, 54–55.

20 For the "costumes" quotation, see "Carl Hagenbeck's Eismeer-Panorama," 975. A similar observation is made of the Leipzig show by Hartung, "Die Sächsisch-Thüringische Industrie- und Gewerbe-Ausstellung," 320. On the use of trainers, see Bolau, "Karl Hagenbeck's Eismeer-Panorama," 59. Adding to the spectacle in Berlin, Castang claims to have bathed the polar bears in blue-colored dye, and "overdid it," leaving them with "a definite blue tinge" on opening day. For the Castang anecdotes, see R. W. Thompson, *Wild Animal Man: Being the Story of the Life of Reuben Castang* (New York: William Morrow, 1934), 57.

21 Reporters linked this display of seals and polar bears back to the live-animal shows of Carl Hagenbeck Sr. See Russ, "Hagenbecks Eismeer-Panorama," 672; and "Carl Hagenbeck's Eismeer-Panorama," *Der Kurier*, 975.

22 The slogan, "Everything living!" comes from a Hamburg poster, which is reproduced in "Carl Hagenbeck's Eismeer-Panorama," *Der Kurier*, 974–75. The Berlin reporter quoted is Russ, "Hagenbecks Eismeer-Panorama," 672. Hagenbeck's biographer, Fischer, describes the process of collecting so many animals of different kinds, and the sort of training that was absolutely necessary in order to be able to exhibit them in the same space (*Aus dem Leben und Wirken*, 55). This biography, it should be noted, was published in 1896, to coincide with the Berlin Trade Exhibition and give Hagenbeck a push there. For a vivid account of mass collection and transport, and their implications for the physical viability of wild animals, see Velvin, *From Jungle to Zoo*, especially 140, 224, 167–69. The estimated number of seals comes from Dittrich and Rieke-Müller, *Carl Hagenbeck*, 138; the "never before" quotation appears on 144.

23 There is no shortage of anecdotes about the loss of animal life. See, e.g., Carl Hagenbeck, *Von Tieren und Menschen*, 116–23; "How to Train Wild Beasts: Carl Hagenbeck Tells a Daily News Reporter All About a Strange Business," *Chicago News*, 14 April 1893; Ellen Velvin, *Behind the Scenes with Wild Animals* (New York: Moffat, Yard, 1906), 189–202.

24 The exception is the very first report, "Hagenbeck auf der Berliner Gewerbe-Ausstellung." For the "unwanted visit" quotation, see Bolau, "Karl Hagenbeck's Eismeer-Panorama," 57. Similar observations can be found in "Carl Hagenbeck's Eismeer-Panorama," *Der Kurier*, 975; Russ, "Hagenbecks Eismeer-Panorama," 672; Hartung, "Die Sächsisch-Thüringische Industrie- und Gewerbe-Ausstellung," 320. At least one journalist, C. J. Cornish, picked up on the novelty of cageless display already in 1895, at Hagenbeck's show in Sydenham ("The Moltke of Menagerie Owners," 83–84).

25 Schwartz, *Spectacular Realities*, 164. Scott B. Wilcox makes a similar point about panoramas of the 1820s in his introduction to *Panoramania! The Art and Entertainment of the 'All-Embracing' View*, by Ralph Hyde (London: Trefoil, 1988), 13–44; here, 37–38.

26 The Hamburg show is discussed in Lorenz Hagenbeck, *Den Tieren gehört mein Herz* (2nd ed.; Hamburg: Hoffmann and Campe, 1955), 25–27. Dittrich and Rieke-Müller have suggested that the ship was probably added at the suggestion of Heinrich Umlauff, who had already created a taxidermy exhibit around this event, including a mock-up of the *Fram*, at his ethnographic museum in Hamburg (*Carl Hagenbeck*, 185). The addition is first mentioned in the unpublished and undated manuscript of Johannes Umlauff's memoir, 12 (TCH). The long quotation appears in "Hagenbeck's Panorama of a Northern Sea," 18098; emphasis added. A detailed list of lantern slides can be found in the program brochure, *La Vie au Pôle Nord* (Paris, 1899) (TCH).

27 The iconography of the Hamburg panorama (fig. 4.5) is vaguely reminiscent of Caspar David Friedrich's famous landscape painting titled "Wreck of Hope" (1823–25). What makes this idea even more intriguing is that Friedrich's painting itself was modeled on earlier Arctic panoramas. Yet the art historical material pulls in very different directions than the present discussion, adding little that was not already implied by the more directly relevant material on panorama painting (and the material on geographical and zoological illustration, discussed in chapter 2). On the German tradition of landscape painting, see Timothy F. Mitchell, *Art and Science in German Landscape Painting, 1770–1840* (Oxford and New York: Oxford University Press, 1993). On Friedrich, see Helmut Börsch-Supan, *Caspar David Friedrich*, trans. Sarah Twohig (2nd ed.; Munich: Prestel, 1990).

28 Rothfels mentions the *Fram* in order to suggest that, even when Hagenbeck's panorama nods to history, it ultimately evacuates history from the scene, creating a timeless space of animals and "paradise," instead (*Savages and Beasts*, 171). Here I would add that the removal of history in this sense of the phrase was neither particular to Hagenbeck's show nor indicative of his approach but rather a common feature of live animal display across many different genres.

29 Eric Baratay and Elisabeth Hardouin-Fugier, *Zoo: A History of Zoological Gardens in the West*, trans. Oliver Welsch (1998; London: Reaktion Books, 2002), 195.

30 But a few streets away, "Carl Hagenbeck's India" was already up and running. Advertisements for each show can be found adjacent to one another in the *Neue Preussische Zeitung*, 17 May 1898, morn. ed.; and in the *Berliner Tageblatt*, 21 July 1898, 1st supplement.

31 "Ein 'Hagenbecksches Tierpanorama,'" *Berliner Tageblatt*, 12 May 1898. See also "In das Paradies der biblischen Schöpfungsgeschichte," *Volks-Zeitung*, 12 May 1898.

32 Quoted in Helga Schmal, "Carl Hagenbecks Tierpark," *Denkmalpflege Hamburg* 15 (June 1997): 15. For a translation of the show's advertising copy, see Rothfels,

Savages and Beasts, 165. For more on this panorama, see Dittrich and Rieke-Müller, *Carl Hagenbeck*, 191–92.

33 On Hagenbeck in St. Louis, see Lorenz Hagenbeck, *Den Tieren gehört mein Herz*, 58; and Pelc, "Hagenbeck auf den Weltausstellungen in Chicago (1893) und St. Louis (1904)." A reproduction of Eggenschwyler's poster is easily available in Rothfels, *Savages and Beasts*, 166. Interestingly, the modern tourist from the patent illustration reappears in this poster, only here he is joined by his wife and two daughters, "the family" being imagined as the ideal audience for Hagenbeck's new park.

34 After the road was built, the consortium sold off the remaining land for profit. "Hagenbecks neuer Tierpark in Stellingen," *Hamburger Fremdenblatt*, 10 March 1903 (SAH, A902 "Hagenbecks Tierpark").

35 For historical accounts of Hagenbeck's different menageries in Hamburg, see Rudolf Mayer, "Ein Gang durch die C. Hagenbeck'sche Handels-Menagerie in Hamburg," *Zoologischer Beobachter* 14 (1873): 25–27; Fritz von Schirp, "Die größte Handelsmenagerie der Erde," *Norddeutsche Allgemeine Zeitung*, 9 March 1884 (SAH, A902 "Hagenbecks Tierpark"). The "largest stock" quotation appears in C. V. A. Peel, *The Zoological Gardens of Europe: Their History and Chief Features* (London: Robinson, 1903), 235. The "pleasure park" quotation appears in Carl Hagenbeck, *Von Tieren und Menschen*, 135.

36 The "fostered" quotation appears in Carl Hagenbeck, *Von Tieren und Menschen*, 135. Here, Hagenbeck or his ghostwriter makes poetic use of the verb *hegen* (pt. pple. *gehegt*), which literally means "to care for" or "to tend," in the context of plant and animal life, and its figurative meaning (in this case, "to harbor" a thought or "to foster" an idea), while punning on the German word for "enclosure" (*Gehege*). The "chaotic confusion" and subsequent quotations appear in "Hagenbecks neuer Tierpark in Stellingen" (1903).

37 The *Tierpark*'s head landscape gardener, who oversaw the initial plantings, was Johannes Hinsch. Scattered details about gardening can be found in "Hagenbecks neuer Tierpark in Stellingen"; "Hagenbecks Tierparadies," *Hamburger Nachrichten*, 24 August 1906, eve. ed. (SAH, A902 "Hagenbecks Tierpark"); "Hagenbecks Tierpark in Stellingen"; *Führer* (1907), xiii.

38 The observations of David Ehrlinger, director of horticulture at the Cincinnati Zoo and Botanical Garden, are particularly helpful in this area: "In addition to the use of appropriate winter-hardy plant species of unusual appearance to give the sense of exotic habitats," archival photographs of the *Tierpark* "show extensive use of large tropical palms and other tender plants." Ehrlinger describes the cultivation species from non-tropical areas as "appropriate" in part because the selected plants suggested exotic habitats in terms of color, shape, and texture, but mainly

because they were made for a sustainable habitat in the northern German climate with its predictably cold winters. The original plantings "appear reasonably naturalistic, particularly around the exhibits" ("The Hagenbeck Legacy," *International Zoo Yearbook* 29 (1989): 6–10; here 8).

39 Schmal, "Carl Hagenbecks Tierpark," 14–15, 39.

40 Mostly deaf since he was a child, Eggenschwyler was an animal lover who opposed the use of small cages; he expressed this opposition creatively through his sculpting of barless enclosures, the first experiments of which took place at his private zoo in Zurich and at a game reserve in St. Gallen, Switzerland. He was still at work on the main cliff formation in Stellingen when Hagenbeck, as a token of his appreciation, gave Eggenschwyler a wild leopard. See Dittrich and Rieke-Müller, *Carl Hagenbeck*, 186, 200; Carl Hagenbeck, *Von Tieren und Menschen*, 214.

41 Here it should be noted that, when the park officially opened to the public, in 1907, it still had two more years of planned construction and expansion, which included a new *Völkerschau* area. See on this point C. Lund, "Aus Hagenbecks Tierpark," *Über Land und Meer* 97, no. 23 (1907): 580–81. On the integration of Hamburg's seawall, see Dittrich and Rieke-Müller, *Carl Hagenbeck*, 200.

42 Zoological gardens would also declare their commitment to the arts. For example, William Hornaday of the New York Zoological Park fostered the work of wildlife artists (especially that of the young German painter Carl Rungius). See on this point Hanson, *Animal Attractions*, 132–40; and esp. Mark Bennett Feldman, "Narrating, Displaying and Spectating the Animal: Frank Norris, Jack London, and the Urban Zoo," Ph.D. diss. (University of California, Berkeley, 2005) 65–75. The sculpture garden quotation appears in *Führer* (1907), xi. On Hagenbeck as "patron of the arts," see "Bei Hagenbeck (Neue Schöpfungen und Pläne)." For an overview of the architects and artists involved in the *Tierpark*, see Pelc and Gretzschel, *Hagenbeck*, 76–79. Short biographies of each appear in Schmal, "Carl Hagenbecks Tierpark," 38–39. Though the sculpture garden was not realized, many statues were eventually added to the park, including memorials to Hagenbeck's father (by Rudolf Franke), Carl Hagenbeck (by Rudolf Marcuse), Hagenbeck's oldest son, Heinrich (by A. W. Goebel), Urs Eggenschwyler, and some of the park's most famous animals (by Josef Pallenberg).

43 The wide use of statuary in zoos today, usually in rest areas or in the transitions between exhibits, is also noteworthy. Animal sculptures are generally there to be touched by spectators, and spectators respond in kind, as evidenced by any number of shiny bronze noses and tails. It is the function of statuary to create a kind of tactile relay, compensating for the fact that the spectator cannot physically handle the zoo animals (apart from the obvious exceptions of petting zoos), while at the same time reinforcing the spectator's tactile relationship to the bodies on display.

44 "Bei Hagenbeck (Neue Schöpfungen und Pläne)"; Oettermann, *The Panorama*, 97.

45 *Führer* (1907), xi–xiii, original emphases. Hagenbeck also endorses this viewing practice in his memoir. "From a certain point in the garden, one should see the animals of all zones, each kind in an environment appropriate to its homeland, moving about freely in big terraces" (*Von Tieren und Menschen*, 134; see also 382–83). For earlier statements on the park as panorama, see "Ein zoologisches Paradies"; and Peel, *The Zoological Gardens of Europe*, 241.

46 Kurt Priemel, "Handelstierpark und Zoologische Gärten," *Frankfurter Zeitung und Handelsblatt*, 24 April 1909, 1st morn. ed.

47 Later commentators would conflate "The Panorama" with the "Africa Panorama," as the complex series of exhibits was renamed in the 1920s, and this conflation has since been perpetuated and retroactively extended back to 1907. Today, scholars routinely mention the "Africa Panorama" as among the park's first attractions, when there was no such thing until long after Hagenbeck's death. During his lifetime, "The Panorama" was the park. The "winding paths" quotation appears in *Führer* (1907), xiii; emphasis added.

48 Ibid., x; see also xiv, 10, 26.

49 John Prest, *The Garden of Eden: The Botanic Garden and the Re-Creation of Paradise* (New Haven: Yale University Press, 1981), 107.

50 At the park's opening ceremony, in 1907, the director of Copenhagen's zoo described Hagenbeck and his wife Amanda as "the Adam and Eve of an animal paradise on the banks of the Elbe [River]" (quoted in Alexander, *Museum Masters*, 323). Neumann-Hofer compares the park to Cranach the Elder's 1526 painting, in "Karl Hagenbeck," 14. For the "Herr Hagenbeck" quotation, a bad pun on the German term for Lord (*Herr*), see "Hagenbecks Tierpark," *Hamburger Echo*, 7 May 1907, 2nd ed. See also Lund, "Aus Hagenbecks Tierpark," 851; Arthur Obst, "Der Schöpfer des Tierparadieses," *Hamburger Fremdenblatt*, 12 November 1908 (SAH, A902 "Hagenbecks Tierpark"); and Jules Huret, *En Allemagne: De Hambourg aux Marches de Pologne* (Paris: Bibliothèque-Charpentier, 1908), especially the chapter on "Le paradis terrestre de M. Hagenbeck," 238–51.

51 Lothar Dittrich, "Zoobauten als Ausdruck geistiger Zeitströmungen: Bemerkungen zum Verständnis der historischen Bausubstanz deutscher Zoos," *Der zoologische Garten* N.F. 68, no. 6 (1998): 325–31; here, 329.

52 For the mud-flat anecdote, see Dittrich, "Zoobauten als Ausdruck geistiger Zeitströmungen," 328. For guidebook text on the "Northern Landscape," see *Führer* (1907), 25; and on the "Hay Eaters," see ibid., 2.

53 Dittrich and Rieke-Müller, *Carl Hagenbeck*, 195; Hanson, *Animal Attractions*, 144.

54 For an exemplary zoogeographical group titled "Africa" (Darmstadt Museum of Natural History, 1908), see fig. 28 in Köstering, *Natur zum Anschauen*. For early

German advocates of zoogeography, see Ludwig Karl Schmarda, *Die geographische Verbreitung der Tiere*, 3 vols. (Vienna: Gerold, 1853); Carl Semper, *Die natürlichen Existenzbedingungen der Thiere* (Leipzig: Brockhaus, 1880); Gottlieb von Koch, *Die Aufstellung der Tiere im neuen Museum zu Darmstadt* (Leipzig: Wilhelm Engelmann, 1899); and Karl Möbius, "Die Tierwelt der Erde," in *Geographisches Handbuch zu Andrees Handatlas*, ed. Albert Scobel (Bielefeld: Velhagen, 1902), 163–75.

55 A proponent of zoogeography with a creative mind for museum work, Möbius played a crucial role in Sokolowsky's development. For more on this figure, see Lynn K. Nyhart, "Civic and Economic Zoology in Nineteenth-Century Germany: The 'Living Communities' of Karl Möbius," *Isis* 89, no. 4 (December 1998): 605–30.

56 For an account of Sokolowsky's youth and his training, see Alexander Sokolowsky, *Carl Hagenbeck und sein Werk* (Leipzig: Haberland, 1928), 15–21.

57 Alexander Sokolowsky, "Die Zoologischen Gärten als Bildungsanstalten," *Natur und Schule* (1905): 555–62, here 562, 561. See also Sokolowsky, "Ein neuer Tierpark nach biologischem Prinzip," *Wild und Hund* 13, no. 22 (1907): 388–89; "Das biologische Prinzip bei der Schaustellung wilder Tiere," *Natur und Haus* 15 (1907): 150–53; and the many essays in his *Gesammelte Aufsätze zoologischen Inhalts: Für Zoologen, Landwirte, Tierzüchter und Kolonialfreunde* (Leipzig: Theodor Oswald Weigel, 1909).

58 The "designs" quotation appears in *Führer* (1911), 26–27; original emphasis.

59 The Berlin plan was drawn up by Johannes Baader, then a young architect, who later became a major figure of Berlin's avant-garde, the future "Oberdada" himself. Though the project had the personal support of Kaiser Wilhelm II, the Berlin Zoological Garden mounted enough resistance at the city level to cause Hagenbeck, who was by then in bad health, to abandon the idea. See Johannes Baader, *Oberdada* (Lahn-Gießen: Anabas-Verlag Kämpf, 1977), 145. For an account of this project, see Dittrich and Rieke-Müller, *Carl Hagenbeck*, 272–90; for a reproduction of the blueprint, see 338. An "India Panorama" was planned at Stellingen in the late 1930s, but it too would be abandoned.

60 Leading up to the 1893 Chicago world's fair, Hagenbeck sent a trained-animal group to Manchester's Blackpool resort and amusement park, as a kind of trial run. After the fair, "Hagenbeck's Trained Animal Show," as the group was generally called, performed at Tattersalls, a vaudeville house, in the winter of 1893, and then at Manhattan Beach on Coney Island, in the summer of 1894, followed by a long run at Madison Square Garden in the fall of 1894, returning to Manhattan Beach in the summer of 1895. Another show (including trainers Reuben Castang and Hermann Boger among others) performed at the New York

Theater for a few weeks in the fall of 1902, and then at Luna Park in the summer of 1903. A number of different shows traveled under the name "Carl Hagenbeck & Co.," but some of them did so illegally, trading on the showman's positive brand image. In his 1896 biography, published shortly before the Berlin Trade Exhibition, Fischer expresses the hope that "a respectable American newspaper will open the public's eyes" to the fact that the current show "carries his name without his authorization, that he has nothing to do with it, and that they [the show's managers] are misusing his name in order to deceive their own people," by which he meant spectators in the United States (*Aus dem Leben und Wirken*, 51).

61 The quotation is from "Hagenbeck's Performing Animals: Wonderful and Thrilling Exhibitions at the Madison Square Garden," *New York Times*, 4 September 1894, 6. See also "Unmuzzled Beasts Run Free," *New York Times*, 1 December 1893, 5; untitled announcement in *The Brooklyn Eagle*, 10 June 1894, 5; "Crowds at Coney Island," *New York Times*, 17 June 1894, 8; "Hagenbeck's Trained Animals: Fast-Growing in Popularity at Manhattan Beach," *New York Times*, 29 July 1894, 8; "More Wonders Promised: The Hagenbeck Arena Company Secures Another Lot of Trained Animals," *New York Times*, 2 August 1894, 8; "Hagenbeck's Animals Take the Stage," *New York Times*, 5 October 1902, 10. For Castang's description of the crowds, see Thompson, *Wild Animal Man*, 91.

62 For a historical postcard showing Hagenbeck's location vis-à-vis Shoot the Chutes, see Richard Snow, *Coney Island: A Postcard Journey to the City of Fire* (New York: Brightwaters Press, 1984), 84. The Surf Avenue slogan is quoted in Gary Kyriazi, *The Great American Amusement Parks: A Pictorial History* (Secaucus, NJ: Citadel Press, 1976), 62–63. For more on Coney, see especially John F. Kasson, *Amusing the Million: Coney Island at the Turn of the Century* (New York: Hill and Wang, 1978), 63–82; Kathy Peiss, *Cheap Amusements: Working Women and Leisure in Turn-of-the-Century New York* (Philadelphia: Temple University Press, 1986); and *The American Experience: Coney Island*, prod. and dir. Ric Burns, 72 min., PBS, 1990, videocassette.

63 The tunnel is described in *Führer* (1907), 26. The toboggan quotation appears in Harold J. Shepstone, "The Completion of Carl Hagenbeck's Novel Zoological Park." *Scientific American Supplement* 64, no. 1649 (10 August 1907): 88–89; here, 88. The slide is mentioned as late as 1914 by Friedrich Knauer in *Der zoologische Garten: Entwicklungsgang, Anlage und Betrieb unserer Tiergärten* (Leipzig: Theodor Thomas, n.d), 170. It closed during or shortly after World War I, never to be reopened, presumably due to risk of injury.

64 Zoo directors dismissed some exhibits as scenified circus acts (see, e.g., Priemel, "Handelstierpark"). Since the late 1800s, however, zoos had also adopted trained-

animal acts on occasion, to attract wider audiences. For an interesting account of this practice written by a Leipzig zoo keeper, see Robert Thomas, *Unter Kunden, Komödianten und wilden Tieren*, ed. Julius R. Haarhaus (Leipzig: Grunow, 1905), 423–38. The "tamed" quotation appears in Harold J. Shepstone, "Carl Hagenbeck's Novel Zoological Park," *Scientific American* (10 November 1906): 345.

65 For the newspaper advertisement, see "Carl Hagenbecks Tierpark, Stellingen" (1906) (available in SAH map room, Sig. 151–21, 15/65); original emphasis. The "turnstile" quotation comes from Shepstone, "Completion," 88. It cost "10 Pfennig per person," the first guidebook stated, adding a cryptic explanation: "This surcharge has become necessary, in order to avoid unpleasantries" (*Führer* [1907], 7).

66 Another safety measure, added later, is worth noting: an abrupt dip or depression (called a *Laufrinne*) spanning the enclosure's perimeter. Should one of the big cats attempt to jump across the trench, the depression was supposed to throw the animal off balance and send it tumbling into the ravine (Zukowsky, *Carl Hagenbeck's Reich*, 164). Carl Hagenbeck acknowledges the moat's visceral effect on spectators in *Von Tieren und Menschen*, 385.

67 Albert G. Krüger, "Ein Tag im Hagenbeckschen Tierpark zu Stellingen bei Hamburg," *Deutscher Hausschatz: Illustrierte Familien-Zeitschrift* 38.3 (1912): 112–16, here 112.

68 The "purely aesthetic" quotation appears in Alfred Freiherr von Berger, "Hagenbeck" (1909), *Gesammelte Schriften*, ed. Anton Bettelheim and Karl Glossy (Vienna and Leipzig: Deutsch-Österreichischer Verlag, 1913), 3:262–78; here, 266. An abridged version of this essay would appear as an obituary for Hagenbeck in Bremen's daily *Nachrichten* on 15 April 1913 (TCH). The "victim/participant" quotation appears in Malcolm Andrews, *Landscape and Western Art*, Oxford History of Art (New York: Oxford University Press, 1999), 134–35. Hanson makes a similar point about the zoo and the sublime with an added claim to American particularity (*Animal Attractions*, 152).

69 The Edison anecdote is from Bernard Livingston, *Zoo: Animals, People, Places* (New York: Arbor House, 1974), 150. The immersive effects of Hagenbeck's park have been strategically understated by contemporary proponents of "landscape immersion." Cf. David Hancocks, *A Different Nature: The Paradoxical World of Zoos and Their Uncertain Future* (Berkeley: University of California Press, 2001), 66–67. Jeffrey Hyson makes a similar point in "Jungles of Eden: The Design of American Zoos," in *Environmentalism in Landscape Architecture*, ed. Michel Conan (Washington, DC: Dumbarton Oaks, 2000), 23–44.

70 The descriptive quotations come from E. Fraas, "Aus der Saurierwelt der Vorzeit in Hagenbecks Tierpark zu Stellingen," *Kolonie und Heimat* 4, no. 1 (1910): 6, 7. For

the official description, see *Führer durch Carl Hagenbecks Tierpark in Stellingen*, 10th ed., revised by Johannes Flemming (Hamburg: Carly, 1914), 44–47 (TCH). The dinosaur-in-a-pond and dinosaur-family poses have become tropes of natural history iconography. See Stephen Jay Gould, *Bully for Brontosaurus: Reflections in Natural History* (New York: Norton, 1991), 96–97. The earliest precedent was the 1854 exhibit built by Benjamin Waterhouse Hawkins at the Crystal Palace Park in Sydenham (which today is advertised as "The World's First Dinosaur Theme Park"). Hagenbeck visited this park many times throughout his career, and at some point—if one of his obituaries is to be believed—he even tried to acquire it. "Maker of Model Zoos.—What Hagenbeck Could Have Done for London.—Unrealized Ambition.—Once Tried to Buy the Crystal Palace," *The Manchester Guardian*, 16 April 1913 (TCH). On Hawkins, see Yanni, *Nature's Museums*, 134–40.

71 "Vergrößerung des Hagenbeckschen Tierparks," *Hamburger Nachrichten*, 5 November 1913, eve. ed.; see also untitled clipping from the *Kölnische Zeitung*, 5 November 1913, 2nd morn. ed. (SAH, A902 "Hagenbecks Tierpark"). In 1922, two years after Hagenbeck's park officially closed, Haase bought Luna Park in Hamburg-Altona and transferred his rides from Stellingen to Altona. The company's biggest contract was to build the amusement park for the 1930 world's fair in Antwerp. On Haase, see Florian Dering, *Volksbelustigungen: Eine bildreiche Kulturgeschichte von den Fahr-, Belustigungs- und Geschicklichkeitsgeschäften der Schausteller vom 18. Jahrhundert bis zur Gegenwart* (Nördlingen: Franz Greno, 1986), 163–76; and Lisa Kosok and Mathilde Jamin, eds., *Viel Vergnügen: Öffentlichen Lustbarkeiten im Ruhrgebiet der Jahrhundertwende* (Essen: Peter Pomp, 1992), 156–57.

72 John F. Kasson, *Amusing the Million*, 82.

73 Details on the "Iron Sea" come from Dering, *Volksbelustigungen*, 127; all of the quotations come from "H. H. Vergnügungs-Park Hugo Haase A.-G. Stellingen," *Hamburger Fremdenblatt*, 21 June 1914.

74 Friedrich Katt, "Hagenbecks Tierparadies," *Zoologischer Beobachter* 50, no. 1 (1909): 370–71.

75 For programmatic German statements on the founding of zoological gardens, see David Friedrich Weinland, "Ueber den Ursprung und die Bedeutung der neueren Zoologischen Gärten," *Der Zoologische Garten* 1, no. 3 (1862): 1–3, and "Zur Rechtfertigung," *Der Thiergarten* 1, no. 1 (1864): 1–4. On the first zoos in German-speaking countries, see Annelore Rieke-Müller and Lothar Dittrich, *Der Löwe brüllt nebenan: Die Gründung Zoologischer Gärten im deutschsprachigen Raum 1833–1869* (Cologne: Böhlau, 1998); and Annelore Rieke-Müller, "Die Gründung Zoologischer Gärten um die Mitte des 19. Jahrhunderts im deutschsprachigen Raum," in *Die Kulturgeschichte des Zoos*, ed. Lothar Dittrich, Dittrich von Engel-

hardt, and Annelore Rieke-Müller (Berlin: VWB-Verlag für Wissenschaft und Bildung, 2001), 83–95. On nineteenth-century zoos generally, see Wilhelm Stricker, "Geschichte der Menagerien und der zoologischen Gärten," in *Sammlung gemeinverständlicher wissenschaftlicher Vorträge*, ed. Rudolf Virchow and Friedrich von Holkendorff, 14, no. 336 (1879): 921–63; Peel, *The Zoological Gardens of Europe*; vol. 3 of Gustave Loisel, *Histoire des menageries de l'antiquité à nos jours* (Paris: Doins, 1912); Knauer, *Der zoologische Garten*; Wilfrid Blunt, *The Ark in the Park: The Zoo in the Nineteenth Century* (London: Hamish Hamilton, 1976); Altick, *The Shows of London*, 302–31; Harriet Ritvo, *The Animal Estate: The English and Other Creatures in the Victorian Age* (Cambridge, MA: Harvard University Press, 1987), 205–42; R. J. Hoage and William A. Deiss, eds., *New Worlds, New Animals: From Menagerie to Zoological Park in the Nineteenth Century* (Baltimore: Johns Hopkins University Press, 1996); Vernon N. Kisling, Jr., *Zoo and Aquarium History: Ancient Animal Collections to Zoological Gardens* (Boca Raton, FL: CRC Press, 2000); Baratay and Hardouin-Fugier, *Zoo*.

76 Shepstone, "Carl Hagenbeck's Novel Zoological Park," 345.

77 The original guidebook was written by Nikolaus Schiller-Tietz—a point which has never been mentioned by other scholars. Dittrich and Rieke-Müller suggest that the biologist Sokolowsky might have drafted the manuscript (*Carl Hagenbeck*, 201), but Schiller-Tietz received the writing credit on the guide's front cover. He was a trained biologist, who turned to writing local travel guides, including, *Kröger's Guide through the Elbe Region* (1900), *Guide through Pinneberg and Its Environs* (1903), Pinneberg being the district in which Stellingen was situated, as well as *Hamburg and Its Environs: A Practical Travel Guide* (23rd ed., 1910). The "straightforward" quotation appears in *Führer* (1907), vii; original emphases.

78 For an interesting early German statement on the aesthetic side of systematic organization, see H. Jäger, "Die Zoologischen Gärten und ihre scenische Anordnung," *Beilage zur Illustrirten Zeitung* (3 January 1863): 19, 22. The "systematic relationship" quotation appears in the Foreword to *Führer* (1912).

79 The animal emporium quotation is from *Führer* (1907), viii. On this point, the guidebook seems to acknowledge that high turnover could have a destabilizing effect on viewers who need certain guarantees. So it offers the following reassurance: "Nevertheless, the animal stock is always so abundant that the character of the park's individual exhibits will at all times be preserved according to their original purpose and arrangement, regardless of which kinds of animals actually inhabit them at a given moment" (viii). The "storehouse" quotation is from von Berger, "Hagenbeck," 264. See also Priemel, "Handelstierpark"; and Knauer, *Der zoologische Garten*, 163.

80 The "unique" quotation appears in "Hagenbecks Tierpark," *Hamburger Echo*, 7 May 1907, 2nd ed. On Hamburg's zoos, see Herman Reichenbach, "A Tale of Two Zoos: The Hamburg Zoological Garden and Carl Hagenbeck's *Tierpark*," in *New Worlds, New Animals: From Menagerie to Zoological Park in the Nineteenth Century*, ed. R. J. Hoage and William A. Deiss (Baltimore: Johns Hopkins University Press, 1996), 51–62.

81 For a detailed account of the debate, see Dittrich and Rieke-Müller, *Carl Hagenbeck*, 243–51; the Schäff quotations appear on 243–44.

82 For Heck's article and Hagenbeck's reply, see "Carl Hagenbeck und die Zoologischen Gärten," *Hamburger Fremdenblatt*, 14 February 1909 (SAH, A902 "Hagenbecks Tierpark"). Priemel's summary appears in "Handelstierpark." The debate continued. See Fritz Grabowsky (director of the Zoological Garden in Breslau), "Noch einmal 'Carl Hagenbeck und sein Tierparadies,'" *Zoologischer Garten* 40 (1909): n. pag.; Em Erich Leonhardt, "Die heutigen Aufgaben der Tiergärten," *Zoologischer Beobachter* 50, no. 11 (1909): 321–28; and Kurt Priemel, "Die heutigen Aufgaben der Tiergärten: Eine Erwiderung," *Zoologischer Beobachter* 50, no. 12 (1909): 354–66.

83 See, e.g., Heini Hediger, *Man and Animal in the Zoo: Zoo Biology*, trans. Gwynne Vevers and Winwood Reade (New York: Delacorte Press, 1969), 188; David Hancocks, *Animals and Architecture* (New York: Praeger, 1971), 126–30; Günter Niemeyer, *Hagenbeck: Geschichte und Geschichten* (Hamburg: Hans Christians Verlag, 1972), 64; Herman Reichenbach, "Carl Hagenbeck's Tierpark and Modern Zoological Gardens," *Journal of the Society for the Bibliography of Natural History* 9, no. 4 (1980): 573–85; Ehrlinger, "The Hagenbeck Legacy," 6–10; Jon C. Coe, "The Evolution of Zoo Animal Exhibits," in *The Ark Evolving: Zoos and Aquariums in Transition*, ed. Christen M. Wemmer (Front Royal, VA: Smithsonian Institution Conservation and Research Center, 1995), 95–128; Harro Strehlow, "The Hagenbeck Revolution," in *Zoo and Aquarium History: Ancient Animal Collections to Zoological Gardens*, ed. Vernon N. Kisling (Boca Raton, FL: CRC Press, 2001), 102–4; and most recently Rothfels, *Savages and Beasts*, 199.

84 All quotations appear in von Berger, "Hagenbeck," 264–67, 274, 277.

85 Tom Gunning, "The Cinema of Attractions: Early Film, Its Spectator and the Avant-Garde," in *Early Cinema: Space, Frame, Narrative*, ed. Thomas Elsaesser (London: BFI, 1990), 58.

5 ✦ The Park and the Cinema

1 "Der Kaiser in Stellingen-Langenfelde," *Lokal-Anzeiger für Stellingen-Langenfelde, Eidelstedt, Lokstedt, Niendorf und Schnelsen*, 21 June 1908 (TCH); original empha-

sis. The various types of nonfiction films mentioned here are based on films produced by Nordisk Films Kompagni at the *Tierpark* between 1907 and 1913. See the following letters from Ole Olsen to Carl Hagenbeck, 22 July 1908, *Breve* 7, 786; 22 October 1909, *Breve* 11 (15.09.09–11.01.10), 323; 29 October 1909, *Breve* 11, 390; 28 May 1910, *Breve* 12 (11.01.10–09.06.10), 904; 10 October 1913, *Breve* 28 (02.10.13–04.12.13), 128; 29 October 1909, *Breve* 11, 390 (all from the unpublished *Nordisk Company Papers* at the Danish Film Institute; hereafter abbreviated as DFI).

2 On film space and diegesis, see especially Jacques Aumont, Alain Bergala, Michel Marie, and Marc Vernet, *Aesthetics of Film*, trans. and rev. Richard Neupert (Austin: University of Texas Press, 1992). On the use of photography to enhance the reality effect of museum habitat displays, see the work of Hiroshi Sugimoto, *http://www.hirshhorn.si.edu/sugimoto/dioramas/index.htm* (accessed 4 March 2007). On the constructed nature of wildlife films, see Derek Bousé, *Wildlife Films* (Philadelphia: University of Pennsylvania Press, 2000), 1–9.

3 Joseph Delmont, *Wilde Tiere im Film: Erlebnisse aus meinen Filmaufnahmen in aller Welt* (Stuttgard: Dieck, 1925), 16. In English, see Joseph Delmont, *Wild Animals on the Films*, trans. G. Morrison Gilmour (London: Methuen, 1925); and *Catching Wild Beasts Alive* (London: Hutschinson, 1931). Cf. Jonathan Burt, *Animals in Film* (London: Reaktion, 2002), 118. Gregg Mitman, *Reel Nature: America's Romance with Wildlife on Film* (Cambridge, MA: Harvard University Press, 1999), 3. For more on wildlife films, see Kevin Brownlow, *The War, the West, and the Wilderness* (New York: Alfred A. Knopf, 1979); and Cynthia Chris, *Watching Wildlife* (Minneapolis: University of Minnesota Press, 2006). In the German context, see Ariane Heimbach, "Die inszenierte Wildnis: Exotische Tierwelt im Film," in *Triviale Tropen: Exotische Reise- und Abenteuerfilme aus Deutschland 1919–1939*, ed. Jörg Schöningh (Munich: edition text + kritik, 1997), 158–66.

4 In the 1890s, Olsen began his career as a showman in Copenhagen. Among his entertainments were a peephole motion picture show, an X-ray machine, and an itinerant troupe of African performers. From 1898 to 1901, he ran an amusement park in nearby Malmö, Sweden. Returning to Copenhagen, in 1905, he opened a motion picture theater and acquired a camera of his own, concentrating initially on nonfiction films. In 1906, he founded Nordisk. Ole Olsen, *Filmens Eventyr og Mit Eget* (Film's Adventure and My Own; Copenhagen: Jespersen og Pios Forlag, 1940), 9–20. In English, see Ebbe Neergaard and Erik Ulrichsen, *The Story of Danish Film* (Copenhagen: Det danske selskab, 1963), 9–19; Bebe Bergsten, *The Great Dane and the Great Northern Film Company* (Los Angeles: Roche, 1973), 2–10; Ron Mottram, *The Danish Cinema Before Dreyer* (Metuchen: Scarecrow, 1988), 16–22. Olsen's collaboration with Hagenbeck represents a forgotten prelude to the Danish-German film relations of the 1910s and 1920s, which other scholars have studied

from various perspectives. See Marguerite Engberg, "The Influence of Danish Cinema on German Film 1910–1920," *Griffithiana* 13, no. 38–39 (October 1990): 127–33; Corinna Müller, *Frühe deutsche Kinematographie: formale, wirtschaftliche und kulturelle Entwicklungen 1907–1912* (Stuttgart: Metzler, 1994), 124–25; Manfred Behn, ed., *Schwarzer Traum und weiße Sklavin: deutsch-dänische Filmbeziehungen 1910–1930* (Munich: edition text + kritik, 1994); Evelyn Hampicke, "The Danish Influence: David Oliver and Nordisk in Germany," in *A Second Life: German Cinema's First Decades*, ed. Thomas Elsaesser (Amsterdam: Amsterdam University Press, 1996), 72–78; and Klaus Kreimeier, *The UFA Story: A History of Germany's Greatest Film Company 1918–1945*, trans. Robert and Rita Kimber (1992; New York: Hill and Wang, 1996), 14, 23–25, 30.

5 The "staging" quotation appears in Bousé, *Wildlife Films*, 56. Film's uncanny relationship to death is one reason why hunting movies are often compared to taxidermy in museum displays—an analogy which has been more than adequately explored. See Donna Haraway, "Teddy Bear Patriarchy: Taxidermy in the Garden of Eden, New York City, 1908–1936," *Social Text* 11 (winter 1984/1985): 20–64; Desmond, "Displaying Death"; Wonders, *Habitat Dioramas*, 155–60; Rony, *The Third Eye*, 99–126; Grifitths, "'Shivers Down Your Spine,'" 30–32.

6 On *The Polar Bear Hunt*, see Mottram, *The Danish Cinema Before Dreyer*, 30; Erik Nørgaard, *Levende Billeder i Danmark* (Copenhagen: Lademann, 1971), 46–47. For correspondence papers concerning *The Lion Hunt* (*Løvejagten*), see Olsen to Hagenbeck, 25 May 1907; 10 June 1907, *Breve* 1 (17.11.06–18.09–07), 315; 16 July 1907, *Breve* 1, 210. On *Bear Hunting in Russia*, see Olsen to Hagenbeck, 9 January 1908, *Breve* 6 (19.09.07–12.03.08), 621; 14 February 1908, *Breve* 6, 836; 12 March 1908, *Breve* 6, 990; 8 April 1908, *Breve* 7, 134; 24 April 1908, *Breve* 7, 200; 29 April 1908, *Breve* 7, 233; 30 April 1908, *Breve* 7, 240; and 2 May 1908, *Breve* 7, 267 (all at DFI). A detailed account of the *Lion Hunt* controversy appears in J. F. Svejgaard Nielsen, *Bogen om Elleore* (Copenhagen: Grafisk Klub Tretten Cicero, 1958), 19–34 (DFI).

7 For a balanced discussion of early editing, see André Gaudreault, "Detours in Film Narrative: The Development of Cross-Cutting," in *Early Cinema: Space, Frame, Narrative*, ed. Thomas Elsaesser (London: BFI, 1990), 133–50. The "problem" quotation appears in Mottram, *The Danish Cinema Before Dreyer*, 31. Engberg is cited in ibid., 75n53. I thank Marguerite Engberg for sharing her unparalleled knowledge of the film with me.

8 An entry from Hagenbeck's 1907 account book indicates that Olsen paid 1,500 Marks for each lion. According to the same entry, Olsen paid 530 Marks for the polar bear used in the previous film. See "Nordische Film Co., Kopenhagen," 31 January 1907, Folio 175, *Hauptbuch 1907*, 107 (TCH)

9 Only the hunters are offered up as relay figures for the spectator; no point-of-view shots issue from the "Negro," whose assigned role is mainly to embody race and servitude, while offering a bit of racial comic relief. When the lion is later spotted by one of the hunters, the servant is fast asleep. The synopsis appears in a program brochure for *Løvejagten paa Elleore* (an alternate title used locally), 1907 (DFI); I thank Elizabeth Stokkebye for translating this text for me. For a detailed shot analysis of the entire film, see Marguerite Engberg, *Dansk Stumfilm* (Copenhagen: Rhodos Internationalt Forlag for Videnskab, Kunst og Debat, 1977), 1:136–46. A partial list of shots is available in Mottram, *The Danish Cinema Before Dreyer,* 31–32.

10 On the spatial implications of centrifugal movement and parallel editing, see Tom Gunning, *D. W. Griffith and the Origins of American Film Narrative: The Early Years at Biograph* (Urbana: University of Illinois Press, 1991), 66.

11 The "roar" quotation appears in *Løvejagten paa Elleore.*

12 Letter from Olsen to the Miles Bros. Co., 26 August 1907, *Breve* 1 (17.11.06–18.09.07), 373 (DFI). The emphasis on shared space also extends to *Bear Hunting in Russia.* The program brochure for this film highlights a moment when one of the five animals to be killed "appears so suddenly and so near to the hunter that, instead of using his gun, he only has time to wield his axe—and with that, he goes for the bear" (*Bjørnejagt i Rusland*, 1908; DFI).

13 André Bazin, "The Virtues and Limitations of Montage," in *What is Cinema?* trans. Hugh Gray (Berkeley: University of California Press, 1967), 1:50.

14 *The Living Bridge* borrowed heavily from the Danish tradition of circus films such as *Mellem Storbyens Artister* (*In the Den of Lions* or *Life in the Circus*, Nordisk, 1912; dir. Edward Schnedler-Sørensen). The German production not only poached plot lines from that film, it also featured a Danish actress, Margot Petersen. On the Danish tradition of circus films, see Mottram, *The Danish Cinema Before Dreyer,* especially chapter 2: "1910–1914." Only a fragment of *The Living Bridge* has survived and it is located at the Bundesarchiv/Filmarchiv in Berlin. Since I was not permitted to view it, my discussion relies necessarily on print material. A program brochure for *Die lebende Brücke* is available at DIF. Advertisements for the film appear in the trade papers *Erste internationale Filmzeitung* 6, no. 42 (19 October 1912): 102–3; *Lichtbildbühne* (2 November 1912): 24–25; *Lichtbildbühne* (16 November 1912): 24–25. A plot summary appears in "Die lebende Brücke," *Lichtbildbühne* (16 November 1912): 21, 26. For production details, see Gerhard Lamprecht, *Deutsche Stummfilme 1903–1912* (Berlin: Deutsche Kinemathek, 1969), 1:259. The "cinematic dramas" quotation appears in "Hagenbeck als Helfer für die Kinematographie," *Lichtbildbühne* (9 November 1912): 8, 17.

15 See Dr. Forch, "Die Sensation im Kinodrama und anderwärts," *Bild und Film* 2, no.

7 (1912/13): 164–65. On the larger debate, see Anton Kaes, ed., *Kino-Debatte: Texte zum Verhältnis von Literatur und Film 1909–1929* (Munich: Deutscher Taschenbuch; Tübingen: Niemeyer, 1978); Sabine Hake, *The Cinema's Third Machine: Writing on Film in Germany 1907–1933* (Lincoln and London: University of Nebraska Press, 1993). The "dramatic plot" quotation appears in "Hagenbeck als Helfer," 8. The censor's notes are reproduced in *Verzeichnis der in Deutschland gelaufenen Filme: Entscheidungen der Filmzensur 1911–1920*, ed. Herbert Birett (Berlin: K. G. Saur, 1980), 120.

16 First references to the cinema appear in "Hagenbecks Kino und die Freilicht-Arena in Stellingen," *Hamburger Fremdenblatt*, 10 May 1913, 5th supplement; and in "Hagenbecks Tierpark," *Hamburger Fremdenblatt*, 17 May 1913. Exact revenue amounts appear under the entry for "Kino" in the account book titled *Tierpark 1913* (TCH). The "death toll" quotation appears in Bousé, *Wildlife Films*, 48. Rainey's film was also exhibited at the American Museum of Natural History. For more on this film, see Mitman, *Reel Nature*, 16–20; and esp. Griffiths, *Wondrous Difference*, 270–76.

17 See Christoph Schulz, *Jagd- und Filmabenteur in Afrika: Streifzüge in das Innere des dunkeln Erdteils* (Dresden: Verlag Deutsche Buchwerkstätten, 1922), 8. For other examples, see Carl Georg Schillings, *Mit Blitzlicht und Büchse* (Leipzig: Voigtländer, 1905); *With Flash-Light and Rifle: Photographing by Flash-Light at Night the Wild Animal World of Equatorial Africa*, trans. Henry Zick (New York: Harper and Brothers, 1905); *Der Zauber des Eleléscho* (Leipzig: Voigtländer, 1906); Hermann Wiele, *Für Hagenbeck in den Urwäldern Indiens: Dreißig Jahre Forscher und Jäger* (Dresden: Verlag Deutsche Buchwerkstätten, 1926); and Hans Schomburgk, *Wild und Wilde im Herzen Afrikas* (Berlin: Fleischel, 1910); *Bwakukama: Fahrten und Forschungen mit Büchse und Film im unbekannten Afrika* (Berlin: Deutsch-Literarisches Institut, 1922). For an account of Schomburgk's films in English, see Oksiloff, *Picturing the Primitive*, 71–95.

18 The names of these early genres are sometimes used interchangeably in the scholarship. On "monumental films" in Germany and Austria, see Helmut Weihsmann, *Gebaute Illusionen: Architektur im Film* (Vienna: Promedia, 1988), 61–99; Rainer Rother, "Monumentalkino: Zum Entstehen des 'Großfilms' in Deutschland," in *Die Modellierung des Kinofilms: Zur Geschichte des Kinoprogramms zwischen Kurzfilm und Langfilm (1905/06–1918)*, ed. Corinna Müller and Harro Segeberg (Munich: Fink, 1998), 375–96; Armin Loacker and Ines Steiner, eds., *Imaginierte Antike: österreichische Monumental-Stummfilme: Historienbilder und Geschichtskonstruktionen in* Sodom und Gomorrha, Samson und Delila, Die Sklavenkönigin *und* Salambô (Vienna: Filmarchiv Austria, 2002).

19 The fascination for "real things" is nowhere reflected in the history of set design.

Cf. Léon Barsacq, *Caligari's Cabinet and Other Grand Illusions: A History of Film Design*, rev. and ed. by Elliott Stein, trans. Michael Bullock (Boston: New York Graphic Society, 1976). For a taxonomic approach to set design and its degrees of realism, see Charles Affron and Mirella Jona Affron, *Sets in Motion: Art Direction and Film Narrative* (New Brunswick, NJ: Rutgers University Press, 1995). For a critique of this approach, and perhaps the most useful study to date, see C. S. Tashiro, *Pretty Pictures: Production Design and the History Film* (Austin: University of Texas Press, 1998). In the German context, scholarship on set design has focused almost exclusively on "Expressionist" films and issues of "architectural" space in canonical films from the 1920s. See, e.g., Michael Esser, "Spaces in Motion: Remarks on Set Design in the German Silent Film," in *Berlin 1900–1933: Architecture and Design*, ed. Tilmann Buddensieg (Berlin: Mann, 1987), 169–83; Weihsmann, *Gebaute Illusionen*; Dietrich Neumann, ed., *Film Architecture: From* Metropolis *to* Blade Runner (Munich: Prestel Verlag, 1999).

20 On the Umlauff family and its various endeavors, see Lange, *Echt, unecht, lebensecht*, 7–26; Hilke Thode-Arora, "Die Familie Umlauff und ihre Firmen: Ethnographica-Händler in Hamburg," *Mitteilungen aus dem Museum für Völkerkunde Hamburg* 22 (1992): 143–58. Heinrich Umlauff's role in film set decoration is first mentioned by Hilke Thode-Arora in "Herbeigeholte Ferne: Völkerschauen als Vorläufer exotisierender Abenteuerfilme," in *Triviale Tropen: Exotische Reise- und Abenteuerfilme aus Deutschland 1919–1939*, ed. Jörg Schöning (Munich: edition text + kritik, 1997), 19–33. On Umlauff as artifact dealer, see Rainer Buschmann, "Exploring Tensions in Material Culture: Commercialising Ethnography in German New Guinea, 1870–1904," and Robert L. Welsch, "One Time, One Place, Three Collections: Colonial Processes and the Shaping of Some Museum Collections from German New Guinea," both in *Hunting the Gatherers: Ethnographic Collectors, Agents and Agency in Melanesia, 1870s–1930s*, ed. Michael O'Hanlon and Robert L. Welsch (New York: Berghahn, 2000), 55–79, and 155–79, respectively. On Umlauff as supplier to German artists, see Jill Lloyd, *German Expressionism: Primitivism and Modernity* (New Haven: Yale University Press, 1991), 10, 30–1, 70, 85–101, 237n44. On Umlauff's life-group exhibits, see Lange, *Echt, unecht, lebensecht*, 67–84, 128–69.

21 "10 Jahre Hagenbecks Tierpark," *Hamburger Correspondent*, 25 May 1917, eve. ed. (SAH A902, "Hagenbecks Tierpark"). The troupes might have been stranded in Germany due to the Allied sea blockade.

22 Only in nonfiction films such as travelogues does the park stand for itself. A rare but useful exception is the provincial comedy *Lucky Mushrooms* (*Glückspilze*, Hamburger Film-Börse, 1912), in which a local comic duo, Leopold and Ludwig Wolf (a.k.a. the Wolf brothers), visit Hagenbeck's *Tierpark*. After drinking copious amounts of alcohol at the park's main restaurant, the brothers proceed to sere-

nade the bronze bust of Hagenbeck Sr. and cavort across the *Völkerschau* area, where the "Bedouins" were then on exhibit. The brothers roam through various huts in the village, dance with female performers, and plant kisses on monkeys and camels. A copy of the program brochure, which includes two photographs of the *Völkerschau* scenes, is available at the TCH. I thank Klaus Gille for bringing this film to my attention.

23 The staircase ascended from the very "ruins" that Umlauff had made for the Burma exhibition of 1913. Publicity stills for this film are available in Walter Bloem, *Seele des Lichtspiels: Ein Bekenntnis zum Film* (Zurich: Grethlein, 1922), fig. 4; in the film's program brochure (TCH); in *Lichtbildbühne* (30 November 1918): 41–43; and in *Lichtbildbühne* no. 49 (7 December 1918): 65–67. The "fidelity" and "massive" quotations appear in *Lichtbildbühne* (5 October 1918): 50. I thank Jörg Schöningh for his assistance in documenting the many films made at Hagenbeck's *Tierpark*.

24 Directed by Iwa Raffay, one of Germany's first female directors, *Eyes of Jade* features an interracial romance between a Norwegian diplomat and a Japanese woman. Only here, in contrast to the Puccini material, the story leads to the death of their child and then to the woman's blindness, to which the film title also alludes. A print of this gorgeous, forgotten film is available at the BA/FA. The text from a program brochure (also available at BA/FA) is reprinted in "Die Augen von Yade," *Das lebende Bild* 28 (5 April 1919): n. pag. The "miniature Japan" quotation appears in Max Prels, *Kino* (Bielefeld and Leipzig: Velhagen & Klasing, 1919), 22; see also 27, 58.

25 According to an untitled notice that ran in the German trade press, "The decorations come in part from the Museum Umlauff, Hamburg," first printed in *Der Kinematograph* (11 September 1918), n. pag.

26 Similarly, one of Hagenbeck's animal panoramas is used to depict "a small cliff island off the South American coast" in *The Prey of the Furies* (an illustrated program brochure is available at TCH).

27 The objects were not de-accessioned from the museum's collections, but rather borrowed and later returned, their usefulness as film props having expired when the shoot was over. The circular logic of collecting and display must also be noted here: Johannes had already rented objects from the Bremen museum for *Mistress of the World*. The museum's director, Schauinsland, was a long-time client of the Umlauffs and the leading practitioner of life-group museum displays in Germany. Information on Johannes Umlauff comes from the unpublished and undated manuscript of his memoir, a photocopy of which is available at the TCH. The "train-wagon" quotation appears on 117–18. The status of this manuscript is such that we must allow for some exaggeration here; his is a rather scurrilous account, particularly when it comes to his rivalry with Heinrich.

28 Reviewing the historical materials on *The Indian Tombstone*, I found a single reference to Johannes: H. L., "Indien in Johannisthal," *Der Film* (7 August 1920): 48, 51. Otherwise, his name goes unmentioned. Instead, the lead architect Martin Jacoby-Boy and his assistant Otto Hunte received exclusive credit for the exotic sets and furnishings. Original credits for *Der goldene See* can be found in the censorship cards for that film, available at BA/FA.

29 The "exemplary" quotation appears in "Harakiri," special issue of *Illustrirte Film-Kurier* no. 11 (1919): 3. The following credit line appears in many other full-page ads: "The Japanese décor was supplied by the Ethnographic Museum J. F. G. Umlauff, Hamburg, whose director, Heinrich Umlauff, also built the Japanese structures." See, e.g., the advertisement for *Harakiri*, in *Der Film* (14 December 1919): n. pag.; which also appears in *Erste internationale Filmzeitung* (20 December 1919): 54.

30 Karl Figdor, "Harakiri," *Erste internationale Filmzeitung* 50 (20 December 1919): 32. See also "Harakiri," *Der Film* 51 (21 December 1919): 40; Fritz Olimsky, "Harakiri," *Berliner Börsen-Zeitung* (21 December 1919); Margot Meyer, "Harakiri," *Film-Kurier* (27 September 1919); "Harakiri," *Lichtbildbühne* (27 December 1919); Ludwig Brauner, "Harakiri," *Der Kinematograph* (31 December 1919); Claus Groth, "Harakiri," *Das Glashaus* 1 (January 1920): 6–7. Further examples are cited by Wolfgang Kabatek in *Imagerie des Anderen im Weimarer Kino* (Bielefeld: transcript Verlag, 2003), 105–8.

31 In his review of *Harakiri* (op. cit.), film critic Fritz Olimsky marveled at the outdoor sets, asking: "Who would have imagined all that could be made out of the delightful landscapes of Woltersdorf?" In so doing, he mistakenly assumed that the sets were built at the May Film City outside of Berlin. Since then, Olimsky's assumption has been perpetuated by other critics, scholars, and archivists. See, e.g., Lotte H. Eisner, *Fritz Lang* (1976; reprint, New York: Da Capo Press, 1986), 28; Frieda Grafe, "Einen Berliner Bären für Madame Butterfly," *Süddeutsche Zeitung*, 27 August 1987; Rolf Aurich, Wolfgang Jacobsen, and Cornelius Schauber, eds., *Fritz Lang: Leben und Werk, Bilder und Dokumente* (Berlin: Jovis, 2001), 56.

32 Barsacq, *Caligari's Cabinet*, 172.

33 Emilie Altenloh, *Zur Soziologie des Kino: Die Kino-Unternehmung und die sozialen Schichten ihrer Besucher* (Leipzig: Spamer, 1913), 34. In English, see Emilie Altenloh, "A Sociology of the Cinema: The Audience," in *Screen* 42, no. 3 (autumn 2001): 249–93. Siegfried Kracauer, "Calico-World: The UFA City in Neubabelsberg," in *The Mass Ornament: Weimar Essays*, ed. Thomas Y. Levin (Cambridge, MA: Harvard University Press, 1995), 281–88; the "collection" quotation appears on 285; "rendezvous" on 281. For a thorough discussion of modern surface culture, see Ward, *Weimar Surfaces*.

34 For an introduction to contemporary studios, see Ben Goldsmith and Tom O'Regan, *The Film Studio: Film Production in the Global Economy* (Lanham, MD: Rowman & Littlefield, 2005). In the German context, see *Babelsberg: Das Filmstudio*, ed. Wolfgang Jacobsen (Berlin: Argon, 1992).

35 There are no surviving records from 1919 in the TCH, so contextualization here is doubly necessary. The Decla Film City in Hamburg-Stellingen is noted in Thode-Arora, "Herbeigeholte Ferne," 23. Selected passages from the trade press are quoted in Georges Sturm, *Die Circe, der Pfau und das Halbblut: Die Filme von Fritz Lang, 1916–1921* (Trier: Wissenschaftlicher Verlag Trier, 2001), 46–49. The film studio is not mentioned in the zoo literature.

36 Accused by British authorities of espionage, John Hagenbeck fled Sri Lanka in 1914 and returned to Hamburg by posing as a Dutch colonial soldier. See John Hagenbeck, *Fünfundzwanzig Jahre Ceylon*, 206–27. On Carl Hagenbeck's debt, see Lorenz Hagenbeck, *Den Tieren gehört mein Herz,* 92–93. On circus income during the war, see Reichenbach, "Carl Hagenbeck's Tierpark," 579–81.

37 The animal statistics are plausible, but the idea that the *Tierpark* hosted five ethnographic troupes ("caravans") is probably an exaggeration. There were, however, two troupes present in the summer of 1917, when *Peer Gynt* was being filmed there. The "housed" quotation appears in "Hagenbeck's Zoo a 'White Elephant,'" *New York Times*, 17 October 1914, 4. Bogus rumors of dire conditions also circulated as war propaganda in England and beyond—evidence of the park's function as a symbolic site of national significance. See, e.g., "Hagenbeck's Near Famine," *New York Times*, 9 October 1914, 3.

38 As late as 1917, Hamburg newspapers claimed that the war had taken no significant toll on the park—claims that turned out to be false and made presumably in response to Allied war propaganda. Lorenz Hagenbeck calculated the (pre-inflation) cost of animals lost as exceeding 960,000 Marks (Niemeyer, *Hagenbeck: Geschichte und Geschichten,* 256). Cf. "10 Jahre Hagenbecks Tierpark"; "Zehn Jahre Stellinger Tierpark," *Hamburger Nachrichten*, 25 May 1917, eve. ed.; "Besichtigung in Hagenbecks Tierpark," *Hamburger Fremdenblatt*, 25 May 1917 (all clippings in SAH A902, "Hagenbeck's Tierpark").

39 For a detailed account of the sea blockade, see C. Paul Vincent, *The Politics of Hunger: The Allied Blockade of Germany, 1915–1919* (Athens, OH and London: Ohio University Press, 1985). See also Anne Roerkohl, "Die Lebensmittelversorgung während des Ersten Weltkrieges im Spannungsfeld kommunaler und staatlicher Massnahmen," in *Durchbruch zum modernen Massenkonsum: Lebensmittelmärkte und Lebensmittelqualität im Städtewachstum des Industriezeitalters*, ed. Hans-Jürgen Teuteberg (Münster: Coppenrath, 1987), 309–70; Richard Bessel, *Germany After the First World War* (Oxford: Clarendon Press,

1993), 1–48; and Belinda J. Davis, *Home Fires Burning: Food, Politics, and Everyday Life in World War I Berlin* (Chapel Hill: University of North Carolina Press, 2000).

40 For a concise statement on the German industry's wartime consolidation, see Sabine Hake, *German National Cinema* (New York: Routledge, 2002), 22–25. For an economic study of the German industry's emergence, see Karl Zimmerschied, *Die deutsche Filmindustrie: Ihre Entwicklung, Organisation und Stellung im deutschen Staats- und Wirtschaftsleben* (Berlin: Poeschel, 1922). The Olimsky quotations appear in "Film-Gründungsfieber!" *Berliner Börsen-Zeitung* (n.d. [1919]), Sammlung Fritz Olimsky (Deutsche Kinemathek, Berlin). On Hamburg's "intoxication" with film, see Margot Meyer, "Film-Kater. . . ," *Film-Kurier* (9 October 1919): n. pag. Here it should be noted that most of the new companies would soon dissolve or move to Berlin. See on this point Friedrich von Zglinicki, *Der Weg des Films: Die Geschichte der Kinematographie und ihrer Vorläufer* (Berlin: Rembrandt, 1956), 363. For a general account of Hamburg's film history, see Michael Töteberg, *Filmstadt Hamburg: Von Emil Jannings bis Wim Wenders: Kino-Geschichte(n) einer Großstadt* (Hamburg: VSA, 1990).

41 On John Hagenbeck, see Jörg Schöning, "Unternehmensgegenstand: Exotik: Der Produzent John Hagenbeck," in *Triviale Tropen: Exotische Reise- und Abenteuerfilme aus Deutschland 1919–1939*, ed. Jörg Schöning (Munich: edition text + kritik, 1997), 111–23; "'Kleines Urwaldreich gedeiht. . .': Die Dschungelfantasien des Filmproduzenten John Hagenbeck," in *Der deutsche Tropenwald: Bilder, Mythen, Politik*, ed. Michael Flitner (Frankfurt am Main: Campus, 2000), 79–93; and John Hagenbeck, "Raubtiere im Film," in *Das Kulturfilmbuch*, ed. Edgar Beyfuss (Berlin: Chryselius & Schulz, 1924), 120–22.

42 Around 1920, there was a general trend toward mergers and acquisitions across the German film industry, which helps explain various moves that Pommer made, including the acquisition—and abandonment—of the *Tierpark* in Stellingen. Although this project is not mentioned anywhere in the literature on Pommer, a discussion of Decla's other mergers and acquisitions around 1920 can be found in Wolfgang Jacobsen, *Erich Pommer: Ein Produzent macht Filmgeschichte* (Berlin: Argon, 1989), 30–31. The "Weißensee" quotation appears in Ursula Hardt, *From Caligari to California: Erich Pommer's Life in the International Film Wars* (Providence: Berghahn, 1996), 35, trans. rev. Here it should also be noted that Decla's relationship to the museum had an American precedent in Kalem Studios, which used costumes and objects from the American Museum of Natural History for various productions between 1907 and 1913. Decla's plan for ownership and expansion takes this idea several steps further. On Kalem, see Griffiths, *Wondrous Difference*, 241, 276–82; and Nanna Verhoeff,

"After the Beginning: Westerns Before 1915" (Ph.D. diss., University of Utrecht, 2002), 279.

43 Details of the first agreement appear in "Das Museum Umlauff als Filmfundus," *Der Film* (10 May 1919): 28. The Hagenbeck agreement is first reported in "Die Expansion der 'Decla,'" *Lichtbildbühne* (11 October 1919): 24. The "subsidiary" quotation appears in "Eine Filmstadt im Hagenbeckpark Stellingen," *Der Film* (12 October 1919): 32.

44 As Corinna Müller has shown, Gad belonged to a generation of directors (including Stellan Rye, Emil Albes, and Max Obal) who took it upon themselves to select furniture and determine its placement on the set. The role of collecting was for them self-evident (*Frühe deutsche Kinematographie*, 25). The "procurement" quotation appears in Urban Gad, *Der Film: Seine Mittel, Seine Ziele*, trans. Julia Koppel (1919; Berlin: Schuster & Loeffler, 1922), 48.

45 Private menageries were a common part of early film studios in the United States, including Universal City, Mack Sennett's Keystone Studios, and the Selig-Polyscope Plant, each located near Los Angeles. The last offers an interesting counterexample to Hagenbeck: Around 1913, Selig established a game farm (for making wildlife adventure films), which later became the studio's menagerie. In 1923, "Selig's Jungle Zoo" was peeled off from the studio to become the Los Angeles Zoo (see Mitman, *Reel Nature*, 9–10).

46 These productions included *The Prey of the Furies* and *Ebb and Flow*, both from 1921. On Decla's termination of the agreement, see Margot Meyer, "Freigabe des Hamburg-Stellinger Terrains," *Film-Kurier* 2, no. 87 (27 April 1920): n. pag. Until his death in 1925, Heinrich Umlauff continued to supply Decla-Bioscop with exotic paraphernalia. His name, and that of his "museum," would also be invoked in publicity materials for Fritz Lang's *Destiny* (*Der müde Tod*, 1921) and *Kriemhilde's Revenge* (*Kriemhilds Rache*, part two of *Die Nibelungen*, 1924), both produced by Eric Pommer. See Lange, *Echt, unecht, lebensecht*, 240–62.

47 T. R. Ybarra, "'Hagenbeck's' Closes Its Doors," *New York Times*, 28 November 1920.

Conclusion ✦ The Future of Nineteenth-Century Theme Space

1 Leutemann, *Lebensbeschreibung*, 78; Kirshenblatt-Gimblett, *Destination Culture*, 159.

2 In this regard, it is worth noting that two imported buildings were recently added to the *Tierpark*, each recalling the original notion of theme space (albeit inadvertently). The one is a gold-covered sala from Thailand, the other an enormous pagoda-temple from Nepal. Designed by a major Bangkok architect, the sala was

a gift of Thailand's honorary consulate in Hamburg, and it was officially inaugurated in 2002 by Princess Maha Chakri Sirindorn. The Nepalese temple was inspired by a similar installation at the EXPO 2000 in Hannover, the first world's fair to be held in Germany. The project's sponsors approached Nepal's honorary consul in Hamburg (a German businessman) about acquiring the temple, but the Hamburg senate balked. Later, the honorary consul raised enough funds to commission a new pagoda for Hagenbeck's *Tierpark*. A Hindu temple dedicated to Shiva, the pagoda stands nearly fifty feet tall. It was built over a period of seventeen months by "three hundred families" in the Katmandu Valley using local materials, then carefully dismantled, packed into ten ship containers, and freighted to Hamburg. A team of sixteen workers was flown from Nepal to reassemble the pieces and add finishing touches. Significantly, this pagoda functions as the park's new main entrance, instead of the original *Jugendstil* gate, which in turn has been displaced and recast as a historical monument—an enormous relic of the park's storied past. See "300 Familien fertigten das Bauwerk," and Claudia Sewig, "Nepal liegt bei Hagenbeck," each in *Hamburger Abendblatt*, 17 May 2003. On the Thai pavilion, see Günter Stiller, "Hagenbeck: das goldene Geheimnis," *Hamburger Abendblatt*, 5 July 2002; and "Goldener Glanz aus Fernost," *Hamburger Abendblatt*, 22 August 2002.

WORKS CITED

Archival Materials

The following abbreviations are used to aid in locating archival materials:

DENMARK

DFI	Danish Film Institute, Copenhagen

GERMANY

BA/FA	Bundesarchiv / Filmarchiv, Berlin (federal film archive)
DIF	Das Deutsche Filminstitut, Frankfurt am Main (German film institute)
DFM	Deutsches Filmmuseum, Frankfurt am Main (German film museum)
DK	Deutsche Kinemathek, Berlin (German cinematheque)
FWMS	Friedrich-Wilhelm-Murnau-Stiftung, Wiesbaden (Murnau foundation)
MfVB	Museum für Völkerkunde, Berlin (ethnological museum of Berlin)
SAH	Staatsarchiv Hamburg (state archive of Hamburg)
TCH	Tierpark Carl Hagenbeck, Hamburg-Stellingen (Hagenbeck's *Tierpark* archive)

UNITED STATES

AMNH	American Museum of Natural History, New York

BBHC-Carver	MS 6, William F. Cody Collection. Series VI: E, W. F. "Doc" Carver scrapbook. Microfilm Roll 1. Buffalo Bill Historical Center, Cody
BBHC-Cody	MS 6, William F. Cody Collection. Series IX: Scrapbooks, ledgers, etc. Germany, 1890. Microfilm Roll 2. Buffalo Bill Historical Center, Cody
DPL	William Fredrick Cody / Buffalo Bill Papers. WH72. Western History Collection. Denver Public Library

Guidebooks and Program Brochures

Aegyptische Ausstellung und Beduinen-Karawane (program brochure). Dir. Ernst Pinkert. 24 May 1890. (TCH)

Am Nil: Bunte Bilder aus Egypten dem Wunderlande der Pyramide: Völkerschau 1912, Carl Hagenbeck's Tierpark, Stellingen (brochure and guidebook). Text by Johannes Flemming. Hamburg: Carly, 1912. (TCH)

Die Augen von Yade (film program brochure). Dir. Iwa Raffay. Hella-Moja-Film, 1918. (BA/FA)

Ausstellung Nordland: Führer durch die Ausstellung: Lappländer, Samojeden, Eskimos, Schweden (program brochure and guidebook, 1911). Text by Johannes Flemming. N.d. (TCH)

Ausstellung Nordland: Rundgang durch die Ausstellung (guidebook, 1911). N.d. (TCH)

Die Beute der Erinnyens (film program brochure). Dir. Otto Rippert. Sächsischer Kunstfilm, 1921. (TCH)

Die Bischaris (program brochure, 1899). Dir. Willy Möller. N.d. (TCH)

Bjørnejagt i Rusland (film program brochure). Dir. Viggo Larsen. Nordisk Films Kompagni, 1908. (DFI)

Die Ceylon-Sammlung des Museum Umlauff, Hamburg. Katalog No. 113 (sales catalog). Hamburg: Friedländer, 1900. (AMNH)

Deutsch-Afrika: Carl Hagenbeck's Kamerun-Expedition (program brochure). Dir. Fritz Angerer. Munich: Verlag von Fritz Angerer, 1886. (TCH)

East African Village and Great Display by the Natives of Somaliland under Direction of Herr Carl Hagenbeck. London, 1895. (TCH)

Ebbe und Flut (film program brochure). Dir. Martin Hartwig. Vera-Filmwerke, 1921. (TCH)

Ethnologischer Garten: Internationale Völkerschau (investment portfolio, brochure, and map, 1912). *Acta betreffend verschiedenen Angelegenheiten der ethnologischen Abteilung*. Vol. 18. 1.8.1911 bis 31.8.1912. Pars III.c. (MfVB)

Führer durch Carl Hagenbecks Tierpark in Stellingen (guidebook). 2nd ed. Hamburg: Hagenbecks Tierpark, 1907. (TCH)

Führer durch Carl Hagenbecks Tierpark in Stellingen. 10th ed. Revised by Johannes Flemming. Hamburg: Carly, 1914. (TCH)

Führer durch Carl Hagenbeck's Tierpark, Stellingen. Text by Nikolaus Schiller-Tietz. 1st ed. Hamburg: Verlag von Carl Hagenbecks Tierpark, 1907. (TCH)

Gebr. Hagenbeck's Indische Carawane: Die Malabaren (program brochure, 1902). N.d. (TCH)

Gebrüder J. & G. Hagenbeck's Indische Völkerschaften (program brochure, 1904) Hamburg: Adolph Friedländer, N.d. (TCH)

Glückspilze (film program brochure). Hamburger Film-Börse, 1912. (TCH)

Hoffmann, M. *Beiträge über Leben und Treiben der Eskimos in Labrador und Grönland: Aus dem Tagebuch des Herrn Carl Hagenbeck in Hamburg mit dem Schiffe "Eisbär" nach Grönland entsandten Herrn J. A. Jacobsen* (pamphlet for the 1880 "Labrador Eskimo" exhibition). Berlin: M. Hoffmann, 1880.

Die lebende Brücke (film program brochure). Dir. Friedrich Müller. Komet, 1912. (DIF)

Løvejagten paa Elleore (film program brochure). Dir. Viggo Larsen. Nordisk Films Kompagni, 1907. (DFI)

Die Neu-Caledonische Sammlung des Museum Umlauff, Hamburg. Katalog No. 107. Hamburg, 1898. (AMNH)

Ein Rückblick (souvenir brochure from Hagenbeck's *Tierpark*, 1907). N.d. (TCH)

Sioux-Indianer: Carl Hagenbeck's Tierpark, Stellingen, 1910 (brochure and guidebook). Text by Johannes Flemming. Hamburg: Carly, 1910. (TCH)

La Vie au Pôle Nord (program brochure) Paris, 1899. (TCH)

Völkerschau Aethiopien (brochure and guidebook). Text by Johannes Flemming. Hamburg: Adolph Friedländer, 1909. (TCH)

Films

Die Augen von Yade (*Eyes of Jade*, Hella-Moja-Film, 1918; dir. Iwa Raffay). (BA/FA)

Aus der afrikanischen Wildnis (*From the African Jungle*, 1914; dir. Christoph Schulz).

Die Beute der Erinnyen (*The Prey of the Furies*, Sächsischer Kunstfilm, 1921; dir. Otto Rippert).

Bjørnejagt i Rusland (*Bear Hunting in Russia*, Nordisk, 1908; dir. Viggo Larsen).

Bontoc Eulogy (Marlon Fuentes, 1995; dir. Marlon Fuentes).

Cabiria (Italia Film, 1914; dir. Giovanni Pastrone).

Darwin (John Hagenbeck-Film, 1919; dir. Fritz Bernhardt).

Ebbe und Flut (*Ebb and Flow*, Vera-Filmwerke, 1921; dir. Martin Hartwig).

Der Fremde: Eine seltsame Geschichte aus Tibet (*The Foreigner: A Strange Story from Tibet*, Decla, 1917; dir. Otto Rippert).

Glückspilze (*Lucky Mushrooms*, Hamburger Film-Börse, 1912).

Der goldene See, part one of *Die Spinnen* (*The Golden Sea*, part one of *The Spiders*, Decla, 1919; dir. Fritz Lang). (FWMS)

Harakiri (Decla, 1919; dir. Fritz Lang). (FWMS)

Die Herrin der Welt (*Mistress of the World*, May-Film, 1919; dir. Joe May). (BA/FA)

Das indische Grabmal (*The Indian Tombstone*, May-Film, 1921; dir. Joe May). (FWMS)

Intolerance (Triangle Film Corp., 1916; dir. D. W. Griffith).

Isbjørnejagt (*Polar Bear Hunt*, Nordisk, 1907; dir. Viggo Larsen).

Die Königstochter von Travankore: Ein indisches Liebesdrama (*The Princess of Travankore: An Indian Love Story*, Decla, 1917; dir. Otto Rippert).

Kriemhilds Rache, part two of *Die Nibelungen* (*Kriemhilde's Revenge*, part two of *The Nibelungen*, Decla-Bioscop, 1924; dir. Fritz Lang).

Die lebende Brücke (*The Living Bridge*, Komet, 1912; dir. Friedrich Müller). (BA/FA)

Die Liebe der Bajadere (*The Love of the Bayadère*, Argus-Film, 1918; dir. Svend Gade).

Løvejagten (*The Lion Hunt*, Nordisk, 1907; dir. Viggo Larsen). (DFI)

Madame DuBarry (*Passion*, Germany, 1919; dir. Ernst Lubitsch).

Maharadjahens yndlingshustru (*The Maharaja's Favorite Wife*, Nordisk, 1917; dir. Robert Dinesen). (DFI)

Mellem Storbyens Artister (*In the Den of Lions* or *Life in the Circus*, Nordisk, 1912; dir. Edward Schnedler-Sørensen). (DFI)

Der müde Tod (*Destiny*, Decla-Bioscop, 1921; dir. Fritz Lang).

Paul J. Rainey's African Hunt (Jungle Film Co., 1912; dir. Paul J. Rainey).

Peer Gynt (Richard Oswald-Film, 1918; dir. Viktor Barnowsky).

Sadja (Ring-Film, 1918; dir. Adolf Gärtner).

Der Tod und die Liebe (*Death and Love*, Vera-Filmwerke, 1919; dir. Paul Otto).

UNPUBLISHED ARCHIVAL PAPERS

Berliner Gesellschaft für Anthropologie, Ethnologie und Urgeschichte. "Erklärung" (declaration of endorsement), 24 May 1878. (TCH)

"Dankschreiben des kalmückschen Fürsten." Letter to Carl Hagenbeck, 30 October 1883. (TCH)

Hagenbeck, Carl. "Instructions for Mr. Adrian Jacobsen for his voyage to South Dakota, U.S.A." Letter to Johan Adrian Jacobsen, 5 January 1910. (TCH)

——. Letter to Johan Adrian Jacobsen, 5 January 1882. (TCH)

Hauptbuch 1907 (account book). (TCH)

"Naturwissenschaftliches Panorama." Patent certificate no. 91492, 6 February 1896. (TCH)

Nordisk Company Papers. (DFI)

Tierpark 1913 (account book). (TCH)

Umlauff, Johannes. Untitled, undated memoir. Typescript. (TCH)

Other Sources

"10 Jahre Hagenbecks Tierpark." *Hamburger Correspondent*, 25 May 1917, eve. ed. (SAH A902, "Hagenbeck's Tierpark").

"300 Familien fertigten das Bauwerk." *Hamburger Abendblatt*, 17 May 2003.

Adams, Bluford. *E Pluribus Barnum: The Great Showman and the Making of U.S. Popular Culture*. Minneapolis: University of Minnesota, 1997.

"Die Aethiopier bei Hagenbeck." *Hamburger Echo*, 16 May 1909, 1st ed.

Affron, Charles, and Mirella Jona Affron. *Sets in Motion: Art Direction and Film Narrative*. New Brunswick, NJ: Rutgers University Press, 1995.

Ahrndt, Wiebke. *Rote Wolke, Blaues Pferd: Bilder aus dem Leben der Sioux*. Hamburg: Christians Verlag and Hamburgisches Museum für Völkerkunde, 1997.

Alexander, Edward P. *Museum Masters: Their Museums and Their Influence*. Nashville, TN: American Association for State and Local History, 1983.

Alloula, Malek. *The Colonial Harem*. Trans. Myrna Godzich and Wlad Godzich. Minneapolis: University of Minnesota Press, 1986.

Altenberg, Peter. *Ashantee*. Berlin: Fischer, 1897.

Altenloh, Emilie. "A Sociology of the Cinema: The Audience." *Screen* 42, no. 3 (autumn 2001): 249–93.

——. *Zur Soziologie des Kino: Die Kino-Unternehmung und die sozialen Schichten ihrer Besucher*. Leipzig: Spamer, 1913.

Altick, Richard D. *The Shows of London*. Cambridge, MA: Harvard University Press, 1978.

The American Experience: Coney Island. Produced and directed by Ric Burns. 72 min. PBS, 1990. Videocassette.

"Die amerikanische Arena." *Münchener Fremdenblatt*, 22 April 1890. (DPL)

Ames, Eric. "From the Exotic to the Everyday: The Ethnographic Exhibition in Germany." In *The Nineteenth-Century Visual Culture Reader*, ed. Vanessa R. Schwartz and Jeannene M. Przyblyski, pp. 313–27. New York: Routledge, 2004.

——. "Seeing the Imaginary: On the Popular Reception of Wild West Shows in Germany, 1885–1910." In *I Like America: Fictions of the Wild West*, ed. Pamela Kort and Max Hollein, pp. 213–29. Munich: Prestel, 2006.

——. "The Sound of Evolution." *Modernism/modernity* 10, no. 2 (April 2003): 297–325.

Andrews, Malcolm. *Landscape and Western Art*. Oxford History of Art. New York: Oxford University Press, 1999.

"Antrag I der Abteilung Metz gegen die Ausfuhr von Eingeborenen aus den deutschen Kolonien zum Zwecke der Schaustellung." *Deutsche Kolonialzeitung* 17, no. 28 (12 July 1900): 329–30.

Apter, Emily, and William Pietz, eds. *Fetishism as Cultural Discourse*. Ithaca: Cornell University Press, 1993.

Artinger, Kai. *Von der Tierbude zum Turm der Blauen Pferde: Die künstlerische Wahrnehmung der wilden Tiere im Zeitalter der zoologischen Gärten*. Berlin: Reimer, 1995.

"Die Augen von Yade." *Das lebende Bild* 28 (5 April 1919).

Aumont, Jacques, Alain Bergala, Michel Marie, and Marc Vernet. *Aesthetics of Film*. Trans. and rev. Richard Neupert. Austin: University of Texas Press, 1992.

Aurich, Rolf, Wolfgang Jacobsen, and Cornelius Schauber, eds. *Fritz Lang: Leben und Werk, Bilder und Dokumente*. Berlin: Jovis, 2001.

"Aus dem Leben eines bekannten Regisseurs: Joseph Delmont." *Der Kinematograph*. (BA-FA, P "Delmont, Joseph")

"Ausstellungen, anthropologische." *Meyers Konversations-Lexikon*, 5th ed. Leipzig: Bibliographisches Institut, 1893.

Baader, Johannes. *Oberdada*. Lahn-Gießen: Anabas-Verlag Kämpf, 1977.

Bachofen, Johann Jakob. *Das Mutterrecht*. Ed. Hans-Jürgen Heinrichs. 1861. Frankfurt am Main: Suhrkamp, 1975.

Bancel, Nicolas, Pascal Blanchard, Gilles Boëtsch, Éric Deroo, Sandrine Lemaire, eds. *Zoos humains*. Paris: La Découverte, 2002.

Baratay, Eric, and Elisabeth Hardouin-Fugier. *Zoo: A History of Zoological Gardens in the West*. Trans. Oliver Welsch. London: Reaktion Books, 2002.

Barker, Andrew and Leo A. Lensing. *Peter Altenberg: Rezept die Welt zu sehen*. Vienna: Braumüller, 1995.

Barnum, P. T. *Selected Letters of P. T. Barnum*. Ed. A. H. Saxon. New York: Columbia University Press, 1983.

Barsacq, Léon. *Caligari's Cabinet and Other Grand Illusions: A History of Film Design*. Rev. and ed. Elliott Stein; trans. Michael Bullock. Boston: New York Graphic Society, 1976.

Baudrillard, Jean. *Simulations*. Trans. Paul Foss, Paul Patton, and Philip Beitchman. New York: Semiotext[e], 1983.

——. *The System of Objects*. Trans. James Benedict. London: Verso, 1996.

Bazin, André. "The Virtues and Limitations of Montage." Trans. Hugh Gray. In *What Is Cinema?* Vol. 1, pp. 41–52. Berkeley: University of California Press, 1967.

Beckmann, L. "Die Hagenbeck'schen Singhalesen." *Die Gartenlaube* 32, no. 34 (1884): 564–66.

Behn, Manfred, ed. *Schwarzer Traum und weiße Sklavin: deutsch-dänische Filmbeziehungen 1910–1930*. Munich: edition text + kritik, 1994.

"Bei Hagenbeck (Neue Schöpfungen und Pläne)." *Hamburger Correspondent*, 1 July 1906, morn. ed. (SAH, A902 "Hagenbecks Tierpark")

Benjamin, Walter. "Charles Baudelaire: Ein Lyriker im Zeitalter des Hochkapitalismus." In *Gesammelte Schriften*, ed. Rolf Tiedemann and Hermann Schweppenhäuser, vol. 1, pp. 509–690. Frankfurt am Main: Suhrkamp, 1991.

——. "Paris, Capital of the Nineteenth Century." In *Reflections: Essays, Aphorisms, Autobiographical Writings*, ed. Peter Demetz, trans. Edmund Jephcott, pp. 146–62. New York: Schocken Books, 1986.

——. "The Work of Art in the Age of Mechanical Reproduction." In *Illuminations*, ed. Hannah Arendt, trans. Harry Zohn, pp. 217–51. New York: Schocken, 1969.

Bennett, Tony. *The Birth of the Museum: History, Theory, Politics*. London: Routledge, 1995.

Berger, Alfred Freiherr von. "Hagenbeck" (1909). In *Gesammelte Schriften*, ed. Anton Bettelheim and Karl Glossy, vol. 3, pp. 262–78. Vienna and Leipzig: Deutsch-Österreichischer Verlag, 1913.

Berges, Philipp. "Hagenbecks Neuschöpfungen: Eröffnung der Völkerschau Aethiopien." *Hamburger Fremdenblatt*, 16 May 1909. (SAH, A902 "Hagenbecks Tierpark")

Bergsten, Bebe. *The Great Dane and the Great Northern Film Company*. Los Angeles: Roche, 1973.

"Besichtigung in Hagenbecks Tierpark." *Hamburger Fremdenblatt*, 25 May 1917. (SAH A902, "Hagenbeck's Tierpark")

Bessel, Richard. *Germany After the First World War*. Oxford: Clarendon Press, 1993.
Bieder, Robert E. "Marketing the American Indian in Europe: Context, Commodification and Reception." In *Cultural Transmissions and Receptions: American Mass Culture in Europe*, ed. Rob Kroes, Robert W. Rydell, and Doeko F. J. Bosscher, pp. 15–23. Amsterdam: VU University Press, 1993.
"Biographisches über Buffalo Bill." *Allgemeine Zeitung* (Munich), 15 April 1890. (DPL)
Birett, Herbert, ed. *Verzeichnis der in Deutschland gelaufenen Filme: Entscheidungen der Filmzensur 1911–1920*. Berlin: K. G. Saur, 1980.
Blackbourn, David. *The Long Nineteenth Century: A History of Germany, 1780–1918*. New York: Oxford University Press, 1998.
Blackstone, Sarah J. *Buckskins, Bullets, and Business: A History of Buffalo Bill's Wild West*. New York: Greenwood Press, 1986.
Blathwayt, Raymond. "Hunting the Beasts: Karl Hagenbeck Tells of His Exploits in Foreign Jungles." *Detroit Journal*, 6 May 1893. (TCH)
———. "Wild Beasts: How They Are Transported and Trained," *McClure's Magazine* 1, no. 2 (July 1893): 130–31.
Bloem, Walter. *Seele des Lichtspiels: Ein Bekenntnis zum Film*. Zurich: Grethlein, 1922.
Blunt, Wilfrid. *The Ark in the Park: The Zoo in the Nineteenth Century*. London: Hamish Hamilton, 1976.
Bogdan, Robert. *Freak Show: Presenting Human Oddities for Amusement and Profit*. Chicago: University of Chicago Press, 1988.
Boger, Hernann [*sic*]. "Training Wild Beasts." *The Independent* 55, no. 2865 (29 October 1903): 2551–57.
Bolau, Heinrich. "Karl Hagenbeck's Eismeer-Panorama." *Illustrirte Zeitung* 108, no. 2793 (9 January 1897): 57–59.
Bolz, Peter, and Hans-Ulrich Sanner. *Native American Art: The Collections of the Ethnological Museum Berlin*. Seattle: University of Washington Press, 1999.
Bormanshinov, Arash. "Kalmyks in Europe in the Nineteenth Century." *Mongolian Studies* 11 (1988): 5–24.
Börsch-Supan, Helmut. "Die Anfänge des Panoramas in Deutschland." In *"Sind Briten hier?" Relations between British and Continental Art, 1680–1880*, ed. Zentralinstitut für Kunstgeschichte in München, pp. 161–80. Munich: Fink, 1981.
———. *Caspar David Friedrich*. Trans. Sarah Twohig. 2nd ed. Munich: Prestel, 1990.
Bousé, Derek. *Wildlife Films*. Philadelphia: University of Pennsylvania Press, 2000.
Brauner, Ludwig. "Harakiri." *Der Kinematograph* (31 December 1919).
Bridges, William. *Gathering of Animals: An Unconventional History of the New York Zoological Society*. New York: Harper & Row, 1974.
Brownell, Charles F. "Marketing Wild Animals." *Leslie's Monthly Magazine* 60, no. 3 (July 1905): 287–95.
Brownlow, Kevin. *The War, the West, and the Wilderness*. New York: Alfred A. Knopf, 1979.
Bruckner, Sierra Ann. "Spectacles of (Human) Nature: Commercial Ethnography between

Leisure, Learning, and *Schaulust*." In *Worldly Provincialism: German Anthropology in the Age of Empire*, ed. H. Glenn Penny and Matti Bunzl, pp. 127–55. Ann Arbor: University of Michigan Press, 2003.

———. "The Tingle-Tangle of Modernity: Popular Anthropology and the Cultural Politics of Identity in Imperial Germany." Ph.D. diss., University of Iowa, 1999.

Bryman, Alan. *Disney and His Worlds*. London: Routledge, 1995.

Buddemeier, Heinz. *Panorama, Diorama, Photographie: Entstehung und Wirkung neuer Medien im 19. Jahrhundert*. Munich: Wilhelm Fink, 1970.

"Buffalo Bill." *Münchener Fremdenblatt*, 20 April 1890. (DPL)

"Buffalo Bill's Wild-Amerika." *Illustrirte Zeitung* (12 July 1890): 41, 46–47.

"Buffalo Bill's Wild West." *Gericht's Zeitung* (Leipzig), 14 June 1890. (BBHC-Cody)

"Buffalo Bills Wild West." *Hamburger Fremdenblatt*, 25 August 1890.

"Buffalo Bill's Wild West." Hannover *Tageblatt*, 29 June 1890. (BBHC-Cody)

"Buffalo Bill's Wild West." Hannover *Courier*, 9 July 1890. (BBHC-Cody)

"Buffalo Bills Wild West." Leipzig *Nachrichten*, 18 June 1890. (BBHC-Cody)

"Buffalo Bill's Wild West." *Lindener Tageblatt* (Hannover), 5 July 1890. (BBHC-Cody)

"Buffalo Bills Wild West." *Münchener Fremdenblatt*, 21 April 1890. (DPL)

"Buffalo Bill's Wild West." *Münchener Tageblatt*, 21 April 1890. (DPL)

"Buffalo Bill's Wild West." *Täglicher Anzeiger* (Düsseldorf), 15 June 1890. (BBHC-Cody)

"Buffalo Bills Wild West in Dresden." *Meitzener Tageblatt*, 3 June 1890. (BBHC-Cody)

"Buffalo Bill's Wild West Journal" (German-language newspaper supplement). *Berliner Tageblatt*, 22 July 1890. (BBHC-Cody)

"Buffalo Bills Wild West-Truppe." Hannover *Presse*, 3 July 1890. (BBHC-Cody)

"Buffalo Bills 'Wilder Westen.'" *Münchener neuste Nachrichten*, 21 April 1890. (DPL)

"Buffalo Bills Wilder Westen." Tharandt and Mohorn *Anzeiger*, 3 June 1890. (BBHC-Cody)

"Buffalo Bill und seine Karawane." *Münchener Tageblatt*, 17 April 1890. (DPL)

Bukatman, Scott. "There's Always Tomorrowland: Disney and the Hypercinematic Experience." *October* 57 (1991): 55–78.

Burt, Jonathan. *Animals in Film*. London: Reaktion, 2002.

Buschmann, Rainer. "Exploring Tensions in Material Culture: Commercialising Ethnography in German New Guinea, 1870–1904." In *Hunting the Gatherers: Ethnographic Collectors, Agents and Agency in Melanesia, 1870s–1930s*, ed. Michael O'Hanlon and Robert L. Welsch, pp. 55–79. New York: Berghahn, 2000.

"Carl Hagenbeck's Eismeer-Panorama." *Der Kurier* 6, no. 53 (31 October 1896): 974–75.

"Carl Hagenbeck's Handelsmenagerie und Thierpark" (advertisement). *Hamburgischer Correspondent*, 25 June 1876.

"Carl Hagenbeck's Indien" (advertisement). *Berliner Tageblatt*, 23 July 1898, 1st supplement.

"Carl Hagenbecks Tierpark, Stellingen" (1906 newspaper announcement). (SAH map room, Sig. 151–21, 15/65)

"Carl Hagenbeck und die Zoologischen Gärten." *Hamburger Fremdenblatt*, 14 February 1909. (SAH, A902 "Hagenbecks Tierpark")

"Carver's Wild-Amerika" (advertisement). *Hamburger Fremdenblatt*, 26 August 1890, 2nd supplement.

"Casanova und Hagenbeck." *Die Gartenlaube*, no. 3 (1869): 42–47.

Chindahl, George L. *A History of the Circus in America*. Caldwell, ID: Caxton Printers, 1959.

Chris, Cynthia. *Watching Wildlife*. Minneapolis: University of Minnesota Press, 2006.

Ciarlo, David M. "Rasse konsumieren: Von der exotischen zur kolonialen Imagination in der Bildreklame des Wilhelminischen Kaiserreichs." In *Phantasiereiche: Zur Kulturgeschichte des deutschen Kolonialismus*, ed. Birthe Kundrus, pp. 135–79. Frankfurt am Main: Campus, 2003.

Clark, Sarah Wood. *Beautiful Daring Western Girls: Women of the Wild West Shows*. Cody, WY: Buffalo Bill Historical Center, 1985.

Clifford, James. *Routes: Travel and Translation in the Late Twentieth Century*. Cambridge, MA: Harvard University Press, 1997.

Coe, Jon C. "The Evolution of Zoo Animal Exhibits." In *The Ark Evolving: Zoos and Aquariums in Transition*, ed. Christen M. Wemmer, pp. 95–128. Front Royal, VA: Smithsonian Institution Conservation and Research Center, 1995.

Cohen, Ed. "The 'Hyperreal' vs. the 'Really Real': If European Intellectuals Stop Making Sense of American Culture Can We Still Dance?" *Cultural Studies* 3, no. 1 (1989): 25–37.

Cohen, Margaret. "Panoramic Literature and the Invention of Everyday Genres." In *Cinema and the Invention of Everyday Life*, ed. Leo Charney and Vanessa R. Schwartz, pp. 227–52. Berkeley: University of California Press, 1995.

Cole, Douglas. *Captured Heritage: The Scramble for Northwest Coast Artifacts*. Norman: University of Oklahoma Press, 1985.

Comment, Bernard. *The Panorama*. London: Reaktion Books, 1999.

Conrad, Rudolf. "Mutual Fascination: Indians in Dresden and Leipzig." In *Indians and Europe: An Interdisciplinary Collection of Essays*, ed. Christian F. Feest, pp. 455–73. Aachen: Rader, 1987.

Cook, James W. *The Arts of Deception: Playing with Fraud in the Age of Barnum*. Cambridge, MA: Harvard University Press, 2001.

———. "Of Men, Missing Links, and Nondescripts: The Strange Career of P. T. Barnum's 'What Is It?' Exhibition." In *Freakery: Cultural Spectacles of the Extraordinary Body*, ed. Rosemarie Garland Thomson, pp. 139–57. New York: New York University Press, 1996.

Coombes, Annie E. *Reinventing Africa: Museums, Material Culture and Popular Imagination in Late Victorian and Edwardian England*. New Haven: Yale University Press, 1994.

Cornish, C. J. "The Moltke of Menagerie Owners." *English Illustrated Magazine* 14 (October 1895): 82–88.

"Cowboys Painting Hamburg." San Francisco *Examiner*, 28 August 1890. (BBHC-Carver)

"Crowds at Coney Island." *New York Times*, 17 June 1894.

Davis, Belinda J. *Home Fires Burning: Food, Politics, and Everyday Life in World War I Berlin*. Chapel Hill: University of North Carolina Press, 2000.

Davis, Susan G. *Spectacular Nature: Corporate Culture and the Sea World Experience*. Berkeley: University of California Press, 1997.

Delmont, Joseph. *Catching Wild Beasts Alive*. London: Hutschinson, 1931.

———. *Wild Animals on the Films*. Trans. G. Morrison Gilmour. London: Methuen, 1925.

———. *Wilde Tiere im Film: Erlebnisse aus meinen Filmaufnahmen in aller Welt*. Stuttgard: Dieck, 1925.

Deloria, Vine Jr. "The Indians." In *Buffalo Bill and the Wild West*. The Brooklyn Museum, Museum of Art at the Carnegie Institute, and the Buffalo Bill Historical Center, pp. 45–56. Brooklyn: Brooklyn Museum, 1981.

Dering, Florian. *Volksbelustigungen: Eine bildreiche Kulturgeschichte von den Fahr-, Belustigungs- und Geschicklichkeitsgeschäften der Schausteller vom 18. Jahrhundert bis zur Gegenwart*. Nördlingen: Franz Greno, 1986.

Desmond, Jane. "Displaying Death, Animating Life: Changing Fictions of 'Liveness' from Taxidermy to Animatronics." In *Representing Animals*, ed. Nigel Rothfels, pp. 159–79. Bloomington: Indiana University Press, 2002.

———. *Staging Tourism: Bodies on Display from Waikiki to Sea World*. Chicago: University of Chicago Press, 1999.

Dittrich, Lothar. "Zoobauten als Ausdruck geistiger Zeitströmungen: Bemerkungen zum Verständnis der historischen Bausubstanz deutscher Zoos." *Der zoologische Garten* N.F. 68, no. 6 (1998): 325–31.

Dittrich, Lothar, and Annelore Rieke-Müller. *Carl Hagenbeck (1844–1913): Tierhandel und Schaustellungen im Deutschen Kaiserreich*. Frankfurt am Main: Peter Lang, 1998.

Dominik, Emil. "Die Nubier im zoologischen Garten Berlins." *Über Land und Meer* 41 (1878): 186–87, 189.

"Dr. Carver's Wild-Amerika." *Hamburger Fremdenblatt*, 25 August 1890, 1st supplement.

"Dr. Carver's Wild-Amerika." *Hamburger Nachrichten*, 22 August 1890, 2nd supplement.

"Dr. Carver's Wild-Amerika." *Hamburger Nachrichten*, 7 September 1890, morn. ed.

Dreesbach, Anne. *Gezähmte Wilde: Die Zurschaustellung "exotischer" Menschen in Deutschland 1870–1940*. Frankfurt am Main: Campus, 2005.

Dunlop, Beth. *Building a Dream: The Art of Disney Architecture*. New York: Harry N. Abrams, 1996.

Eco, Umberto. *Travels in Hyperreality: Essays*. Trans. William Weaver. San Diego: Harcourt Brace Jovanovich, 1986.

Edwards, Elizabeth, ed. *Anthropology and Photography, 1860–1920*. New Haven: Yale University Press, 1992.

———. "Photographic 'Types': The Pursuit of Method." *Visual Anthropology* 3 (1990): 235–58.

Ehrlinger, David. "The Hagenbeck Legacy." *International Zoo Yearbook* 29 (1989): 6–10.

Eisner, Lotte H. *Fritz Lang*. 1976; New York: Da Capo Press, 1986.

Engberg, Marguerite. *Dansk Stumfilm*. Vol. 1. Copenhagen: Rhodos Internationalt Forlag for Videnskab, Kunst og Debat, 1977.

———. "The Influence of Danish Cinema on German Film 1910–1920." *Griffithiana* 13, no. 38–39 (October 1990): 127–33.

"Die Eröffnung von Hagenbecks Tierparadies." *Hamburger Nachrichten*, 7 May 1907, eve. ed.

"Die Eskimofamilie im zoologischen Garten zu Berlin." *Daheim* 14, no. 28 (1878).

Esser, Michael. "Spaces in Motion: Remarks on Set Design in the German Silent Film." In *Berlin 1900–1933: Architecture and Design*, ed. Tilmann Buddensieg, pp. 169–83. Berlin: Mann, 1987.

"Die Expansion der 'Decla.'" *Lichtbildbühne* (11 October 1919): 24.

Farquhar, Peter H. "Managing Brand Equity." *Marketing Research* (September 1989): 24–33.

Feldman, Mark Bennett. "Narrating, Displaying and Spectateing the Animal: Frank Norris, Jack London, and the Urban Zoo." Ph.D. diss., University of California, Berkeley, 2005.

Ferdinand, Miriam. "'Völkerschauen' in Hamburg im Spiegel der Lokalpresse während des Kaiserreichs (1875–1917)." Master's thesis, Universität Hamburg, 2004. (TCH)

Fiedler, Leslie. *Freaks: Myths and Images of the Secret Self.* New York: Simon & Schuster, 1978.

Fienup-Riordan, Ann. "Johan Adrian Jacobsen Brings Treasures from Alaska." In *Yup'ik Elders at the Ethnologisches Museum Berlin: Fieldwork Turned on Its Head*, with Yup'ik trans. Marie Meade and German trans. Sonja Lührmann, Anja Karlson, and Adelaid Pauls, pp. 3–34. Seattle: University of Washington Press, 2005.

Figdor, Karl. "Harakiri." *Erste internationale Filmzeitung* 50 (20 December 1919): 32.

"Eine Filmstadt im Hagenbeckpark Stellingen." *Der Film* (12 October 1919): 32.

Fischer, Wilhelm. *Aus dem Leben und Wirken eines interessanten Mannes*. Hamburg: Baumann, 1896.

Fjellman, Stephen M. *Vinyl Leaves: Walt Disney World and America*. Boulder, CO: Westview Press, 1992.

Flint, Richard W. "American Showmen and European Dealers: Commerce in Wild Animals in Nineteenth-Century America." In *New Worlds, New Animals: From Menagerie to Zoological Park in the Nineteenth Century*, ed. R. J. Hoage and William A. Deiss, pp. 97–108. Baltimore: Johns Hopkins University Press, 1996.

Forch, Dr. "Die Sensation im Kinodrama und anderwärts." *Bild und Film* 2, no. 7 (1912/13): 164–65.

Foucault, Michel. "Of Other Spaces." *Diacritics* 16, no. 1 (spring 1986): 22–27.

Fox, Charles Philip, and Tom Parkinson. *The Circus in America*. Waukesha, WI: Country Beautiful, 1969.

Fraas, E. "Aus der Saurierwelt der Vorzeit in Hagenbecks Tierpark zu Stellingen." *Kolonie und Heimat* 4, no. 1 (1910): 6, 7.

Friebe, Wolfgang. *Buildings of the World Exhibitions*. Trans. Jenny Vowles and Paul Roper. Leipzig: Edition Leipzig, 1985.

Friedberg, Anne. *Window Shopping: Cinema and the Postmodern*. Berkeley: University of California Press, 1993.

Fusco, Coco. "The Other History of Intercultural Performance." In *English Is Broken Here: Notes on Cultural Fusion in the Americas*, pp. 37–63. New York: The New Press, 1995.

Gad, Urban. *Der Film: Seine Mittel, Seine Ziele*. Trans. Julia Koppel. Berlin: Schuster & Loeffler, 1922.

Garelick, Rhonda. "*Bayadères*, *Stéréorama*, and *Vahat-Loukoum*: Technological Realism in the Age of Empire." In *Spectacles of Realism: Gender, Body, Genre*, ed. Margaret Cohen and Christopher Prendergast, pp. 294–319. Minneapolis: University of Minnesota Press, 1995.

Gaudreault, André. "Detours in Film Narrative: The Development of Cross-Cutting." In *Early Cinema: Space, Frame, Narrative*, ed. Thomas Elsaesser, pp. 133–50. London: BFI, 1990.

Goldmann, Stefan. "Wilde in Europa: Aspekte und Orte ihrer Zurschaustellung." In *Wir und die Wilden: Einblicke in eine kannibalische Beziehung*, ed. Thomas Theye, pp. 243–69. Reinbek: Rowohlt, 1984.

Goldsmith, Ben, and Tom O'Regan. *The Film Studio: Film Production in the Global Economy*. Lanham, MD: Rowman & Littlefield, 2005.

Gottdiener, Mark. *The Theming of America: Dreams, Visions, and Commercial Spaces*. Boulder, CO: Westview Press, 1997.

Gould, Stephen Jay. *Bully for Brontosaurus: Reflections in Natural History*. New York: Norton, 1991.

Grabowsky, Fritz. "Noch einmal 'Carl Hagenbeck und sein Tierparadies.'" *Zoologischer Garten* 40 (1909).

Grafe, Frieda. "Einen Berliner Bären für Madame Butterfly." *Süddeutsche Zeitung*, 27 August 1987.

Grau, Oliver. *Virtual Art: From Illusion to Immersion*. Trans. Gloria Custance. Cambridge, MA: MIT Press, 2003.

Greenhalgh, Paul. *Ephemeral Vistas: The Expositions Universelles, Great Exhibitions and World's Fairs, 1851–1939*. Manchester: Manchester University Press, 1988.

Gretzschel, Matthias, Klaus Gille, and Michael Zapf. *Hagenbeck: Ein zoologisches Paradies: Hundert Jahre Tierpark in Stellingen*. Hamburg: Carl Hagenbeck, 2007.

Griffiths, Alison. "'Shivers Down Your Spine': Panoramas and the Origins of the Cinematic Reenactment." *Screen* 44, no. 1 (spring 2003): 1–37.

———. *Wondrous Difference: Cinema, Anthropology, and Turn-of-the-Century Visual Culture*. New York: Columbia University Press, 2002.

"Grosse Völkerschau: Birma." *Hamburger Fremdenblatt*, 10 May 1913.

Groth, Claus. "Harakiri." *Das Glashaus* 1 (January 1920): 6–7.

Gunning, Tom. "The Cinema of Attractions: Early Film, Its Spectator and the Avant-Garde." In *Early Cinema: Space, Frame, Narrative*, ed. Thomas Elaesser, with Adam Barker, pp. 56–62. London: BFI, 1990.

———. *D. W. Griffith and the Origins of American Film Narrative: The Early Years at Biograph*. Urbana: University of Illinois Press, 1991.

———. "From the Opium Den to the Theatre of Morality: Moral Discourse and the Film Process in Early American Cinema." In *The Silent Cinema Reader*, ed. Lee Grieveson and Peter Krämer, pp. 145–54. London and New York: Routledge, 2004.

———. "Weaving a Narrative: Style and Economic Background in Griffith's Biograph Films." In *Early Cinema: Space, Frame, Narrative*, ed. Thomas Elsaesser, pp. 336–47. London: BFI, 1990.

"H. H. Vergnügungs-Park Hugo Haase A.-G. Stellingen." *Hamburger Fremdenblatt*, 21 June 1914.

Haberland, Wolfgang. "Adrian Jacobsen on Pine Ridge Reservation, 1910." *European Review of Native American Studies* 1, no. 1 (1988): 11–15.

———. "'Diese Indianer sind falsch': Neun Bella Coola im Deutschen Reich 1885–86." *Archiv für Völkerkunde* 42 (1988): 3–65.

———. "Nine Bella Coolas in Germany." In *Indians and Europe: An Interdisciplinary Collection of Essays*, ed. Christian Feest, pp. 337–74. Aachen: Edition Herodot, Rader Verlag, 1987.

Haenlein, Carl-Albrecht, and Wolfgang Till, eds. *Menschen, Tiere, Sensationen: Zirkusplakate 1880–1930*. Hannover: Kestner-Gesellschaft, 1978.

"Hagenbeck als Helfer für die Kinematographie." *Lichtbildbühne* (9 November 1912): 8, 17.

"Hagenbeck auf der Berliner Gewerbe-Ausstellung." *Hamburger Correspondent*, 11 June 1896, eve. ed., 1.

Hagenbeck, Carl. *Beasts and Men: Being Carl Hagenbeck's Experience for Half a Century among Wild Animals*. Trans. Hugh S. R. Elliott and A.[rthur] G.[ordon] Thacker; introduction by P. Chalmers Mitchell. London: Longmans, Green, and Co., 1909.

———. *Von Tieren und Menschen: Erlebnisse und Erfahrungen von Carl Hagenbeck*. Rev. and enl. ed. Berlin-Charlottenburg: Vita Deutsches Verlagshaus, 1909.

Hagenbeck, John. *Fünfundzwanzig Jahre Ceylon: Erlebnisse und Abenteuer im Tropenparadies*. Ed. Viktor Ottmann. Dresden: Verlag Deutsches Buchwerkstätten, 1922.

———. *Kreuz und Quer durch die indische Welt: Erlebnisse und Abenteurer in Vorder- und Hinterindien, Sumatra, Java und auf den Andamanen*. Ed. Victor Ottmann. Dresden: Verlag Deutsche Buchwerkstätten, 1922.

———. "Raubtiere im Film." In *Das Kulturfilmbuch*, ed. Edgar Beyfuss, pp. 120–22. Berlin: Chryselius & Schulz, 1924.

Hagenbeck, John George. *Mit Indiens Fahrendem Volk*. Berlin: Scherl, 1932.

Hagenbeck, Lorenz. *Den Tieren gehört mein Herz*. 2nd ed. Hamburg: Hoffmann and Campe, 1955.

"Hagenbeck's Animals Take the Stage." *New York Times*, 5 October 1902.

"Hagenbecks Kino und die Freilicht-Arena in Stellingen." *Hamburger Fremdenblatt*, 10 May 1913, 5th supplement.

"Hagenbeck's Near Famine." *New York Times*, 9 October 1914.

"Hagenbecks neuer Tierpark in Stellingen." *Hamburger Fremdenblatt*, 10 March 1903. (SAH, A902 "Hagenbecks Tierpark")

"Hagenbeck's Panorama of a Northern Sea." *Scientific American Supplement*, 11 September 1897, 18098–99.

"Hagenbeck's Performing Animals: Wonderful and Thrilling Exhibitions at the Madison Square Garden." *New York Times*, 4 September 1894.

"Hagenbecks Tierparadies." *Hamburger Nachrichten*, 24 August 1906, eve. ed. (SAH, A902 "Hagenbecks Tierpark")

"Hagenbecks Tierpark." *Hamburger Echo*, 7 May 1907, 2nd ed. (SAH, A902 "Hagenbecks Tierpark")

"Hagenbecks Tierpark." *Hamburger Fremdenblatt*, 17 May 1913.

"Hagenbecks Tierpark in Stellingen." *Hamburger Correspondent*, 6 May 1907, morn. ed. (SAH, A902 "Hagenbecks Tierpark")

"Hagenbeck's Trained Animals: Fast-Growing in Popularity at Manhattan Beach." *New York Times*, 29 July 1894.

"Hagenbeck's Zoo a 'White Elephant.'" *New York Times*, 17 October 1914.

"Ein 'Hagenbecksches Tierpanorama.'" *Berliner Tageblatt*, 12 May 1898.

Hake, Sabine. *The Cinema's Third Machine: Writing on Film in Germany 1907–1933*. Lincoln and London: University of Nebraska Press, 1993.

——. *German National Cinema*. New York: Routledge, 2002.

Hampicke, Evelyn. "The Danish Influence: David Oliver and Nordisk in Germany." In *A Second Life: German Cinema's First Decades*, ed. Thomas Elsaesser, pp. 72–78. Amsterdam: Amsterdam University Press, 1996.

Hancocks, David. *Animals and Architecture*. New York: Praeger, 1971.

——. *A Different Nature: The Paradoxical World of Zoos and Their Uncertain Future*. Berkeley: University of California Press, 2001.

"Hanseatisches Panopticum." *Hamburger Fremdenblatt*, 29 November 1885, 1st supplement.

Hanson, Elizabeth. *Animal Attractions: Nature on Display in American Zoos*. Princeton: Princeton University Press, 2002.

"Harakiri." *Der Film* 51 (21 December 1919): 40.

"Harakiri." *Illustrirte Film-Kurier* no. 11 (1919): 3.

"Harakiri." *Lichtbildbühne* (27 December 1919).

Haraway, Donna. "Teddy Bear Patriarchy: Taxidermy in the Garden of Eden, New York City, 1908–1936." *Social Text* 11 (winter 1984/1985): 20–64.

Hardt, Ursula. *From Caligari to California: Erich Pommer's Life in the International Film Wars*. Providence: Berghahn, 1996.

Harper, Warren. "Hagenbeck of Hamburg: The Modern Noah." *Men and Women for November 1904*, 8. (TCH)

Harris, Neil. "Expository Expositions: Preparing for the Theme Parks." In *Designing Disney's Theme Parks: The Architecture of Reassurance*, ed. Karal Ann Marling, pp. 19–27. Paris: Flammarion, 1997.

——. *Humbug: The Art of P. T. Barnum*. Chicago: University of Chicago Press, 1973.

Harrison, Mark. *Climates and Constitutions: Health, Race, Environment and British Imperialism in India, 1600–1850*. New Dehli and New York: Oxford University Press, 1999.

Hartung, Max. "Die Sächsisch-Thüringische Industrie- und Gewerbe-Ausstellung in Leipzig." *Die Gartenlaube* (1897): 316–20.

Headrick, Daniel R. *The Tentacles of Progress: Technology Transfer in the Age of Imperialism, 1850–1940*. New York: Oxford University Press, 1988.

———. *The Tools of Empire: Technology and European Imperialism in the Nineteenth Century*. New York: Oxford University Press, 1981.

Hediger, Heini. *Man and Animal in the Zoo: Zoo Biology*. Trans. Gwynne Vevers and Winwood Reade. New York: Delacorte Press, 1969.

Heimbach, Ariane. "Die inszenierte Wildnis: Exotische Tierwelt im Film." In *Triviale Tropen: Exotische Reise- und Abenteuerfilme aus Deutschland 1919–1939*, ed. Jörg Schöningh, pp. 158–66. Munich: edition text + kritik, 1997.

Hellwald, Friedrich von. "Die Kalmücken." *Die Gartenlaube* 32, no. 39 (1884): 644–45.

Heyden, Ulrich van der. "Südafrikanische 'Berliner': Die Kolonial- und Transvaal-Ausstellung in Berlin und die Haltung der deutschen Missionsgesellschaften zur Präsentation fremder Menschen und Kulturen." In *Fremde Erfahrungen: Asiaten und Afrikaner in Deutschland, Österreich und in der Schweiz bis 1945*, ed. Gerhard Höpp, pp. 135–56. Berlin: Das Arabische Buch, 1996.

Hinsley, Curtis M., Jr. *Savages and Scientists: The Smithsonian Institution and the Development of American Anthropology 1846–1910*. Washington, DC: Smithsonian Institution Press, 1981.

Hoage, R. J., and William A. Deiss, eds. *New Worlds, New Animals: From Menagerie to Zoological Park in the Nineteenth Century*. Baltimore: Johns Hopkins University Press, 1996.

Hobsbawm, Eric. *The Age of Capital, 1848–1875*. 1975. New York: Vintage, 1996.

———. *The Age of Empire 1875–1914*. New York: Vintage, 1987.

"How Animals are Tamed: A Talk with Carl Hagenbeck, the European Barnum." *New York Sun*, 17 July 1893. (TCH)

"How to Train Wild Beasts: Carl Hagenbeck Tells a Daily News Reporter All About a Strange Business." *Chicago News*, 14 April 1893. (TCH)

Huret, Jules. "Le paradis terrestre de M. Hagenbeck." In *En Allemagne: De Hambourg aux Marches de Pologne*, pp. 238–51. Paris: Bibliothèque-Charpentier, 1908.

Hyde, Ralph. *Panoramania! The Art and Entertainment of the 'All-Embracing' View*. London: Trefoil, 1988.

Hyson, Jeffrey. "Jungles of Eden: The Design of American Zoos." In *Environmentalism in Landscape Architecture*, ed. Michel Conan, pp. 23–44. Washington, DC: Dumbarton Oaks, 2000.

"In das Paradies der biblischen Schöpfungsgeschichte." *Volks-Zeitung*, 12 May 1898.

"In Umlauff's Weltmuseum." *Hamburger Fremdenblatt*, 30 November 1891, 2nd supplement. (SAH L 2/1)

"Die Indianer im Gärtnerplatzthater und im Orpheum." *Münchener Bote*, 30 April 1890. (DPL)

"Die Indianer im Zoologischen Garten." *Frankfurter Journal*, 9 May 1879.

"Indianer in der Stadt." *Münchener Nachrichten*, 25 April 1890. (DPL)

"Indianer in Hagenbeck's Thierpark." *Hamburger Fremdenblatt*, 26 August 1890, 1st supplement.

"Indianer-Spielen." *Tageblatt* (Dresden), 4 June 1890. (DPL)

Ingram, Susan, and Markus Reisenleiter, eds. *Placing History: Themed Environments, Urban Consumption and the Public Entertainment Sphere / Orte und ihre Geschichte(n): Themenwelten, urbaner Konsum und Freizeitöffentlichkeit*. Vienna: Turia + Kant, 2003.

Jacobsen, Adrian. *Die weiße Grenze: Abenteuer eines alten Seebären rund um den Polarkreis*. Ed. Albrecht Janssen. Leipzig: Brockhaus, 1931.

Jacobsen, Johan Adrian. *Alaskan Voyage 1881–1883: An Expedition to the Northwest Coast of America*. Trans. Erna Gunther from the German text of Adrian Woldt. 1884. Chicago: University of Chicago Press, 1977.

Jacobsen, Wolfgang. *Babelsberg: Das Filmstudio*. Berlin: Argon, 1992.

——. *Erich Pommer: Ein Produzent macht Filmgeschichte*. Berlin: Argon, 1989.

Jäger, H. "Die Zoologischen Gärten und ihre scenische Anordnung." *Beilage zur Illustrirten Zeitung* (3 January 1863): 19, 22.

Jansen, Wolfgang. *Das Varieté: Die glanzvolle Geschichte einer unterhaltenden Kunst*. Berlin: Edition Hentrich, 1990.

Joeden-Forgey, Elisa von. "Race Power in Postcolonial Germany: The German Africa Show and the National Socialist State, 1935–1940." In *Germany's Colonial Pasts*, ed. Eric Ames, Marcia Klotz, and Lora Wildenthal, pp. 167–88. Lincoln: University of Nebraska Press, 2005.

Kabatek, Wolfgang. *Imagerie des Anderen im Weimarer Kino*. Bielefeld: transcript Verlag, 2003.

Kadich, H. M. von. "Gastliche Tage bei Karl Hagenbeck." *Der Zoologische Garten* 64, no. 2 (February 1903): 37–42; no. 3 (March 1903): 83–88.

Kaes, Anton, ed. *Kino-Debatte: Texte zum Verhältnis von Literatur und Film 1909–1929*. Munich: Deutscher Taschenbuch; Tübingen: Niemeyer, 1978.

"Der Kaiser in Stellingen-Langenfelde." *Lokal-Anzeiger für Stellingen-Langenfelde, Eidelstedt, Lokstedt, Niendorf und Schnelsen*, 21 June 1908. (TCH)

Kasson, John F. *Amusing the Million: Coney Island at the Turn of the Century*. New York: Hill and Wang, 1978.

Kasson, Joy. *Buffalo Bill's Wild West: Celebrity, Memory, and Popular History*. New York: Hill and Wang, 2000.

Katt, Friedrich. "Hagenbecks Tierparadies." *Zoologischer Beobachter* 50, no. 1 (1909): 370–71.

Kaufmann, Edward N. "The Architectural Museum from World's Fair to Restoration Village." *Assemblage* 9 (June 1989): 21–39.

Keller, Kevin Lane. *Strategic Brand Management: Building, Measuring, and Managing Brand Equity*. Upper Saddle River, NJ: Prentice Hall, 1998.

"'King of the Zoos': Death of Herr Hagenbeck." *The Daily Mail* (London), 16 April 1913. (TCH)

Kirchhoff, Alfred. "Die Nubier in Halle." *Mittheilungen des Vereins für Erdkunde zu Halle* (1879): 49–64.

Kirshenblatt-Gimblett, Barbara. *Destination Culture: Tourism, Museums, and Heritage.* Berkeley: University of California Press, 1998.

———."The Ethnographic Burlesque." *TDR: The Drama Review* 42, no. 2 (summer 1998): 175–80.

Kisling, Vernon N., Jr. *Zoo and Aquarium History: Ancient Animal Collections to Zoological Gardens.* Boca Raton, FL: CRC Press, 2000.

Klein, Naomi. *No Logo.* 1st rev. ed. New York: Picador, 2002.

Knauer, Friedrich. *Der zoologische Garten: Entwicklungsgang, Anlage und Betrieb unserer Tiergärten.* Leipzig: Theodor Thomas, n.d. (1914).

Kober, August Heinrich. "Carl Hagenbeck 1844–1913." In *Die Großen Deutschen: Neue Deutsche Biographie*, ed. Willy Andreas and Wilhelm von Scholz, vol. 4, pp. 301–14. Berlin: Propyläen, 1936.

Koch, Gottlieb von. *Die Aufstellung der Tiere im neuen Museum zu Darmstadt.* Leipzig: Wilhelm Engelmann, 1899.

Kocks, Katinka. *Indianer im Kaiserreich: Völkerschauen und Wild West Shows zwischen 1880 und 1914.* Gerolzhofen: Oettermann, 2004.

König, Eva. "Johan Adrian Jacobsen: Impresario und Sammler (1853–1947)." In *Indianer 1858–1928: Photographische Reise von Alaska bis Feuerland*, ed. Eva König, pp. 31–35. Heidelberg: Edition Braus, 2002.

Kopas, Cliff. *Bella Coola.* Vancouver: Mitchell Press, 1970.

Kort, Pamela, and Max Hollein, eds. *I Like America: Fictions of the Wild West.* Munich: Prestel, 2006.

Kosok, Lisa, and Mathilde Jamin, eds. *Viel Vergnügen: Öffentlichen Lustbarkeiten im Ruhrgebiet der Jahrhundertwende.* Essen: Peter Pomp, 1992.

Köstering, Susanne. *Natur zum Anschauen: Das Naturkundemuseum des deutschen Kaiserreichs 1871–1914.* Cologne: Böhlau, 2003.

Kracauer, Siegfried. "Calico-World: The UFA City in Neubabelsberg." In *The Mass Ornament: Weimar Essays*, ed. Thomas Y. Levin, pp. 281–88. Cambridge, MA: Harvard University Press, 1995.

Kramer, Paul. "Making Concessions: Race and Empire Revisited at the Philippine Exposition, St. Louis, 1901–1905." *Radical History Review* 73 (1999): 74–114.

Kreimeier, Klaus. *The UFA Story: A History of Germany's Greatest Film Company 1918–1945.* Trans. Robert and Rita Kimber. New York: Hill and Wang, 1996.

Kreis, Karl Markus. "Indians Playing, Indians Praying: Native Americans in Wild West Shows and Catholic Missions." In *Germans and Indians: Fantasies, Encounters, Projections*, ed. Colin G. Calloway, Gerd Gemünden, and Susanne Zantop, pp. 195–212. Lincoln: University of Nebraska Press, 2002.

Krüger, Albert G. "Ein Tag im Hagenbeckschen Tierpark zu Stellingen bei Hamburg." *Deutscher Hausschatz: Illustrierte Familien-Zeitschrift* 38.3 (1912): 112–16.

Kuenheim, Haug von. *Carl Hagenbeck*. Hamburg: Ellert & Richter, 2007.

Kyriazi, Gary. *The Great American Amusement Parks: A Pictorial History*. Secaucus, NJ: Citadel Press, 1976.

L., H. "Indien in Johannisthal." *Der Film* (7 August 1920): 48, 51.

Lamprecht, Gerhard. *Deutsche Stummfilme 1903–1912*. Vol. 1. Berlin: Deutsche Kinemathek, 1969.

Landes, David S. *The Unbound Prometheus: Technological Change and Industrial Development in Western Europe from 1750 to the Present*. 2nd ed. Cambridge: Cambridge University Press, 2003.

Lange, Britta. *Echt, unecht, lebensecht: Menschenbilder im Umlauf*. Berlin: Kadmos, 2006.

Lant, Antonia. "The Curse of the Pharaoh, or How Cinema Contracted Egyptomania." *October* 59 (Winter 1992): 87–112.

"The Late Carl Hagenbeck: 'King of the Zoos.'" *The Daily Telegraph* (London), 16 April 1913. (TCH)

"Leben wie ein Film: Joseph Delmont, ein jünger 60-jähriger." N. pub., 6 May 1933 (BA-FA, P "Delmont, Joseph")

"Die lebende Brücke." *Lichtbildbühne* (16 November 1912): 21, 26.

Lehmann, Alfred. "Schaustellungen im Leipziger Zoo." In *Vom Leipziger Zoo: Aus der Entwicklung einer Volksbildungsstätte*, ed. Karl Max Schneider, pp. 72–92. Leipzig: Geest & Portig 1953.

——. "Zeitgenössische Bilder der ersten Völkerschauen." In *Von fremden Völkern und Kulturen: Hans Plische zum 65. Geburtstag*, ed. Werner Lang, Walter Nippold, and Günther Spannaus, pp. 31–44. Düsseldorf: Droste, 1955.

Leonhardt, Em Erich. "Die heutigen Aufgaben der Tiergärten." *Zoologischer Beobachter* 50, no. 11 (1909): 321–28.

Leutemann, Heinrich. "Die Eskimos in Deutschland." *Daheim* 14, no. 28 (1878).

——. *Lebensbeschreibung des Thierhändlers Carl Hagenbeck*. Hamburg: Hagenbeck, 1887.

——. *Leutemann's Bilder aus dem Völkerleben mit erläuterndem Text von Prof. Dr. Alfred Kirchhoff*. Fürth: Löwensohn, 1888.

——. "Nordische Gäste." *Die Gartenlaube* 75 (1875): 742–44.

——. *Zonen-Bilder: Nach Aquarellen von Heinrich Leutemann, mit erklärenden Schilderungen für die Jugend von Hermann Wagner*. Stuttgart: Julius Hoffmann, 1876.

Lindenberg, Paul. *Pracht-Album photographischer Aufnahmen der Berliner Gewerbe-Ausstellung 1896*. Berlin: Werner, 1896.

Livingston, Bernard. *Zoo: Animals, People, Places*. New York: Arbor House, 1974.

Lloyd, Jill. *German Expressionism: Primitivism and Modernity*. New Haven: Yale University Press, 1991.

Loacker, Armin, and Ines Steiner, eds. *Imaginierte Antike: österreichische Monumental-Stummfilme: Historienbilder und Geschichtskonstruktionen in* Sodom und Gomorrha, Samson und Delila, Die Sklavenkönigin *und* Salambô. Vienna: Filmarchiv Austria, 2002.

Loisel, Gustave. *Histoire des menageries de l'antiquité à nos jours*. Vol. 3. Paris: Doins, 1912.

Loring, Stephen. "In Torngak's Realm: The Nineteenth-Century Photography of Moravian Missionaries in Labrador." In *Imaging the Arctic*, ed. Jonathan C. H. King and Henrietta Lidchi, pp. 207–20. Seattle: University of Washington Press, 1998.

Lund, C. "Aus Hagenbecks Tierpark." *Über Land und Meer* 97, no. 23 (1907): 580–81.

Lutz, Hartmut, ed. and trans. *The Diary of Abraham Ulrikab: Text and Context*. Ottawa: University of Ottawa Press, 2005.

MacCannell, Dean. *The Tourist: A New Theory of the Leisure Class*. 1976. Berkeley: University of California, 1999.

"Maker of Model Zoos.—What Hagenbeck Could Have Done for London.—Unrealized Ambition.—Once Tried to Buy the Crystal Palace." *The Manchester Guardian*, 16 April 1913. (TCH)

Malhotra, Ruth. *Manege frei: Artisten- und Circusplakate von Adolph Friedländer*. Dortmund: Harenberg, 1979.

"A Man Called Apache George." San Francisco *Times*, 18 June 1893. (BBHC-Carver)

Marcus, Greil. "Forty Years of Overstatement: Criticism and the Disney Theme Parks." In *Designing Disney's Theme Parks: The Architecture of Reassurance*, ed. Karal Ann Marling, pp. 201–7. Paris: Flammarion, 1997.

Marling, Karal Ann. "Imagineering the Disney Theme Parks." In *Designing Disney's Theme Parks: The Architecture of Reassurance*, ed. Karal Ann Marling, pp. 29–176. Paris: Flammarion, 1997.

Martin, Philipp Leopold. *Die Praxis der Naturgeschichte*. Vol. 2. Weimar: Voigt, 1870.

Marx, Karl. "The Fetishism of the Commodity and Its Secret." In *Capital*, vol. 1, pp. 163–77. London: Verso, 1976.

Mathur, Saloni. "Living Ethnological Exhibits: The Case of 1886." *Cultural Anthropology* 15, no. 4 (November 2000): 492–524.

Mayer, Rudolf. "Ein Gang durch die C. Hagenbeck'sche Handels-Menagerie in Hamburg." *Zoologischer Beobachter* 14 (1873): 25–27.

McClintock, Anne. *Imperial Leather: Race, Gender and Sexuality in the Colonial Contest*. New York: Routledge, 1995.

"A Menagerie Monarch—Training Wild Beasts—The Methods Pursued by Karl Hagenbeck, the King." *New York Journal*, 16 July 1893. (TCH)

Menges, Josef. "Bemerkungen über den deutschen Thierhandel von Nord-Ost-Afrika." *Der Zoologische Garten* 17 (1876): 229–36.

Meyer, Margot. "Film-Kater. . . ." *Film-Kurier* (9 October 1919).

———. "Freigabe des Hamburg-Stellinger Terrains." *Film-Kurier* 2, no. 87 (27 April 1920).

———. "Harakiri." *Film-Kurier* (27 September 1919).

Mitchell, Timothy. *Colonizing Egypt*. Cambridge: Cambridge University Press, 1988.

Mitchell, Timothy F. *Art and Science in German Landscape Painting, 1770–1840*. Oxford and New York: Oxford University Press, 1993.

Mitman, Gregg. *Reel Nature: America's Romance with Wildlife on Film*. Cambridge, MA: Harvard University Press, 1999.

Möbius, Karl. "Die Tierwelt der Erde." In *Geographisches Handbuch zu Andrees Handatlas*, ed. Albert Scobel, pp. 163–75. Bielefeld: Velhagen, 1902.

"A Modern Noah." *Minneapolis Spectator*, 1 June 1893. (TCH)

Mohr, Erna. "Das Geschlecht Hagenbeck." *Der Zoologische Garten*, N. F., 21, no. 1 (1954): 2–9.

"More Wonders Promised: The Hagenbeck Arena Company Secures Another Lot of Trained Animals." *New York Times*, 2 August 1894.

Morgan, Lewis Henry. *Systems of Consanguinity and Affinity of the Human Family*. Smithsonian Contributions to Knowledge 218. Washington, DC: Smithsonian Institution, 1871.

Moses, L. G. *Wild West Shows and the Images of American Indians, 1883–1933*. Albuquerque: University of New Mexico Press, 1996.

Mottram, Ron. *The Danish Cinema Before Dreyer*. Metuchen: Scarecrow, 1988.

"Mr. Carl Hagenbeck, the King of Wild Animal Trainers." *Tit-Bits* (28 July 1900): 413.

Müller, Corinna. *Frühe deutsche Kinematographie: Formale, wirtschaftliche und kulturelle Entwicklungen 1907–1912*. Stuttgart: Metzler, 1994.

Murphy, David Thomas. *German Exploration of the Polar World: A History, 1870–1940*. Lincoln: University of Nebraska Press, 2002.

"Das Museum Umlauff als Filmfundus." *Der Film* (10 May 1919): 28.

Musser, Charles. "Moving Towards Fictional Narratives: Story Films Become the Dominant Product, 1903–1904." In *The Silent Cinema Reader*, ed. Lee Grieveson and Peter Krämer, pp. 87–102. London and New York: Routledge, 2004.

Myers, Arthur B. R. *Life with the Hamran Arabs*. London: Smith, Elder, 1876.

Neergaard, Ebbe, and Erik Ulrichsen. *The Story of Danish Film*. Copenhagen: Det danske selskab, 1963.

"Die neue Völkerschau bei Hagenbeck" (review of the Egyptian show). *Hamburger Echo*, 7 May 1912.

Neumann, Dietrich, ed. *Film Architecture: From* Metropolis *to* Blade Runner. Munich: Prestel Verlag, 1999.

Neumann-Hofer, Otto. "Karl Hagenbeck und sein Tierparadies." *Daheim: Ein deutsches Familienblatt und Illustrationen* no. 23 (6 March 1909): 11–15.

Nielsen, J. F. Svejgaard. *Bogen om Elleore*. Copenhagen: Grafisk Klub Tretten Cicero, 1958. (DFI)

Niemeyer, Günter. *Hagenbeck: Geschichte und Geschichten*. Hamburg: Hans Christians Verlag, 1972.

Nissen, Claus. *Die zoologische Buchillustration: Ihre Bibliographie und Geshichte*. Vol. 1. Stuttgart: Anton Hiersemann, 1966.

Nørgaard, Erik. *Levende Billeder i Danmark*. Copenhagen: Lademann, 1971.

The North-West Coast of America: Being the Results of Recent Ethnological Researches from the Collections of the Royal Museums at Berlin, Published by the Directors of the Ethnological Department, Translated from the German. New York: Mead, 1883.

Nye, David E. *Electrifying America: Social Meanings of a New Technology, 1880–1914*. Cambridge, MA: MIT Press, 1990.

Nyhart, Lynn K. "Civic and Economic Zoology in Nineteenth-Century Germany: The 'Living Communities' of Karl Möbius." *Isis* 89, no. 4 (December 1998): 605–30.

Obst, Arthur. "Der Schöpfer des Tierparadieses." *Hamburger Fremdenblatt*, 12 November 1908. (SAH, A902 "Hagenbecks Tierpark")

Oettermann, Stephan. *The Panorama: History of a Mass Medium*. Trans. Deborah Lucas Schneider. New York: Zone Books, 1997.

———. "Die Reise mit den Augen: 'Oramas' in Deutschland." In *Sehsucht: Das Panorama als Massenunterhaltung des 19. Jahrhunderts*, ed. Marie-Louise von Plessen, pp. 42–51. Basel and Frankfurt am Main: Stroemfeld/Roter Stern, 1993.

Oksiloff, Assenka. *Picturing the Primitive: Visual Culture, Ethnography, and Early German Cinema*. New York: Palgrave, 2001.

Olsen, Ole. *Filmens Eventyr og Mit Eget*. Copenhagen: Jespersen og Pios Forlag, 1940.

Olimsky, Fritz. "Film-Gründungsfieber!" *Berliner Börsen-Zeitung* (n.d. [1919]). Sammlung Fritz Olimsky. (DK)

———. "Harakiri." *Berliner Börsen*-Zeitung, 21 December 1919.

Peel, C. V. A. *The Zoological Gardens of Europe: Their History and Chief Features*. London: Robinson, 1903.

Peiss, Kathy. *Cheap Amusements: Working Women and Leisure in Turn-of-the-Century New York*. Philadelphia: Temple University Press, 1986.

Pelc, Ortwin. "Hagenbeck auf den Weltausstellungen in Chicago (1893) und St. Louis (1904)." *Zeitschrift des Vereins für Hamburgische Geschichte* 86 (2000): 89–113.

Pelc, Ortwin, and Matthias Gretzschel. *Hagenbeck: Tiere, Menschen, Sensationen*. Hamburg: Hamburger Abendblatt, Axel Springer Verlag, 1998.

Penny, H. Glenn. *Objects of Culture: Ethnology and Ethnographic Museums in Imperial Germany*. Chapel Hill: University of North Carolina Press, 2002.

Pfening, Fred D., Jr. "How Wallace Bought Hagenbeck." *Bandwagon* (July–August 1964): 11–12.

"Pfingsten in Hagenbecks Tierpark in Stellingen." *Hamburger Nachrichten*, 18 May 1910.

Philips, Deborah. "Narrativised Spaces: The Functions of Story in the Theme Park." In *Leisure/Tourism Geographies: Practices and Geographical Knowledge*, ed. David Crouch, pp. 91–108. London: Routledge, 1999.

Pierard, Richard Victor. "The German Colonial Society, 1882–1914." Ph.D. diss., State University of Iowa, 1964.

Plessen, Marie-Louise von. *Sehsucht: Das Panorama als Massenunterhaltung des 19. Jahrhunderts*. Basel and Frankfurt am Main: Stroemfeld/Roter Stern, 1993.

Potter, Russell A. "Arctic Spectacles: Visions of the North in Panoramas, 1820–1874." In *The North in Film: Papers Presented at "Visions of the North, Voices of the North," Northern Culture Conference*, ed. A. W. Plumstead, pp. 9–36. North Bay, Ont.: Nipissing University, 1999.

Prager, Erich. *Die deutsche Kolonialgesellschaft, 1882–1907*. Berlin: Reimer, 1908.

Pratt, Marie Louise. *Imperial Eyes: Travel Writing and Transculturation*. London and New York: Routledge, 1992.

Prels, Max. *Kino*. Bielefeld and Leipzig: Velhagen & Klasing, 1919.

Prest, John. *The Garden of Eden: The Botanic Garden and the Re-Creation of Paradise*. New Haven: Yale University Press, 1981.

Priemel, Kurt. "Handelstierpark und Zoologische Gärten." *Frankfurter Zeitung und Handelsblatt*, 24 April 1909, 1st morn. ed.

——. "Die heutigen Aufgaben der Tiergärten: Eine Erwiderung." *Zoologischer Beobachter* 50, no. 12 (1909): 354–66.

Raibmon, Paige. *Authentic Indians: Episodes of Encounter from the Late-Nineteenth-Century Northwest Coast*. Durham: Duke University Press, 2005.

Reddin, Paul. *Wild West Shows*. Urbana: University of Illinois Press, 1999.

Reichenbach, Herman. "Carl Hagenbeck's Tierpark and Modern Zoological Gardens." *Journal of the Society for the Bibliography of Natural History* 9, no. 4 (1980): 573–85.

——. "A Tale of Two Zoos: The Hamburg Zoological Garden and Carl Hagenbeck's *Tierpark*." In *New Worlds, New Animals: From Menagerie to Zoological Park in the Nineteenth Century*, ed. R. J. Hoage and William A. Deiss, pp. 51–62. Baltimore: Johns Hopkins University Press, 1996.

Richards, Thomas. *The Commodity Culture of Victorian England: Advertising and Spectacle, 1851–1914*. Stanford: Stanford University Press, 1990.

Richter, Roland. "Die erste deutsche Kolonial-Ausstellung 1896: Der 'Amtliche Bericht' in historischer Perspektive." In *Kolonialausstellungen: Begegnungen mit Afrika?* ed. Robert Debusmann and János Riesz, pp. 25–42. Frankfurt am Main: IKO-Verlag für Interkulturelle Kommunikation, 1995.

Rieke-Müller, Annelore. "Die Gründung Zoologischer Gärten um die Mitte des 19. Jahrhunderts im deutschsprachigen Raum." In *Die Kulturgeschichte des Zoos*, ed. Lothar Dittrich, Dittrich von Engelhardt, and Annelore Rieke-Müller, pp. 83–95. Berlin: VWB—Verlag für Wissenschaft und Bildung, 2001.

Rieke-Müller, Annelore, and Lothar Dittrich. *Der Löwe brüllt nebenan: Die Gründung Zoologischer Gärten im deutschsprachigen Raum 1833–1869*. Cologne: Böhlau, 1998.

——. *Unterwegs mit wilden Tieren: Wandermenagerien zwischen Belehrung und Kommerz 1750–1850*. Marburg: Basilisken-Presse, 1999.

Ritvo, Harriet. *The Animal Estate: The English and Other Creatures in the Victorian Age*. Cambridge, MA: Harvard University Press, 1987.

Roerkohl, Anne. "Die Lebensmittelversorgung während des Ersten Weltkrieges im Spannungsfeld kommunaler und staatlicher Massnahmen." In *Durchbruch zum modernen Massenkonsum: Lebensmittelmärkte und Lebensmittelqualität im Städtewachstum des Industriezeitalters*, ed. Hans-Jürgen Teuteberg, pp. 309–70. Münster: Coppenrath, 1987.

Roller, Kathrin. "'Wir sind Deutsche, wir sind Weiße und wollen Weiße bleiben': Reichstagsdebatten über koloniale 'Rassenmischung.'" In *Kolonialmetropole Berlin: Eine Spurensuche*, ed. Ulrich van der Heyden and Joachim Zeller, pp. 73–79. Berlin: Berlin-Edition, 2002).

Rony, Fatimah Tobing. *The Third Eye: Race, Cinema, and Ethnographic Spectacle*. Durham, NC: Duke University Press, 1996.

Rosa, Joseph G., and Robin May. *Buffalo Bill and His Wild West: A Pictorial Biography*. Lawrence: University Press of Kansas, 1989.

Rother, Rainer. "Monumentalkino: Zum Entstehen des 'Großfilms' in Deutschland." In *Die Modellierung des Kinofilms: Zur Geschichte des Kinoprogramms zwischen Kurzfilm und Langfilm (1905/06–1918)*, ed. Corinna Müller and Harro Segeberg, pp. 375–96. Munich: Fink, 1998.

Rothfels, Nigel. *Savages and Beasts: The Birth of the Modern Zoo*. Baltimore: Johns Hopkins University Press, 2002.

Russ, Karl. "Hagenbecks Eismeer-Panorama auf der Berliner Gewerbeausstellung." *Über Land und Meer: Deutsche Illustrirte Zeitung* 76, no. 42 (October 1896): 679.

Russell, Don. *The Lives and Legends of Buffalo Bill*. Norman: University of Oklahoma Press, 1960.

——. *The Wild West: A History of the Wild West Shows*. Fort Worth, TX: Amon Carter Museum of Western Art, 1970.

Rydell, Robert W. *All the World's a Fair: Visions of Empire at American International Expositions, 1876–1916*. Chicago: University of Chicago Press, 1984.

——. "The Literature of International Expositions." In *The Book of the Fairs: Materials about World's Fairs, 1834–1916, in the Smithsonian Institution Libraries*, pp. 1–62. Chicago: American Library Association, 1992.

S., G. "Eine Kalmückenkarawane in Deutschland." *Illustrirte Zeitung* (8 September 1883): 213–14.

Saltarino, Signor. *Fahrend Volk: Abnormitäten, Kuriositäten und interessante Vertreter der wandernden Künstlerwelt*. Leipzig: Weber, 1895.

Sammons, Jeffrey L. "Nineteenth-Century German Representations of Indians from Experience." In *Germans and Indians: Fantasies, Encounters, Projections*, ed. Colin G. Calloway, Gerd Gemünden, and Susanne Zantop, pp. 185–93. Lincoln: University of Nebraska Press, 2002.

"Samoaner in Umlauff's Welt-Museum." *Hamburger Fremdenblatt*, 16 November 1889, 1st supplement. (SAH 11859)

"Samoaner in Umlauff's Welt-Museum." *Hamburger Fremdenblatt*, 18 November 1889, 1st supplement. (SAH 11859)

Sandberg, Mark B. *Living Pictures, Missing Persons: Mannequins, Museums, and Modernity*. Princeton: Princeton University Press, 2003.

Schechner, Richard. *Between Theater and Anthropology*. Philadelphia: University of Pennsylvania Press, 1985.

——. *Environmental Theater*. New and exp. ed. New York: Applause, 1994.

Schillings, Carl Georg. *With Flash-Light and Rifle: Photographing by Flash-Light at Night the Wild Animal World of Equatorial Africa*. Trans. Henry Zick. New York: Harper and Brothers, 1905.

——. *Mit Blitzlicht und Büchse*. Leipzig: Voigtländer, 1905.

——. *Der Zauber des Eleléscho*. Leipzig: Voigtländer, 1906.

Schirp, Fritz von. "Die größte Handelsmenagerie der Erde." *Norddeutsche Allgemeine Zeitung*, 9 March 1884. (SAH, A902 "Hagenbecks Tierpark")

——. "Die Hagenbeck'sche Singhalesenkarawane." *Illustrirte Zeitung* (3 October 1885): 338.

Schivelbusch, Wolfgang. *Disenchanted Night: The Industrialization of Light in the Nineteenth Century*. Trans. Angela Davies. Berkeley: University of California Press, 1995.

——. *The Railway Journey: The Industrialization of Time and Space in the Nineteenth Century*. Berkeley: University of California Press, 1986.

Schlör, Joachim. *Nights in the Big City: Paris, Berlin, London 1840–1930*. Trans. Pierre Gottfried Imhof and Dafydd Rees Roberts. London: Reaktion Books, 1998.

Schmal, Helga. "Carl Hagenbecks Tierpark." *Denkmalpflege Hamburg* 15 (June 1997).

Schmarda, Ludwig Karl. *Die geographische Verbreitung der Tiere*. 3 vols. Vienna: Gerold, 1853.

Schmidt-Linsenhoff, Viktoria, Kurt Wettengl, and Almut Junker, eds. *Plakate 1880–1914*. Kleine Schriften des Historischen Museums Frankfurt 29. Frankfurt am Main: Pippert + Koch, 1986.

Schneider, William H. *An Empire for the Masses: The French Popular Image of Africa, 1870–1900*. Westport, CT: Greenwood Press, 1982.

Schomburgk, Hans. *Bwakukama: Fahrten und Forschungen mit Büchse und Film im unbekannten Afrika*. Berlin: Deutsch-Literarisches Institut, 1922.

——. *Wild und Wilde im Herzen Afrikas*. Berlin: Fleischel, 1910.

Schöning, Jörg. "'Kleines Urwaldreich gedeiht. . . .': Die Dschungelfantasien des Filmproduzenten John Hagenbeck." In *Der deutsche Tropenwald: Bilder, Mythen, Politik*, ed. Michael Flitner, pp. 79–93. Frankfurt am Main: Campus, 2000.

——. "Unternehmensgegenstand: Exotik: Der Produzent John Hagenbeck." In *Triviale Tropen: Exotische Reise- und Abenteuerfilme aus Deutschland 1919–1939*, ed. Jörg Schöning, 111–23. Munich: edition text + kritik, 1997.

"Der Schöpfer des Tierparadieses." *Hamburger Fremdenblatt*, 12 November 1908. (SAH, A902 "Hagenbecks Tierpark")

"Die Schuli in Hamburg." *Der Kurier* 2, no. 5 (5 December 1891): 75. (SAH L 2/1)

Schulz, Christoph. *Jagd- und Filmabenteur in Afrika: Streifzüge in das Innere des dunkeln Erdteils*. Dresden: Verlag Deutsche Buchwerkstätten, 1922.

Schwartz, Vanessa R. *Spectacular Realities: Early Mass Culture in* Fin-de-Siècle *Paris*. Berkeley: University of California Press, 1998.

Schwarz, Werner Michael. *Anthropologische Spektakel: Zur Schaustellung "exotischer" Menschen, Wien 1870–1910*. Vienna: Turia + Kant, 2001.

Semper, Carl. *Die natürlichen Existenzbedingungen der Thiere*. Leipzig: Brockhaus, 1880.

Sewig, Claudia. "Nepal liegt bei Hagenbeck." *Hamburger Abendblatt*, 17 May 2003.

Shepstone, Harold J. "Carl Hagenbeck's Novel Zoological Park." *Scientific American* (10 November 1906): 345.

———. "The Completion of Carl Hagenbeck's Novel Zoological Park." *Scientific American Supplement* 64, no. 1649 (10 August 1907): 88–89.

———. "The Trade in Wild Animals." *Scientific American* 88, no. 20 (16 May 1903): 376–78.

"Die Sioux-Indianer." *Hamburger Fremdenblatt*, 20 November 1885.

"Sioux-Indianer bei Hagenbeck." *Hamburgischer Correspondent*, 16 April 1910.

Sippel, Harald. "Rassismus, Protektionismus oder Humanität? Die gesetzlichen Verbote der Anwerbung von 'Eingeborenen' zu Schaustellungszwecken in den deutschen Kolonien." In *Kolonialausstellungen: Begegnungen mit Afrika?* ed. Robert Debusmann and János Riesz, pp. 43–64. Frankfurt am Main: IKO-Verlag für Interkulturelle Kommunikation, 1995.

Snow, Richard. *Coney Island: A Postcard Journey to the City of Fire*. New York: Brightwaters Press, 1984.

Sokolowsky, Alexander. "Akklimatisations-Erfolge im Hagenbeck'schen Tierpark." *Hamburger Nachrichten*, 18 September 1907, morn. ed. (SAH, A902 "Hagenbecks Tierpark")

———. "Das biologische Prinzip bei der Schaustellung wilder Tiere." *Natur und Haus* 15 (1907): 150–53.

———. *Carl Hagenbeck und sein Werk*. Leipzig: Haberland, 1928.

———. *Gesammelte Aufsätze zoologischen Inhalts: Für Zoologen, Landwirte, Tierzüchter und Kolonialfreunde*. Leipzig: Theodor Oswald Weigel, 1909.

———. "Hagenbecks Tierpark im Schnee." *Hamburger Nachrichten*, 4 January 1906, eve. ed. (SAH, A902 "Hagenbecks Tierpark")

———. "Ein neuer Tierpark nach biologischem Prinzip." *Wild und Hund* 13, no. 22 (1907): 388–89.

———. "Die Zoologischen Gärten als Bildungsanstalten." *Natur und Schule* (1905): 555–62.

"Somaliland at Sydenham." *The Graphic* (3 August 1895): 139.

Sorkin, Michael. "See You in Disneyland." In *Variations on a Theme Park: The New American City and the End of Public Space*, ed. Michael Sorkin, pp. 205–32. New York: Hill and Wang, 1992.

Staehlin, Balthasar. *Völkerschauen im Zoologischen Garten Basel 1879–1935*. Basel: Basler Afrika Bibliographien, 1993.

Steele, Jeffrey. "Reduced to Images: American Indians in Nineteenth-Century Advertising." In *Dressing in Feathers: The Construction of the Indian in American Popular Culture*, ed. S. Elizabeth Bird, pp. 45–64. Boulder, CO: Westview Press, 1996.

Sternberger, Dolf. "Panorama of the 19th Century." Trans. Joachim Neugroschel. *October* 4 (fall 1987): 3–20.

Stiller, Günter. "Goldener Glanz aus Fernost." *Hamburger Abendblatt*, 22 August 2002.

———. "Hagenbeck: das goldene Geheimnis." *Hamburger Abendblatt*, 5 July 2002.

Stoecker, Helmuth. "The Annexations of 1884–1885." In *German Imperialism in Africa: From the Beginnings until the Second World War*, ed. Helmuth Stoecker, trans. Bernd Zöllner, pp. 21–38. London: Hurst; Atlantic Highlands, NJ: Humanities Press International, 1986.

———. "German Empire in Africa before 1914: General Questions." In *German Imperialism in Africa: From the Beginnings until the Second World War*, ed. Helmuth Stoecker, trans. Bernd Zöllner, pp. 185–229. London: Hurst; Atlantic Highlands, NJ: Humanities Press International, 1986.

Strauch, D. "Zur Frage der Ausfuhr von Eingeborenen aus den deutschen Kolonien zum Zwecke der Schaustellung." *Deutsche Kolonialzeitung* 17, no. 44 (1 November 1900): 500; no. 45 (8 November 1900): 511, 513; no. 46 (15 November 1900): 520.

Strehlow, Harro. "The Hagenbeck Revolution." In *Zoo and Aquarium History: Ancient Animal Collections to Zoological Gardens*, ed. Vernon N. Kisling, pp. 102–4. Boca Raton, FL: CRC Press, 2001.

Stricker, Wilhelm. "Geschichte der Menagerien und der zoologischen Gärten." *Sammlung gemeinverständlicher wissenschaftlicher Vorträge*, ed. Rudolf Virchow and Friedrich von Holkendorff, vol. 14, no. 336 (1879): 921–63.

Sturm, Georges. *Die Circe, der Pfau und das Halbblut: Die Filme von Fritz Lang, 1916–1921.* Trier: Wissenschaftlicher Verlag Trier, 2001.

Sugimoto, Hiroshi. *http://www.hirshhorn.si.edu/sugimoto/dioramas/index.htm* (accessed 4 March 2007).

Tashiro, C. S. *Pretty Pictures: Production Design and the History Film.* Austin: University of Texas Press, 1998.

Thacker, Christopher. *The History of Gardens.* Berkeley: University of California Press, 1979.

Thinius, Carl. *Damals in St. Pauli: Lust und Freude in der Vorstadt.* Hamburg: Christians, 1975.

Thode-Arora, Hilke. "'Charakteristische Gestalten des Volkslebens': Die Hagenbeckschen Südasien-, Orient- und Afrika-Völkerschauen." In *Fremde Erfahrungen: Asiaten und Afrikaner in Deutschland, Österreich und in der Schweiz bis 1945*, ed. Gerhard Höpp, pp. 109–34. Berlin: Verlag das Arabische Buch, 1996.

———. "Das Eskimo-Tagebuch von 1880: Eine Völkerschau aus der Sicht eines Teilnehmers." *Kea: Zeitschrift für Kulturwissenschaften* 2 (1991): 87–115.

———. "Die Familie Umlauff und ihre Firmen: Ethnographica-Händler in Hamburg." *Mitteilungen aus dem Museum für Völkerkunde Hamburg* 22 (1992): 143–58.

———. *Für fünfzig Pfennig um die Welt: Die Hagenbeckschen Völkerschauen.* Frankfurt am Main: Campus, 1989.

———. "Die Hagenbeckschen Völkerschauen: Indianer Nordamerikas in Europa." In *Indianer Nordamerikas: Kunst und Mythos*, ed. Patricia Rochard, pp. 80–87. Mainz: Schmidt, 1993.

———. "Herbeigeholte Ferne: Völkerschauen als Vorläufer exotisierender Abenteuerfilme." In *Triviale Tropen: Exotische Reise- und Abenteuerfilme aus Deutschland 1919–1939*, ed. Jörg Schöning, 19–33. Munich: edition text + kritik, 1997.

———. "Indianer und Inuit in Europa: Völkerschauen." In *Indianer 1858–1928: Photographische Reisen von Alaska bis Feuerland*, ed. Eva König, pp. 69–73. Heidelberg: Edition Braus, 2002.

Thomas, Robert. *Unter Kunden, Komödianten und wilden Tieren*. Ed. Julius R. Haarhaus. Leipzig: Grunow, 1905.

Thompson, R. W. *Wild Animal Man: Being the Story of the Life of Reuben Castang*. New York: William Morrow, 1934.

Thomson, Rosemarie Garland, ed. *Freakery: Cultural Spectacles of the Extraordinary Body*. New York: New York University Press, 1996.

Thorp, Raymond W. *Spirit Gun of the West: The Story of Doc W. F. Carver*. Glendale, CA: Arthur H. Clark, 1957.

Töteberg, Michael. *Filmstadt Hamburg: Von Emil Jannings bis Wim Wenders: Kino-Geschichte(n) einer Großstadt*. Hamburg: VSA, 1990.

"Trained Animal Exhibit." *Chicago Dispatch*, 2 May 1893. (TCH)

"Unmuzzled Beasts Run Free." *New York Times*, 1 December 1893.

Velvin, Ellen. *Behind the Scenes with Wild Animals*. New York: Moffat, Yard, 1906.

——. *From Jungle to Zoo*. London: S. Paul & Co., 1914.

Venturi, Robert, Denise Scott Brown, and Steven Izenour. *Learning from Las Vegas*. Cambridge, MA: MIT Press, 1972.

"Vergrößerung des Hagenbeckschen Tierparks." *Hamburger Nachrichten*, 5 November 1913, eve. ed. (SAH, A902 "Hagenbecks Tierpark")

Verhoeff, Nanna. "After the Beginning: Westerns Before 1915." Ph.D. diss., University of Utrecht, 2002.

"Veteran Animal Trainer Wonders Why Rich Americans Don't Adopt His Idea and Lay Out Private Parks to be Stocked with Wild Animals and Birds." *New York Times*, 16 October 1904, SM5.

Vincent, C. Paul. *The Politics of Hunger: The Allied Blockade of Germany, 1915–1919*. Athens, OH, and London: Ohio University Press, 1985.

"Völkerschau: Birma" (advertisement). *Hamburger Fremdenblatt*, 11 May 1913, morn. ed.

Wagner, Hermann. Foreword to *Zonen-Bilder: Nach Aquarellen von Heinrich Leutemann, mit erklärenden Schilderungen für die Jugend von Hermann Wagner*. Stuttgart: Julius Hoffmann, 1876.

Wahrman, Dror. *The Making of the Modern Self: Identity and Culture in Eighteenth-Century England*. New Haven: Yale University Press, 2004.

Wakefield, Neville. *Postmodernism: The Twilight of the Real*. London: Pluto Press, 1990.

Walker, Derek. Ed. *Animated Architecture*. New York: St. Martin's Press, 1982.

Wallace, Alfred Russel. *The Geographical Distribution of Animals*. New York: Harper and Brothers, 1876.

——. *Die geographische Verbreitung der Thiere*. Trans. A. B. Meyer. Dresden: Zahn, 1876.

Ward, Janet. *Weimar Surfaces: Urban Visual Culture in 1920s Germany*. Berkeley: University of California Press, 2001.

Warren, Louis S. *Buffalo Bill's America: William Cody and the Wild West Show*. New York: Knopf, 2005.

Weihsmann, Helmut. *Gebaute Illusionen: Architektur im Film*. Vienna: Promedia, 1988.

Weinland, David Friedrich. “Über den Ursprung und die Bedeutung der neueren Zoologischen Gärten.” *Der Zoologische Garten* 1, no. 3 (1862): 1–3.

———. “Zur Rechtfertigung.” In *Der Thiergarten* 1, no. 1 (1864): 1–4.

Welsch, Robert L. “One Time, One Place, Three Collections: Colonial Processes and the Shaping of Some Museum Collections from German New Guinea.” In *Hunting the Gatherers: Ethnographic Collectors, Agents and Agency in Melanesia, 1870s–1930s*, ed. Michael O’Hanlon and Robert L. Welsch, pp. 155–79. New York: Berghahn, 2000.

Wiele, Hermann. *Für Hagenbeck in den Urwäldern Indiens: Dreißig Jahre Forscher und Jäger*. Dresden: Verlag Deutsche Buchwerkstätten, 1926.

Wilcox, Scott B. Introduction to *Panoramania! The Art and Entertainment of the ‘All-Embracing’ View*, by Ralph Hyde. London: Trefoil, 1988.

Wildenthal, Lora. *German Women for Empire, 1884–1945*. Durham, NC: Duke University Press, 2001.

“Wild-West.” *Freisinnige Zeitung*, 24 July 1890. (BBHC-Cody)

“Wild-West bei Hagenbeck.” *Hamburger Nachrichten*, 16 April 1910.

“‘Wild-West’ in Berlin.” *Lokal-Anzeiger* (Berlin), 24 July 1890. (BBHC-Cody)

Williams, Rosalind H. *Dream Worlds: Mass Consumption in Late Nineteenth-Century France*. Berkeley: University of California Press, 1982.

“Die Wirkungen der Vorstellungen Buffalo Bill’s.” *Nachrichten* (Leipzig), 22 June 1890. (BBHC-Cody)

Wolf, Eric. *Europe and the People without History*. Berkeley: University of California Press, 1982.

Wonders, Karen. *Habitat Dioramas: Illusions of Wilderness in Museums of Natural History*. Acta Universitatis Upsaliensis, Figura Nova Series 25. Uppsala: Almqvist and Wiksell, 1993.

Wörner, Martin. *Vergnügung und Belehrung: Volkskultur auf den Weltausstellungen 1851–1900*. Münster: Waxmann, 1999.

Wyl, Wilhelm. “Der ‘Wilde Westen’ in Berlin.” *Berliner Tageblatt*, 23 July 1890. (BBHC-Cody)

Yanni, Carla. *Nature’s Museums: Victorian Science and the Architecture of Display*. London: Athlone Press, 1999.

Ybarra, T. R. “‘Hagenbeck’s’ Closes Its Doors.” *New York Times*, 28 November 1920.

Zantop, Susanne. *Colonial Fantasies: Conquest, Family, and Nation in Precolonial Germany, 1770–1870*. Durham: Duke University Press, 1997.

“Zehn Jahre Stellinger Tierpark.” *Hamburger Nachrichten*, 25 May 1917, eve. ed. (SAH A902, “Hagenbeck’s Tierpark”)

Zeller, Joachim. “‘Das Interesse an der Kolonialpolitik fördern und heben’: Das Deutsche Kolonialmuseum in Berlin.” In *Kolonialmetropole Berlin: Eine Spurensuche*, ed. Ulrich van der Heyden and Joachim Zeller, pp. 142–49. Berlin: Berlin-Edition, 2002.

Zglinicki, Friedrich von. *Der Weg des Films: Die Geschichte der Kinematographie und ihrer Vorläufer*. Berlin: Rembrandt, 1956.

Zimmerman, Andrew. *Anthropology and Antihumanism in Imperial Germany*. Chicago: University of Chicago Press, 2001.

Zimmerschied, Karl. *Die deutsche Filmindustrie: Ihre Entwicklung, Organisation und Stellung im deutschen Staats- und Wirtschaftsleben.* Berlin: Poeschel, 1922.

Zuckmayer, Carl. "Hamburg, Hafen, Hagenbeck." *Arche Noah* 1 (1949): 3. (TCH)

Zukin, Sharon. *Landscapes of Power: From Detroit to Disneyworld.* Berkeley: University of California Press, 1991.

Zukowsky, Ludwig. *Carl Hagenbeck's Reich: Ein deutsches Tierparadies.* Berlin: Volksverband der Bücherfreunde Wegweiser-Verlag, 1929.

"Zur Eingeborenenfrage." *Deutsche Kolonialzeitung* 18 (25 May 1901): 203.

Zwernemann, Jürgen. *Hundert Jahre Hamburgisches Museum für Völkerkunde.* Hamburg: Hamburgisches Museum für Völkerkunde, 1980.

Zwick, Jim. *Inuit Entertainers in the United States: From the Chicago World's Fair through the Birth of Hollywood.* West Conshohocken, PA: Infinity Publishing, 2006.

INDEX

The abbreviation pl. *indicates a color plate;* f *indicates figure.*

A

B

C

D

E

F

G

H

I

J

K

L

M

N

O

S

T

U

V